An Analysis of
Thinking and Research
About
Qualitative Methods

LEA's COMMUNICATION SERIES
Jennings Bryant/Dolf Zillmann, General Editors

Select titles in General Theory and Methodology
(Jennings Bryant, Advisory Editor) include:

Vocate • Intrapersonal Communication: Different Voices, Different Minds

Perloff • The Dynamics of Persuasion

Heath/Bryant • Human Communication Theory and Research:
Concepts, Contexts, and Challenges

Casmir • Building Communication Theories: A Socio/Cultural Approach

For a complete list of other titles in LEA's Communication Series, please contact
Lawrence Erlbaum Associates, Publishers.

An Analysis of Thinking and Research About Qualitative Methods

W. James Potter
University of California, Santa Barbara

 LAWRENCE ERLBAUM ASSOCIATES, PUBLISHERS
1996   Mahwah, New Jersey

Lawrence Erlbaum Associates, Inc., Publishers
10 Industrial Avenue
Mahwah, New Jersey 07430

Library of Congress Cataloging-in-Publication Data

Potter, W. James
    An analysis of thinking and research about qualitative methods /
W. James Potter.
        p.   cm.
    Includes bibliographical references (p.) and index.
    ISBN 0-8058-1750-6. — ISBN 0-8058-1751-4 (pbk.)
    1. Communication—Research—Methodology. I. Title.
P.91.3.P68 1996
302.2′072—dc20   95-44514
                                                                            CIP

Books published by Lawrence Erlbaum Associates are printed on acid-free paper,
and their bindings are chosen for strength and durability.

Printed in the United States of America
10 9 8 7 6 5 4 3 2 1

CONTENTS

PART III: ILLUSTRATIONS OF DECISION MAKING

PART IV: CRITICAL INSIGHTS

PREFACE

This book is my story about how I make sense of the qualitative approach. Before I tell you my story, there are a few things you should know. First, my goal in conducting the *research* for this book was to find out how qualitative researchers construct meaning in their research; that is, I attempted to do a qualitative analysis of qualitative research. My purpose in *writing* this book then was to clarify what the qualitative method is for those scholars who want to learn how to use it to conduct research or how to become better consumers of that type of research. This is not to say that there are not clear writings that define what qualitative research is. There are many such writings. The problem is that there is not a consistent picture across the writings in this set. Thus scholars who read one of these writings might feel that they are clear about qualitative thinking, but when they continue to read other descriptions, they will likely become confused. I wanted to illuminate as wide a span of these ideas and interpretations as possible in a single forum so they could be compared and contrasted.

Second, in order to make sense of my interpretations, you need to understand my interpretive stance. In writing this book, I have tried to maintain a perspective that is neither purely qualitative nor purely quantitative; that is, it sits somewhere between the two. To clarify, my perspective is based on the following four premises:

Premise 1: There is a material reality that exists apart from our interpretation of it.

Premise 2: We, as humans, can never experience the phenomenon directly or completely, because (a) our conduits of information (the five senses) are limited, and (b) the way we make meaning from the raw sense data is subjective. For these reasons, there will always be a range of interpretations about physical phenomena (such as the movement of electrons, chemical reactions, nature of living cells, etc.) and an even wider range of interpretations about social phenomena (human conversations, meaning of texts, construction of institutions, and cultural artifacts).

Premise 3: All scholarship necessarily is composed of the components of speculation and empiricism. In the speculation phase, the scholar constructs an interpretation of the phenomenon. In the empirical phase, the scholar cites observed characteristics about the phenomenon to illustrate and support the interpretation.

Premise 4: Among the various interpretations of a phenomenon, some are better than others; that is, all are not equally useful. In all research communities, scholars have developed norms for what constitutes acceptable research and what does not. These norms are often difficult to discern (because they consist of multiple elements, the elements vary in importance, and some elements are unwritten; i.e., they are only observable in the practices), but they still exist. Underlying these norms is the idea of utility. Useful scholarship accounts for what is known and either (a) extends the reader's knowledge of the topic, and/or (b) presents the reader with some intriguing new way to look at the phenomenon.

There are a variety of perspectives that I could have used to write this book. I chose the one I did (as illustrated by the four premises just discussed) so as to have the greatest appeal to scholars in media studies.

Third, this book focuses on the qualitative approach in the realm of media studies. This "home base" of media studies is an especially rich area for qualitative thinking and research. There are many active scholars working here, and their output displays a wide range of assumptions and practices. To do a good job of illuminating this home base, I must acknowledge many important ideas of scholars in the broader area of communications as well as some contiguous fields. For example, the foundations of qualitative research cannot be adequately understood without a grounding in certain important issues in the field of philosophy and philosophy of science. Also, the use and development of qualitative methods in media studies cannot be adequately presented without tracing their origins back to sociology and anthropology. And, many scholars in education have produced a rather large literature that runs parallel to the concerns about the method as expressed in media studies.

Fourth, I need to tell you something about me. I first became intrigued with the idea of making sense of the qualitative approach almost two decades ago while I was working on a PhD and took various courses in linguistics, communication, and education that referred to these "new" methods. Prior to that time, I had been an English literature major as an undergraduate where we grappled with questions such as: What makes a novel, play, or poem great? Why do different readers have different reactions to the same book or movie? Why do I have different reactions to certain books each time I read them? In my struggle to answer these questions, I used many different methods, all of them qualitative. After graduation, I found myself working full time as a newspaper reporter. The questions were more applied and numerous, but the methods were still qualitative, even though I had never heard the term. But in graduate school I heard the term all the time and tried to figure out what all it meant. My dissertation was an interpretative analysis. As a graduate student and then as a full-time consultant on a major faculty development grant, I conducted several ethnographic projects, but I still found myself continually surprised by new meanings for "qualitative."

After several years of chafing under the limitations of the methods, I went back to graduate school to study more "scientific" topics of social psychology, communication theory, research design, and statistics. Since the completion of that PhD, I have been most visible as a quantitative researcher. Over the past 8 years, I have published several dozen articles in the mainstream communication journals that are considered primarily outlets for quantitative research studies, such as *Communication Research, Human Communication Research, Journal of Advertising Research, Journal of Broadcasting & Electronic Media,* and *Journalism Quarterly.* To many qualitative scholars, my published research might represent the very antithesis of what they believe; that is, my quantitative work demonstrates a belief in intersubjectivity, the enumeration of qualitative properties, reductionistic focus, statistical analysis, and hypothetico-deductive reasoning.

When I became the editor of the *Journal of Broadcasting & Electronic Media,* I began reading much more of the published qualitative research so that I could create for myself a more developed and current context from which to evaluate qualitative manuscripts that would be submitted to the journal. The more I read, the more impressed I became about many of the developments in thinking and research findings produced by qualitative methods. However, at the same time, I was becoming puzzled about how to make sense out of all this activity.

This book is my story about what I have found useful in navigating the qualitative literature. At times in this journey, I have found it useful to think like a quantitative researcher so as to set up contrasts with (or analogies for) the qualitative approach to achieve a deeper insight. However, I do not use the quantitative insights to argue against the qualitative approach. That is not my purpose. I do not use the quantitative approach as my locus, nor am I interested in using the qualitative approach as my guiding point. Instead, my locus is a curiosity about what constitutes meaning, and I use the methods and methodologies of both approaches as tools. When I or someone else uses one of these tools, I ask: How well does the researcher follow the rules and achieve the standards of their chosen methodology? And, on a meta-level, the question for me is: How well does the design of the chosen methodology serve to generate a useful answer to the question being examined? To provide answers to these questions, I find myself very critical of particular claims or practices within the qualitative approach. But this should not be interpreted by readers to mean that I am critical of the qualitative approach in general. I think the qualitative approach can be very useful; however, I see some misuses. I also think the quantitative approach can be very useful, but that there are some misuses of it (for examples of my perceptions of misuses, see Potter, 1993, 1994; Potter, Cooper, & Dupagne, 1993). But even more troublesome than the misuses is a lack of understanding among researchers under one approach for the goals and practices of the researchers operating under the other approach. I hope this book will help those favoring the quantitative approach to understand better the thinking and practices of those researchers within the qualitative approach.

And fifth, I am not writing this book to convince you that mine is the only interpretation of the qualitative approach. To the contrary, I show that there are many interpretations of what *qualitative* means. Also, I am not arguing that my interpretation is the one you should believe over all others. Although there are arguments presented in the book, the book itself is not an argument for a particular interpretation. The arguments that are presented are used as devices to illustrate a progression of thought on a certain topic; that is, they begin with premises and then progress to a conclusion. If you, the reader, do not first accept the premises, then you will not accept the conclusion that follows. That is fine with me; I am not writing the book to persuade you to change your beliefs. Instead, my aim is to show what the fundamental premises are and further to show how the acceptance of various sets of premises leads to certain conclusions. Therefore the arguments are used for the purpose of illustration rather than persuasion. This is what I mean when I say that the book itself is an interpretation rather than an argument.

WHO IS THE BOOK FOR?

I had two target audiences in mind when writing the book. One audience is the so-called "quantitative" scholar who wants a "different" interpretation of the qualitative approach. By different I mean an interpretation that is neither (a) a condemnation of qualitative thinking written by a quantitative scholar, nor (b) a glorification of qualitative thinking by a scholar who feels that the quantitative approach is bankrupt and that the qualitative approach is the only legitimate one. I expect that quantitative scholars will find my interpretive *stance* fairly close to their own, and this sharing of a perspective should lead to a more understandable interpretation for them. A second primary audience is the student who wants to enter the qualitative realm through a portal that is close to their own thinking. Even in our postmodern world, there are many students who accept the four premises outlined earlier.

Qualitative theoreticians and researchers who have strong ideas of their own about the purpose and structure of their methodologies and practices will find my treatment of topics fairly introductory and not substantive enough for their needs. Also, their belief system will undoubtedly be very different from the interpretive stance I use in this book. If these scholars do find themselves reading this book and disagreeing with my interpretations, I welcome their comments and look forward to beginning a heuristic process that might stimulate an interesting debate. Such a debate, if conducted constructively, will serve to increase our literacy about this very intriguing, and often puzzling, approach to research.

I hope that this book will be able to show readers that the approaches share some important commonalities and that the actual practices are not as far apart as some of the rhetoric would have us believe. This is not to say that the approaches are identical; we should not minimize the fundamental differences that do exist. If scholars are able to develop a clearer picture about where the differences and similarities are, then future researchers may be more willing and able to pass back and forth between the two approaches—thus being guided much more by their curiosity about the phenomenon than by the limitations imposed by adhering to only one approach.

OVERVIEW OF CHAPTERS

The book presents 17 chapters organized into four sections: foundations, interpretive analysis, illustrations of decision making, and critical insights. Each of these four sections is very different in both purpose and tone.

Part I: Foundations

The purpose of the five chapters in this section is to illuminate the fundamental issues that lay the groundwork for the book. They are primarily descriptive and interpretive in tone. In the first chapter, I use a metaphor to address some of the perceived barriers to entry into the realm of qualitative thinking. Some of these barriers are philosophical in nature and some are revealed in the practices of scholars writing about the qualitative approach. These are the barriers that cause problems of understanding for quantitative researchers as well as students new to qualitative thinking.

Chapter 2 presents the proliferation of definitions, then shows that the elements in those definitions are usefully organized when they are separated into three categories: axiomatic issues, methodologies, and methods.

In chapter 3, I explore the fundamental reasons for the split between the qualitative and quantitative approaches. To do this, I show how the different beliefs on these axioms have influenced the history of foundational thinking concerning the suitability of using scientific methods to examine humans as social entities. Then I lay out the philosophical issues of ontology and epistemology that underlie qualitative thinking. Both of these issues offer a variety of positions, and it is the selection of a position on these issues that indicates the most fundamental difference between the quantitative and qualitative thinkers. Once we understand the differences at this fundamental level, it becomes much clearer why the research produced by the two approaches is so different.

Chapter 4 focuses on seven qualitative methodologies. The foundations of each are first presented and then the methods that matched with the methodology are listed. Chapter 5 presents the perspective that the area of media studies is composed of three facets: focus on texts, focus on audiences, and focus on institutions. Each of these facets is illuminated in terms of how the seven methodologies can contribute to their understanding.

Part II: Interpretive Analysis

The purpose of the seven chapters in this section is to present my interpretation of the major issues involved in doing qualitative research. This set of issues represents a synthesis of the ideas raised by qualitative theoreticians. Examples from the qualitative research literature are presented to show how these points are addressed by practitioners of the qualitative approach.

In chapter 6, I explore the answers to the question: What constitutes evidence of the phenomenon? These answers deal with the issues of the type of evidence, broadness of the evidence, and the use of numbers. Chapter 7 focuses on six issues of evidence gathering: types of data gathering, researcher identification, researcher activity, sampling, collaboration, and length of the evidence collection. Chapter 8 deals with the issues of data analysis: expectations, process, conceptual leverage, and generalization. Chapter 9 lays out the methods available for qualitative data analysis.

Chapter 10 focuses on the writing purposes: description, interpretation, explanation, criticism, and action advocacy. Chapter 11 lays out four issues encountered in the writing of qualitative research reports: contextualization, locus of the argument, forms of expression, and degree of self-reflexivity. Chapter 12 raises the issue about whether standards can be developed for qualitative research reports, and, if so, what those internal and external standards might be.

Part III: Illustrations of Decision Making

The purpose of the two chapters in this section is to illustrate how research decisions are made under the two approaches. The tone is self-analytical as I reveal the process of decision making I undertook throughout two separate research projects, one using a methodology from the quantitative approach and the second using a methodology from the qualitative approach. Chapter 13 presents the report of a study conducted using the quantitative methodology of content analysis. This report is written so as to illuminate the decisions that had to be made in applying the methodology. In contrast, chapter 14 illuminates the decisions that I had to make in conducting the textual analysis that resulted in the interpretations of chapters 6–12. In this self-reflexive chapter, I explicate the how and why of the project by presenting an overview of the process, purpose, evidence, analysis, writing, and standards.

Part IV: Critical Insights

This section presents a critical analysis in three chapters. The intention here is to point out specific problems in thinking and in practices and to call for some sort of corrective action. Chapter 15 is a critical assessment of the thinking and research on foundational issues. The main questions addressed are: What are the common assumptions among the theoreticians? What are the most prevalent assumptions underlying the empirical work? Is there a correspondence between qualitative theorizing and practices? Should there be correspondence?

Chapter 16 presents a critique of the thinking and research on methodological issues. This chapter deals with the same type of questions as laid out in the previous chapter, but instead of critiquing assumptions, the critical focus is on methods and techniques.

Finally, in the 17th chapter, I attempt a synthesis. The synthesis is not between the qualitative and quantitative approach. Instead, I focus on the correspondence between qualitative thinking and practice. This comparison highlights the places where the prescriptions of the theoreticians are not followed in practice by qualitative researchers. I conclude with an assessment about the degree of similarity between qualitative and quantitative practices.

ACKNOWLEDGMENTS

There are five sets of people I must thank for providing me with considerable help in making this book. First, there are the communication scholars—especially Tom Lindlof and James Anderson—who have written so insightfully about the usefulness of the qualitative approach for addressing communication issues. Although I have not always agreed with everything they have written (nor will they agree with all my positions), I have always found their work very stimulating. Their writings have set in motion for me a process of thinking that results in the criticisms and positions that appear in this book.

Second, in the Department of Telecommunications at Indiana University, there was a handful of very intelligent and motivated graduate students who were interested in learning more about the qualitative approach. Karen Riggs, Cathy Troiano, Mike Robinson, and Greg Newton are each very different in their temperament and approach to research, and this made for an extremely interesting research team in 1991–1992. Our freewheeling discussions eventually found a common track that led us to complete a research project, which is described in chapter 13.

Third, there are Jennings Bryant, who as editor of this series, and Hollis Heimbouch, who as senior acquisitions editor at Lawrence Erlbaum Associates, encouraged me early in the writing process. Also, there is Amy Olener and then Kathleen O'Malley, who took over for Hollis, and Sondra Guideman, who as production editor guided this project smoothly and quickly into print.

Fourth, there is the wide range of colleagues in the field who read part or even all of the manuscript. This includes qualitative scholars (Tom Lindlof at the University of Kentucky and Ellen Seiter at Indiana University), quantitative scholars (Ed Wotring at Florida State University and Walt Gantz at Indiana University) and scholars who seem equally comfortable with both approaches (Dan Berkowitz at the University of Iowa and Chuck Whitney at the University of Texas).

And fifth, there are nine special graduate students in the Department of Communication Studies at the University of California at Santa Barbara: Shari Altarec-Ross, Eva Blumenthal, Cathy Boggs, Travis Dixon, Tim Gray, Dean Krikorkian, Patrick O'Sullivan, Sunwolf, and Karen Tanski. They took a seminar with me where they read and critiqued the ideas throughout the entire manuscript, which enabled me to understand the areas where readers would need the greatest help in following the ideas.

To all of these people, I am extremely grateful. Each contributed an important piece to the mosaic that formed the intellectual context within which this book began, germinated, and took shape. However, despite their best guidance, I realize there are places where I have departed from their wisdom. For those places where I do not seem to have "gotten it right," I will not offer the standard caveat that "all errors are mine." Instead, I'll say let's celebrate our differences of interpretation by undertaking a dialogue where we help each other construct a higher ground of understanding.

W. James Potter

FOUNDATIONS

1

WHETHER TO ENTER?

INTO THE GARDEN

Qualitative research is less like a field than a garden. When we view it meta-phorically it looks like a large hilly area with an incredible variety of plants—all shapes, sizes, and colors. Some of the plants appear majestic and timeless like ancient sequoias, whereas others appear fragile and exotic like jungle orchids.

The qualitative garden is not like a Japanese garden where a single person toils throughout the years to impose his or her unfolding vision on the design until perfection of form is reached. Instead, there are many gardeners working to bring their favorite forms of vegetation to life. There are different visions across plots so the overall garden grows, mutates, and evolves unevenly. The sights are constantly changing. If we photograph one section then return to it later, we are likely to see many differences; or perhaps it is instead our perspec-tive that has changed as we view it from a different angle.

If we try to pull one plant out of the ground to examine its roots we might find them entangled with the roots of many of the other plants. If we continue to pull up roots, we see an ongoing entanglement where all the roots seem to be joined. But it is a mistake to jump to that conclusion. There is no common root. Each plant has its own root system and requires its own special nutrients and attention.

The garden has an amorphous and ever changing perimeter. Sometimes we can see the boundaries marked by berms that obscure our vision; in some places there are moats to make it difficult for us to get into the garden; and in other places there are no easily discernible boundaries so we are not sure whether we have entered the garden or not.

Some people admire the garden and are irresistibly drawn to it. They like the activity, the mass of color and form that is constantly changing. They open themselves to all the experiences therein and feel at home. Others look at the garden and merely see a vacant lot full of weeds that need to be pruned, trimmed, and plotted, but they hesitate to undertake such a task for fear of an allergic reaction. They might feel it would be better to level the lot, then erect buildings of brick, steel, and glass with straight edges of right angles creating structures that are stable and dependable.

Then there are the others, perhaps you, who have gazed from afar at this garden of qualitative ideas and wondered whether you should enter. The activities inside the garden appear intriguing, but they raise questions you would like answered before you enter: What are the boundaries so that I can tell when I have entered? Is there a single ecosystem (or climate) that is common to all the differing plots? If I just want to travel through and experience the place, how can I get around without getting lost? If I want to stay, what will be expected of me and how can I begin to think like a native? Many students and quantitative researchers stand outside, ambivalent about entering, looking for a friendly entry point—away from the more intimidating aspects of the terrain.

INTIMIDATING ASPECTS

What are the characteristics of the garden that intimidate those students and scholars? In this section, I address four such characteristics. First, there is a reluctance by some scholars to provide a definition of *qualitative*. Second, among those scholars who do provide a definition, there is a wide range of meanings attributed to qualitative. Third, there is a lack of consistency in the usage of important terms; that is, there are many examples where a single term is used to refer to very different concepts and where different terms are often used to evoke the same idea. Fourth, there is a political purpose underlying much of the writing, especially attacks on nonqualitative research, and this alarms scholars who do not agree with these politics. Let's examine each of these four characteristics in some detail.

Reluctance in Providing Definitions

What is the qualitative approach? Metaphorically, what are the boundaries of the garden; how do we know when we have entered the garden and how far can we wander without finding ourselves outside the fence; and what are the different component regions within this garden?

Attempts at answering these types of questions require some careful thinking about definitions. There are many scholars who attempt such definitions, as we see in the next section of this chapter. However, there are also a fair number of scholars who think all attempts to define the garden are foolhardy. For example:

- Marshall and Rossman (1989) wrote an entire book on qualitative methods without defining "qualitative." Instead they said, "throughout the text we refer to *qualitative research* and *qualitative methods* as if these were one agreed-upon set that everyone understands. We intend no such implication" (p. 9).
- Lincoln and Guba (1985) were proud of resisting a simple definition. In the preface to their long book, they warned readers that they will not find a simple direct definition. They said, "it is not possible to provide a simple definition. . . . Instead a proper impression . . . can be gleaned only as an overall perspective" (p. 8).
- Wolcott (1992) said that the qualitative approach:

    . . . is not a field of study, and there is no clearly specified set of activities or identifiable group of specialists who practice them. To claim competence in qualitative research is, at most, to claim general familiarity with what is currently being done, coupled perhaps with experience in one or two particular facets (e.g., to "be good at" collecting and interpreting life histories or to "be" a symbolic interactionist). Claims to familiarity often amount to little more than a sympathetic attitude toward descriptive or interpretive work, accompanied by a far more deeply expressed antagonism for that "other kind" of research to which we have begun attaching the negative label "positivist." (p. 4)

- Denzin and Lincoln (1994c) observed that "the 'field' of qualitative research is far from a unified set of principles promulgated by networked groups of scholars" but that it is instead "defined primarily by a series of essential tensions, contradictions, and hesitations" (p. ix).
- M. L. Smith (1987) observed that in educational research, "the body of work labeled qualitative is richly variegated and its theories of method diverse to the point of disorderliness" (p. 173).

There are also many examples of scholars who are reluctant to provide a definition of subareas of the qualitative approach, such as:

- cultural studies (Fiske, 1994);
- critical studies (Real, 1986);
- discourse analysis (Gee, Michaels, & O'Conner, 1992);
- feminism (Bowen & Wyatt, 1993);
- history (Nord, 1989; Tuchman, 1994);
- semiology (Berger, 1982);
- symbolic interactionism (Schwandt, 1994);
- myth analysis (Breen & Corcoran, 1986).

For example, Breen and Corcoran (1986) said:

> [The] problem of definition in myth studies is yet to be solved. Paradoxically, the deeper one delves into the studies of myth, the more one returns to the problem of definition. While this approach is anathema to logic and the physical or social sciences, it nevertheless remains the state-of-the-art. Because myth deals with language, description, and ways of thinking and expressing, it is, of its essence, an elusive concept which reflexively draws attention to the fact that it can only be defined by the idea of myth itself. (p. 198)

Also, Berger (1982) said he is not sure whether semiology "is a subject, a movement, a philosophy, or a cult-like religion" (p. 14). Bowen and Wyatt (1993) took the position that there "is no single definition of 'feminism' or 'feminist' precisely because it is the nature of 'feminism' and 'feminist' thought and inquiry to resist definitive statements" (p. 2). Fiske (1994), in his chapter entitled "Audiencing: Cultural Practice and Cultural Studies," said "cultural *studies* is such a contested and currently trendy term that I must disclaim any attempt to either define or speak for it" (p. 189). And Real (1986) said "no widely accepted definition of 'the critical approach' exists, but there is documentable consensus about its general meaning" (p. 460). But although such a consensus might exist among experts, it cannot exist among potential visitors to the area, and these are the people who must need a clear definition in order to orient themselves.

There are some very good reasons why many qualitative scholars do not want to provide a definition. Many feel that the task of defining their area is so complex and fraught with danger that they may end up misleading the reader. But the problem is more than a matter of a high degree of difficulty; for some scholars, the quest for a definition is a useless and even dangerous task, because they believe that definitions serve only to limit the organic nature of the subjective and creative process of meaning making. Definitions have a static nature whereas the qualitative approach is organic. Definitions reflect a linear process of presenting words and concepts, whereas the qualitative approach is nonlinear, multidirectional, an asymmetrical bundling of nonessential conditions. Scholars with this perspective on the qualitative approach think the quest for a set of definitions is foolhardy.

Although there are very good reasons why those expert in qualitative scholarship would resist definitions of their approach, this is of very little comfort to students and other scholars trying to understand it. When humans enter situations that are new or ambiguous to them, they seek organizing principles and definitions of key elements around them in order to become oriented. Without a clear orientation to a system of thinking, readers fear they will wander through the literature aimlessly and not be able to make sense of what they experience or even know if they have, without realizing it, wandered outside that literature into another realm.

Wide Range of Definitions for *Qualitative*

In contrast to the scholars who resist formulating a definition for qualitative, there are many scholars who find definitions important. Nevertheless, managing the range of definitions can be daunting to the new student or the quantitative scholar who is looking for a standard, accepted definition. For example, the following is a partial list of synonyms that have been used to describe the qualitative approach: phenomenology, interpretation, humanism or humanistic studies, naturalism, hermeneutics, ethnography, critical theory, cultural science, postpositivism, interactionism, and ethnomethodology. Although these terms overlap somewhat, their individually subtle and sometimes nuanced elements distinguish them from one another.

There are many scholars who have presented definitions of qualitative, as illustrated in the following partial list:

- Strauss and Corbin (1990) defined qualitative research as "any kind of research that produces findings that are not arrived at by means of statistical procedures or other means of quantification" (p. 17).
- Jensen and Jankowski (1991) said that qualitative is concerned with "meaning in phenomenological and contextual terms," not information "in the sense of discrete items transporting significance through mass media." It also requires an internal approach to looking at indivisible experience through exegesis with a focus on process "which is contextualized and inextricably integrated with wider social and cultural practices" (p. 4).
- Jankowski and Wester (1991) said that the qualitative approach relies on the idea of *verstehen*, which "refers to an understanding of the meaning that people ascribe to their social situation and activities. Because people act on the basis of the meanings they attribute to themselves and others, the focus of qualitative social science is on everyday life and its significance as perceived by the participants" (pp. 44–45).
- Pauly (1991) saw qualitative as a five-step process: (a) finding a topic, (b) formulating research questions, (c) gathering the evidence, (d) interpreting the evidence, and (e) telling the researcher's story.
- Bogdan and Taylor (1975) maintained that the qualitative approach refers to research procedures that examine "settings and the individuals within those settings holistically; that is, the subject of the study, be it an organization or an individual, is not reduced to an isolated variable or to an hypothesis, but is viewed instead as part of a whole" (p. 2).
- Lofland (1971) said "qualitative analysis is addressed to the task of delineating forms, kinds of social phenomena; of documenting in loving detail the things that exist" (p. 13).

The point of presenting this list is to demonstrate the range of thinking about what qualitative is. Although this diversity bothers some, it does not bother scholars such as Evans (1990), who said, "In routine academic discourse, this terminological conflation is not too problematic, because like-trained scholars usually have a tacit but mutual understanding of the invoked terms" (p. 155). Evans' observation is most likely a shared one—by like-trained scholars. But to the untrained scholar, there is no tacit understanding. Instead, it is more likely that what they see is inconsistency and confusion among theoreticians.

Lack of Consistency in Usage of Important Terms

Readers of the qualitative literature will usually encounter some technical terms that the author uses to refer to some specialized meaning. Technical terms are not unique to the qualitative approach—all scholarly fields and professions have them. Technical terms are the tools that define the substance and boundaries of a field. Students must learn the meaning of these terms before they can grasp the essence of a field. Some fields, like law or medicine, have very long lists of technical terms, thus requiring a high level of commitment from potential novices; students must learn the specialized meanings of the terms in order to be considered for inclusion in the field.

With the qualitative approach, the list of technical terms is moderate. The problem is that for many of the terms, the scholars in the field are not consistent in the meaning they ascribe to these terms. For example, a very important term within the qualitative approach is *naturalism*. Lincoln and Guba (1985) wrote a widely disseminated book entitled *Naturalistic Inquiry*, in which they defined naturalism as a belief in multiple realities where the knower and the known are inseparable. The goal of naturalistic inquiry is to produce idiographic knowledge (the particulars about how an individual in a special situation produces meaning), rather than generalizable principles (laws of human behavior that apply to everyone). Alternatively, other qualitative scholars in education and communication may use the term naturalism to mean the belief that the world should be studied in its natural state, undisturbed by the researcher, "rather than an artificially constrained one such as an experiment" (Marshall & Rossman, 1989, pp. 10–11). Also, in the communications field, Christians and Carey (1989) maintained that researchers must "pitch their tents among the natives, must enter the situation so deeply that they can recreate in imagination and experience the thoughts and sentiments of the observed" (p. 360). Other communication scholars also use the term naturalism in this sense (Jankowski & Wester, 1991; Lindlof, 1991; Lindlof & Meyer, 1987).

But in a 1989 book chapter, Giddens chose to define naturalism as "the notion that the social sciences should be modeled after the natural sciences and that the logical framework of social science addresses problems similar to those of natural science" (p. 53). In essence he was using naturalism as a synonym for positivism saying "it means the same thing" (p. 53). This radical shift in meaning, first introduced by Giddens, was immediately adopted by others such as Krippendorf (1989), who referred to it in the next chapter of the very same book. "Anthony Giddens (in this volume) prefers the term *naturalistic paradigm* to refer to the same and I have no quarrel with that" (p. 70). The problem here is not who is defining the term correctly; scholars can create terms and define them any way they find useful. The problem instead is that a contrary definition can easily get into the literature and get picked up by other scholars immediately. This creates a condition where readers need to be continually skeptical of the meaning of all terms, even those terms they think they understand.

There is also a range of meaning applied to the term *discourse*. Vande Berg and Wenner (1991) observed that:

> In many instances the same term refers to rather different notions as part of the critical vocabulary of adjacent approaches. Take, for example, the term *discourse*. In a rhetorical or conversational approach, discourse analysis is concerned with the study of message structure from a phenomenological perspective. Discourse is regarded as an active, intentional, strategic communicative action. The critic's purpose in such discourse analysis is the discovery of rules or principles that the discourse communicator knew and used. On the other hand, in cultural studies, discourse is defined more broadly as a socially produced and conventionalized representation system which coneys a set of power relationships. (p. 29)

Another example is with the term *critical*. Seiter, Borchers, Kreutzner, and Warth (1989b) pointed out that there are at least four different uses of this term. First, it "may simply mean pertaining to the practice of criticism" (p. 6) such as that practiced by the professionals, for example, television critics and film critics. The second use refers to the Frankfurt School tradition, which criticized society at large using psychoanalytical and Marxist ideas. Third, poststructuralists use the term to contrast their ideology with what they call empiricism and positivism. Fourth, "scholars sometimes use the term 'critical' to identify any research which has something negative to say about the media: as though all that is called for is taking a moral stand against the media" (p. 8). My argument is not that some of these definitions are faulty or useless. Instead, I question why there are not four technical terms to refer uniquely to each of these important ideas. Given the current abuse, an author's meaning may be obscured rather than illuminated when he or she uses this term.

Arguably the most problematic term is *empirical*. For example, Allen (1985) labeled some of his work a "critique of the empiricist methods usually employed by American media researchers to study fictional programming" (p. 5). Readers who look up the term *empiricism* in the dictionary will find: "the practice of emphasizing experience, esp. of the senses or the practice or method of relying on observation, experimentation, or induction rather than upon intuition, speculation, dialectic or other rationalistic means in the pursuit of knowledge" (Gove, 1986, p. 743). These readers will then be very puzzled trying to imagine what nonempirical research is. There is no help to sort out this puzzle in Allen's own book, because after he made his argument for the uselessness of empiricism, he presented observations and quotes from interviews and even 25 pages of scripts in his appendices. Clearly Allen was not using *empirical* in an ordinary way that would refer to our common understanding of the term. He changed the definition, but he did not tell the reader what his special definition was. He *may* have been referring to the idea of splitting communication research into two camps and labeling them *empirical* and *critical*—a distinction put forth by Rogers (1982). However, this labeling is very misleading and the dichotomy itself is wrong as pointed out quickly in Slack and Allor (1983). But the terms got picked up and used by others like Allen, who did not even cite their origin. Perhaps the meaning of the term is specialized to subgroups within the field of communication. But this does not appear to be the case, because some critical scholars *do* use the term in its ordinary, nonspecialized sense. For example, Silverstone (1988) described his work on television and myth as "both theoretical and empirical. It has involved narrative-semiotic analysis, the study of the production process, and some work with audiences" (p. 20).

Political Context

Many qualitative scholars view the purpose of their research in a consciously political context. Because the focus of their research is on how humans construct meaning, they feel that those people who seem to have more power in this process should be the focus of criticism. The writings take on an adversarial tone. Some of these scholars are very convincing, but others generate more heat than light, especially among readers who do not accept their premises. For example, quantitative scholars find some qualitative researchers difficult to read when those researchers seem to characterize science unfairly. Some qualitative writers set up a rigid distinction between quantitative and qualitative research in which all quantitative research is argued to be reductionistic number crunching done by researchers operating under the false consciousness that they are in the objective pursuit of discovering truth. Such an argument can appear powerful to the new student in the field; however, its claims are hyperbolic and obfuscate the important distinctions across the varieties of research. To illustrate, Allen (1985) said, "the battles against exclusively quantitative analysis, the presumed objectivity of the investigator, and appropriateness of research models based on the natural sciences for the study of cultural phenomena, and other tenets of empiricism are no longer being fought; the war is over, and the antiempiricists now occupy the field" (p. 5). This statement displays a combatant nature, rather than a cooperative perspective, and reveals an elitism in which he placed his position beyond question. This attitude is not constructive, and the perspective expressed there does not seem to fit what either qualitative or quantitative scholars do. For example, Gerbner (1983) clearly showed why this false dichotomy of qualitative-quantitative is very misleading:

> Qualitative distinctions and judgments (as in labeling or classifying) are prereq-
> uisites to quantitative measurements; the two are inseparable. To say that one can
> only measure what exists and, therefore, quantitative efforts can only support the
> status quo, is sophistry. The careful observation of existing conditions is necessary
> to support any judgment of or strategy for change, and judgment is not hurt by
> some attempt at precision. . . . Qualitative change cannot be understood, let alone
> achieved, without noting the accumulation of quantities. Add heat (quantity) to
> water and it changes to steam (quality). To consider quantification only mindless
> counting or number crunching is both a philosophical and strategic fallacy. (p. 361)

The criticism of this dichotomy cuts both ways. Quantitative researchers who characterize qualitative methods as not being rigorous are also creating a false distinction. Rosengren (1989) argued that qualitative methods are no less rigor-ous than quantitative methods: "The most 'humanistic' of activities, the inter-pretation of texts, may be carried out in a very systematic and rigorous way" (p. 26).

The adversarial nature of some of the qualitative writing does not try to establish a common ground with quantitative researchers and thereby take them step by step into the garden where the quantitative scholars can begin to appreciate the qualitative perspective more fully. The oppositional nature serves instead to intimidate or anger those quantitative scholars browsing at the gate to the garden.

A GUIDE

From afar, the qualitative garden can seem intimidating to new students and to quantitative researchers. There are many reasons why people are scared away from entering this garden. But unless you are willing to enter the garden, it is impossible to get past these negative perceptions, which lead to a very unflat-tering stereotype that qualitative thinking is a swirl of unformed ideas that draw visitors into a vortex of unproductive activity.

My purpose is not to be a botanist who attempts to catalog each species and thereby develop *the list* of plants. Instead, I attempt to be a guide who provides descriptions of the different plants as a means for illustrating the main features of the garden. These chapters should be read as a guidebook to the garden as I point out what you should *look* for and what you should *look out* for. In this book, I share the contexts I have found useful. I hope you will find those contexts of use to you when you construct your own interpretations.

There are many different places where one could enter the garden. I present some gateway ideas in the first five foundational chapters of this book. In the second section (chapters 6–13) of the book, I illustrate the fundamental issues underlying the qualitative approach and show how they are exemplified in the research literature. These gateway ideas and issues should not be regarded as a system of categories for memorization but as a list of suggestions that may be modified as you learn your way around. To understand the qualitative approach, you must ultimately make your own interpretations. The greater your exposure to this garden's creativity and vitality, the more ideas you will find that resonate with your own experience, and the more you will come to appreciate the strengths of an often misunderstood approach that has a unique power to guide our understanding about what makes us human.

SUMMARY

It is the thesis of this chapter that there are some intimidating aspects to learning about the qualitative approach. Among these aspects are a reluctance by some scholars to provide a definition of *qualitative*, whereas among other scholars there is a proliferation of definitions, some of which use the same term differently and others who use different terms to mean the same thing. Also, there is a political purpose underlying much of the writing, especially attacks on nonqualitative research, and this alarms scholars who do not find such a confrontational approach constructive.

Despite its apparent intimidating nature, the qualitative approach provides an enormously useful variety of means for examining how humans make sense out of their world. It is the purpose of the following chapters to help readers make sense out of the qualitative writings and thereby be able to appreciate and use the strengths of this approach to research.

CHAPTER

2

A POTPOURRI
OF DEFINITIONS

Qualitative theoreticians have presented a very wide array of views about what the qualitative approach is or should be. By *qualitative theoretician*, I do not mean someone who has developed a theory about how humans construct meaning; instead, I use the term throughout this book to mean a scholar who focuses on the qualitative approach *as the phenomenon of interest* and seeks to describe what it is or prescribe what it should be. This is in contrast to a qualitative researcher who is a scholar who *uses* some aspect of the approach as a tool to examine social phenomena. Of course, some scholars are both theoreticians and researchers.

Also, I prefer to use the term *qualitative approach*, because the word *approach* is much less formal than *paradigm* and a more general term than *technique*, *method*, or *methodology*. It is a perspective on research that is conducted by scholars who want to examine some phenomenon, develop insights, and report those insights to others. Scholars must have some sort of approach to this task. An approach is composed of a set of assumptions, goals, and methods. Qualitative is one kind of approach.

Fortunately, there are many good theoreticians who have written about what the approach should be. Although there are many clear ideas in these writings, it is difficult to see a consensus about what the approach is across all the theoreticians. Some sort of a synthesis is needed to help readers orient to the structure of the approach. The purpose of this chapter is to illustrate the wide range of thinking about what the qualitative approach is or should be as envisioned by those theoreticians. I do this by first presenting different definitions of qualitative. Then I present the different schemes qualitative theoreticians have proposed to organize thinking *about* the research. Like the definitions, the schemes display more variety than consensus.

CHAPTER 2

WIDE RANGE OF THINKING ABOUT DEFINITIONS FOR QUALITATIVE

Some scholars are uncomfortable with the term *qualitative* but continue to use it for want of a better term. For example, as Lindlof (1991) put it, "although the term is not used universally by those who engage in non-quantitative audience studies (ethnography or naturalistic inquiry are others that are preferred), qualitative inquiry is probably the best single descriptor for what the great majority of them do" (p. 25). For better or worse, this term is the most popular among all the alternatives.

Although the term qualitative is the one that is most often used, it appears to have many synonyms as can be seen in the following list:

- Interpretive (Christians & Carey, 1989; Jankowski & Wester, 1991; J. K. Smith, 1983; M. J. Smith, 1988);
- Humanism or humanistic studies (Jankowski & Wester, 1991; Lincoln & Guba, 1985; M. J. Smith, 1988);
- Phenomenology (Bogdan & Taylor, 1975; Jankowski & Wester, 1991; Lincoln & Guba, 1985);
- Naturalistic (Jankowski & Wester, 1991; Lincoln & Guba, 1985; Lindlof, 1991; Lindlof & Meyer, 1987; M. L. Smith, 1987);
- Hermeneutic (Christians & Carey, 1989; Lincoln & Guba, 1985);
- Ethnography (Lincoln & Guba, 1985; Lindlof, 1991; Lindlof & Meyer, 1987; M. L. Smith, 1987);
- Ethnomethodology (Lindlof, 1991);
- Critical theory and cultural science (Christians & Carey, 1989);
- Postpositivistic, subjective, and case study (Lincoln & Guba, 1985);
- Interactionist (Jankowski & Wester, 1991).

It appears that many of these synonyms have an asymmetric relationship to the term qualitative. For example, we might agree that ethnography is subsumed under the term qualitative, but that qualitative means more than just ethnography. By this reasoning, ethnography would be a better synonym for qualitative (because its characteristics are fully encapsulated in the more general term of qualitative) than qualitative would be for ethnography (because there is much more to qualitative than just ethnography). This asymmetry leads to only partially fitting terms together, and this can be confusing to readers struggling to piece together all the elements of meaning for qualitative.

There are many scholars who regard a good definition of qualitative as very important, and a great deal of work has gone into the task of defining qualitative. However, these definitions exhibit a variety that can be daunting to the new student or to the quantitative scholar who is looking for a standard, accepted definition. Many of these definitions exhibit the characteristics of asymmetry and partial meaning like was the case with synonyms. When looking at the variety of definitions, it helps to sort them into type (see Table 2.1). Following is a comparison across the types of definitions.

Direct Definition

A direct definition attempts to explicate the full meaning of a term by laying out the complete set conditions that must be met in order for something to be included in the class of things referenced by that term. This direct type of definition usually takes the form of "Qualitative research is defined as. . . ." This type of definition is the most useful type, because it focuses the reader's attention on the boundaries, and it provides a foundation for the reader to judge what should be included and what should not. It is rare to find a simple, direct definition of qualitative, but there are a few. For example, see the general definition offered by Pauly (1991). Its strength is its simplicity, however it leaves the reader feeling that this definition could also apply to much of the quantitative approach. The other examples are more wordy, but they also have the advantage of providing more detail to help the reader see the boundaries in a more concrete fashion.

Indirect Definitions

In contrast to the direct definition, an indirect definition gives the reader a flavor for the meaning of the term, but because the guidance is partial, the reader does not have enough information to feel confident about classifying examples. The indirect definition has the advantage of being more specific and concrete. Qualitative writers provide many kinds of indirect definitions, such as a contrasting definition, a component definition, a procedural definition, or a product-oriented definition.

Contrasting-Type Definition. The contrasting definition is very popular, especially when writers are more interested in showing that there is an alternative method to traditional media research. This traditional research or standard for comparison is almost always quantitative research. The simplest form of contrast is then on the matter of using numbers. For example, Strauss and Corbin (1990) defined qualitative research as "any kind of research that produces findings that are not arrived at by means of statistical procedures or other means of quantification" (p. 17).

The contrast is not always in terms of the use of numbers. For example, Lancy (1993) provided a contrast of qualitative with quantitative focusing on the choice of topics, sampling, role of investigator, bias, context, length of study, and report. The contrasting definition of Jensen and Jankowski (1991) highlights the differ-

TABLE 2.1
Types of Definitions of *Qualitative*

A. *Formal Definition:* This is a dictionary-type of definition where the essence of the concept is made explicit. This type of definition "centers" readers by telling them what to focus on and where the boundaries are; it provides a foundation for the reader to judge what should be included and what should not.

---

1. J. A. Anderson (1987): "A research paradigm which emphasizes inductive, interpretive methods applied to the everyday world which is seen as subjective and socially created" (p. 384). He also provided an oppositional definition (see Item B.1).
2. Bogdan and Taylor (1975): "Qualitative methodologies refer to research procedures which produce descriptive data: people's own written or spoken words and observable behavior." It "directs itself at settings and the individuals within those settings holistically; that is, the subject of the study, be it an organization or an individual, is not reduced to an isolated variable or to an hypothesis, but is viewed instead as part of a whole" (p. 2).
3. Lindlof (1991): "Qualitative inquiry examines *the constitution of meaning in everyday social phenomena....* Probably the fundamental touchstone for the term is methodological. Qualitative research seeks to *preserve the form, content, and context of social phenomena and analyze their qualities*, rather than separate them from historical and institutional surroundings" (italics in original; p. 24).
4. Lindlof (1995): "Qualitative researchers seek to preserve the form and content of human behavior and to analyze its qualities, rather than subject it to mathematical or other formal transformations" (p. 21).
5. Lofland (1971): "Qualitative analysis is addressed to the task of delineating forms, kinds of social phenomena; of documenting in loving detail the things that exist" (p. 13).
6. Pauly (1991): "Qualitative studies investigate meaning-making" (p. 2).

B. *Contrasting Definition:* Some scholars define qualitative in contrast to something else. That something else is usually quantitative, but the term quantitative is usually a synonym for something such as reductionism, radical empiricism, and so forth.

---

1. J. A. Anderson (1987) defined qualitative (in contrast to quantitative) as inductive (deductive), eidetic (atomistic), subjective (objective), contextual (generalizable), mundane (purified), textual (measurable), preservationistic (aggregated), interactive (independent), and interpretive (material).
2. J. A. Anderson and Meyer (1988) declared, "Qualitative research methods are distinguished from quantitative methods in that they do not rest their evidence on the logic of mathematics, the principle of numbers, or the methods of statistical analysis" (p. 247).
3. Bogdan and Taylor (1975), in their book *Introduction to Qualitative Research Methods: A Phenomenological Approach to the Social Sciences*, made a contrast on the philosophical level. They contrasted the positivism of Comte with the phenomenological approach of Weber and Deutscher: "The positivist seeks the facts or causes of social phenomena with little regard for the subjective states of individuals" (p. 2). They stated that "Durkheim advised the social scientist to consider 'social facts,' or social phenomena, as 'things' that exercise an external and coercive influence on human behavior" (p. 2). In contrast, phenomenologists are "concerned with understanding human behavior from the actor's own frame of reference.... The important reality is what people imagine it to be" (p. 2). They also defined the phenomenon as "the process of interpretation" (p. 14).
3. Christians and Carey (1989) contrasted physical sciences with social sciences—a distinction such as made in Europe.

(Continued)

TABLE 2.1
(Continued)

4. Jensen and Jankowski (1991): In contrasting qualitative with quantitative they asserted that qualitative is concerned with "meaning in phenomenological and contextual terms," not information "in the sense of discrete items transporting significance through mass media" (p. 4). "Qualitative analysis focuses on the *occurrence* of its analytical objects in a particular context, as opposed to the *recurrence* of formally similar elements in different contexts" (p. 4). It also requires an internal approach to looking an indivisible experience through exegesis with a focus on process "which is contextualized and inextricably integrated with wider social and cultural practices" (p. 4). They further stated that "there seems to be no way around the quantitative-qualitative distinction. Although it sometimes serves to confuse rather than clarify research issues, the distinction is a fact of research practice which has major epistemological and political implications that no scholar can afford to ignore" (p. 5).
5. Lancy (1993) provided a contrast of qualitative with quantitative focusing on the choice of topics, sampling, role of investigator, bias, context, length of study and report.
6. Lindlof and Meyer (1987) drew a distinction between what they called deterministic, functionalist, and interpretive paradigms: "The deterministic paradigm responds to the perceived need for universal probability statements regarding audience behavior that can be applied to transient social problems. Emphasis is placed on the types of attitudinal or behavioral effects that *can* be produced under certain optimal conditions" (p. 3). "The functionalist paradigm, on the other hand, casts the audience member as a 'free agent' media user whose goal is to assess the utility of more or less equivalent sources of social and psychological gratification" (p. 3). The interpretive paradigm focuses on the "fields of meaning" that people construct in their social lives (p. 4).
7. Schwartz and Jacobs (1979) asserted that quantitative researchers assign numbers to qualitative observations and thereby produce data by counting and measuring things. Qualitative researchers report observations in their natural language. They defined quantitative researchers in sociology as positivists. They stated that positivists are concerned with:

> the sharpening up of an otherwise fuzzy picture of "what's really going on out there." The picture is fuzzy because lay persons have their own practical ways of describing the particulars of the world they inhabit. . . . That is, it displays inconsistency, vagueness, multiple meanings, and other characteristics that contribute to a blurred and sketchy picture. It is therefore understood that one of positivistic sociology's services to society is to provide more accurate information. A familiar procedure is to take a lay concept, such as crime or suicide, and repair it or "clean it up" by precise definition and the development of measurement procedures in the hope that it will become capable of being used in scientific theory. With its new definition and new use, the altered concept can be presented to colleagues and the society at large as contributing to a clearer, more valid picture of the world than its lay counterpart. (pp. 5–6)

8. J. K. Smith (1983) compared qualitative and quantitative on the issues of (a) the relationship of the investigator to the phenomenon, (b) the relationship between facts and values in the process of investigation, and (c) the goal of the investigation.
9. J. K. Smith and Heshusius (1986) cited Dilthey's position of an interpretive or hermeneutical approach, which is a direct challenge to positivism. Positivism might work with physical sciences that focus on "inanimate objects that could be seen as existing outside of us (a world of external, objectively knowable facts)" (p. 5). In contrast, social science focuses on "the products of the human mind with all its subjectivity, emotions, and values" (p. 5).

(Continued)

TABLE 2.1
(Continued)

10. Strauss and Corbin (1990) defined qualitative research as "any kind of research that produces findings that are not arrived at by means of statistical procedures or other means of quantification" (p. 17). They clarified this position by adding that qualitative reports may contain some numbers, such as census data, "but the analysis itself is a qualitative one" (p. 17).

11. Wimmer and Dominick (1991) saw three main differences between qualitative and quantitative. First, they asserted that qualitative believes that there is no single reality, and that each person creates a subjective reality that is holistic and not reducible to component parts. Second, qualitative believes that individuals are fundamentally different and that they cannot be categorized. And third, qualitative strives for unique explanations about particular situations and individuals.

C. Component Definition: Some scholars illuminate some components or characteristics. This gives readers a sense of the parts or concerns within the qualitative domain, but it does not provide a sense of the boundaries or limits.

---

1. Bogdan and Taylor (1975), who used phenomenology as a synonym for qualitative research, argued that phenomenology itself has two components: symbolic interactionism and ethnomethodology. In their view, ethnomethodology means qualitative methods, but qualitative methods does not mean ethnomethodology because there is more to qualitative research than the component of ethnomethodology.

2. Christians and Carey (1989) mentioned four subsets as follows: symbolic interactionism, ethnomethodology, humanistic sociology, and cultural hermeneutics.

3. Jacob (1988) perceived six domains: human ethology, holistic ethnography, ethnography of communication, cognitive anthropology, ecological psychology, and symbolic interactionism. However, she asserted that human ethology is based on positivist traditions and is not really a form of qualitative research. There are then five qualitative components as she presented in her earlier treatment (Jacob, 1987).

4. Jankowski and Wester (1991) presented two unique elements in their definition. First is the idea of *verstehen,* which "refers to an understanding of the meaning that people ascribe to their social situation and activities. Because people act on the basis of the meanings they attribute to themselves and others, the focus of qualitative social science is on everyday life and its significance as perceived by the participants" (pp. 44–45). The second element is role taking, which expresses the idea that people are active and their roles change across situations.

5. Jensen and Jankowski (1991) examined discourse analysis, textual analysis, reception analysis, ethnography, and history.

6. Lancy (1993) identified ethnography, ethnomethodology, ecological psychology, and history.

7. Lindlof and Meyer (1987) broke down their interpretive paradigm into ethnomethodology, ecological psychology, symbolic interactionism. Lindlof (1991) divided qualitative research in media audience studies into five components, each of which is composed of subcomponents. Those five components are: social-phenomenological (which includes social reality construction, ethnomethodology, symbolic interactionism, and cultural hermeneutics), communication rules (which includes rules theory, ethnography of communication, and conversational analysis), cultural studies (which appears to include discourse analysis, social-structuralism, political economy criticism, poststructuralism, and ethnography again), reception study (which includes the antecedents of literary theory and criticism), and feminist research (which "in many respects . . . shares the same goals and methods as cultural studies" (p. 29). His structure provides a generally neat categorization scheme, but some terms overlap (such as ethnography) into more than one superordinate area.

(Continued)

TABLE 2.1
(Continued)

8. Strauss and Corbin (1990) stated that "some of the different types of qualitative research are: grounded theory, ethnography, phenomenological approach, life histories, and conversational analysis" (p. 21).

D. Procedural Definition: Qualitative can be defined in terms of a list of steps.

1. Lincoln and Guba (1985) offered two prime tenets: that "first, no manipulation on the part of the inquirer is implied, and, second, the inquirer imposes no *a priori* units on the outcome" (p. 8).
2. Pauly (1991) attempted to "guide the work of beginners" who want to try qualitative research by providing a "step by step explanation of how one might do qualitative research" (pp. 1–2). He presented five steps: (a) finding a topic, (b) formulating research questions, (c) gathering the evidence, (d) interpreting the evidence, and (e) telling the researcher's story.

E. Product Definition: Some theoreticians define *qualitative* in terms of the end point of a process.

1. Bogdan and Taylor (1975) asserted that "qualitative methodologies refer to research procedures which produce descriptive data: people's own written or spoken words and observable behavior." It "directs itself at settings and the individuals within those settings holistically; that is, the subject of the study, be it an organization or an individual, is not reduced to an isolated variable or to an hypothesis, but is viewed instead as part of a whole" (p. 2).
2. Lofland (1971) stated, "Qualitative analysis is addressed to the task of delineating forms, kinds of social phenomena; of documenting in loving detail the things that exist" (p. 13).

ences in the assumptions researchers make, whereas differences in practices are the focus of the contrasting definitions of J. K. Smith (1983) as well as Wimmer and Dominick (1991). Some theoreticians make a contrast at the philosophical level (Bogdan & Taylor, 1975; Schwartz & Jacobs, 1979; J. K. Smith & Heshusius, 1986).

J. A. Anderson (1987) contrasted qualitative with quantitative along many different kinds of dimensions. He included fundamental axioms along with procedures by saying that qualitative is primarily inductive, whereas quantitative is deductive; qualitative is eidetic, compared to quantitative being atomistic; subjective, not objective; contextual, not generalizable; mundane, not purified; textual, not measurable; preservationistic, not aggregated; interactive, not independent; and interpretive, not material.

Lindlof and Meyer (1987) referred to qualitative method as an interpretive paradigm and drew a double comparison of it with both a deterministic and a functionalist paradigm. "The deterministic paradigm responds to the perceived need for universal probability statements regarding audience behavior that can be applied to transient social problems. Emphasis is placed on the types of attitudinal or behavioral effects that *can* be produced under certain optimal conditions" (p. 3). "The functionalist paradigm, on the other hand, casts the audience member as a 'free agent' media user whose goal is to assess the utility of more or less equivalent sources of social and psychological gratification" (p.

tion" (p. 3). The interpretive paradigm focuses on the "fields of meaning" that people construct in their social lives (p. 4).

Some scholars seem to define qualitative in a contrasting fashion but they do not use the terms qualitative or quantitative. For example, Lincoln and Guba (1985) drew a contrast between naturalism and positivism in education. Also, Ang (1989) drew a contrast between what she called mainstream and critical research. She said that mainstream and critical are relative terms that can only be applied in the context of other research. She proposed "an *open* and *contextual* definition of critical research, one that does not allow itself to rest easily on pre-existent epistemological foundations, but—on the contrary—engages itself in reflecting on the ways in which it contributes to our understanding of the world" (p. 98). She did back off from this purely relativistic position by providing a sort of definition of critical saying:

> [I]t refers first of all to a certain intellectual-political *orientation* toward academic practice: whatever its subject matter or method of analysis, essential to doing "critical" research would be the adoption of a self-reflexive perspective, one that is, first, conscious of the social and discursive nature of any research practice, and second, takes seriously the Foucaultian reminder that the production of knowledge is always bound up in a network of power relations. (p. 97)

And, Jensen (1993) presented multiple contrasts: "our field is divided up into qualitative or quantitative, interpretive or social science, expressivist or objectivist approaches" (p. 69).

The prededing descriptions of contrasting definitions show how difficult it is to put these examples on a common ground. Although each is contrasting, each seems to make a comparison at a different level or with different characteristics. Also, the terms used are different enough to indicate that maybe the two "paradigms," "approaches," or "methods" are not the same two across each example. That is, a large part of the confusion generated with the contrasting definitions is with what is chosen as the other. Sometimes, this other is referred to as quantitative (J. A. Anderson, 1987; Jensen & Jankowski, 1991; Lancy, 1993; Schwartz & Jacobs, 1979; Strauss & Corbin, 1990; Wimmer & Dominick, 1991), positivism (Bogdan & Taylor, 1975; Carey, 1977; Lincoln & Guba, 1985; Lutz, 1989; Schwartz & Jacobs, 1979; J. K. Smith & Heshusius, 1986), empiricist (Allen, 1987; Carey, 1977), even pragmatist, which includes behavioral psychology and functional sociology (Carey, 1977). So the definitions vary with the characterization of the other.

Component-Type Definition. The component definition characterizes qualitative in terms of its parts. This type of definition is more concrete than an abstract, direct definition, but it usually gives the reader an incomplete feeling, because it does not illuminate clearly what it is the components share that warrants them being considered a set. For example, Jankowski and Wester (1991) presented two unique elements in their definition. First is the idea of *verstehen*, which refers to an understanding of the meaning that people ascribe to their social situation and activities. The second element is role taking, which expresses the idea that people are active and their roles change across situations. The two components of meaning in the Jankowski and Wester definition are important elements of qualitative; that is, almost all qualitative theoreticians would agree that those elements are part of the qualitative approach. However, the definition is unsatisfying in the sense that it would seem possible to follow the definition and still not formulate an example of qualitative research. Many quantitative social scientists design questionnaires and observational protocols to measure the way their research subjects see their world and to analyze the data in a way to respect the dynamic nature of role playing; however, qualitative researchers who look at such a study might see elements in it that disqualify it from being qualitative—even though it exemplified the two components in the Jankowski and Wester definition.

Procedural-Type Definition. The procedural definition describes the method by illuminating a sequence of tasks. An example is Pauly (1991), who attempted to "guide the work of beginners" who want to try qualitative research by providing a "step by step explanation of how one might do qualitative research" (pp. 1–2). He presented five steps: (a) finding a topic, (b) formulating research questions, (c) gathering the evidence, (d) interpreting the evidence, and (e) telling the researcher's story. Like the component type of definition, this is more concrete than a direct type definition, but it leaves the reader with a feeling that he or she could follow each of these steps in sequence and still not produce a qualitative research study.

Product-Type Definition. The product-oriented definition focuses on what is produced by the qualitative method. According to Bogdan and Taylor (1975), "qualitative methodologies refer to research procedures which produce descriptive data: people's own written or spoken words and observable behavior." It "directs itself at settings and the individuals within those settings holistically; that is, the subject of the study, be it an organization or an individual, is not reduced to an isolated variable or to an hypothesis, but is viewed instead as part of a whole" (p. 2). And, as Lofland (1971) put it, "Qualitative analysis is addressed to the task of delineating forms, kinds of social phenomena; of documenting in loving detail the things that exist" (p. 13).

These types of definitions demonstrate a range of thinking about qualitative methods. As can be seen from those examples, some of the theoreticians offer more than one type of definition, and this is evidence for the struggle in determining what the qualitative approach really is. Providing a definition for qualitative research is a very difficult task.

ANALYSIS OF EXISTING ORGANIZATIONAL SCHEMES

Many of the component type definitions lay out a set of elements that the authors feel define the full extent of subdomains within the qualitative approach. Although these sets vary across authors, there are some commonalities, as can be seen in the following list of elements:

- Ethnomethodology (Bogdan & Taylor, 1975; Christians & Carey, 1989; Jankowski & Wester, 1991; Lancy, 1993; Lindlof, 1991; Lindlof & Meyer, 1987);
- Symbolic interactionism (Bogdan & Taylor, 1975; Christians & Carey, 1989; Jacob, 1987; Jankowski & Wester, 1991; Lindlof, 1991; Lindlof & Meyer, 1987);
- Ethnography (Jacob, 1987; Jankowski & Wester, 1991; Jensen & Jankowski, 1991; Lancy, 1993; Strauss & Corbin, 1990);
- Ecological psychology (Jacob, 1987; Lancy, 1993; Lindlof & Meyer, 1987);
- Phenomenology (Lindlof, 1991; Strauss & Corbin, 1990);
- Cultural studies (Christians & Carey, 1989; Lindlof, 1991);
- Reception studies (Jensen & Jankowski, 1991; Lindlof, 1991);
- History (Jensen & Jankowski, 1991; Lancy, 1993);
- Conversational analysis (Lindlof, 1991; Strauss & Corbin, 1990).

But there are also some lone elements that are mentioned by only one theoretician. These include: humanistic sociology (Christians & Carey, 1989), cultural hermeneutics (Christians & Carey, 1989), holistic ethnography (Jacob, 1987), cognitive anthropology (Jacob, 1987), communication rules (Lindlof, 1991), feminist research (Lindlof, 1991), discourse analysis (Jensen & Jankowski, 1991), textual analysis (Jensen & Jankowski, 1991), grounded theory (Strauss & Corbin, 1990), and life histories (Strauss & Corbin, 1990). If we include the most popular synonyms (interpretive, humanism or humanistic studies, naturalistic, hermeneutic, critical theory, and case study) noted in chapter 1, we have quite a list of terms for the qualitative enterprise.

KINDS OF KEY IDEAS

It is not surprising that readers of this literature become confused about what is regarded as qualitative research. It seems like each theoretician has his or her own view of definitions, synonyms, and structure of methods.

How can we make sense out of all these terms? Separating the definitions into types helps illuminate the differences in the definitions, but it does not point to a path to a synthesis. Instead, we need to break these definitions down into their key components. When we conduct such an analysis, it becomes clear that those elements cannot be arrayed on a single dimension. Nor can they be mapped out in two dimensions; that is, we cannot draw a map on a sheet of paper to show in an adequate manner how the various elements in the definitions form different domains of activity. If some definitional elements addressed data gathering, some addressed analysis, and some addressed writing issues, we could sketch out three domains and place all the definitional elements within one of the areas; however, if we were to try this, we would be left with many definitional elements that would not fit in any of the areas on our two-dimensional map. So, we need more than two dimensions to think about all the elements.

When we add a third dimension (such as abstraction of the elements), we can envision a cube like a room where the definitional elements can be perceived in three-dimensional space. There may be those who would argue that we need four, five, or many more dimensions to capture all the definitional elements, but for purposes of illustrating a useful analysis, I stop at three dimensions. If we regard the "third dimension" as the level of abstraction, we can see that the elements in the definition do in fact vary along this dimension.

The terms in the most abstract group would include those that present a broad, foundational perspective on the qualitative approach. They refer to *axiomatic* positions about the nature of the research enterprise. This includes the philosophical issues of ontology and epistemology. Ontology is the concern with what exists and what the nature phenomenon is that the qualitative approach is employed to examine. Epistemology is the concern with how meaning is constructed by humans. This axiomatic group also includes the terms of phenomenology, hermeneutics, interpretive, humanistic studies, and naturalism; these are assumptions that scholars make about the nature of research. Making a certain set of assumptions would define a scholar as a quantitative researcher; making another set of assumptions would define one as a qualitative one.

There are other terms that refer to fairly concrete practices—terms such as interviewing, discourse analysis, and case study. These are methods or the specific tools of gathering data, analyzing data, and forms of writing reports.

In the middle between the highly abstract axioms and the fairly concrete methods are terms that refer to methodologies. An important distinction is made between methodology and method similar to that illuminated by Craig (1989). Method refers to "any explicit, orderly procedure" such as "data collection and analysis" (p. 101). A methodology is more concrete than an axiom, but more abstract than a method. Methodologies are based on assumptions that researchers must hold; they are strategies that lay out blueprints for scholars who must then use the tools of methods to build the design. The selection of a methodology is a more involved decision by scholars who must consider their beliefs about the nature of research—this requires attention to axioms. Methodologies are perspectives on research that deal with issues at the juncture of axioms and methods. The qualitative methodologies are ethnography, ethnomethodology, reception studies, ecological psychology, symbolic interaction-ism, textual analysis, and cultural studies.

Each of the seven methodologies rest on the foundation of the axioms in the first group (phenomenology, interpretation, hermeneutics, naturalism, and hu-manism), but each of these seven is unique in terms of the value each places on these axioms. For example, with ethnomethodology, the assumptions of phenomenology and naturalism are most important; with cultural studies, inter-pretation and humanism are the most salient axioms. The seven are also very different in terms of their preferred methods.

This three-level scheme is a useful heuristic device, because it can be used to show that decisions made within one group influence the decisions that will be made in another group. For example, a scholar who holds strong beliefs (axiom group) about phenomenology and naturalism would be likely to choose an ethnographic methodology and a participant observation method for the purpose of interpreting a culture. Notice that there is a fairly wide (but not complete) degree of choice within each group—that is, a decision among axioms narrows (but does not direct) the choice of methodology, and the choice of methodology narrows (but does not direct) the choice of method.

IS SYNTHESIS POSSIBLE?

A Single Definition?

Can we take the elements analyzed previously and assemble them all into a single grand definition of qualitative? If I did so, the result would truly be a cumbersome agglomeration, because there are so many different synonyms, types of definitions, and organizational schemes to fit together. Even if such a result were to illuminate the meaning of qualitative, its utility would be short lived. The thinking about the qualitative approach is in dynamic flux where ideas are constantly being mixed and where perspectives suddenly erupt then splinter. Also, and perhaps even more important, you as a reader will change your perceptions of the meaning of the qualitative approach as you learn more and view it from differing and more valued perspectives.

A Set of Issues?

Although it is not useful to synthesize all this thinking into a single definition, another kind of synthesis will result in something more useful. The synthesis that follows is not an authoritative distillation of all elements into a single definition. Instead, the synthesis is a distillation of qualitative thought into a set of issues that can serve as a template. The difference between a definition and a template can be highlighted as an analogy with the agenda-setting theory of the media. A definition would serve to tell readers what to think whereas the template instead serves to guide readers in what to think *about*.

A template would be an orientation for the reader to raise certain questions and consider particular elements when reading the qualitative literature (those writings of both the theoreticians as well as the researchers). The template is like an agenda that highlights certain issues for readers to attend to as they work through the literature and construct their own meaning. As each individual reader answers those questions for him or herself, he or she is building a unique, individualized interpretation of the literature. By so doing, the process respects the aims of the qualitative approach itself.

The template is the set of foundational issues raised in the following three chapters and the practical issues of design and practices raised in the seven chapters in Part II—the interpretive analysis.

3

ISSUES OF BELIEF

The problem of finding a consistent definition of the qualitative approach across all theoreticians can be traced to the strong valuing of individual interpretation. The individual interpretations about what the qualitative approach is or should be then leads to many different definitions among the theoreticians. However, when these differing interpretations are analyzed, we can see some commonalities that exist at a deeper level of belief—that is, there are some shared beliefs about how research should be conducted and the contributions the research can make. The purpose of this chapter is to illuminate those beliefs that underlie the qualitative approach: first, by looking at how fundamental beliefs about research have generated a debate between the use of scientific or humanistic approaches to examining human behavior; second, by examining the philosophical issues of ontology and epistemology; and third, by illuminating the axioms that form the foundation for the qualitative approach.

THE SOCIAL SCIENCE–HUMANIST DEBATE

For the last century, scholars have been debating whether human behavior can be examined using a scientific approach or whether it requires a humanistic one. Some scholars argue that the scientific approach, which has been used successfully to increase our understanding about the physical world (such as the structure of the universe, the composition of matter, reactions among molecules and among subatomic particles, the chemical nature of plant and animal systems), offers such powerful methods that it can be useful to help increase our understanding about how humans behave. The scientific approach is regarded as powerful because it has been found successful in predicting and explaining broad, general patterns in the aggregate. This function is accomplished by using what has been referred to as "the scientific method," the inductive process of observing a phenomenon and looking for patterns. A statement of these patterns is a general prediction or explanation about what happens in the aggregate. Related statements are arranged into a set of predictions, known as a theory. After a theory is constructed, its statements are tested through a process of deduction, where the statements are translated into a specific setting, with specific people subject to specific conditions so that the predictions can be formally tested. The tests usually, but not always, translate concepts into mathematical values (a process called enumeration), which are then subjected to quantitative analyses.

In contrast, humanists are more concerned with the diversity among people. Each human is unique in how he or she creates meaning, because each person is operating from a different set of experiences. In order to understand why a person has a certain meaning for a specific object, scholars must examine the unique history of that person and the special contexts in which the object holds meaning for that person.

The foundations of the debate between scientists and humanists began back in the Renaissance with the rise of empiricism, but it was not until the 19th century that this grew to a heated debate as some scholars became interested in the scientific study of human behavior, a debate still going on today. The debate focuses on whether science is a useful tool for examining human activity. There was (and still is) a range of opinion about the appropriateness of using scientific methods to examine how humans make meaning of their worlds. This range was anchored by positivists at one extreme and idealists at the opposite end. The positivists (especially Mill, Comte, and Durkheim) believed that it was not only permissible, but highly desirable, for social scientists to use the proven methods of the physical sciences. On the other side of the debate were idealists (Dilthey, Rickert, Husserl, Weber, and Schutz) who traced their thoughts back to Kant. They believed it was useless to look for general laws governing behavior, and science therefore was not a useful method for studying human behavior. Over time the debate grew, and various ideological camps, or schools of thought, formed.

Rise of Empiricism

Until the 1500s, the rationalist method was the dominant form of scholarship and knowledge production. Scholars believed that the human mind, when properly trained, was all that was needed to discover God's truths about how the world was ordered. This tradition led to the discovery of knowledge that, although logical and rational, sometimes did not conform to what people could see in the world.

The scientific revolution was essentially a call for empirical confirmation of mental speculations. Galileo, a key figure in this revolution, began his investigations by speculating about the nature of the world, but he would not stop with his guesses. He would also derive tests to see if physical phenomena performed in the world as he had speculated they should. The results of his tests were often at odds with his speculations. Rather than reject his observation, he modified his speculations. This method of speculation and testing, the scientific method, was used successfully by the great scientists of the time—people like Copernicus, Kepler, Boyle, and Newton.

By the 17th century, the scientific method with its empirical component was well established. The scientific method was regarded as being very successful in generating useful information about the natural world, especially in the areas of astronomy, physics, and chemistry. Philosophers of the time (such as Locke, Berkeley, and Kant) struggled with the epistemological question about the extent to which our understanding of phenomena is generated by the phenomena themselves and to what extent humans must construct their own meaning. In a radical break with rationalism, Locke said the mind was a *tabula rasa* that had no preconceptions of any kind; he maintained that everything humans know comes into our minds as sensory data from which we must construct ideas. Also, Berkeley believed that the essence of something is our perceptions of it; we have no other way of knowing something.

Then in the late 18th century, Kant published the *Critique of Pure Reason* in which he constructed a position between the extremes of pure empiricism and pure rationalism. He set himself apart from pure empiricism by arguing that the mind was not a *tabula rasa* where only sense perceptions are written. Instead, he believed the mind to have some a priori reasoning powers that enable it to screen and order the sense stimuli. However, he did not go to the extreme of rationalism. Although he believed, like the rationalists, that the human mind was a very important tool in the understanding of meaning, he did not accept the rationalist claim that thinking about the phenomenon would result in an objective view of truth; not every human's thought processes lead to discoveries of universal truth. Instead, thought processes are individual and subjective, because they are influenced by the experiences and perceptions of each person. Therefore, different people arrive at different interpretations of the phenomenon. This idea has led scholars such as Hamilton (1994) to say "the epistemology of qualitative research, therefore, had its origins in an epistemological crisis of the late eighteenth century" (p. 63).

The Positivists

Some scholars credit John Stuart Mill's *A System of Logic*, published in 1843, as the first strong statement to advocate the use of the empirical physical science methods to examine human behavior (Lincoln & Guba, 1985). Mill argued that there is a uniformity in nature and time that applies to the objects of study in both the social and natural sciences. He believed that the physical and social sciences have identical aims—the discovery of general laws—so their methods can be the same. When social scientists use the methods of the natural sciences, they will find laws that will explain behavior, make predictions, and improve society by changing social conditions.

In the early 19th century, the term *positivist* was coined by Comte to refer to a strict form of empiricism. He argued that scholarship had developed from a theological basis of explanation to a metaphysical one to a positive one. The high point in this evolution was positivism or science. He also placed sociology on the same path as the other sciences, despite its newness compared to physics and astronomy, because its methods and aims were the same.

Comte argued that the objects of study in social science are the same as in the physical sciences. There is the knower (the researcher) and the object of study, two separate entities. Comte argued that social science must not be bound by individual contexts, but instead must get beyond the specifics in different contexts and move to a more general perspective of broad principles. "The positivist maintains that only those knowledge claims which are founded directly on experience are genuine" (H. I. Brown, 1977, p. 21). Positivism meant that claims for truth had to be verified empirically; it ruled out philosophy and mentalism. If something cannot be verified, it is non-sense by definition. The early positivists fixated on the empirical component of science and virtually ignored the theorizing/speculation component.

Another prominent positivist figure was Durkheim who held the view that certain influences in society (he called them social facts) exercised constraints over individuals. Social facts are things such as population density, prevailing religion, or the level of industrialization. He said it was the role of the sociologist to study social facts and that science was the method to use. In his view, science was an activity conducted by objective, unbiased observers in the search for documenting truth. He believed that eventually sociology would develop a set of laws to explain all human behavior.

The Idealists

On the other side of the argument were the idealist scholars in Germany. Idealism is the belief that social science is profoundly different from physical sciences. In the social sciences, humans are both the subject and object of the investigation, so the investigation itself must be subjective; research about humans requires a process of inquiry that recognizes that human experience is strongly influenced by contexts, and the product of that investigation must be description and interpretation, not explanation.

The key figures of the idealist scholars were Dilthey, Weber, and Husserl. Drawing their ideas from the philosophy of Kant, they argued that our knowledge of the world is shaped by our own interpretations; that is, perceptions are not accurate and clear views of an external reality. Instead, there is a circular process where we use our interpretations to order and filter our perceptions which in turn results in additional interpretations.

First to challenge the positivist side was Dilthey who argued that science might be a good method for dealing with physical objects, but it is not a good method in dealing with humans and cultures. He said that physical sciences focused on inanimate objects that clearly exist outside us. But with social sciences we are studying a creation of human minds (such as behavior or culture), and there can be no objectivity. In Dilthey's view, it is not possible to separate the investigator from what is being investigated; that is, we are the subject and the object of our investigation. Because the object of study is a product of human minds, it is inseparably connected to our minds, and therefore we cannot remove the subjectivity, values, and emotions. And because the social world changes over time, it is impossible to discover laws such as those in the physical sciences. Hence, social sciences cannot be explanatory or predictive, only descriptive and concentrated on interpretive understanding—or *verstehen,* the process of re-creating the experience of others within oneself. The researcher engages in a hermeneutic process where there is constant movement between the parts and the whole and where there are no clear beginning or ending points. Dilthey distinguished between two ways of experiencing: sensory experience and inner-lived experience. Sensory experience is within the domain of the physical sciences and can therefore be understood using scientific methods. However, with inner-lived experience, investigators of the social world can only attain an understanding of that world through a hermeneutic process of interpretation. Researchers cannot understand an individual expression until they understand the context, but in order to understand the context, they must understand the individual expressions. Dilthey recognized that this hermeneutic process allowed for differing interpretations, and that it was impossible to say that any one of these interpretations was the correct one.

Then in the late 19th century, Weber built on the ideas of Dilthey, especially the idea of *verstehen.* He said that nothing could be understood without interpreting the action within its context. In contrast to other idealists, Weber felt that researchers could use hypotheses and that they should be checked empirically. Weber was also bothered by Dilthey's problem of determining the value among differing interpretations. In an attempt to solve this, Weber constructed a synthesis of the realist and idealist positions. However, most scholars do not feel this synthesis was successful (J. K. Smith, 1983). His major contribution was his attempt "to link the scientific concepts of general laws and causal analysis with the purportedly unique subject matter of social science—human beings" (Schwartz & Jacobs, 1979, pp. 17–18).

Husserl, a contemporary of Weber, argued that the methods of science were useful, but incomplete. To show this, he developed a phenomenological philosophy, which is the study of how humans attach meaning to experiences in their own minds. In order for researchers to understand how another person interprets the world, they must bracket (set aside) their own interpretations and get into the mind of the person they are examining.

Middle Positions Develop

In reaction to this extreme position of empiricism, a group of thinkers formed calling themselves logical positivists. Logical positivism allows for two sources of knowledge: empirical data and logical analysis. This logical positivism was based on the ideas of Wittgenstein and developed by the members of the Vienna Circle, who were philosophers of science trained primarily in mathematics and physics. Their purpose was to unite philosophy and science into a common critical discipline. They argued that neither logic nor experience, by themselves, were adequate tools for generating knowledge; both of these were needed. Logical positivists would philosophize about systems of explanations or theories, then deduce tests from the theory. If an empirical test could be deduced, then the theoretical statement was meaningful; if not, the statement was non-sense. An important feature of the logical positivism of the Vienna Circle was its focus on the analysis of language. They recognized that there is no point in arguing whether a thesis is true unless you know what it means. So, according to logical positivism, the primary task for philosophy was to develop tools for the analysis of meaning.

Logical positivists rely primarily on two tools of analysis: the technique of operational analysis and the verification principle. Operational analysis required a translation of general terms into measurements. Operationalism is based on the assumption that all concepts in theoretical statements must be specified by the operations that the scientist performs in order to observe them. Concepts have no other meaning or existence than their measurement. For example, shyness is a person's score on a shyness test. A good example of this position is the persuasion research of Carl Hovland, a very popular model of social science in the 1960s.

Verification focused on what it means to support a general statement. Logical positivists reasoned that verification was a goal that could never be attained; that is, general principles can never be fully tested, because their generalness means they have no boundaries in time or space. For example, you could take a theoretical proposition, deduce a hypothesis, and test it in a limited sample. If you find support for the hypothesis, then you have found support for the theoretical proposition—but you have not gone so far as to verify it. For verification, you must test that hypothesis on all possible samples of people. Such a complete test is not possible, because there are too many people, some of whom are no longer living and are beyond such a test. Therefore, verification is not possible.

However, it is possible to falsify a theoretical proposition, as Karl Popper demonstrated in his logic of falsifiability. He argued that if your test does not find support for your hypothesis, then you have found a condition where the theory does not hold. This means the theory is not as general as previously thought and must be modified. This reasoning illustrates why falsifiability is regarded as a more powerful tool than is verification.

The logical empiricists took a more moderate position compared to the logical positivists. The logical empiricists believed that it is impossible to verify conclusively any scientific proposition. Because scientific propositions are general statements, it is impossible to perform all the possible tests to confirm that the statement holds in an infinite set of instances and times. The logical empiricists then were satisfied with a process of gradual confirmation.

The ideas of the Vienna Circle spread throughout the scientific community in the early 20th century, and a new perspective arose among philosophers and scientists who were calling into question the status of scientific findings. "Scientific truth was found not to be absolute, enduring, and ontologically basic, but rather to be contingent upon the frames of references, the constructions, the conceptual premises that give to the scientific argument its unique possibility" (Turner, 1965, p. 105). In physics, Einstein and Mach made corrections to Newton's mechanics and in so doing revealed that a change in assumptions required a change in theory and explanation. Their new theories were found to be more useful than Newton's theory, because they could explain the same phenomenon that Newton explained (mechanics on earth) along with additional phenomena (mechanics in the universe) and do so more parsimoniously. Science was shifting to the newer criterion of utility, thus abandoning claims of truth. Members of the Vienna Circle reasoned that humans have limited perceptions and will never be able to perceive natural phenomena in an unfiltered, completely accurate manner. Instead, they set out a criterion of utility, reasoning that it is possible for scientists to improve their explanations. Improved explanations are those that more clearly and more parsimoniously account for broader phenomena.

In this quest for more useful explanations, logical empiricists set out to show that the scientific-empirical method was a superior method to the alternatives. But they did not go so far as to argue for cause–effect influences. They reasoned that causation is a process that can never be observed. Covariation can be observed, but that is not the same as causation. For example, we can observe that in the spring when the weather gets warmer, college students leave town. There is covariation between the warmer temperatures and students leaving town. However, it is wrong to conclude that the warm weather *causes* students to leave town. There might be a third variable (such as classes coming to an end for the academic year) that serves as the influence. In order to make a case for causation, we first need to demonstrate covariation; then we need to argue that the causal variable (and not some other third variable) is a meaningful and significant influencer of another variable. The members of the Vienna Circle felt that scientists can never rule out all possible third variables, so it is pointless to argue for causation.

Recent Perspectives on the Debate

The debate between positivism and idealism in the late 19th century has evolved into a debate between scientific realism and idealism. This evolution is not a simple translation of positivism into realism. Realists believe in a material world that is unaffected by the values of the researcher; things exist apart from the perceptions of them. Under realism, the ontological question of "what is" can be separated from the epistemological question about the ability of our perceptions to come to know "what is." So knowledge and truth are questions of correspondence between what is and our understanding of what is.

In contrast, idealism is the belief that existence is mind dependent; there is no reality independent of the perceptions of it. J. K. Smith (1983) characterized the distinction as: "Idealism focuses on what we know and then moves to construct an 'outer' reality from the point; whereas realism, reversing the direction, presupposes an independent reality and then investigates how we are a part of that reality and how we can come to know that reality" (pp. 8–9).

There are some scholars who now argue that the differences between the sciences and the humanities are not as great as previous debates would have us believe. For example, Toulmin (1983) said that when Dilthey drew a "sharp distinction between scientific explanation and hermeneutic interpretation" (p. 100) a century ago, that distinction might have held at the time but that it certainly does not hold now with postmodern science. However, many people still subscribe to this distinction. Toulmin said, "It is a pity then for scholars working in the humanities to continue shaping their critical attitudes and theories by relying on a contrast with a modern science that—among scientists themselves—no longer even *seems* to exist" (p. 101). He pointed out that significant changes have occurred in scientific thinking. In the classical period from the mid-17th century until around 1920, scientists were regarded as pure spectators, looking at the universe as if from outside it somehow. However, this perspective broke down when "the scope of investigation was extended to include systems and subjects whose behavior may be changed by the very fact that they are being investigated" (p. 102). Physical scientists found this to be true when studying subatomic particles, and this is certainly true when studying even more complex phenomena such as human behavior.

Toulmin (1983) presented several principles to support his argument of a convergence. First, he said that "the doctrines of the natural sciences are critical interpretations of their subject matter, no less than those of the humanities" (p. 101). He also said that scientists are enculturated into their professional community, and once they are fully inside that community, their work takes on the same interpretive processes as others in that community. He also tried to debunk the belief that interpretation is always personal and idiosyncratic. He asserted that scholars in well-defined disciplines draw from the accumulated experience of other scholars, so their own interpretations conform to those of the community and are therefore not purely personal or arbitrary. The community standard determines what is the correct interpretation. This does not rule out alternative interpretations within a community, but each alternative interpretation has its own scope and justification. "In sciences and humanities alike, we must be prepared to consider the products of human imagination and creation—whether ideas or artifacts, poems or theories—from a variety of different points of view" (Toulmin, 1983, p. 110).

Toulmin (1983) argued that the division between the natural sciences and the humanities is not as strong or rigid as people think. Both employ a hermeneutic process of discovery. On the science side, he said, people give too much credence to the position that science is objective and rational. Physics, for example, "has always asked its participants to adopt an interpretive standpoint" (Toulmin, 1983, p. 100). This interpretive standpoint is used to construct reality. As Toulmin said, "the supposed contrast between the scientists' claim to rational objectivity (which requires no interpretation) and the humanists' rival claim to subjective sensibility (in which interpretation is all) shows *on its face* its essential irrelevance to the actual work of art and science. At most, there is a difference of balance or emphasis" (p. 111).

As Toulmin (1983) further argued:

> We should ask scholars to pay more attention to the elements of interpretation—even of hermeneutics—that have nowadays become essential to both the natural and human sciences and to base their comparisons between the sciences and humanities not on the assumed *absence* of hermeneutic interpretation from natural science but rather on the different *modes* of interpretation characteristic of the two general fields. (p. 101)

The Quantitative-Qualitative Distinction

Now that we have laid out the science-humanities debate, it is tempting to make a direct translation into the quantitative-qualitative distinction, where the quantitative approach follows science and the qualitative approach favors the humanistic tradition. But such a translation is too simple and it ignores the complexity of the qualitative approach. Let's look at this translation more critically.

It is relatively safe to conclude that the quantitative approach follows the scientific traditions of induction and deduction as well as its orientation for searching for aggregate patterns across empirical observations. And it is safe to say that much of the qualitative approach follows the traditions of humanism, but there is also a sizable scholarly community of qualitative researchers (such as ethnographers in sociology and anthropology) who consider themselves as following the traditions of science more so than the traditions of humanism.

As far as the science-humanism debate is concerned, there are two types of qualitative scholars. One type sides with the arguments of the humanist position, and the research produced by this side appears to follow those traditions while rejecting the scientific approach as a useful one for studying human behavior. A second type accepts the basic goals of science but rejects some of its procedures. For example, an ethnographer can accept the scientific goal of building theory through a process of inducing general explanations by looking for patterns in the aggregate across observations of individuals' behaviors. But at the same time, this ethnography might reject some of the procedures of science, such as the hypothetico-deductive method of beginning with a general explanation then testing it through operationalization, the practice of reductionism that narrows the research focus down into microunits, the enumeration procedure of translating qualities into numerals, and the use of statistics that mathematically manipulates the enumerated data. Therefore, it is possible to be scientific without being quantitative.

PHILOSOPHICAL ISSUES

In order to understand the fundamental difference between the qualitative and the quantitative approaches, we must examine the philosophical issues of ontology and epistemology. This is not to say that qualitative scholars all share one view on each of these issues; to the contrary, there is a range of opinion, but this range is fairly distinct from the range of opinion among quantitative scholars.

These issues of ontology and epistemology are so fundamental to our everyday behavior that we may rarely bother to examine them; in fact, the questions themselves are so fundamental that we might think it silly even to ask them seriously in everyday conversation. We tell ourselves that, of course, we believe in an external reality that exists apart from us. If a tree falls in the woods and we do not hear it, was there a sound? We answer: Of course! A tree can make a sound even if we aren't there to hear it. Furthermore, if someone tells us there is a tree in the woods, we can accept this to be true. We don't have to see the woods or tree to accept their existence. We don't have to perceive something directly to be convinced that it exists; indirect evidence will do, especially in our mediated world. For example, there is no question in our minds that the President of the United States exists, even though we did not experience his swearing in directly; we might have experienced his swearing in indirectly by seeing it on television or having read about the ceremony in the newspaper. We believe the indirect sources of experience, and we believe in the existence of the events, people, and behaviors they depict or recount. In the case of our everyday thinking, the question of existence is not dependent on our perceiving something directly. For example, we all believe we have a brain although we will never see it, touch it, smell it, taste it, or hear it.

We accept certain rules and follow certain conventions in the belief that it will allow us to organize and integrate our world into a shared community with others. For example, when we see a long piece of bark-covered wood with branches sprouting on one end and roots on the other, we know this means tree. We also have faith that other people in our culture share the same meaning for this object and will use the same word to express this meaning.

For most of us in everyday life, the words *ontology* and *epistemology* do not arise, nor do the questions they pose. Our lack of concern for them derives from axiomatic nature; they require us to take a position based on belief, not proof. Similar axiomatic questions include, Is there a supreme being?, What is beauty?, and What is a moral life? The answers to these questions are beyond fact and logic; they require an answer based on belief. Once we have recognized our belief, then we can use logic to fashion arguments and practices to follow from it. When these practices become established we need not think about them; we take them for granted.

However, when we enter the world of formal scholarship, it is essential that we examine the foundations of our thinking. When we do this, we discover that there exist alternative answers to each foundational question. Two scholars who hold different beliefs of ontology and epistemology may be interested in examining the same phenomenon, but their beliefs will lead them to set up their studies very differently because of their differing views of evidence, analysis, and purpose of the research.

The Issue of Ontology

Ontology is the concern about whether the world exists, and if so, in what form. It is what we call an axiomatic issue, because there is no way we can experience the answer to this question while we are trapped inside our five senses. Our sensory organs may be imperfect filters that may distort external stimuli. Because we cannot experience the world directly (unfiltered through our senses), we will never know for sure what the world really is. Therefore, there is no correct and no wrong position about the nature of the world. There is no convincing evidence that can be used to prove or justify one position as being more truthful or accurate than another. It is a matter of belief, and all scholars have a position, whether or not they realize it or can articulate it.

With the question of ontology, the central distinction seems to be on the matter of materialism versus idealism. Materialism is the belief that there is a fixed material reality that is external to people. In contrast, idealism is the belief that reality is in one's mind; nothing exists apart from the mind knowing it.

We can pose the following questions to determine whether someone is a materialist or an idealist: If a tree falls in the woods and no one is around to hear it, did it really fall? Or did the tree really exist? The idealist would answer no to these questions; the tree has no existence until it is perceived by a human mind, and sound waves do not exist unless sense organs are stimulated and the mind can attribute meaning to them. In contrast, the materialist would answer yes to both of these questions. Furthermore, the materialist may regard the questions as rather silly while thinking, "Of course, the tree exists. I don't have to perceive something directly to know that it exists."

Materialism is a popular, commonsensical position with regard to physical sciences; most people believe that there exists a material world of rocks, trees, houses, and other people whether they perceive them or not. However, the materialist position comes under question when we enter into the social sciences, and the phenomenon shifts from physical substances to human constructions. Some scholars believe that human behavior is relatively fixed (or at least ordered) and can be explained in terms of general patterns. People are members of classes, and the meaning making across people in the same class is relatively similar. But, in contrast, there are other scholars who believe that there is no social world; instead there are many social worlds, each one a human construction that is nonrational and quickly changing.

To illustrate the major points of thinking across the alternative positions on the ontological issue, we can envision a continuum (see Table 3.1). On one side of the continuum is idealism, the belief that the "mind is the primary reality and that matter cannot exist independently of minds capable of knowing it" (Powers, 1982, p. 5). On the other side of the continuum is materialism, which is based on two propositions. First, there is a physical world consisting of objects that exist independent of our experience of them. Second, these objects have their own properties, and these properties exist independent of our experience of them.

Across this ontological continuum there are five positions worth noting. At the far left, there is *solipsism,* which is the belief that nothing exists outside of the individual and that all perceptions are false signals. For a human being, the mind with its constructed meanings is all that exists. A second position is an *idiographic* type of idealism that reflects a belief that there is something that exists apart from the individual, but because that something can never be experienced objectively

TABLE 3.1
The Major Points of Thinking Across the Alternative Positions
on the Ontological and Epistemological Issues

The Ontological Continuum				
Idealism			*Materialism*	
Solipsism	Idiographic Idealism	Actionalism	Dialectical Materialism	Mechanistic Materialism
The Epistemological Continuum				
Constructivism			*Realism*	
Pure Subjectivity		Intersubjectivity		Pure Objectivity

(outside the limitations and influence of one's own perceptions), it is pointless to grant it a materialistic ontological status. Individuals' perceptions of the some-thing are based on their varying abilities to perceive and their own interpretive processes so that an individual's understanding of the something is subjective and varies across individuals. Therefore we cannot say that what the something really is, and we conclude that there are multiple somethings.

Third, there is the idealist position of *actionalism* where humans are believed to be active agents who possess goals and have the capacity to choose goal-maximizing actions. Humans are regarded as being subject to situational and social forces that they cannot control, but they are also subject to their own choice-making behavior. Aristotle and Kant are examples of thinkers who held this position. Much of the mass media research exhibits a belief in this position.

Fourth, there is *dialectic materialism,* which is the belief that there is a material reality but that it is constantly changing and new properties continually evolve. This view, which was developed by Hegel and Marx, rejects the need for reduc-tionism, so that larger scale systems can be studied intact without having to focus on the component parts.

At the right extreme, there is the position of *mechanical materialism,* which is the belief that not only does everything have a physical existence, but that everything that happens in the world is determined by prior physical causes acting according to invariable laws. Part of this mechanical view is the belief that the behavior of any complex whole can be explained in terms of its basic, elementary parts. This second belief is the foundation for reductionism—the practice of taking a phenomenon and breaking it down into its elementary parts so that each finite part can be studied parsimoniously. Under the mechanistic materialism view, humans are regarded as machines whose behaviors are de-termined by conditioning as well as outside stimulus. A good example of this position is the work of B. F. Skinner, who isolated discrete behaviors of rats and pigeons, then generalized those findings to human behavior. He used the ration-ale that all organisms are mechanistically driven and are therefore locked into responding in certain predictable ways to certain stimuli.

Ontology Under the Qualitative Approach

It is difficult to find a direct treatment of ontology in the qualitative literature, because it is such a fundamental assumption, and writers seldom feel the need to address such issues. However, there are some instances where ontological positions can be inferred. For example, Pauly (1991) revealed an idealist perspec-tive when he said, "Humans fabricate rather than discover reality. They use symbols to construct the worlds in which they live. In this view, reality is an accomplishment rather than an entity out there, waiting to be uncovered" (p. 2). The idealist position is what is usually espoused by most qualitative theoreticians. To people who hold this position, the reality is what exists in a person's mind about the somethings—not the somethings themselves.

In contrast, there are some examples of a materialist position in the qualitative literature. Strauss and Corbin (1990) appeared to take a materialist approach, which can be seen in the statement "if theory is faithful to the everyday reality of the substantive area and carefully induced from diverse data, then it should fit that substantive area" (p. 22). Garfinkel (1967) said the purpose is to discover the formal properties of commonplace actions from within actual settings. In both of these statements, the word *discovery* is used, implying that there exists something to be discovered—hence a belief in materialism. Also, Jensen (1991a), in trying to link qualitative methods to humanistic scholarship, implied the existence of reality accessible through language, "the primary medium of interchange between humans and reality (in processes of perception, cognition, and action) . . . verbal texts may become vehicles of knowledge and truth" (p. 19). Again, there is not a direct treatment of ontology, but a materialist position can be inferred through his references to a reality and the quest for a truth.

The Issue of Epistemology

The epistemological issue poses the question: Can an observer come to "know" the phenomenon? It is quite different from the ontological one, which is the more fundamental of the two. Scholars who hold an idealist ontological position have limited options epistemologically. In contrast, materialists have a wide range of epistemological positions open to them.

The epistemological question is a foundational one and is not related to how well a researcher applies methods. On the philosophical level, we are not concerned with the problem about whether the researcher has used the correct sample, a good measurement instrument or protocol, and therefore gathered valid data; instead, the issue is whether or not it is even possible to gather data that are somehow free of the perceptual predispositions of the person gathering that data. On an operational level, we may be concerned with data gathering and analyses, but this is a distinct issue, secondary—in the philosophical sense—to epistemological concerns.

An early epistemological view was based on rationalism in which creative human thought is viewed as the key to unlocking the secrets of the empirical world. Understanding of the world is gained not through scattered observations but by reasoned contemplation of the logical structure of the world. Scholars move from one clear idea to another and arrive at some indubitable knowledge and at the construction of a unified, all-embracing body of knowledge. Primary adherents are Plato and Descartes. For example, Descartes, in his *Discourse on Method* published in 1637, argued that abstract reasoning, such as that afforded by mathematics, was the most useful tool of science because it allowed scholars to gain their distance from physical objects. He said that scholars should avoid the temptation of empirical observation to corrupt pure analysis.

The epistemological issue became an important problem in the social sciences since the late 19th century where there was a split between two camps of thinkers. I refer to these camps as realists and constructivists (see Table 3.1 for the epistemological continuum). The realists were those who believed it was possible to know reality, whereas the constructivists believed that reality was not something to be known, but instead something to be constructed through a creative process.

Realists are empiricists. They believe it is important to observe the world; although observations are distorted due to the limitations of the senses, it is still better to make observations than to resort to pure speculation. The realist position is not a monolithic one. An early and dominant realist position in social science was known as positivism.

In contrast to the realists are the constructivists who do not believe in an objective way of knowing. Constructivists believe that scholarly inquiry is conducted from within a global perspective or world view that shapes the process of research. They reject the logical positivist view of an objectively real world, believing instead that the world is subjectively constructed by the meanings that people assign to observations. Therefore, the empirical world is not independent of people's observations.

Constructivists use some of the methods of traditional science, but they reject many of those practices in order to accommodate the belief that communication is not mechanistic but rather a creative social construction. For example, they reject reductionism, preferring instead to look at integrated wholes, and they reject operationalism, saying that theoretical constructs are fundamentally different than their indicators.

J. A. Anderson (1987) displayed a constructivist position in his argument that "material reality intersects but does not contain the world of meaning. . . . That is not to say that there is no material existence outside of the human conscious. It is to say that the way we make sense of that material existence is the product of our conscious efforts not of the structure of the universe" (p. 78). He said with qualitative research, the researcher "holds to a contingent reality where meaning is embedded in context, and behavior must be interpreted within it" (p. 47). Human behavior exists in a material form but that its existence is dynamic, so changeable across people and even across time (within a person), so complex and idiosyncratic that researchers who attempt to interpret human behavior will not all perceive the same thing. The reality of the perceptions is therefore contingent on the context they use to interpret the phenomenon.

There is an intermediate position between the extremes of realism and constructivism. For example, Bogdan and Taylor (1975) argued that although humans create meaning through their interpretations, this meaning making need not be solely idiographic or completely unique to each individual so that the process is guaranteed to be purely subjective. Instead, two people may develop shared definitions and shared perspectives, which can be social norms, values, and goals that exert influence on people in a nondeterministic way. People are not purely creative in their interpretations, but they are joined in common patterns of meaning making. If researchers can "get on the same wavelength" as their subjects, then researchers can provide an accurate account of how those subjects use symbols; the researchers' accounts need not be their purely subjective, creative interpretations.

Another argument for an intermediate position is that human consciousness approaches reality with certain embedded interpretations. Leiter (1980) argued that some knowledge of the external world can be gained empirically, but not all knowledge, because perceptions impose limits and distortions. So how can we explain a substantial agreement of interpretations about many things? There must be some imbedded interpretations in the human consciousness.

The Relationship of Epistemological and Ontological Issues

Often, qualitative scholars do not separate the ontological question from the epistemological question of "Can we 'know' the material reality?" These are two quite different issues, but often they become confused in the literature. Several theoreticians argue that the issues of ontology and epistemology, which are two quite different issues for realists, are the same for idealists. For example, Lincoln and Guba (1985) asserted that rationalism assumes that a single reality exists, whereas naturalism assumes there are multiple realities. With positivism, there is a single tangible reality "out there," fragmented into independent variables and processes, any of which can be studied independently of the others. With naturalism, there are multiple constructed realities that can be studied only holistically; inquiry into these multiple realities will inevitably diverge. With science, they do make a distinction by using two different terms (rationalism for the ontological concern and positivism for the epistemological one), but they use one term (naturalism) for both concerns when dealing with qualitative research. With naturalism, the inquirer and the "object" of inquiry interact to influence one another; knower and known are inseparable.

Also, J. K. Smith (1983) said that for realists, the "ontological questions concerning 'what is' can be kept separate from the epistemological questions about how we come to know 'what is' " (p. 8). But with idealists, the subject and object become one and they therefore "perceive no reality independent of the shaping of creating efforts of the mind" (p. 8). Smith argued there is a range of positions within idealism from ontological idealism to conceptual idealism. Ontological idealism is the belief that reality does not exist independent of people; it is a pure creation of individuals. Conceptual idealism is the belief that reality is shaped by our minds. This contrast can be made at the epistemological level also. Realists believe that explanations should correspond to the external reality that exists. But correspondence has no meaning for idealists who do not believe in a knowable external reality. Instead, idealists have a different version of epistemology. The conceptual idealist uses a standard of coherence in an explanation. Because the explanation is a construction, it cannot represent anything outside itself, but it should be internally coherent. The ontological idealist looks for agreement with other researchers.

But some writers seem to move away from a purely subjective position on epistemology. For example, Lancy (1993) drew the distinction between the emic and etic perspectives that researchers can take. The emic is the insider's (or research subject's) perspective, whereas the etic is the outsider's (or objective) perspective. Lancy said that when the researcher writes from the emic perspective, the insights should be shown to the subjects to cross-check the accuracy of the description. This would imply the existence of the possibility of a shared perspective.

Positions on the Epistemological Continuum

When reading the qualitative literature, it is helpful to keep in mind three positions on the epistemological continuum. First, a writer can exhibit an *objective* belief that researchers can provide a factual, value-free description of the phenomenon. It is possible for researchers to be neutral, objective observers. With scientific training, researchers can develop neutral and objective data-gathering instruments/procedures and analytical schemes. Bias is an operational (not epistemological) problem that can be solved. So a researcher who uses accepted methods systematically will arrive at findings that are precisely the same as any other researcher following the same procedures.

Second, there is the position of *intersubjectivity,* which says that researchers can never be purely objective, but they are not limited to pure subjectivity either. It is possible for several researchers to perceive the same thing, to arrive at the same meaning, but it is also possible for several researchers to have different interpretations. When this occurs, it is possible to apply certain accepted standards to determine the relative values of the interpretations. Some observations are better than others. Better observations mean that they more accurately reflect the external reality; evidence comes from agreement among researchers. Although subjectivity is an integral part of any human activity, in scholarly research we strive to achieve agreement in our use of language, methods, and standards, thus leading to a convergence in our findings.

Third, there is the position of *pure subjectivity.* This position holds that it is never possible to be objective. Qualitative researchers can only provide their own idiographic, subjective interpretations. Researchers make no attempt to argue (or in any way make a case) that their interpretation of the phenomenon is anything but their own personal interpretation. Furthermore, there are no standards that can be used to judge the value of their interpretation in comparison to the interpretation of others, because all interpretations are subject and have value.

AXIOMATIC PERSPECTIVES

This section addresses the assumptions that scholars make about the qualitative approach. Five such assumptions are prevalent in the writings of qualitative theoreticians. They are phenomenology, interpretive, hermeneutics, naturalism, and humanistic studies. Following are definitions of each of these.

Phenomenology is the belief that the object of interest be examined without any preconceived notions or a priori expectations. Researchers attempt to get inside the mind of the actor to understand what the actor sees and believes. This understanding leads the researcher to explain how the actor constructs reality and why the actor behaves as he or she does.

In defining phenomenology, there are five main facets. First, the focus is on "the very commonplace, common sense, unclarified, taken-for-granted features of the world in which we pass our everyday lives" (Morris, 1977, p. 11). The task for the phenomenologist "is to reconstruct the ways in which human beings go about this interpreting in their daily lives, a task which involved *direct intuition* as the source and final test of all knowledge, and *insight* into essential structures derived from such intuition" (Morris, 1977, p. 10).

Second, phenomenology is the "understanding of human behavior from the actor's own frame of reference . . . how the world is experienced . . . the important reality is what people imagine it to be" (Bogdan & Taylor, 1975, p. 2). It requires the researcher to get into the perspective of the actor (person being studied). All the description of the social action is then from the view of the actor as if the researcher were a camera (Wolcott, 1982).

Third, the focus is on meaning. "The phenomena of phenomenology are not the *facts* of experience, but the *meaning*. When we 'bracket the existence' of the content of any given experience, we put aside all questions of fact—of truth or falsity—to concentrate exclusively on the meaning of the experience to the one or ones experiencing it" (Morris, 1977, p. 12).

Fourth, the phenomenon is examined without any preconceived notions in the form of assumptions or a priori expectations (Lancy, 1993). And fifth, researchers avoid reducing complex reality to a few variables (Lancy, 1993).

Some writers refer to this as social phenomenology, because it is applied to human interactions. When research is called social phenomenological, it focuses on the study of how language and interactions are used to construct reality in social situations. According to Lindlof (1991):

> [It] conceives of humans as uniquely able to account for past and future actions of themselves and others in coordinating present behavior. Language is the primary medium in which this accounting is done. It is the means by which intentions are expressed and generalized to routine social situations. Language and other symbol systems also enable humans to invent new modes of being. . . . The main task and accomplishment of all social life is making meanings. (p. 26)

Interpretive assumptions refer to the belief that the researcher, while trying to see the situation from the point of view of those who are being studied, cannot escape from providing his or her own interpretation of the situation (Denzin & Lincoln, 1994c; Morris, 1977). Researchers, like all humans, must use subjective methods and their own interpretations to try to understand what is happening in the social settings they observe. As J. A. Anderson (1987) put it, "Meaning is promiscuous and prolific; it is the product of human consciousness and is not contained in objects" (p. 253). Meaning comes from the interaction of the person with the object so that if either the person or the object is changed, so is their meaning. If there are three qualitative researchers all examining the exact same text, it is possible that there will be three interpretations of that text. This situation, when viewed from a scientific perspective, would be unacceptable, but from the qualitative perspective, a multiplicity of interpretations is seen as a strength. Within the qualitative approach, the role of human interpretation is highlighted, not ignored.

Hermeneutics is the perspective that humans view the world as an interaction of parts and wholes. The part is only understood in the context of the whole, and the whole is constructed of the parts. There is no beginning or end in this circular process of interpretation. As J. K. Smith (1983) explained, "In this circular process, the meaning of any particular part of a text, such as a word or a sentence, requires an understanding of the meaning of the whole and vice versa. Achieving a meaningful interpretation is a process of constant movement between parts and whole in which there is no absolute starting point and no absolute ending point" (p. 12).

This term comes from literary criticism in which texts are analyzed to determine their meaning (Orr, 1991; J. K. Smith, 1983). Smaller units, such as words and images, are interpreted in the overall context of the work; the overall work is a whole composed of its individual words and symbols. The scholar asks questions about the parts and uses the whole to provide the context for the answer. The scholar also asks questions about the whole and uses the parts to construct those answers. In this process, there are always more questions to be asked of a text and more contexts to be considered in interpreting it. Therefore, no criticism is ever final or complete.

Naturalism refers to the belief that the world should be studied in its natural state, undisturbed by the researcher (Denzin & Lincoln, 1994c). Christians and Carey (1989) said that researchers must "pitch their tents among the natives, must enter the situation so deeply that they can recreate in imagination and experience the thoughts and sentiments of the observed" (p. 360). Marshall and Rossman (1989) argued that all qualitative approaches assume "that systematic inquiry must occur in a natural setting rather than an artificially constrained one such as an experiment" (pp. 10–11).

Lincoln and Guba (1985) extended the idea of naturalism to a paradigm that rests on five fundamental beliefs. First, ontologically there are multiple realities, not one ultimate truth. Second, epistemologically the knower and the known are inseparable. Third, the goal is to produce idiographic knowledge, not generalizable principles. Fourth, researchers cannot establish a claim of causal linkages, because the phenomenon is in a state of mutual simultaneous shaping so it is impossible to distinguish cause from effect. And fifth, inquiry is value bound.

Humanistic studies is a very old (perhaps 2,500 years) scholarly tradition in which the texts of interpersonal communications and literary works have been studied from a cultural or historical perspective. To make the definition more concrete or specific beyond this point is very difficult. In grappling with this definitional problem, Nord (1989) called the term "maddeningly ambiguous" (p. 295). He then said the term evokes three characteristics. First, it focuses on human values as an answer to the question of what does it mean to be human? Second, there is a conception of the individual as a causal force in human affairs. And third, the goal is to illuminate individual experience, not to generalize.

According to Jensen (1991a), that which we regard as humanities began to emerge as a separate scholarly tradition in the early 19th century when social science began to establish its own scholarly identity. In distinguishing humanities, he said, "Perhaps the key contribution of the humanities to qualitative research is an emphatic commitment to studying the *language* of particular texts and genres in their social setting. . . . From a humanistic perspective, the contents (of media) must be conceptualized as the expression of a particular subjectivity and aesthetics, and as the *representation* of a particular context" (p. 18).

Nord (1989) added that within journalism history there have been four types of humanistic study: (a) descriptions of technological developments and their effects on humans, (b) the study of the development of media organizations, (c) cultural studies (the ways in which humans in the past have grasped reality), and (d) political studies (relationship between journalism and government).

In summary, these five terms convey five major complementary ideas that are axiomatic to qualitative research. This is not to say that every scholar who considers himself or herself a qualitative researcher holds all of these foundational beliefs. However, most hold almost all of these beliefs, and it would be inconceivable for a qualitative researcher *not* to hold any of them. Simply put, these beliefs are: (a) Researchers should not have preconceived notions about the phenomenon, but keep themselves open to the experience fully, (b) researchers should strive to see the situation from the perspective of the other, (c) research is a never-ending process of observing an instance and interpreting it in terms of a context that is itself a construction of instances, (d) researchers need to go to the phenomenon and experience it in its natural, undisturbed state, and (e) the focus is on language as a demonstration of meaning, and this language must be interpreted in cultural and historical contexts.

SUMMARY

This chapter illuminates the fundamental issues of belief in three areas: the debate between science and humanities, the philosophical issues of ontology and epistemology, and five axioms underlying the qualitative approach. This examination reveals the foundational commonalities among scholars who favor the qualitative approach. (See Table 3.2 for an outline of the key terms and concepts and Table 3.3 for an outline of the foundational issues.)

TABLE 3.2

Dictionary of Key Terms and Concepts in the Philosophy of Science

Ontological Issues

Materialism - the belief in a physical world consisting of objects that exist independent of our experience of them. Also, these objects have their own properties and these exist independent of our experience of them.

Mechanistic materialism - a form of materialism that holds that everything that happens in the world is determined by prior physical causes acting according to invariable laws. Also, behavior of any complex whole can be explained in terms of its basic, elementary parts (reductionism). Under the mechanistic materialism view, humans are regarded as machines whose behaviors are determined by conditioning and outside stimulus. The behaviorism of B. F. Skinner is a good example of research conducted under this view.

Reductionism - the practice of taking a phenomenon and breaking it down into its elementary parts so that each finite part can be studied parsimoniously.

Dialectical materialism - the belief that regards matter as existing but that it changes and evolves so that new properties emerge. This view rejects the need for reductionism, so that larger scale systems can be studied intact without having to focus on the component parts.

Actionalism - the belief that humans are active agents who possess goals and have the capacity to choose goal-maximizing actions. Explanations for humans' actions refer to humans' goals and intentions rather than external factors. Examples of this position are Aristotle and Kant.

Actional realism - the belief that humans are believed to be subject to situational and social forces that they cannot control, but they are also subject to their own choice-making behavior. Much of the mass communication research exhibits a belief in this position.

Idealism - the belief that social science is very different from physical sciences because people are both the subject and object of the investigation. The physical sciences deal with inanimate objects that clearly exist outside of humans. But with social sciences the focus is on humans and cultures. Because the object of study was a product of human minds, it is inseparably connected to our minds, and therefore we cannot remove the subjectivity, values, and emotions. There is an interrelationship between the knower and the object; that is, we are the subject and object of the investigation. Because the social world changes over time, it is impossible to discover laws like there are in the physical sciences.

Solipsism - the belief that nothing exists outside of one's self and that all perceptions are false signals.

Epistemological Issues

Positivism - the belief that physical science methods could be used. Includes Comte, Mill, and Durkheim. Based on empiricist tradition established by Newton, Locke, and others. Comte established a hierarchy of sciences placing sociology on it. Comte also said that the objects of study in social science are the same as in the physical sciences. There is the knower (the researcher) and the object of study, and these two can be separated. Social science must not be context bound and must find broad principals that would span across large groups.

Logical positivism - the belief that neither logic nor experience, by themselves, were adequate tools for generating knowledge; both of these were needed. They place a strong focus on the analysis of language, believing that there is no point in arguing whether a thesis is *true* unless you know what it *means*. So, according to logical positivism, the primary task for philosophy was to develop tools for the analysis of meaning. Logical positivists philosophize about systems of explanations or theories, then deduce tests from the theory. If an empirical test could be deduced, then the theoretical statement is meaningful; if not, the statement is non-sense. Furthermore, they abandoned claims of truth, reasoning that humans have limited perceptions and will never be able to perceive natural phenomena in an unfiltered completely accurate manner. Instead, they set out a criterion of utility, reasoning that it is possible for scientists to improve their explanations. Improved explanations are those that more clearly, more parsimoniously accounted for broader phenomena.

(Continued)

TABLE 3.2

(Continued)

Operationalism - the technique of translating of general terms into measurements.

Logical empiricists - a group of thinkers who took a more moderate position compared to the logical positivists. The logical empiricists recognized that it is impossible to conclusively verify any scientific proposition. Because scientific propositions are general statements, it is impossible to perform all the possible tests to confirm that the statement holds in an infinite set of instances and times. The logical empiricists then were satisfied with a process of gradual confirmation.

Rationalism - the belief that creative human thought is the key to unlocking the secrets of the empirical world. Understanding of the world is gained not through scattered observations but by reasoned contemplation of the logical structure of the world. Scholars move from one clear idea to another and by so doing arrive at not only some indubitable knowledge, but at the construction of a unified, all-embracing body of knowledge. Primary adherents are Plato, Descartes, Einstein, and Chomsky.

Rational empiricism - the belief that human understanding is best achieved by applying rational thought to observational data. Aristotle is usually credited with originating this position. Third, there is *mechanistic empiricism,* which is a subset of empiricism based on the belief that knowledge is best derived from empirical observations with a minimal intrusion of rational thought. This is a "data-to-theory" approach. The empirical world is ordered like a machine, consisting of sequences of cause-to-effect relationships, and the business of science is to discover the causes of sensible events. Much of the persuasion research of the 1950s and 1960s is an example of this. (Francis Bacon; Newton).

Logical positivism - a school of thought developed in the 1920s by a group of philosophers and mathematicians known as the Vienna Circle. They sought to unify science with a general method of inquiry based on two fundamental premises: (a) that "a real objective world" of empirical phenomena exists independent of individual perceivers, and (b) that an understanding of the objective world can be based on empirical inquiry. They did not accept arguments for cause and effect, because causation is a process that can never be observed, but covariation can be observed. Committed to the principles of reductionism and operationalism. Reductionism assumes that the smallest units of observation are the most meaningful (atomism). Operationalism assumes that all concepts in theoretical statements must be specified by the operations that the scientist performs to observe them, and that they have no other meaning or existence; for example, "shyness" IS a person's score on a shyness test. A good example of this position is the work of Carl Hovland and his persuasion research, which was very popular as a model of social science in the 1960s.

Constructivism - the belief that scholarly inquiry is conducted from within a global perspective or world view that shapes the process of research. It rejects the logical positivist view of an objectively real world, believing instead that the world is subjectively constructed by the meanings that people assign to observations. Therefore, the empirical world is not independent of people's observations. It also rejects reductionism (prefers to look at integrated wholes) and operationalism (theoretical constructs are fundamentally different than their indicators). It was developed as a reaction to radical empiricism, and is a compromise between scientific empiricism and humanism. It embraces traditional science, but it also tempers scientific assumptions to accommodate the socially constructed nature of communication. Kant is a primary figure in this position.

Constructive realism - the belief founded on the basic tenets of constructivism, but is careful not to go so far as the radical constructivists where scholarship is a subjective enterprise with each researcher applying idiosyncratic interpretations of the same phenomenon. They believe that communication phenomena are prestructured by meanings that communicators assign to them and they also rely on shared interpretations presented by other researchers so as to achieve intersubjectivity.

Empiricism - the belief that knowledge is gained from experience and observation.

TABLE 3.3
Foundational Issues

Issue I: Ontology

Key Question: Does the author regard the phenomenon to exist apart from humans' perceptions of it?

Alternative Answers:
1. Radical Materialism: There is a material world apart from a person's perceptions. There is no nonmaterial world (if it can't be observed, it does not exist).
2. Dialectic Materialism: This is the belief that there is a material reality but that it is constantly changing.
3. Actional Idealism: Humans are believed to be active agents who possess goals and have the capacity to choose goal-maximizing actions. Humans are regarded as being subject to situational and social forces that they cannot control, but they are also subject to their own choice-making behavior.
4. Idiographic Idealism: There is an external reality that is very complex and dynamic; it varies substantially across individuals and across time. There is a material and nonmaterial reality. The nonmaterial reality is very complex and dynamic, because it varies substantially across individuals and across time. The perception of meaning making is very sensitive to context and changes substantially across contexts.
5. Solipsism: There is no reality external to the researcher; the research creates everything through perceptions, and these perceptions are the only reality.

Issue II: Epistemology

Key Question: To what degree are humans limited from knowing (making meaning about) the phenomenon?

Alternative Answers:
1. Objective: Researchers can approach an objective interpretation through the use of systematic methods.
2. Intersubjectivity: Researchers can never be purely objective, but they can demonstrate that people share interpretations.
3. Pure subjectivity: It is not possible to be objective, and qualitative researchers can only provide their own idiographic, subjective interpretations.

Issue III: Axioms

Key Question: What are the key assumptions underlying the qualitative approach?

Alternative Answers:
1. Phenomenology: Researchers should not have preconceived notions about the phenomenon, but keep themselves open to the experience fully.
2. Interpretive: Researchers should strive to see the situation from the perspective of the other.
3. Hermeneutics: Research is a never-ending process of observing an instance and interpreting it in terms of a context that is itself a construction of instances.
4. Naturalism: Researchers need to go to the phenomenon and experience it in its natural, undisturbed state.
5. Humanistic studies: The focus is on language as a demonstration of meaning, and this language must be interpreted in cultural and historical contexts.

For over a century there has been a debate about whether the scientific approach is useful for examining human thought and behavior. The positivists support the use of science, whereas the idealists argue against its use. The qualitative tradition grows out of the idealist argument that humans creatively and subjectively construct meaning for themselves, and this phenomenon cannot be captured using a scientific approach.

The debate over the usefulness of the qualitative and quantitative approaches is grounded in the axiomatic issues of ontology and epistemology. As axioms, they require us to take a position based on our beliefs. The ontological issue is the concern with what exists. In this chapter four positions were illuminated: materialism, actionalism, actional realism, and idealism. The epistemological issue is the concern about how we come to know our world and how we make sense of it. To illuminate this issue, brief histories of empiricism and positivism were presented. The three positions were laid out: objective, intersubjective, and subjective.

As awareness about the numerous positions available on ontology and epistemology has grown, the debate about scientific methods has evolved. Scholars who hold extreme positions have a more and more difficult time defending their beliefs; scientists now recognize the importance of interpretation in their processes. And humanist scholars recognize the essential nature of empirical observation.

Finally, five axioms of qualitative research were illuminated. They are phenomenology, interpretive, hermeneutics, naturalism, and humanistic studies. Given the variety of qualitative thinking, these assumptions vary in importance across scholars. However, they are all essential in distinguishing the qualitative approach from the quantitative one.

4

THE QUALITATIVE METHODOLOGIES

Methodologies are perspectives on research; they set out a vision for what research is and how it should be conducted. They are the connection between axioms and methods; methods are tools—techniques of data gathering, techniques of analysis, and techniques of writing. Because it is a tool, a particular method can often be used by many different methodologies (both qualitative and quantitative). Therefore, methodologies are at a more abstract (or general) level than are methods. Methodology is like a strategy—or plan—for achieving some goal; methods are the tactics that can be used to service the goals of the methodology. In essence, methodologies provide the blueprints that prescribe how the tools should be used. Those prescriptions can be traced to the axioms—beliefs about how research should be conducted.

The predominate qualitative methodologies are: ethnography, ethnomethodology, reception studies, ecological psychology, symbolic interactionism, cultural studies, and textual analysis. There may be other methodologies at the fringes of qualitative approach, and there might be qualitative scholars developing other methodologies. However, these seven are currently the dominant ones—the ones you will see time and again when you read the work of theoreticians as well as the qualitative research itself.

These seven methodologies vary among themselves to a degree that they can be considered distinct from one another—each presents a different strategy for research. However, there are also some overlaps in their prescriptions, because each rests on the fundamental axioms of the qualitative approach, although they do differ in the emphasis placed on various axioms. Also, within a methodology, there are preferred methods, but in almost all instances, researchers have a variety of methods from which to choose; no methodology prescribes one and only one method. It is for this reason, that a methodology should not be defined solely in terms of the methods it prescribes.

In this chapter, each of these seven methodologies is introduced. A methodology is first defined, then its foundations are presented, and finally the methods typically used with it are outlined. The chapter concludes with a comparison across methodologies as an illustration of how each would approach several research topics.

ETHNOGRAPHY

Ethnography is a methodology focused on exploring how communities are created and held together with human interactions. It is different from other forms of qualitative research in terms of its focus on long-term observation of cultural forms from everyday behavior to large-scale and arcane institutions such as religion and the arts (Jankowski & Wester, 1991). Also, ethnographers seek to document the cosmology, that is, the knowledge and belief systems that contribute to the coherence of the group. Van Maanen (1988) defined ethnography as the search for culture where "culture refers to the knowledge members ('natives') of a given group are thought to more or less share; knowledge of the sort that is said to inform, embed, shape, and account for the routine activities of the members of the culture" (p. 3). Culture is regarded as a "loose, slippery concept" because it is not tangible and it continually changes and is only visible through its representations, which require interpretation.

Ethnography has four core features, according to Atkinson and Hammersley (1994). First, it is inductive rather than deductive. Second, the data are open to many interpretations and are not collected in a closed set of analytical categories. Third, investigation is intensive on a small number, even as small as one, of cases. And fourth, the analysis is an explicit interpretation of meanings of language and human actions. When statistical analyses are used, they play a subordinate role.

Various theoreticians illustrate the facets of ethnography by adding detail to this general definition just presented. Van Maanen (1988) asserted that ethnographies "pose questions at the margins between two cultures. They necessarily decode one culture while recoding it for another" (p. 4). Vidich and Lyman (1994) placed ethnography within a "subdiscipline known as descriptive anthropology—in its broadest sense, the science devoted to describing ways of life of humankind" (p. 25), and Wolcott (1982) defined ethnography simply as cultural interpretation.

Some theoreticians point out that defining this term has been somewhat controversial. For some scholars, ethnography refers to a philosophical paradigm to which one makes a total commitment, but for other scholars it refers to a particular method of gathering data that is useful in certain situations (Atkinson & Hammersley, 1994).

Although ethnography can be used to examine a wide variety of phenomena, ranging from everyday behavior to large-scale institutions such as religion and the arts (Jankowski & Wester, 1991), it is useful to make a distinction between macroethnography and microethnography. Macroethnography, often called holistic ethnography, focuses on broad-scope inquiry in human culture. Holistic ethnographers "seek to describe and analyze all or part of a culture or community by describing the beliefs and practices of the group studies and showing how the various parts contribute to the culture as a unified, consistent whole" (Jacob, 1987, p. 10). In contrast, microethnography focuses more on particular behaviors or certain symbols (semiotics). A great deal of the ethnography of communication occurs at the microlevel. Drawing on ideas from nonverbal communication, sociolinguistics, sociology, and anthropology, the ethnography of communication focus on particular verbal (linguistics) and nonverbal interactions (Jacob, 1987). Researchers look at the rules of interactions that are exhibited in face-to-face communication within cultural groups then relate these rules to patterns of larger scale social and cultural processes. In short, researchers examine these microinteractions to see how they are related to macropatterns in the culture. For example, cultural anthropologists focus on "understanding the cognitive organization of cultural knowledge through the study of semantic schemata, with a consequent emphasis on the relationships among words" (Jacob, 1987, p. 22). In analyzing discourses, they seek to find the cultural categories that people use to organize their world.

Foundations. At its foundation, ethnography is primarily an anthropological approach, but it draws on a wide range of philosophical and sociological ideas, such as symbolic interactionism, phenomenology, hermeneutics, linguistic philosophy, and ethnomethodology. Perhaps its strongest foundational concept is naturalism where the social world should be studied in its natural state, undisturbed by the researcher. The social researcher respects the social world being examined; the allegiance is to the natural world where the information exists, not to any one particular set of methodological principles (Hammersley & Atkinson, 1983).

Methods. The ethnographic researcher's methods are to go into the field to live with the people in their natural community for a long enough period of time in order to understand how they construct meaning about their communities and their own places in those communities. Ethnographic researchers almost always use the data-gathering methods of observation and interview. The particulars of ethnographic observation were developed primarily in anthropology and the Chicago School of sociology (Wolcott, 1982).

As for analysis, the case study is a popular method. With case studies, the focus is on one person or one program that is then followed through time (Schwartz & Jacobs, 1979; Wolcott, 1982).

ETHNOMETHODOLOGY

Ethnomethodology is a methodology focused on the study of *how* people make sense out of everyday life. It seeks to identify and understand the methods people use to analyze behaviors and construct their own practical explanations. Perhaps the simplest and clearest definition was offered by Morris (1977) who conceptualized ethnomethodology as the study of procedures, which are essentially methodologies, used by humans (ethnics) in their effort to make meaning of the world. These procedures of meaning making result in commonsense knowledge, and it is a person's stock of knowledge that influences the practices of commonsense reasoning.

Ethnomethodologists attempt to assess a person's stock of knowledge, which consists of social types or idealizations of people, objects, and events that serve as points of inference and action. This knowledge is multifaceted and consists of recipes (ways of going about doing things), rules of thumb, social types, maxims, and definitions. The stock of knowledge has six properties. First, it is socially derived; that is, it is handed down by parents and friends. Little of it comes through personal experience. Second, it is socially distributed. What each person knows is different from others; we are all experts and novices on different things. Third, the social distribution of knowledge is itself part of the stock of knowledge at hand. Fourth, the stock of knowledge is built upon and expressed in everyday language. Everyday language is the medium of the stock of knowledge at hand. Fifth, this knowledge has an "open horizon of meaning"—that is, every element is potentially equivocal, lending itself to multiple meanings. Two people can have totally opposite beliefs, but each belief makes sense in that person's situation. And sixth, the stock of knowledge is not a neatly and logically ordered storehouse of information and typifications; it is not ordered by formal logic, because formal logic attempts to be situation free.

The emphasis is on process over product. The question of *what* (commonsense knowledge) is less important than the question of *how* (procedures used in constructing meaning) (Bogdan & Taylor, 1975; Garfinkel, 1967; Leiter, 1980; Morris, 1977; Wolcott, 1982). Researchers focus on the *practices* of commonsense reasoning and the cognitive style through which people experience the social world. To do this, researchers examine the relatively unnoticed, routine, informal interactions that take place in human communities, such as how people do their jobs, shop, watch television, talk to other people, cook, eat, and the other practical accomplishments of everyday life (Morris, 1977).

Foundations. At its foundation, ethnomethodology grew out of sociology. But it is very different from the social science of sociology in that sociology is the study of the causes of social action, whereas ethnomethodology is the study of how members of a society perceive behavior as social action (Leiter, 1980).

Ethnomethodology rests most strongly on a belief in hermeneutics, humanism, and phenomenology. As for hermeneutics, ethnomethodologists concentrate on the relationships between contexts and particulars; events are examined as embedded in their contexts, rather than as independent entities to be experimentally isolated in the laboratory.

It also might appear to take a strongly humanistic position in which communication interactions are viewed as creative human constructions grounded in the demands of particular situations, not determined by rules or norms that are outside of the actors. However, some theoreticians maintain that such rules may exist and exert an influence on human interactions. For example, Jankowski and Wester (1991) asserted that ethnomethodology seeks to identify the rules people apply in making sense of their world. Bogdan and Taylor (1975) argued that the focus is on "the ways people apply abstract rules and commonsense understandings in situations in order to make actions appear routine, explicable, and unambiguous" (p. 16).

According to Holstein and Gubrium (1994) the most important axiom is phenomenology, because ethnomethodology grew out of Schutz's social phenomenology. Interpretation is also important because "the world of 'social facts' is accomplished through members' interpretive work—activity through which actors produce and organize the very circumstances of everyday life" (p. 264).

Methods. The methods used by ethnomethodologists are primarily the interview method in gathering data, because their data consist of talk (Lindlof & Meyer, 1987). But in examining talk, ethnomethodologists do *not* look at extraordinary utterances; instead they focus on the ordinary (Garfinkel, 1967), such as everyday conversations (Jankowski & Wester, 1991).

An important analysis method is discourse analysis. Although ethnomethodologists focus on talk in their data gathering, their analysis focuses less on the words than on the context of the conversations (Lindlof, 1991). Ethnomethodologists attempt to use the context of the talk in order to derive understandings about how discourse structures the talk. This makes discourse analysis a popular analytical method within this methodology.

RECEPTION STUDY

Reception study is a methodology that focuses on how readers of texts construct meaning from that activity. Because the meaning making is believed to be strongly influenced by interpretive communities, the "text-audience encounter" is very important (Lindlof, 1991, p. 28). And the key to explaining that audience-text encounter is to focus on the context of the interpretation rather than the texts themselves.

Researchers examine how the ideas in a text are brought to life in a reader's imagination. As Allen (1987) put it, "The relationship between text and reader can be conceptualized in a number of ways—as a sort of mutually sustaining collaboration, a surrender to the thoughts of another, or even a battle of wills between the intentions of the reader and those of the author" (p. 77). When an author finishes a work (a novel, a musical score, or a script), it represents a schemata or a "skeletal structure of meaning possibilities" (p. 77) awaiting concretizing by the reader. Therefore, the text is only "one-half of the perceptual dynamic; it is an object, yet without a perceiving subject" (p. 78).

This methodology is sometimes referred to as reader-response studies. In their book on television criticism, Vande Berg and Wenner (1991) referred to reader-response studies saying that "texts provide parameters—narrative structuring of characters, actions, and settings which entail normative hierarchies of values, attitudes, and beliefs—and a preferred spectator position relative to these structures" (p. 34). But readers can reject this "written in" point of view and take an opposing position. Here, meaning is believed to come from the interpretation of the reader rather than being something that resides in the text.

Foundations. This methodology's foundation is in literary theory and criticism, which provides perspectives on how to understand texts. But with reception analysis, the reader of the text is foregrounded, whereas literary criticism focuses primarily on the text itself. Around the 1960s, this reader-oriented criticism became popular as it grew from the phenomenological ideas of Husserl, especially his belief that reality "has no meaning for us except as individually experienced phenomena" (Allen, 1987, p. 76). In 1980, Stuart Hall was credited with introducing the idea that television programs do not have a single meaning, but are relatively open texts, capable of being read in different ways by different people.

The reception study methodology is similar to ethnography, because both focus on people as members of interpretive communities; however, ethnography is a broader methodology. Reception study is limited to examining how individuals use their communities to help them interpret certain types of media messages. Ethnography looks at a much wider range of community use and community making and does so over a longer time period. The reception study has some overlap with ethnomethodology because they both look at how people make sense of messages, but ethnomethodology is much broader with its interest on a wide spectrum of meaning making in everyday life.

The focus on interpretive communities as a context for the meaning making reflects a strong hermeneutic perspective. Also, the caution to focus on the meaning in the interpretations, rather than the texts themselves, shows a foundation of phenomenology.

Methods. In their data gathering, researchers must look at both the texts and the readers of those texts. For example, Allen (1987) likened reception scholars to archaeologists as they critically search through a text to discover the keys to its meaning. The methods of in-depth interviews and participant observations are used to gather data from the readers of the texts.

The primary analysis method is the comparison of the data gathered from the texts with the data gathered from the readers to determine what is assimilated by the viewers. One technique of making this comparison is for the analyst to "type" the reader, such as the fictive reader, model reader, intended reader, characterized reader, ideal reader, inside and outside reader, implied reader, and superreader. The most popular typing scheme is that of Hall (1980), who suggested three types of readings: the dominant, the negotiated, and the oppositional. The dominant reading is exhibited by a viewer who accepts (either consciously or unconsciously) the dominant ideology in the text. A negotiated reading is one produced by viewers who fit into the dominant ideology in general, but who need to translate it into their own context in order to take into account their own social position. Finally, there are those readings produced by people whose social situation puts them into direct conflict with the dominant ideology; these readings are termed oppositional. The type of reading is traced to a person's social situation, which forms his or her interpretive community.

ECOLOGICAL PSYCHOLOGY

Ecological psychology is a methodology that focuses on culturally patterned behavior and uses biological constructs as metaphors to explain how environments affect different species-specific behaviors. In short, researchers focus on how the environment influences behavior. The biological constructs and assumptions are used in an analogous rather than literal manner.

In this view, behavior has objective and subjective components (Jacob, 1987). Objective elements occur at the molecular (or micro) level and are usually the movements of the body (e.g., the movement of tongue and lips when speaking), which are taken for granted by the person. Subjective elements occur at a molar level where the person's behavior is goal directed and requires cognitive awareness (such as giving a speech).

Foundations. This approach comes from psychology—especially its concern for human behavior and how internal mental states (or traits) can be used to explain that behavior. But whereas traditional psychology focuses on the degree to which individual variables have an influence on behavior, ecological psychology is more concerned with the pattern of influences in naturally occurring settings.

Ecological psychology is similar to ethnomethodology in the sense that it focuses on the examination of "the situational influences on behavior through naturalistic inquiry" but unlike ethnomethodology, it "conceptualizes those influences in terms of developmental effects of person-environment systems" (Lindlof & Meyer, 1987, p. 5). It is also different from reception studies because it focuses on behaviors as influenced by biological as well as cultural factors, whereas reception studies focus on interpretations of meaning as influenced by a person's interpretive community, and to a lesser extent, the text itself.

The foundational ideas of naturalism, phenomenology, and especially hermeneutics are important to ecological psychology. Researchers identify a behavior setting, such as the family television-viewing room, a public movie theater, or a bookstore. Because these behavior settings are nested within larger contexts, researchers seek to identify those contexts that influence behaviors. For example, the family television-viewing room is part of the family's home, which in turn is part of a particular neighborhood. Each of these levels influences the other. Human behavior is affected by elements in the setting such as physical properties (furniture and size of the room), human elements (family roles and personalities), and programmatic elements (family viewing rules and norms).

Methods. The methods employed by ecological psychologists primarily include data gathering through direct observation, but they also use specimen records and behavior-setting surveys (Marshall & Rossman, 1989). The specimen record is the researcher's field notes inconspicuously recorded while watching the subject behave in his or her natural environment.

The analysis of these notes is oriented toward examining the goal-directed behavior of the subject. The behavior-setting survey catalogs in detail the behavior settings within a particular community. Also, researchers focus their analyses on the interaction of the person and environment in the shaping of behavior. There are both subjective aspects about people (such as their goals for behavior) as well as subjective aspects in the environment (such as people's reactions to their surroundings). The goal of the analysis is to "produce detailed, objective descriptions of naturally occurring behavior that are amenable to quantitative analysis" (Jacob, 1987, p. 3), as well as having the power to discover the laws of behavior.

SYMBOLIC INTERACTIONISM

Symbolic interactionism is a methodology that focuses on meaning in social settings, that is, how individuals are able to assume other people's perspectives to learn about the meanings behind the use of symbols in human interactions. In short, it is concerned primarily with meaning as a product of human interactions and how that meaning influences behavior in social situations. It is assumed that people do not act randomly; instead, behavior is influenced by the meanings humans ascribe to objects and situations when they are in interactions with others (Bogdan & Taylor, 1975; Jacob, 1987; Jankowski & Wester, 1991; Lindlof & Meyer, 1987; Marshall & Rossman, 1989).

In this way, actors have different histories of experiences, so they each bring a different perspective to each situation; therefore, the meaning of a given situation will vary across actors as well as across situations. Sometimes per-situation will vary across actors as well as across situations. Sometimes perspectives can be shared, but often they are not, and this can be traced to an actor's position in the situation. "Social roles, norms, values, and goals may set conditions and consequences for action, but do not determine what a person will do" (Bogdan & Taylor, 1975, p. 15). Instead, a person's behavior is determined by his or her own personal interpretation, not the organization of which the person is a part.

Symbolic interactionists see humans "as qualitatively different from other animals. Whereas animals act in response to other objects and events based on factors such as instinct or previous conditioning, humans act toward things on the basis of the meanings those objects have for them" (Jacob, 1987, p. 27). The meanings arise through social interactions with others, so the meanings are regarded as social products. Those meanings constitute a symbolic environment in which humans live along with their physical environment and its physical stimuli. Meaning making is not automatic, objective, or deterministic. Individuals consciously screen and organize information, and they perform this ongoing task using their subjective interpretations.

Foundations. When symbolic interactionism was popularized in the 1920s and 1930s, it was very different from the current approaches "that argued that human behavior was the product of internal psychological drives or that it was determined by structural forces in society" (Woods, 1992, p. 338). Instead, symbolic interactionism viewed the person as a creator of meaning who was continually interacting with others in the world, then readjusting the meaning. People were not only influenced by social structures; they influenced them also.

The major thinkers of the movement were George Herbert Mead, W. I. Thomas, William James, Herbert Blumer, and Erving Goffman. For Mead, the focus of symbolic interactionism was on the self in interaction with others. The self, a uniquely human characteristic, is not present at birth, but develops in each individual through the process of social experience and social communication. The self is a process, so it changes over time.

Blumer's main contribution was to move meaning making into a sociological context (Schwartz & Jacobs, 1979). Before Blumer there were two positions on meaning making: inherent and psychological. The inherent position was the belief that the meaning of an object was in the object itself. The psychological position was the belief that the meaning was determined by the person's mind, his or her mental schema based on past experiences. Blumer defined meaning as the process of a person watching how others react to the object. Other people's reactions are social products that are generated in social interactions. Blumer (1969), drawing from the ideas of Mead, asserted that symbolic interactionism rests on three premises. First, human behavior can be traced to the meanings people attribute to their actions, other people, and things. Second, humans construct their meaning from social interactions, through the creation and use of symbols such as language. Third, humans continually modify their meanings as they check them out in social situations.

Morris (1977) drew a distinction between ethnomethodology and symbolic interactionism in terms of scope, method, theory, subject matter, and of the confusion of topic and resource in the research activity. The scope of symbolic interactionism is broader. Ethnomethodology makes no claim to investigate the question: How is the social order possible? As for method, ethnomethodology is broader. Symbolic interactionism requires that the researcher see the action from the actor's point of view, so participant observation is the dominant method. With ethnomethodology the researcher listens to talk, watches how records are kept and decisions made; ethnomethodology gathers accounts both written and verbal. Use of language is another distinction. Ethnomethodology focuses on what is said as a guide, whereas symbolic interactionism is rarely concerned with language and instead places more emphasis on information that is expressed through body language and behavior. Finally, ethnomethodology does not assume a shared language between participants and researchers; what is said cannot be taken at face value. However, with symbolic interactionism researchers assume there is a shared meaning, and they do not analyze it.

The reference to people as actors underscores behavior as the focus of investigation. With symbolic interactionism, human behaviors are interpreted in terms of the process of meaning making in situations. This process is also a focus of ethnomethodology, but in symbolic interactionism the emphasis is placed on symbols outside of the person and how these symbols accrue meaning in conversations and other forms of interpersonal interactions. In ethnomethodology the focus is on the individual's internal processing of all forms of information on a day-to-day basis. Ethnography and reception studies also have a stronger external focus, but they are not redundant with symbolic interactionism. Ethnography looks at social communities and larger scale structures such as cultures and institutions, whereas symbolic interactionism focuses on interpersonal interactions.

Symbolic interactionism uses all five axioms as a foundation. It is concerned with the inner phenomenological aspects of human behavior, so the focus is on meanings experienced by the participants themselves (Morris, 1977). It focuses on the interpretations of humans in social situations. Hermeneutics is also very important. Jacob (1987) stated, "Symbolic interactionists view the individual and society as inseparable units. To understand one completely you need to understand the other" (p. 28). As for naturalism, Woods (1992) said symbolic interactionism "required studying people in their natural environment" (p. 338). And Schwartz and Jacobs (1979) took a very humanistic approach by saying that the goal of symbolic interactionism is "precisely opposite to that of scientific sociology" (p. 7). They asserted that scientists try to discover "things about the social world that those within it do not know," but symbolic interactionist researchers instead "want to know what the actors know, see what they see, and understand what they understand" (p. 7).

Methods. According to Denzin (1970), there are seven principles to consider when selecting methods to pursue the goals of the symbolic interactionist methodology. First, any method examining symbolic interactionism must look both at symbols and at interactions (behaviors). Second, the researcher must assume the perspective of his or her subjects and view their world through their eyes. Third, the researcher must relate the subject's symbols and definitions with the social relationships that provide those conceptions. Fourth, the researcher must record the dynamics of the particular observational situations. Fifth, research methods must reflect the process of change as well as static behavioral forms. Sixth, researchers must realize that their own definitions, values, and ideologies shape their investigations. And seventh, concepts are sensitizing, not operational; theory is formal, not grand; and causation is seen as interactional. "Sensitizing" concepts (directions in which to look) are used in place of operational definitions (Jacob, 1987).

Even when researchers are willing to follow the aforementioned seven principles, they still need to realize that there is a great deal of latitude with this methodology. For example, symbolic interactionism is a methodology broad enough to span two levels of inquiry (Lindlof & Meyer, 1987). On the large scale (analysis of belief systems of entire cultures or societies), the method of semiotics is used. When it is used on a small scale, ethnographic case study methods are used, especially the technique of participant observation (Jacob, 1987; Morris, 1977), life histories, and open interviews (Jacob, 1987). Another analytical device used is dramaturgy. This approach, developed by Erving Goffman, focuses on how actors project their images as they perform on the various stages of their lives.

Analysis begins with data collection as a researcher relates observations to one another, develops new concepts, and links extant ones. These procedures continue until the researcher has a guiding metaphor, general scheme, or overall pattern that illuminates significant classes of things, persons, and events and the properties characterizing them. Because the role of theory is important and because the goal of the research is to produce verifiable knowledge, symbolic interactionism has been placed within "the realm of empirical science" (Jacob, 1987, p. 29). Theory is inductive and grounded in its ability to yield generalizable statements, rather than a deductive axiomatic system that would require some a priori reasoning.

CULTURAL STUDIES

Cultural studies examines how people interpret their culture and how they interact with it through the creation and use of symbols. It focuses on social practices from a holistic cultural perspective, and it emphasizes the importance of the intervention of culture as an influence on how people live their lives (Jensen, 1991a).

Cultural studies exists at the border between textual and social research by looking at the everyday social practices among objects of textual analysis. It is not confined to high culture, but also includes popular culture.

Christians and Carey (1989) placed the focus on the "creative process whereby people produce and maintain forms of life and society and systems of meaning and value. This creative activity is grounded in the ability to build cultural forms from symbols that express this will to live and assert meaning" (p. 358). They asserted that the phenomenon includes a concern for how individuals create culture and society, where society is seen not as a body of contingent and neutral factors to be charted, but as an active creation of its members.

Fiske (1987) pointed out that with the term cultural studies, culture has a political emphasis, not an aesthetic or humanist one. He perceived the focus not on the study of artistic products of the human spirit as much as on the way people live in an industrial society. Cultural studies is concerned with the generation and circulation of meanings in industrial societies.

Foundations. The foundation of cultural studies is difficult to trace, because there are so many different perspectives on it. For example, according to Jensen (1991a), it originated with certain versions of structuralism and semiology, and along the way it has assimilated French social and psychoanalytical theory. Lindlof (1991) argued that cultural studies represents a "confluence of many different, but compatible schools of thought" consisting of the three primary components of cultural criticism, "how dominant ideology and class consciousness are learned and enacted in everyday life" (includes Raymond Williams, E. P. Thompson, and Richard Hoggart); hegemony, "how *consent* and *resistance* to dominant ideas occur in capitalist society" (Gramsci); and semiology, "the language like codes which underlie the production of popular culture" (p. 27).

Vande Berg and Wenner (1991) divided cultural studies into two camps: British and American. They argued that British cultural studies, which developed in the 1970s at the University of Birmingham Centre for Contemporary Culture Studies, is based on the belief that ideology, economic structures, social structure, and culture are inseparable. Its central constructs are ideology, hegemony, and discourse. Its critical perspectives are primarily neo-Marxism, feminism, Freudian psychoanalytical analysis, reception theory, structural analysis, ethnography, and discourse analysis. In contrast, the American cultural studies "tend to make structural characteristics and ritual functioning of programs more central" (p. 28).

The empirical research had its programmatic start with the Birmingham school in the late 1960s under Stuart Hall (Fiske, 1987). Then in 1973 Hall published "Encoding/Decoding in the Television Discourse," in which he argued that people do not necessarily decode messages to mean what the creators had in mind when they encoded the messages. From its roots in cultural criticism and ideology (usually political economy), the cultural perspective evolved into the poststructuralist view that the audience is more active in its reading of discourses with the theories of Foucault, Bourdieu, Bakhtin, and de Certeau and the work of Fiske and Ang. Culturalism and structuralism are distinct, however. Culturalism emphasizes the relative autonomy of culture as a site of social struggle and as an agent of change; structuralism emphasizes the relatively determined nature of social life and cultural forms under industrial capitalism.

Cultural studies has also been gaining popularity in the field of sociology. Wuthnow and Witten (1988) perceived four types of cultural studies in sociology depending which methods are employed. First, there is a group of studies, the most well established of the four approaches, that focuses on the subjective meanings of cultural objects. Culture is regarded as an implicit feature of social life that is taken for granted. Second, there is a focus on internal patterns or structures evident among those objects themselves. Here, content analysis is employed to look at the elements (thematic, semantic, or lexical) in cultural material as well as the relationships among those elements. Third is the dramaturgic (expressive, communicative) functions performed by those objects in social settings. The focus here is on social uncertainties that give rise to ritual and ideology. And fourth is the institutional contexts in which those objects are produced and disseminated. Here, the focus is on the allocation of social resources among the different competing claims to those resources.

The key axiom is interpretation. Christians and Carey (1989) stated, "Humans live by interpretations. They do not merely react or respond but rather live by interpreting experience through the agency of culture. This is true of the microscopic forms of human interaction (conversation and gatherings) as it is of the most macroscopic forms of human initiative (the attempt to build religious systems of ultimate meaning and significance)" (p. 359).

Methods.   Researchers focus their examinations on broad social and cultural practices, instead of on the texts or media. They might gather data about a text, but the analysis is directed toward making interpretations or criticisms of society or culture as an influencer of the text.

TEXTUAL ANALYSIS

Textual analysis is a methodology that focuses on texts and seeks to understand them from a literary point of view (Jensen & Jankowski, 1991) and to understand how they define culture (Jensen, 1991a). Instead of focusing on people as constructors of culture, texts themselves can be viewed as cultural influencers. Texts have been used to define culture "in anthropological terms as a set of communicative practices constituting a way of life" (Jensen & Jankowski, 1991, p. 8).

With television, textual analysis deals with three issues: "the formal qualities of the television programs and their flow; the intertextual relations of television within itself, with other media, and with conversation; and the study of socially situated readers and the process of reading" (Fiske, 1987, p. 16).

Foundation. Textual analysis has its roots in literary criticism and structuralist linguistics. Literary criticism follows the practice of looking at texts as constructed works of art that can be compared to some set of aesthetic standards. The scholar must make some judgment about the quality or merit or the scholar can become an advocate for change. Structural linguistics have introduced four assumptions that now underlie much of textual analysis of the media. First, the media are believed to be one of a number of complex sign systems through which we experience and come to know the world. Second, with most of the media, especially television and film, the traditional notion of author or artist as the source of meaning is changed, because the mass media involve so many people in the production of messages. Third, the focus is not on an independent piece of work (one TV show or one scene) but on the symbolic structures and the systems of relationships among those symbols that create meaning. And fourth, the representation of reality is not recognized as a criterion, because programs are products of people's imagination and also because words acquire meaning by virtue of their positions with a conceptual system of similarity and difference and not through any direct relationship with reality.

The primary axioms of textual analysis are hermeneutics and interpretation. In analyzing texts, scholars must attribute meaning to large-scale units (such as entire stories or genres) by interpreting the meaning of smaller scale units (such as narrative elements or character depictions). But in interpreting the meaning of the smaller scale units, scholars need to assess how they fit as examples of the broader scale units. The interpretation is usually limited to the researchers themselves; that is, the researchers do not interview or observe audience members to gather their interpretations.

Methods. Data are almost exclusively the elements in the texts. The analysis is performed primarily from a literary point of view (Jensen, 1991) using the analysis of discourse, narrative, genre, and auter among others.

COMPARATIVE ILLUSTRATIONS

The seven methodologies have been introduced in the preceding sections, but you the reader might be feeling uneasy with the abstract nature of the introduction and might want more concrete examples about how these methodologies differ. So let's consider two examples of research topics and look at how useful each methodology would be in approaching that research.

Example I. Let's say you are interested in examining the phenomenon of family communication patterns while watching television. All of the methodologies with the exception of textual analysis would offer a useful strategy. Textual analysis focuses on the meaning in texts and would not be broad enough to encompass family communication patterns. Although the other six methodologies would be useful, they are not interchangeable; each presents a unique strategy for focusing on what is important. Ethnography focuses the research on the "community" of family members that is formed during the viewing. Who controls the set? What are the rules of who can talk and what can be said? Ethnomethodology focuses more on what goes on inside the head of each person as they decide for themselves how to make meaning about the mundane things of deciding where to sit and how to respond to what others say. How do parents create and communicate the rules about TV use and how do children interpret the rules? The focus is more on the how than on the rules themselves. With ecological psychology, the researcher focuses on the environment, such as how the size of the room, the arrangement of furniture, possible distractions (windows, telephone, etc.) influence the viewing and the communication. Symbolic interactionists look at how meaning is negotiated through interpersonal interactions. A symbol of power might be the recliner chair; if a child jumps in the chair and claims it for her own, what meaning does this communicate to others and how do they behave and talk in order to attempt to change (or restore) the meaning of that chair? How does the child respond to these behaviors and words? As the negotiation continues, does the meaning of the chair change and/or do the meanings of other symbols change?

The methodologies of reception studies and cultural studies are different than the four previously exemplified because they each bring another important element into the mix. With reception studies, the researcher will carefully analyze texts of particular programs that the family watches. He will then observe how the family members construct meaning for themselves given the particular images, characters, and plots of those programs. He will examine the meaning construction to see the extent to which each family member is influenced by the other members in that group. With cultural studies scholars, the additional element is a broad cultural (political-economic) context that is used to interpret the patterns within the family. In the earlier examples, the context is the family, its history, its structure, its environment, and so forth. With cultural studies, the context must be something outside the household. For example, if the researcher were interested in a Marxist context, she would interpret the family viewing patterns as being determined by the political and economic influences of living in a capitalist society. If instead, she were interested in a feminist context, she would observe how the males possessed the most power in the setting and how they used conversation and control of the TV set to exercise their power over the females.

In each of the preceding six examples, the topic of the research was the same, but the use of different methodologies would lead the researcher to select different types of evidence and subject the evidence to different kinds of analysis to arrive at divergent conclusions as prescribed by the differing purposes of the methodologies. However, the differences are not so great as to lead one to believe that any of these methodologies has strayed outside the qualitative approach as defined by its fundamental assumptions.

Example 2. Let's say you are interested in examining the phenomenon of how women have been portrayed in film. Several of the methodologies (textual analysis, cultural studies) would be useful, some (reception studies, symbolic interactionism) might be useful, and several (ethnography, ethnomethodology, ecological psychology) would not be of help.

Textual analysis would focus on the symbols in particular films and show how they are used to connote certain meanings. These meanings can be interpreted in many ways (feminist, myth, psychoanalytical) depending on the analytical techniques chosen by the researcher. A cultural studies scholar would identify certain elements in the film texts and use them to show that they are evidence of patterns in the culture (such as the fragmentation of society or the exploitation of women).

A researcher using the reception study methodology would analyze certain characteristics of film texts but would also want to observe and interview audience members to see how they interpret those characteristics for themselves. A scholar using symbolic interactionism would want to listen to people discussing film to determine what were the symbols with which they are most concerned and how they conveyed the meaning of those symbols to others through conversations.

As with the first example, there are many ways of approaching a research topic. The choosing of a methodology serves to narrow the topic (by focusing attention on a certain part of the phenomenon), and serves to move the researcher out of a condition of having an abstract interest in doing a study and onto a more concrete path of decision making about evidence, analysis, and writing.

SUMMARY

Methodologies and methods are not the same thing. Methodologies are strategies that lay out the means for achieving the goals of research, whereas methods are the techniques used in the service of achieving those goals. Methodologies are the blueprints; methods are the tools.

Within the qualitative approach, there are currently seven predominate methodologies: ethnography, ethnomethodology, reception studies, ecological psychology, symbolic interactionism, cultural studies, and textual analysis. Although each of these shares a common set of axioms and draws from a common pool of methods, each has a different vision for what qualitative research should contribute to scholarship.

In the next chapter, the focus shifts to an examination of the primary facets of the phenomenon of how humans construct meaning from the media. These seven methodologies can be used to guide the research into any of these facets; however certain methodologies are more useful than others with certain facets.

5

THE QUALITATIVE PHENOMENON

What is the subject of qualitative research; that is, what should qualitative research focus on as a subject of investigation? Many different writers have attempted to provide a definition of the phenomenon of interest in qualitative research. At the most general level, qualitative research focuses on meaning making by humans and this meaning is seen best through examining the symbols and language (J. A. Anderson, 1987; Jankowski & Wester, 1991; Lincoln & Guba, 1985; Lindlof, 1991; Lindlof & Meyer, 1987; Pauly, 1991; J. K. Smith, 1983). For example, Jensen (1991a) argued that "language is the primary medium of exchange between humans and reality (in processes of perception, cognition, and action), and that, accordingly, verbal texts may become vehicles of knowledge and truth" (p. 19). He stated, "Through language, reality becomes social. Equally, it is through language that reality becomes intersubjective and accessible for analysis. Hence, for the purpose of qualitative research, language and other semiotic systems represent both an analytical object and a central tool of analysis" (p. 19). According to Lindlof and Meyer (1987), the phenomenon includes a concern about "under what conditions communicative acts occur, how it is that people account for their acts, what versions of the world are proposed and negotiated through communication" (p. 6). Lincoln and Guba (1985) espoused the position that the phenomenon is social reality, and that this is purely mind-dependent, because people (including investigators) construct and shape reality, and this changes over time and is sensitive to situations.

The characteristics just illuminated are shared perspectives among qualitative researchers. Looking at this general phenomenon of the qualitative approach at a more specific level—media studies—there appear to be three important facets: texts, institutions, and people. When viewed from the text

67

perspective, the focus is on the messages in the media. Researchers analyze the symbols in those written and visual texts and infer either what the authors had in mind (consciously or unconsciously) or what meanings the audience members would make from the texts.

When the phenomenon is viewed from the perspective of institutions, the focus is on large-scale meaning production. For example, researchers might examine the news production industry and analyze how that culture shapes newsworkers' behavior and how those behaviors influence the meaning of the news.

The third perspective focuses on people as the primary facet. When the phenomenon of meaning making is viewed from this perspective, the focus is on how ordinary individuals use the media and how they construct their personal meanings from the symbols they see.

All three facets are integral parts of the phenomenon. This is why I use the term facet, not components. Facets cannot be pulled apart and examined separately as components can. Instead, a researcher rotates the phenomenon so he or she can bring a facet of interest into clearer focus. Although the examination focuses on a primary facet, the researcher must deal with the other facets as contexts for interpreting the central facet of interest.

The phenomenon of meaning making is too large a thing to be examined in total, so a researcher must choose one facet on which to focus his or her investigation. The choosing of a facet must be done carefully, because it influences the nature of the research. The phenomenon of meaning making will look different from a text perspective than from a people perspective, just like the skyline of Manhattan will look different from the Hudson River than it will from Central Park. The phenomenon being viewed is the same in both cases, but the different perspectives offer a foreground for examining certain features while obscuring and even hiding others.

These three facets are intricately intertwined, and each forms a context for the others. However, when a researcher undertakes a project, he or she usually focuses on one of these and chooses one methodology as a strategy for examining the facet of interest. Let's look at how the methodologies match up with the facets.

Most of the seven methodologies focus on people as the creators of meaning. All seven methodologies must deal with people, but some focus their attention more on texts or institutions. Those that give the people facet primacy are ethnography, ethnomethodology, reception studies, and ecological psychology.

When the primary facets of media research are used as a context for comparison among the qualitative methodologies, some interesting patterns emerge (see Fig. 5.1). The seven qualitative methodologies vary in terms of their broadness; some allow for a focus on all three areas of media research (industry issues, people, and texts), whereas others have a more narrow focus.

The seven methodologies can be compared in a second way (see Fig. 5.2). One dimension is the source of data. Some methodologies rely primarily on human

| | Primary Focus of Research | | |
Methodology	Text	Industry	Audience
Reception studies			XXXXXXXX
Ecological psychology			XXXXXXXX
Ethnography			XXXXXXXXXXXXXXXXX
Ethnomethodology			XXXXXXXXXXXXXXXX
Symbolic interactionism	XXXXXXXXXXXXXXXXXXXXXXXXXXXX		
Cultural studies	XXXXXXXXXXXXXXXXX		
Textual analysis	XXXXXXXXX		

FIG. 5.1. Comparisons of methodologies, methods, and purpose by primary focus of research.

sources; others rely more on texts and cultural artifacts. A second dimension is the humanistic-to-scientific continuum. Some methodologies are very focused on humanistic foundations; others are more broad—reaching into the scientific realm. When we plot the seven methodologies on these two dimensions, their differences and similarities become clearer. The horizontal axis shows a range of approaches from a humanistic extreme at the left to a scientific one at the right. The humanistic extreme is characterized by those approaches that focus on the idiographic and unique elements in particular humans, whereas the scientific extreme focuses on approaches concerned with uniform patterns in the aggregate. Also humanistic approaches focus more on a phenomenological approach (no a priori expectations) compared to the scientific front end theorizing and deductive reasoning. The vertical axis sets up a range of possibilities for data gathering and the focus of the analysis. At the top, the focus is exclusively on humans and the source of information and as the subject of the investigation. At the bottom, the focus is exclusively on texts and cultural artifacts. Each methodology is plotted on its own line. However, it would have been more accurate to plot the methodologies so that the lines overlap to indicate a range in the data sources. This was not done in order to focus the graphic more cleanly on the differences rather than the similarities among the methodologies.

The broadest methodologies appear to be ethnography and symbolic interactionism, both of which are firmly planted in the humanistic tradition but that span into scientific applications. Ecological psychology, not surprisingly, resides closer to science, but it allows for a humanistic approach also. The methodolo-

Data Source	Humanistic	Scientific
People	+++++Ecological Psychology+++++	
	+++++++++++++Ethnography+++++++++++++	
	++++++++++Ethnomethodology+++++++++++	
	+++++++Reception Studies++++++++	
	+++++Cultural Studies+++++	
Texts & Artifacts	+++Textual Analysis+++	
	Pure Humanism	Pure Science

FIG. 5.2. Comparison of methodology by source of data and type of approach.

gies with the least tolerance for scientific analysis are cultural studies and textual analysis.

When looking at the patterns across both dimensions together, it appears that those methodologies that focus most strongly on people are the broadest; that is, they allow for both humanistic and scientific approaches. In contrast, the use of texts as a data source is associated with an exclusively humanistic form of analysis.

The graphics of Figs. 5.1 and 5.2 are oversimplifications, but they can serve as tools to help us begin to understand the gross differences among the methodologies. To understand the finer differences, we need to conduct more careful analysis of what qualitative theoreticians say about the enterprise and compare these prescriptions to what researchers seem to do when they conduct qualitative studies—a task that is addressed in the second part of this book. In the meantime, let us turn our attention to comparing and contrasting the seven methodologies as alternative strategies for examining each of the three facets.

THE AUDIENCE FACET

The examination of the audience facet has been growing in popularity recently. D. Morley (1980) saw the shift from text-based research to audience-focused inquiry as a positive change, saying that scholars should not prescribe how audiences interpret messages; instead, empirical work is needed to discover the readings. He stressed the role of social factors in the production of meaning by individuals but cautioned against "universalist" generalizations. He said the "most useful work which has been conducted within audience studies in the last few years is that which has taken on board the questions raised about the flow of television, the positioning of the subject, the contextual determinations operating on different types of viewing of different media, alongside a close attention to the varieties of patterns of taste, response, and interpretation on the part of specific members of the audience" (pp. 38–39). He showed how some ideas (semiotics, cultural studies, film theory, psychoanalysis) have had an influence on audience studies.

This shift in thinking most likely began in 1978 with the publication of *Reading Television* in which Fiske and Hartley advanced the thesis that people need a certain type of literacy to be able to understand the messages on television. People who are literate at reading novels are not necessarily literate at reading television, because the two tasks require different skills. To be literate at reading television, people must learn the culturally generated codes and conventions. Hall (1980) built on this work by adding the ideas of encoding and decoding. He said that audiences employ competencies for decoding television that do not necessarily correspond to the way messages are encoded.

Each of the qualitative methodologies (with the exception of textual analysis and cultural studies) is useful in examining the audience facet of the phenomenon.

To contrast how scholars using the five methodologies would proceed, let's consider a research project with the goal of determining how adolescents use television news to learn about current events. A researcher using the ethnography methodology would first attempt to gain access to the lives of some adolescents. She would visit their households frequently and observe how the adolescents watched television news and what they said during the exposure. She could follow the adolescents outside the home and observe whether they talked about any current events when they interacted with other adolescents in school or in social situations. She would look for patterns in the way the adolescents constructed meaning for the current events stories and how those constructions were influenced by peers as well as the institutions of family and school.

In contrast, a researcher using the reception study methodology would typically have a more narrow focus than a researcher using the ethnographic methodology. He would accomplish this by exercising more control over the adolescents in research settings. For example, he would invite groups of adolescents to a common area to view news programs on television; thus he would control the setting, the timing, and the news material. Like the ethnographer, the reception study researcher would observe the adolescents during the viewing to see how they interacted with one another and how they expressed meaning for what they were seeing. Although the central focus of reception studies is the text-person interaction, the social environment is a very important context. So the researcher might generate discussions among the adolescents following the viewing in order to watch for the formation of what are called interpretive communities—socially constructed support systems for certain meanings. For example, adolescents who are politically conservative would reinforce each other's opinions about which stories were biased and which were good. The researcher looks for these social support systems and documents how they influence the meaning a viewer has constructed in the person-text interaction.

A researcher using ethnomethodology would appear to be similar to an ethnographer on the surface with her procedures of gaining access to adolescents in naturalistic settings and unobtrusively observing them over a long period of time. However, the ethnomethodologist, by observing adolescents as they perform their everyday activities, is less interested in documenting the meaning adolescents have for current events than in documenting how they arrive at that meaning. So the ethnomethodologist looks for the rules and practices of meaning making.

The symbolic interactionist would begin by following the same procedures as the ethnographer or a researcher using the reception study methodology. But while observing the adolescents, the symbolic interactionist would focus on symbols and how they influenced the meaning making. A symbol could be the image on the television screen during a news story or it could be the way a particular adolescent dressed or a word he used. For example, if an adolescent wore a suit and tie, some adolescents might interpret this dress pattern as revealing a thoughtful, mature, and intelligent boy whose opinion about current events should be respected. However, other adolescents might regard this symbol of dress as pretentious, elitist, and out of step so his opinion should be scorned. Another example of a symbol is the word *news*. To some adolescents it might mean interesting and important information about how the world operates; to others it might mean boring facts that only adults care about; and to others it might mean nothing. The symbolic interactionist observes adolescents in social situations first to parse out the important symbols, second to examine how the adolescents attach meaning to these symbols, and third to study how those meanings are reinforced or altered in social interactions.

A researcher using the ecological psychology methodology would attempt to get access to a person's life like an ethnographer. In her observations, the ecological psychologist would focus her attention on the person-environment interaction. For example, she would study the layout of an adolescent's home to determine how the arrangement of rooms and placement of the television sets serves to foster (or inhibit) discussions about the news. Also, she would look at how the neighborhood, the transportation system (car pools, bus, walking routes), and the school layout provide adolescents with opportunities to talk with particular kinds of people.

The preceding examples illustrate that there is considerable overlap among the methodologies but that each is unique in its plan for what the researcher should focus on most strongly and therefore which methods will be most useful. Now let's leave the hypothetical example of adolescents' constructions of meanings for television news and look at how the methodologies have been used by researchers to examine the audience facet. A very good example of an ethnography is provided by Turkle (1984), who lived in a computer culture for 6 years, observing and interviewing 400 people. She looked at how the medium of the computer helped define people and create communities of users who held the same meaning for the computer.

Rakow (1992) conducted an ethnomethodology focusing on how various women in a small town make meaning of the telephone in their everyday lives. While living in a community of 1,000 people for 6 weeks, Rakow interviewed 43 women in depth. She reported on how these women used their gender experiences through the telephone to extend their place in the community. Taking an historical perspective, she said "the telephone was introduced into a gendered world, within which it became embedded, and hence it has become a site at which gender relations are organized, experienced, and accomplished in both the family and the larger community and political world" (p. 154). Gender is then the key to understanding how women construct meaning about and through the telephone.

Also, a good example of an ethnomethodology is a study by Traudt and Lont (1987), who said they were doing an ethnography but this was really more of an ethnomethodology because they were interested primarily in determining "how social reality is constructed by members of the family household, and how television contributes to the common stock-of-knowledge shared by family members within this process of social construction" (p. 140). They visited five family members in their home 14 times within 3 months and observed behavior. They also audiotaped interviews and had the family fill out quarter-hour viewing diaries for 2 weeks. The concluded that television use is the key to understanding how families construct meaning for individuals, one's role as a family member, and one's role in life outside the home" (p. 159). Also, "television's presentational logic comes to represent a media consciousness on the part of family members" (p. 159).

Lull (1987) used symbolic interactionism to examine communication within the San Francisco punk subculture. He spent hundreds of hours over 2 months of participant observation and interviewing in locations where punks congregate, such as where they live, eat, hang out, and attend music shows. He focused primarily on "the domains of symbolic interaction, where so many of their images are nurtured" (p. 226). He defined the punk lifestyle in terms of the symbols of appearance, clothing, living quarters, food, school, religion, money, drugs, gender relations, their enemies, their music, and media habits. He showed that their symbols have a special meaning to the members of that community and this shared meaning is opposite to how outsiders would interpret the meaning. For example, their talk appears very aggressive and violent, but to insiders, the meaning is the opposite.

As for ecological psychology, Barrios (1988) observed 13 Venezuelan families in their homes so he could see how the houses were laid out, the arrangement of television sets, and the patterns of accessibility. A primary finding was that children were found to be passive when viewing alone, but active when viewing with others. Also, Pardun and Krugman (1994) observed 40 American families in their homes to determine how the architectural style of a home is related to how families use the television. They reported that families who live in transitional-style homes treat the TV as a common hearth for family gatherings. In contrast, families who live in traditional-style homes treat the TV as a retreat; that is, individuals use the TV to get away from the family.

The most popular methodology among audience-focused scholars seems to be the reception study. Because there are so many examples of this methodology, I break it down into two subsets, one that includes the studies that focus on how individuals receive meaning and the other that includes studies where reception is couched in terms of interpretive communities.

An example of the subset of reception studies that focus on the individual would be a study by Hobson (1982), who interviewed English housewives about their viewing of soap operas. She watched shows with them and asked them about what the shows meant to them. She found that viewers had a keenly developed sense of what was real and did not like it when the portrayals veered into fantasy. Also, Radway (1984) interviewed avid readers of romance novels. The interviews were not conducted in the natural setting of the women, nor were the women members of an interpretive community where they would discuss the novels with each other; they were interviewed individually. Radway also generated data from 42 responses to her 53-item questionnaire, which was fairly quantitative in nature. She reported that women interact with the romance novel text primarily as a way of creating their own space in their confining daily routines as wives and mothers. The reading is a gesture of protest against the strictures of a patriarchal society.

The interpretive community subset includes those studies that look at how individuals make sense out of media messages. The authors of these studies argued that this sense making is traceable to various types such as a person's gender group, ethnic group, or culture. For example, Jhally and Lewis (1992) showed people an episode of "The Cosby Show," then asked them questions about their attitudes toward race, gender, and class. They found that African-Americans did not see the show as a celebration of African-American upward mobility. In contrast, Whites liked the idea of seeing African Americans succeed without affirmative action help. Also, Liebes and Katz (1988, 1989) showed Israelis (Moroccan Jews, Arabs, Russian Jews, and people living in an Israeli kibbutz) an episode of "Dallas," then asked them to discuss it. They concluded that American programs like "Dallas" "invite multiple levels of understanding and involvement, offering a wide variety of different projects and games to different types of viewers" (p. 114). They found three major patterns in the decodings. First were the traditional viewers who remain in the "real" world and "mobilize values to defend themselves against the program" (p. 116). Second, the more Western groups deal with its reality in a playful fashion. And third, the Russians are the most serious as they focus on the underlying message rather than the structure of the program. Finally, the authors explained the show's appeal in terms of its primordiality (echoing fundamental myths) and its seriality (familiarity builds from repeated contact with characters and situations).

THE TEXT FACET

When the text is to be the focus of research, the qualitative approach offers three methodologies: textual analysis, symbolic interactionism, and cultural studies. To contrast how scholars using these three methodologies would proceed, let's consider a research project with the goal of determining how situation comedies on television have changed over time. A researcher using the textual analysis methodology would first attempt to assemble scripts or tapes of situation comedies from each of the five decades of commercial television. He would look for patterns of changes in terms of characterization, plot, conversation, themes, use of humor, and so on.

A researcher using symbolic interactionism would also begin by assembling texts, but he would focus on key symbols in the show such as the use of taboo words and examine how the meaning of such symbols change over time as different kinds of characters use them. In contrast, a researcher using the cultural studies methodology would assemble texts but also gather a great deal of information about the texts to use as context. This contextual information could include interviews with writers and producers, ratings of programs, industry trends, and views of social critics. She would then highlight some change in situation comedies and present this change within a web of contextual influences.

The aforementioned examples illustrate that there are alternative strategies to use in studying texts. Now let's leave the hypothetical example of examining changes in situation comedies and look at how the methodologies have been used by researchers to examine the text facet. A good example of a textual analysis is a study by Schwichtenberg (1987), who analyzed the opening sequence of the "Love Boat" to show how those images create a promise of love. Barker (1987) used textual analysis to render a close reading of two television programs ("All in the Family" and "M*A*S*H"). His purpose was to examine camera space and performer space in a comparative analysis of the two shows. Esslin (1987) examined the texts of television ads to provide a foundation for his argument that it is advertising that presents the basic myths of our society. Notice in these examples that the textual analysis methodology is a general strategy guiding the examination but that within the strategy there is room for the use of very different analytical techniques such as criticism (Schwichtenberg), comparative analysis (Barker), and myth analysis (Esslin).

Although all of the examples just mentioned focus on the facet of texts, there is a range of degree to which the focus stays on the texts themselves or to which the focus is broadened to provide a significant cultural context for the text. With textual analysis, the scholar keeps the focus on the text in an attempt to show patterns internal to the text. With cultural analysis, the scholar shifts the focus more onto examining how the text was influenced by or how it fits into the larger context of culture. An example of a cultural analysis is C. Anderson (1987), who provided a reading of "Magnum, P.I." text to show how it fits into and breaks the mold of detective series. His analysis links the show to historical and cultural events of the time as well as to previous detective programs. But his treatment goes well beyond the text itself (and even the genre) to provide an interpretation of television in general. He asserted "television is a distinctly new form which has developed during the most intense and disorienting period of change in recorded history" (p. 117). Also, Lipsitz (1992) interpreted 1950s working-class sitcoms in terms of the economic, political, and cultural environment of the time. His primary data are elements of the programs, but he also cited economic trends, political positions, and cultural patterns as context.

As for symbolic interactionism, Bird and Dardenne (1988) looked for symbols in the narrative qualities of news and inferred how viewers interact with those symbols to construct meaning from them. They regarded the news genre as a particular kind of symbolic system, and they explored the difference between the reality of events and the symbols that are used to construct stories about that reality.

THE INSTITUTION FACET

When the institution facet is the focus, there are four useful qualitative methodologies: ethnography, ethnomethodology, symbolic interactionism, and cultural studies. To contrast how scholars using the four methodologies would proceed, let's consider a research project with the goal of determining how an advertising agency produces a television commercial. A researcher using the ethnography methodology would first attempt to gain access to the agency where she could observe all facets of the production process. During those observations, she might look for the social structure of who had formal status (account executives, producers, and directors) and informal status (those with no titles but with good ideas) in the production culture. She would examine the dynamics within the culture that influenced the production process.

A researcher using ethnomethodology would also seek access to the production team to be able to make observations, but he would be more interested in uncovering the procedures about how the various team members come to their decisions, that is how each person constructed meaning from their everyday conversations during the production.

As for symbolic interactionism, the researcher would try to identify the key symbols in the culture. For example, how do the members of the production team know who has the power to control the decisions and how does that power get negotiated in their interpersonal interactions? What are the symbols indicating power? Is it dress, the way a person speaks, body language?

A cultural studies researcher would focus primarily on the institution of advertising and reveal its mechanisms within different contexts, such as historical, political, and economic. Then she could present a case study of the production she observed and contrast it with the larger patterns in the institutional culture of advertising in general.

The preceding examples illustrate that there are alternative strategies to use in studying institutions. Now let's leave the hypothetical example of examining the production of a television commercial and look at how the methodologies have been used by researchers to examine the institution facet. A good example of an ethnography is Altheide (1976), who spent a year in a network affiliate newsroom (and 2 more years in other newsrooms). He observed how news workers created a community of rules in order to get their daily work done. This set of rules and procedures, which he called the "news perspective," is constructed by the constraints of commercialism, scheduling, technology, and competition. Also, Elliott (1979) was a participant observer in an English television studio during the production of seven programs for an adult education project entitled, "The Nature of Prejudice." He shows how the production of the programs were strongly influenced by the production community that evolved throughout the project.

Using ethnomethodology, Tuchman (1978) gathered her data over a 10-year period (not continuously) at four sites in New York City. In examining how news workers create categories in their everyday commonsensical construction of the news, she found that the news workers' personal sense of professionalism guided their construction of meaning.

Symbolic interactionism was used by Altheide and Snow (1979) to examine how the media symbols reveal a special logic of their own. Altheide (1985) dealt "with mass communication, and especially television, as a piece of culture" (p. 12). He tried to get beyond the political ideological arguments to look at whether there is "a cultural consideration lurking within the symbolic, semantic, and syntactic structure of these media" (p. 12). Snow (1983) examined how "the language and perspectives of present-day mass media have produced *media culture*" (p. 9).

The most prevalent methodology used by institution-focused scholars is cultural studies. Because there are so many examples of cultural studies, I subdivide the examples into cultural history, cultural interpretation, and critical analysis. The examples of each of these is briefly described next.

Cultural History. The examples in this set focus on studies that are primarily descriptive; that is, there is little interpretation or theorizing by the authors—they are primarily journalistic. The broadest of these cultural histories was presented by Innis (1950), who interpreted the development of empires and examined the role of communication within them. Barnouw (1975) was also fairly broad in his description of the development of American broadcasting from its inception to the early 1970s. Other historians have focused on a piece of this topic. For example, Metz (1975) focused on CBS from its beginning to the mid-1970s. Spigel (1993) provided a cultural history of the way children were treated during the development of television. Baughman (1990) traced ABC's rise to prominence in the early 1950s through its use of Hollywood studios' production of TV shows. And Auletta (1991) updated part of Barnouw's history of broadcasting by examining the three commercial TV networks in the later 1980s.

Several scholars look at the economics of the industry. Litman (1990) provided an economic analysis of the development of the TV industry. And Brown (1971) examined the business of television during the 1970 season.

Some historians have focused on the press or newspaper moguls. Altschull (1984) provided a history of the press in different countries and classified those systems into three categories. Pauly (1988) presented a cultural history of Rupert Murdoch's media acquisitions and their effect on the public.

Cultural Interpretation. The most popular form of cultural interpretation of the media industries focuses on how messages are produced. Because this is a complex process involving many different kinds of people and many influences (overt as well as subtle), the task of making sense of this process requires interpreting patterns within various contexts. For example, Turow (1984) interpreted how the mass media industries create their messages within a resource dependency context. In a later book, Turow (1989) showed that his interpretive scheme works in analyzing the production of TV doctor programs. Cantor (1980) studied "the production of television drama, how it is produced, by whom, under what conditions, and for whom" (p. 11). Her findings are strongly contextualized within a traditional occupational sociology perspective on the television industry.

Critical Analysis. The writings in this set feature arguments by authors who believe there are weaknesses or dangerous trends in the media industries. For example, some use an economic perspective. Bagdikian (1987) laid out the case against the desirability of media monopolies by showing that the culture of the media industries has drastically changed over time. His context for these changes is not a conspiracy theory but rather a response to good business principles of efficiency; however, he still perceived the trend as dangerous and argued for an alternative. Gandy (1982) argued that government policymakers provide an information subsidy to certain industries that results in a widening of the information gap. His contexts of analysis are the dominant corporate, political, and bureaucratic entities in this country.

Some researchers focus their criticism on the manufacturing of content. Bagdikian (1972) criticized press coverage. Parenti (1986) argued that media do not meet their own standards of objectivity, informativeness, truthfulness, or independence. Dates and Barlow (1990) criticized the media for their portrayals and treatment of African Americans. Gitlin (1983) provided a critical view of how messages get selected for television broadcast. Gitlin (1980) argued that the public's image of the New Left was created and maintained by the mass media. And Kellner (1987) argued that the television industry maintains myths although some of the messages are not reflective of the dominant ideology.

Some authors are critical of the scholarship about the media industries. In a criticism of the literature, Collins (1989) called for a postmodern interpretation that regards culture as a complex of conflictive power relations, not just one. Ang (1991) criticized the industry's emphasis on decontextualized quantitative data and recommended ethnographic work instead. Browne (1987) was critical of using an aesthetic analysis of television texts; instead, he said the megatext of television should only be analyzed from a political economic point of view. Corcoran (1987) argued against the use of both positivist and film criticism approaches to analyzing television. Gitlin (1987) argued that Gramsci's idea of hegemony can be adapted to answer the question: What do television programs mean?

SUMMARY

There are three interrelated facets to the single phenomenon of mass media research: audiences, texts, and institutions. Each of the seven qualitative methodologies are variously useful across these facets. Some of these methodologies are more narrow in their usefulness than others. For example, the methodologies of reception analysis and ecological psychology are extremely useful in examining elements within the audience facet, but they have little or no usefulness with the other facets. Narrow in this context means the number of facets the methodology has potential usefulness within. It does not refer to a limit on the number of methods that can be employed in the service of the methodology, because each of the seven methodologies allows for a very wide range of latitude in purposes and techniques. The next section of this book, with its eight chapters, demonstrates the alternative conceptions of evidence, the options for data gathering, the variety of analytical schemes, the methods for analysis, purposes, and approaches to writing. Within any of these seven methodologies, a researcher has an almost limitless combination of techniques that can be assembled.

INTERPRETIVE ANALYSIS

6

NATURE OF QUALITATIVE EVIDENCE

Anyone who intends to undertake a research project must address the following question early in the planning phase: What should be regarded as evidence of the phenomenon being researched? Experienced researchers have usually developed habits of using certain techniques with which they are most familiar and comfortable. So the aforementioned question is not one they typically deal with in an explicit manner; rather, the use of their chosen techniques guides the nature of their evidence.

However, the nature of the evidence is a more fundamental concern than the techniques employed. In determining the nature of evidence, researchers need to be concerned with at least three issues: type of evidence, level of evidence, and the use of numerical evidence (see Table 6.1 for a breakdown of these three issues).

TYPE OF EVIDENCE

The essence of the type of evidence concern lies in the degree to which researchers believe they can be objective. The researcher's position on this is traced to his or her answer to the epistemological question about the way humans make sense of their world. As was illuminated in chapter 3, there is a range of opinion about the degree to which humans can be objective. Some scholars argue that humans are always subjective and can never attain any degree of objectivity, whereas others argue that objectivity is possible under certain conditions.

This epistemological issue is further complicated when we bring it into the research arena, where there are two, not just one, steps of meaning making.

TABLE 6.1
Nature of Qualitative Evidence

---

1. Type of Evidence

Key Question: What does the researcher believe to be the nature of evidence?

Alternative Answers:

(1) Researcher construction: The phenomenon of interest is unknowable through empirical means, therefore all research must be a subjective interpretation of the researcher.

(2) Subjective valuing: There are tangible, material artifacts that reflect the phenomenon of interest, but each researcher has his or her own subjective manner for valuing each bit of evidence.

(3) Contingent accuracy: Empirical evidence is important and valued. It is checked for accuracy.

---

2. Level of Evidence

Key Question: At what level does the researcher feel the evidence is best gathered?

Alternative Answers:

(1) Micro: When examining audiences, evidence is gathered from people, one person at a time. When the focus of the research is texts, the evidence is from very small units, such as scenes within individual shows.

(2) Mid: When examining audiences, evidence is gathered from groups of people; includes observations of individual and group dynamics. With the focus on texts, the evidence is from units such as series of television shows.

(3) Macro: When examining audiences, evidence is aggregated patterns of exposure or public opinion in general. When the focus is texts, evidence is on genres or all messages in a medium. With institution-focused research, the evidence is from large-scale structures such as organizations and institutions.

---

3. Numerical Evidence

Key Question: Does the researcher allow for enumeration?

Alternative Answers:

(1) No numbers are used.

(2) Numbers are used but no ennumeration: Numbers that refer to real mathematic properties (dates, ages, quantities, monetary figures, etc.) are used, but no translations are made of qualities into quantities.

(3) Enumeration: Qualities (such as motives, attitudes, etc.) are translated into numbers.

One step is concerned with how humans interpret meaning for themselves in any experience. When a researcher observes this step, the researcher then enters a second step of making meaning of how the observed person made meaning. Some researchers try not to take the second step; they try to faithfully report in the observed people's own words how they interpreted meaning for themselves. However, many qualitative researchers do take the second step and present their own interpretations of the observed people's interpretations. This subtle, but very important, distinction was termed *etic* and *emic* by M. L. Smith

(1987). When a researcher uses expressions in his or her language or from his or her own perspective, the evidence is etic. In contrast, evidence is emic when it is composed of the expressions in the categories and meanings of the object—that is, the person being studied.

How does the etic-emic distinction relate to the objective–subjective debate? If the phenomenon being examined is the verbal language of a television viewer, then emic evidence (quotes from the television viewer if they are faithfully reproduced) can be regarded as being a fairly objective account of the phenomenon itself. If the researcher presents the complete set of direct quotations and describes how they were taken, then the research report can be viewed as an uninterpreted picture of what happened, hence objective. If instead, the researcher wrote up the interview with an interspersing of his or her interpretations (where the researcher challenges the quotes as being inconsistent or superficial, etc.; or where the researcher rearranges the quotes to fit an argument the researcher is trying to make), then the researcher's interpretations become more prominent and the report reflects more etic evidence.

But let's say that the phenomenon is not the language of television viewers, as was the case in the preceding example. Let's say the phenomenon of interest is television-viewing motives and that the researcher is distrustful of the language of television viewers; the researcher does not trust viewers to know or be able to express their viewing motives. This researcher would focus on his or her interpretations (etic evidence of the motives) and reject what the television viewers say (emic evidence of the motives). In this case the match between emic evidence and objectivity is not as clear, if objectivity is equated with realist accuracy; the researcher's interpretation may be closer to the truth than the perceptions and words of the television viewers being studied. However, in qualitative research the assumption of interpretation reminds us that there is no ultimate, defensible truth; there are only interpretations of it. Therefore, objectivity must not be viewed as a fixed position reflecting truth, but instead as a relative position on a continuum. On that continuum, objectivity is a position that is closest to the phenomenon being examined. So in this sense, the emic evidence of the television viewers' own accounts of their motives can be regarded as being more objective than the researcher's interpretation of that phenomenon filtered through the words of the television viewers. The television viewers' verbal accounts are once removed from their motives themselves, but the researcher's interpretation of the phenomenon is twice removed from the phenomenon; and a reviewer's interpretation of the researcher's interpretation is three times removed. With each step removed there is an additional layer of interpretation that serves to shift the balance from the phenomenon toward the interpretation of the phenomenon. Therefore, it would be best not to use the terms objective and subjective to capture this continuum but to use the following three categories that serve to emphasize differences in the degree of interpretation: *researcher construction* (the researcher's personal, subjective position, which is purely etic), *subjective valuing* (a combination of etic and emic evidence), and *contingent accuracy* (primarily emic).

The first conception—researcher construction—regards evidence as a total construction of the researcher. It is based primarily on the idea that the human senses are not trustworthy, so that all observations are subjective. The focus is on the inner experiences of the researcher (J. K. Smith & Heshusius, 1986). In this conception, etic evidence—perceptions and insights of the researcher—are the focus.

In contrast to the first conception, most qualitative theoreticians recognize the importance of evidence that has an existence outside of the researcher's experience. Using one's senses to observe the phenomenon (or empiricism) is especially important to physical scientists (J. K. Smith & Heshusius, 1986), but it is also important in qualitative research (M. L. Smith, 1987). The second and third conceptions of evidence are empirically based.

The second conception—subjective valuing—is based on the belief that there are tangible artifacts (memos, video images, spoken words, observed behaviors, etc.) that reflect the phenomenon of interest. These artifacts have a material existence, but the researcher's ability to perceive these artifacts is limited and his or her interpretations of them are subjective. The artifacts can be a starting place to suggest what the phenomenon is like, but they require much interpretation. For instance, five researchers may look at the same artifacts and arrive at five different interpretations, because each researcher has his or her own subjective manner for valuing each bit of evidence.

The third conception—contingent accuracy—is the belief that artifacts are relatively accurate reflections of the phenomenon, some more so than others. It is the most objective of the three positions, but it should be characterized as intersubjective rather than objective. Researchers must make judgments about which bits of evidence to use and which to discard. When the proper selection is made, little interpretation is needed in the analysis. With training and experience, researchers will be able to make the correct decisions in selecting evidence. The selected evidence is then regarded as being the most accurate until countervailing evidence is found. In this manner, the focus is placed on the evidence more than on the researcher. In this conception, emic evidence—direct quotes from that which is being researched—would be favored.

Now let's take a look at the qualitative research to see how these types of evidence are exemplified.

Researcher Construction. A strong focus on researchers' constructions are found within text-based research. For example, Deming (1992) chose to focus on the phenomenon of a television series ("Kate and Allie") as a text. Although he did not interview any audience members of the show, he argued, "female spectators can read TV programs differently because their own social, political, and historical situations vary. In addition, women have different levels of reading competencies depending on their memories of and familiarity with inter/extra-textual discourses" (p. 212). He did not interview anyone connected with the creation or production of the series, so his evidence for the points he made is solely his interpretations as well as the interpretations of other scholars whom he cited. Another example is Horowitz (1987), who constructed her own personal interpretation of the genre of situation comedies as a text. As with Deming, her evidence is exclusively her interpretation.

Subjective Valuing. When presented a subjective valuing perspective on evidence, a researcher treats the evidence as idiosyncratic elements needing interpretation. A good example is Lindlof's (1987) study of prisoners and their use of the media. He presented direct quotes from the prisoners but he mixed in his own observations and interpretations to build to his conclusions. None of the prisoners was quoted as saying that they used media to satisfy their situational needs of diversion from predictability, to gain control over environmental stimuli, to maintain artifactual continuity with the former life, to provide them material for learning, and to gain control over the degree and type of social affiliation. These were Lindlof's conclusions—hence his interpretations.

Another example is a study by Jhally and Lewis (1992), who presented quotes from viewers of "The Cosby Show" then interpreted those reactions to the series in terms of their race, class, and gender. Also, Rakow (1992) presented long passages of interviewees talking, but she also provided her own interpretation along a feminist perspective.

Within institution-focused research, Gitlin (1983) said that most of the people he interviewed told him they had no idea how TV shows get on the air or how decisions are made about what images are used. Acknowledging this finding made him elevate the subjective nature of the evidence to an important issue in his overall argument. He had to infer a deeper meaning from their apparent ignorance (or evasions) by examining patterns in their idiosyncratic comments.

Contingent Accuracy. There are many examples of qualitative scholars approaching the phenomenon as if it consisted of ordered elements that needed a clear description. These researchers present their evidence as if it were facts that speak for themselves and require little or no interpretation; that is, the facts are presented as accurate reflections of the phenomenon being examined. Of course, the tasks of selecting which facts to present and how to order them require a certain degree of interpretation, and the accuracy of the facts is contingent on their ability to make interpretations. However, the researchers who present this perspective of contingent accuracy foreground the facts and rarely present to the reader any description about the decisions they made in their interpretive deliberations. For example, Hobson (1989) reported the quotes of the women she interviewed; these quotes are ordered to provide answers to a series of questions about why women watch soap operas. Also, Barker (1987) looked at elements of camera space and performer space, which are physical properties in the production and require little interpretation. Bodroghkozy (1992) presented a series of quotes from letters about the television show "Julia."

The clearest examples of evidence treated with contingent accuracy are those studies that appear to emulate mainstream social science. For example, Chesebro (1978) set up his study by posing four research questions about the portrayal of characters on popular television series. He developed his primary types (ironic, mimetic, leader, romantic, mythical) early then conducted a content analysis to look for the prevalence of these types. Liebes and Katz (1988, 1989) created an analytical scheme then applied it to the diverse responses from 65 focus group members. It does not appear that the scheme was developed in a hermeneutic process during the data collection; instead, it is presented independent of the evidence, then the evidence is brought in as examples to illustrate the usefulness of the scheme. D. Morley (1980) appeared to use his a priori hypotheses through an ordering of his quotations into different forms of decoding. He did recognize that there are exceptions to his categorization scheme, but his focus is more on aggregate patterns, that is, on the characteristics that viewers share rather than their idiosyncratic differences.

LEVEL OF EVIDENCE

Evidence differs in terms of its level. Some evidence has a fairly microlevel; some is very macro; and some is midlevel. With people or institutions as the subject of study, the microlevel evidence consists of quotations, answers to questions, diaries, memos, letters, and the like. Midlevel evidence includes social interaction patterns, structures of conversations (rather than single quotes), and leadership behaviors. Macrolevel evidence includes institutional norms, cultural values, and broadly practiced rituals. With texts as the subject of study, microlevel evidence consists of an individual text such as a book, a television program, or a film. Midlevel evidence would be genres of television shows or an auteur's body of work. Macrolevel evidence would be cultural values exhibited through a variety of texts.

The level of evidence is a different issue than the facet of the phenomenon that the researcher addresses. For example, the facet of interest might be institutions, but the evidence might be from a microlevel—people or specific texts. Although it is usually a better practice to gather evidence of the same level as the research focus, sometimes a match is not possible. For example, Lindlof and Meyer (1987) argued that with mediated communication, there are not discrete events that can be easily operationalized at a macrolevel, so there is often a need to gather evidence at a microlevel (analysis of an individual television show's episode) over time so as to be sensitive to "the temporal and interactive nuances of its enactments" (p. 6), then to construct a pattern to reflect the broad-scale changes in television programming. So it is possible to gather evidence at one level and use it to make a case for a pattern at another level. However, we need to be aware of the distinction between level of evidence and facet of the phenomenon; when the level of data is not appropriate for the facet of the phenomenon to be examined, greater care can be applied in assessing the degree to which the researcher is able to move across levels from data to purpose.

Microlevel. With text-focused research, an example of microlevel evidence is in a study by Flitterman-Lewis (1992), who looked at only one television program ("General Hospital") and within that at only two weddings. Several scholars limit their analysis to one program but look at the entire run of the program (not just one episode) as the text. For example, C. Anderson (1987) examined "Magnum, P.I.," Deming (1992) interpreted "Kate and Allie," D'Acci (1992) examined "Cagney and Lacey," Schwichtenberg (1987) criticized "Love Boat," and Zynda (1988) focused on the "Mary Tyler Moore Show."

With audience-focused research, there are many examples of the microlevel. Lindlof (1987) interviewed inmates individually. Tulloch (1989) interviewed elderly people individually in their homes. Lewis (1991) interviewed people one at a time for reactions to a particular news show. Radway (1984) interviewed romance readers individually. Rakow (1992) interviewed individual women. Ang (1985) examined individual letters written to her by viewers of "Dallas." Although some of these letters were written by more than one person, there were still individual opinions expressed in them. Bodroghkozy (1992) also used letters from individuals as the database.

Midlevel. Some researchers look at groups of texts. Chesebro (1978) presented a scheme that can be used to group all entertainment shows; that is, he drew lines for the groupings on the basis of individual shows. But his focus was on groups, not individual shows. Bird and Dardenne (1988) treated all TV news shows as a group. They did not even mention a particular type of news show, nor did they analyze any examples. Esslin (1987) dealt with a "group of texts" of TV ads but he never mentioned one by name. He talked about the structure of coffee ads as well as ads for other products without mentioning a particular brand or particular ad. Still this article is empirical, but his evidence comes from categories of ads rather than single ads, and his conclusions are reflected to all TV ads. Lipsitz (1992) interpreted 1950s working-class sitcoms in terms of the economic, political, and cultural environment of the time. His primary data are elements with the programs, but he also cited economic trends, political positions, and cultural patterns as context.

Some researchers gathered their data from people in groups, usually families (Barrios, 1988; Lull, 1980; Pardun & Krugman, 1994; Rogge, 1989; Rogge & Jensen, 1988; Traudt & Lont, 1987), coworkers (Altheide, 1976; Elliott, 1979; Fishman, 1988; Gitlin, 1983; Hobson, 1989; Tuchman, 1978), friends (Liebes & Katz, 1988, 1989), or children in school (Wolf, 1987). D. Morley (1980) used relatively intact groups for his focus group interviews and the presumption is that the culture of the groups is in part responsible for the type of readings.

Macrolevel. Some scholars select very broad-scale texts. For example, Him-melstein (1984) took all of television as his text in arguing for its demythologiza-tion. He carefully analyzed eight types of programming (situation comedies, social comedies, melodrama, news and documentaries, sports and live events, religious shows, game shows, and talk shows) in a cultural context. Also, Rowland (1983) took the entire debate about violence on television as his text. Because that text does not exist in a material form anywhere, he assembled it from the "hearings, records, and reports of the various congressional committees and national commissions involved in federal attempts to grapple with television and the question of its content. These records are examined for the patterns of argument advanced by the leading research spokesmen, industry representatives, public interest group leaders, and political figures" (p. 17).

Lull (1987) looked at San Francisco punk culture by participating and inter-viewing, but he never quoted any individuals and his descriptions seem to apply to all members of the subculture. He presented examples about the behavior of particular individuals, but this is done to illuminate what he presented as overall patterns in the subculture. There is no focus on documenting the variety of individuals within that subculture.

Most often the evidence in institution-focused research is from a broad scale. For example, Turow (1984) looked at industry trends and relationships among the principal players. Evidence comes from almost all 55 doctor shows—inter-views with actors and producers, reading scripts, and reading popular press treatments of the shows. Some scholars examined existing documents and in-terviewed people to get their information about large-scale structure of the broadcasting industry (Auletta, 1991; Barnouw, 1975; Brown, 1971; Collins, 1989; Kellner, 1987) or some large segment of it (Allen, 1985; Bagdikian, 1972, 1987; Litman, 1990; McChesney, 1993; Meehan, 1993; Metz, 1975; Reeves, 1988; Spigel, 1993). Altschull (1984), Baughman (1990), and Bernhard (1993) studied press systems. Barnouw (1978), Berman (1981), and Clark (1988) examined a wide range of documents about the broadcast advertising industry. Jowett and Linton (1980) looked at the film industry. Ewen and Ewen (1992) examined the culture broadly to include media and fashion in dress. Collins (1989) was very broad with his focus on popular culture and the scholarship that addresses it. Corcoran (1987) and Gitlin (1987) focused on the connections between ideologies and television texts. Browne (1987) examined the mega texts of television. Perhaps the broadest scale was exhibited by Innis (1950), who looked at the role of communication in empires of Egypt, Babylonia, Greece, and Rome.

NUMERICAL EVIDENCE

Most qualitative theoreticians are generally skeptical about the use of numbers in qualitative analysis preferring instead the use of interviews, documents, books, videotapes, social actions, speech, gestures, body movements, and artifacts—all of which are kept in their qualitative form and not translated into numbers. But these scholars do recognize that the use of some numbers (such as data quantified for other purposes, e.g., census data) are important (Lindlof, 1991; M. L. Smith, 1987; Strauss & Corbin, 1990). No one would argue that the numbers in the following statements are antithetical to qualitative research: "Interviews were conducted with 12 members of the community over 15 months" or "John spent $10 a week to rent a television set so he could view for 2 or 3 hours each evening."

The use of numbers is not the problem, per se. What bothers most qualitative theoreticians is the practice of enumeration, the translation of concepts or qualities into numerals so that they can be analyzed using statistical procedures. For example, a researcher might be interested in a person's reaction to a television show. She could ask the person about the show and copy down his reactions in his own words. Or she could ask the person to standardize his reaction using five answer choices as follows: 1 = hated the show, 2 = disliked the show, 3 = was neutral, 4 = liked the show, and 5 = loved the show. Asking the person to translate a reaction to the show into a number is asking the person to enumerate his qualitative feeling about the show. Quantitative researchers frequently ask their respondents to enumerate their reactions, motives, attitudes, and so forth, so that the numbers can be subjected to mathematical manipulation and thus parsimoniously reveal the degree of dispersion as well as the central tendency of reactions.

This practice of enumeration is usually rejected by qualitative researchers. Jensen (1991b) pointed out that qualitative researchers do not use numerical analysis, because the translation from concepts to numbers decontextualizes the meaning, and this is a key problem in the study of human communication. Pauly (1991) objected to enumeration, because the translation of qualities into quantities can "truncate reality to make it amenable to statistical manipulation" (p. 5).

There are a few qualitative theoreticians who argue for enumeration, but only under certain conditions. For example, Marshall and Rossman (1989) asserted that enumeration is best for dealing with frequency distributions, adequate in dealing with institutionalized norms and statuses, but not adequate in dealing with incidents and histories. They found value in enumerated data in certain situations and did not rule it out of the qualitative method.

There are three categories of thinking about this issue of ennumeration. The first, and strictest position, prohibits the use of all numbers, reflecting the researcher's belief that all numbers are suspect. The second, and perhaps the most prevalent position, allows for the use of numbers where they represent mathematical properties (dates, ages, quantities, monetary figures, etc.). This position does not allow for translations of qualities into quantities. A third, and perhaps rarest position among qualitative thinkers, permits ennumeration where qualities (such as motives, attitudes, etc.) are translated into numbers.

No Numbers. Some researchers not only avoid using numbers but also make a point of arguing against their use. For example, Wolf (1987) eschewed numbers. She said she tried to use the results of "traditional tests of cognitive skills to place the children in distinct, qualitatively different stages, but test scores were useless for explaining how the children varied in performing complex cognitive tasks" (p. 93). Instead, she argued that her qualitative analysis was superior to identify the methods children used to make sense out of fictional narratives on television. Children varied in their constructions, but these variations were not attributable to age or other numbers-based distributions.

Numerical Properties. The use of numbers to reflect truly quantitative properties is frequent in qualitative research. For example, Chesebro (1988) used lots of numbers in one study. He cited Gallup poll results and compared those data against percentages of various demographics of characters on television. He also made demographic comparisons across years. And he reported tests of reliability as percentage of agreements among coders. Horowitz (1987) made the point that sitcoms are losing viewership by tabulating the number of shows that are ranked in the top 10 as determined by Nielsen ratings.

As for audience-focused research, Liebes and Katz (1989) presented tables of counts and percentages, but stopped short of presenting inferential statistics to examine the tables for patterns. Barrios (1988) included numbers indicating percentage of households with televisions, amount of exposure, and like information.

Within institution-focused research, cultural historians frequently use numbers to express audience sizes, audience compositions, company profitability, and the like (Auletta, 1991; Barnouw, 1975; Baughman, 1990; L. Brown, 1971; Clark, 1988; Gitlin, 1987; Litman, 1990; Metz, 1975; Turow, 1981). Also, numbers are essential to economic analyses, such as Browne's (1987) analysis of advertising revenues and audiences, Bagdikian's (1987) analysis of media concentration patterns, as well as the analysis of the film industry by Jowett and Linton (1980).

Enumeration. There are examples of enumeration of qualities. For example, in audience studies, Radway (1984) presented the results of her questionnaires in four quantitative tables. She did not run inferential tests nor did she run data reduction procedures. However, there is a form of reductionism implicit in her questionnaire where answer-sanctioned choices were provided thus limiting the range of responses from the women.

In institution-focused research, Turow (1981) developed something he called a diversity index. Although diversity can be regarded as a qualitative concept, it still has a mathematical component to it. So the computation of the diversity index is not as much of a translation from a qualitative concept into a number as would be the translation of an attitude into a number, for example.

CHAPTER

7

ISSUES OF
EVIDENCE GATHERING

Now that we have examined the nature of the evidence in chapter 6, it becomes important to deal with the topic of how to gather the required evidence. This too is a complex topic that raises several issues. In this chapter, we examine six of those issues: types of evidence-gathering methods, researcher identification, researcher activity, selection of samples, collaboration in data gathering, and length of data gathering (see Table 7.1 for a breakdown of these six issues).

TYPES OF EVIDENCE-GATHERING METHODS

There is a wide range of data-gathering techniques mentioned in the qualitative literature. Every theoretician has his or her own list. For example, Jankowski and Wester (1991) talked about in-depth interviewing, document analysis, and unstructured observations. Lindlof and Meyer (1987) mentioned participant observation, life history interview, the depth interview, the informant interview, and unobtrusive measures, which include institutional as well as personal documents and artifacts, representational maps, diaries, and audiovisual records. Denzin and Lincoln (1994b) mentioned case study, personal experience, observational, historical, international, and visual texts. They also argued that:

> qualitative researchers use semiotics, narrative, content, discourse, archival, and phonemic analysis, even statistics. They also draw upon and utilize the approaches, methods, and techniques of ethnomethodology, phenomenology, hermeneutics, feminism, rhizomatics, deconstructionism, ethnographies, interviews, psychoanalysis, cultural studies, survey research, and participant observation, among others. (p. 3)

TABLE 7.1

The Template for Issues of Data Gathering

---

1. Types of Data Gathering

Key Question: What methods of gathering data are available to the qualitative researcher?

Alternative Answers:
(1) Document Examination
(2) Interviewing
(3) Observation

---

2. Researcher Identification

Key Question: To what extent does the researcher identify himself or herself?

Alternative Answers:
(1) Unidentified: No one in the situation knows the researcher is there to gather data (examples: watching people in a crowded public park; reading a text).
(2) Identified as a Member of the Group: People are aware of the presence of the researcher as a person, but do not know he or she is there to gather data.
(3) Identified as a Researcher: People regard the researcher as an outsider (nonmember of the group) who is there only to gather data.
(4) Identified as a Group Member and a Researcher: People accept researcher as a group member even knowing that he or she is there to gather data.

---

3. Researcher Activity

Key Question: How active does the researcher feel he or she should be?

Alternative Answers:
(1) Passive Observer: The researcher's presence is known (as a researcher) but relatively ignored by those who are being observed; it has some, but little effect on those being observed (example: students hang out in the home of a family to observe them watching television).
(2) Active Observer: The researcher remains active (such as asking questions) so that the research subjects cannot forget the intruder is there for a different purpose than they are.
(3) Active Participant: The researcher continually engages in behavior to alter the situation so as to find out what the reaction of the people will be (example: taking the television set out of the home then observing what the family does).

---

4. Sampling

Key Question: How does the researcher select evidence?

Alternative Answers:
(1) No information on evidence selection.
(2) Some information provided; selection usually based on convenience.
(3) Argument for representative sample.
(4) Population study.

(Continued)

94

TABLE 7.1
(Continued)

---

5. Collaboration

Key Question: To what extent do others work with the researcher in gathering the data?

Alternative Answers:
(1) No collaboration; all evidence is gathered by the author.
(2) Collaboration among researchers; evidence gathering is shared by more than one researcher.
(3) Collaboration of researcher with subjects; subjects become partners with the researcher(s) in the evidence gathering.

---

6. Length of Data Gathering

Key Question: For how long does the researcher believe he or she should maintain contact with sources of evidence?
a. What is the span of the total data-gathering effort from first observation/interview to last?
b. What is the amount of contact during each observation/interview session?

Despite the proliferation of terms and ideas, the qualitative approach essentially relies on three types of evidence-gathering methods: document examination, interview, and observation. The second and third of these, which identify people as the subject of the investigation, often show considerable overlap. For example, a researcher who spends time with families in their homes so she can determine patterns of controlling television viewing may constantly engage the family members in conversations and at the same time observe their reactions to her questions and suggestions. In this case, and many like it, it is impossible to separate the insights gained from interviewing from those gained through observation.

Each of these three major types is presented individually in the sections that follow so that their main characteristics can be clearly highlighted. Each type has its own special strengths and weaknesses. Many research projects use more than one type of method, because a combination of methods will provide the researcher with more different kinds of evidence thus making comparisons richer and more contextualized. However, in this chapter, each of these types of evidence collection methods is considered separately so that their strengths and weaknesses can be more clearly compared.

Document Examination

When texts are the focus of the investigation, documents must be examined. There is a wide variety of documents, including diaries, letters, memos, notes, photographs, audiotapes, videotapes, films, articles, books, manuscripts, and the list goes on. In general, documents are any preserved recording of a person's thoughts, actions, or creations.

The examination of documents is especially important to historians who investigate patterns and trends from the past. If no humans remain alive to provide primary evidence, then documents are the only source of data. But documents are also important to researchers who have humans available; the documents may provide confirmatory evidence and strengthen the credibility of the results of interviews or observations. With textual analysis, documents are always the primary source of data.

Within audience-focused research, document examination was the primary source by Bodroghkozy (1992) who looked at viewers' reactions to "Julia" by examining 151 letters and postcards in the archives of the show's producer. Ang (1985) examined 42 letters written to her from viewers of "Dallas." The analysis in these two studies was limited to texts, but the statements made by the researchers focused much more on inferences about the people who wrote the letters rather than the texts themselves. These two studies raise an interesting issue and that is: Can audience studies be conducted on documents or must the researchers have direct contact with people? With audience-focused research, direct contact with the audience members is required for primary data. However, Bodroghkozy was interested in a television show that had been off the air for several decades so there was not much of an opportunity to gather primary data. This is an example of an historical analysis and the best data available at the time were the secondary data of letters written at the time the show was on the air. In contrast, the Ang study was conducted at the time "Dallas" was still running in Holland, but rather than conduct a reception study, as others have done, she decided to solicit letters by placing an ad in a newspaper. She had a choice to collect either primary data, secondary data, or both.

With institution-focused research, reliance on existing documents is the most prevalent method. For example, Barnouw (1975, 1978) relied on a great deal of primary and secondary sources in preparing his history of broadcasting in the United States. Litman (1990) looked primarily at legal and policy documents.

Interviewing

Interviewing is the technique of gathering data from humans by asking them questions and getting them to react verbally. There are several ways of characterizing interviews. For example, interviews can be structured or unstructured. They can be casual or in-depth. Marshall and Rossman (1989) explained: "Typically, qualitative in-depth interviews are much more like conversations than formal, structured interviews. The researcher explores a few general topics to help uncover the participant's meaning perspective, but otherwise respects how the participant frames and structures the responses" (p. 82).

Another form of interviewing is called the ethnographic interview, which differs from friendly conversation in several important ways. It is not balanced as most conversations are. Instead, the ethnographer informs the interviewee of the purpose of the interview and then takes control by asking questions and probing the person's responses. This type of interviewing is structured like survey interviewing; the key difference is that it is responsive to situations rather than standardized. Nondirective questions are open-ended and designed to get the interviewee talking about a broad topic area. Directive questions are designed to get a specific fact or opinion. Interviewers must be careful not to ask leading questions, and the accounts produced by the interviewees must never be dismissed as ideological distortions; even inaccuracies are themselves data.

The ethnographic interviewer probes the subject seeking five types of explanation: project explanation, recording explanation, native language explanation, interview explanation, and question explanation (Spradley, 1979). Also, the interviewer seeks to gather cultural data by asking three types of questions: descriptive (to collect a sample of the subject's language), structural (to discover the basic units of a subject's cultural knowledge), and contrast (to reveal the meaning of the terms in the subject's native language). In creating an "ethnographic context," qualitative researchers must recognize that the person being studied "decides both what to say to the interviewer and the precise meaning and significance of what he is saying" (Schwartz & Jacobs, 1979, p. 42). The subject is not forced to answer questions that have no meaning for him or her. In order to maintain the value of the ethnographic context, the researcher must cross-examine the subject so the researcher is sure he or she understands the subject's meanings.

The life history or oral history is a form of interviewing where a researcher records the details of a person's entire life. It is "a deliberate attempt to define the growth of a person in a cultural milieu and to make theoretical sense of it" (Marshall & Rossman, 1989, p. 96). It is "an account of how a new person enters a group and becomes an adult capable of meeting the traditional expectations of that society for a person of that individual's sex and age. Life history studies emphasize the experiences and requirements of the individual—how that person copes with society" (Marshall & Rossman, 1989, p. 96). They are particularly helpful in studying how changes in people occur over time as they gain experience with culture. It is a very useful data-gathering tool in ethnography (Wolcott, 1982) and symbolic interactionism (Denzin, 1970).

There are two types of life histories: nomothetic and idiographic (Lincoln & Guba, 1985; Schwartz & Jacobs, 1979). The nomothetic, which is used by positivists, assembles facts about a person on reductionistic-type variables. These are used in the fields of psychology (test scores) and medicine (physiological measures, demographics, etc.) where the purpose is to locate the person on a general continuum and make comparisons of that person with other people on that continuum. The idiographic, which is used by naturalists, focuses on building a narrative of a person's life in some area, thereby relocating reductionistic variables to the background. Denzin (1970) made a distinction among the complete, the topical, and the edited life history. The complete life history attempts to cover the entire sweep of the subject's life experiences. The topical life history is limited to one phase of a person's life, and the edited life history can be complete or topical, but it displays an interspersing of questions and explanations of someone besides the focal subject.

With audience-focused studies, interviewing is used very frequently. Sometimes the interviews are rather informal. For example, Hobson (1989) invited a group of six women who work together to a pub for lunch and to talk about the television programs they watch. Sometimes the interviewing is more formal such as when the research uses focus groups. Liebes and Katz (1988, 1989) assembled particular kinds of people into focus groups where they showed them an episode of "Dallas" then asked them questions. Other audience researchers have used focus groups to get people talking about what they like about the television shows they have watched regularly in their own homes (Jhally & Lewis, 1992; Morley, 1980; Seiter, Borchers, Kreutzner, & Warth, 1989a). Sometimes the interviewing is very formal, as exemplified by Tulloch (1989) who met with 20 elderly people in their homes to talk with them about their television use.

In institution-focused research, some scholars will act like journalists in interviewing large numbers of key people so as to get a full picture of an event or development. For example, Auletta (1991) conducted 1,500 interviews with 350 people, and Metz (1975) conducted 120 major interviews for his book on CBS. Sometimes a scholar will submerge himself in an environment and continually ask questions of the people. For example, news organizations are a popular place for this (Altheide, 1976; Elliott, 1979; Fishman, 1988).

Observation

Observation is the technique of gathering data through direct contact with an object—usually another human being. The researcher watches the behavior and documents the properties of the object. It is a very important method of data collection used by both qualitative and quantitative researchers. Quantitative scholars usually have an a priori highly structured plan that directs them to remain aloof (such as in laboratory experiments) and observe certain behaviors. In contrast, qualitative researchers usually observe from a phenomenological perspective; they immerse themselves in natural environments and watch a situation as a diffuse, ambiguous entity and allow themselves to be struck with certain peculiarities or interesting happenings.

As for researcher activity, some observers are unobtrusive as they watch from outside the group being studied; sometimes the people in the group are not even aware they are being observed. Other observers are intrusive, as in the case of participant observation where the observer is present on site to participate, observe, and/or interview.

Participant observation has been called "a special form of observation" that "demands firsthand involvement in the social world chosen for study. Immersion in the setting allows the researcher to hear, see, and begin to experience reality as the participants do.... This technique for data gathering is basic to qualitative research studies" (Marshall & Rossman, 1989, p. 79). Another view of participant observation is provided by Atkinson and Hammersley (1994), who tried to address the question about how active a researcher should be. According to them, researchers must decide for themselves how much of a participant to be and this decision is based on several factors. One factor is the degree to which the researcher wants to be known as a researcher—either to some or all of those being studied. Another factor is how much the researcher already knows about the research topic and how much he or she wants to learn. The researcher must decide on what activities he or she wants to participates in and what his or her orientation (insider or outsider) is to be. All of these factors together are important. On balance, they concluded that participant observation "is not a particular research technique but a mode of being-in-the-world characteristic of researchers" and "that in a sense *all* social research is a form of participant observation" (p. 249).

With the data-gathering technique of observation, researchers make the assumption that behavior is purposive and expressive of deeper values and beliefs (Marshall & Rossman, 1989). The primary advantage of this technique, then, is that it gives the researcher the ability to see if people "say what they mean and mean what they say" (Schwartz & Jacobs, 1979, p. 46).

The observations are usually recorded as field notes, which can be free-form jottings that one takes down, on the spot, or lengthier, but perhaps less detailed reconstructions after the fact (Lancy, 1993). They are often written on two levels. On the surface level are the facts, which are direct descriptions of what was observed and/or verbatim recordings of what was overheard. On another level are the observer's comments about the events and interviews. These are recorded in order to provide a context for the raw facts and to add speculations about what the researcher thinks it means.

With institution-focused research, observation is very important although it is not the only method used; it is usually used in conjunction with interviewing. For example, Altheide (1976) spent a year in a television network affiliate newsroom (and 2 more years in other newsrooms) where he was a participant observer; of course, he conducted interviews, but his primary mode of evidence gathering appeared to be observation. Elliott (1979) also conducted a participant observation during the making of a British television series of seven programs for an adult education project entitled, "The Nature of Prejudice."

Multiple Methods

In audience analysis, many studies use more than one method. Lull (1987) relied primarily on observation in his examination of punk culture but he also conducted interviews. Turkle (1984) observed, interviewed, and examined documents—probably the best (and most complete) example of an ethnography in this set of readings. Also, Pardun and Krugman (1994) conducted in-depth interviews as their primary source of data, but they also visited people's houses, took pictures, and had respondents fill out a questionnaire about demographics.

Lewis (1991) interviewed people individually and in focus groups, but he also reported in detail about the struggle to interpret the audiotaped transcriptions of those interviews, so there is a focus on document examination also—however these documents are not produced as cultural artifacts by the respondents. Traudt and Lont (1987) observed a family's TV-viewing behavior, audiotaped interviews, and examined viewing diaries completed by the family members. Hobson (1982) conducted unstructured interviews, observed people watching television, and read the letters sent to the producers of "Crossroads," a British television series. Barrios (1988) used primarily observations (taken as notes and audiotapes), but also used photographs, family home maps, family daily schedules, and other documents.

More on the social scientific side were a few studies using multiple methods, one of which was a questionnaire. For example, Rogge (1989) gathered data using a standardized questionnaire, participant observation, a media journal, and the qualitative interview, which "addressed the multiple aspects of concrete living situations of everyday life" (p. 174). Radway (1984) used in-depth interviews and a questionnaire of 53 closed-ended items.

Multiple methods were also used by several researchers who conducted institution-focused research. For example, Fishman (1988) worked as a journalist on one newspaper for about 7 months, then went to a competing newspaper where he observed for about 5 months during which time he conducted interviews and observations. He also had access to 400 pages of field notes of a researcher who had conducted a participant observation at the same newspaper several years earlier. Tuchman (1978) gathered data "by participant observation and interviews over a period of ten years" (p. 9) at four different sites: TV station, newspapers, and city hall press room. Turow (1989) interviewed 109 actors, producers, and members of the medical profession. He read scripts or viewed tapes of the 55 medical programs aired on network prime time. And he looked at the writings about these shows in the popular press over 40 years. Cantor (1980) conducted interviews with actors, union officials, directors, writers, and producers; she also got secondary data from the popular press, scholarly articles, congressional hearings, and court decisions; and she conducted a content analysis of prime-time television programs. Allen (1985) combed through the trade and general press for material on the history of soap operas, interviewed the cast and staff of a major soap opera, and analyzed scripts.

RESEARCHER IDENTIFICATION

In many examples of qualitative research, especially ethnography, the researcher goes into the field to observe and interview people. This raises an important concern about how the researcher is to present him or herself in the community being studied. One option is that researchers could be anonymous so no one in the situation being studied would know the researcher is there to gather data. An example of this would be a researcher watching people in a crowded public park. Another option is that researchers identify themselves as a member of the group they are studying. In this case, people in the group are aware of the presence of the researcher as a person, but do not know he or she is there to gather data. A third option is that researchers identify themselves as researchers. In this case, the people in the group regard the researcher as an outsider (nonmember of the group) who is there only to gather data.

With textual analysis, researcher identification is not a concern, but it is very important with audience-focused research. Let's see how these questions are answered in practice. In focus groups, researchers are, of course, identified as being researchers (Jhally & Lewis, 1992; Lewis, 1991; Liebes & Katz, 1988, 1989; Seiter et al., 1989a; Tulloch, 1989). Researchers who interviewed people in the field usually identified themselves (Hobson, 1989; Lindlof, 1989; Morley, 1980; Pardun & Krugman, 1994; Radway, 1984).

Sometimes deception is used. For example, studies by Barrios (1988) and Lull (1980) used college students to make observations of families in their homes while they watched television. These students identified themselves as researchers looking into "family daily life," which was a bit of deception so that families would not realize that the focus was on their daily viewing habits and therefore be tempted to alter their behavior in that area. Rakow (1992) told the people she lived with in a town called Prospect that she was a researcher, but she did not tell them that she was a feminist who wanted to find examples to support her ideological perspective. Wolf (1987) and her student researchers were identified as researchers to the children at the day-care center; it is not clear from the article if the children (4–12 years) really understood what this meant.

The questions about researcher identification can also be important ones in institution-focused research. Auletta (1991) and L. Brown (1971) were both known as a journalists to those they were interviewing. Elliott (1979), who worked for the British government as a television audience researcher, was invited to observe the production of a new series and report his observations.

But sometimes, a researcher's identification is not believed or can lead to skepticism. For example, Altheide (1976) was known as a researcher in the newsrooms, although some were skeptical that he was trying to get a job there. Fishman (1988) joined the staff of a competing newspaper and was known as a reporter, then he quit and hung out at the larger paper identifying himself as a sociologist. It is likely that journalists at the second newspaper were skeptical about Fishman's motives.

RESEARCHER ACTIVITY

To what extent should the researcher be active in the data-gathering situation? J. A. Anderson (1987) argued that the main form of qualitative research is "participant observation, but there is considerable variation in what is permitted under that rubric" (p. 235). What is essential, according to Anderson, is that the researcher gain access to the phenomenon and then gain acceptance by legitimizing his or her presence within the routine of the "other"—that is, the person or people being observed. The researcher must also demonstrate the proper level of competence in the group/situation.

Because the qualitative approach rests on the axiom of naturalism, researchers need to observe phenomenon in its natural state as undisturbed as possible (Christians & Carey, 1989; Jankowski & Wester, 1991; M. L. Smith, 1987). To do so, it is important that researchers maintain what is called marginality—a distance between themselves and that which is being studied. As Hammersley and Atkinson (1983) argued, there is often a real danger of "going native" or of exhibiting "overrapport," both of which may force the researcher to lose his or her objectivity. In order to guard against this, they suggested careful ethnographic interviewing. The theoreticians espousing this position are sensitive to the fact that researchers are human, thereby, are active constructors of meaning. On the one hand, the researcher must maintain a marginal status within the situation so as not to unduly influence behaviors. But he or she must also be active in generating conversations and stimulating behaviors that he or she wants to observe. But how far can a researcher go without losing marginality? This is an important question, but one that cannot be answered in a general manner. The most we can do on the general level is to lay out the available options: passive observer, active observer, and active participant.

Passive Observer

The safest way to maintain marginality is for researchers to be passive observers while they simply gather documents and observe actions without asking questions or otherwise doing anything to make the least disturbance in the situation. Passive observer activity is exemplified in studies where the observers simply look at the phenomenon in a way that does not affect it. For example, in audience-focused research, Bodroghkozy (1992) was passive, because all she did was read letters sent to the producers of "Julia" 24 years earlier. Likewise Ang (1985) was passive; she solicited letters from a newspaper ad and merely read the responses without contacting the writers. In text-focused research, scholars are passive in the sense that their gathering of evidence (memos, videotapes, etc.) does not have a potential to change the evidence in the same way that a scholar would have if he or she were interviewing people.

Also, this passive category could be stretched to include researchers who asked open-ended questions, then sat back and observed. Hobson (1989) began her focus groups as a questioner, but the group took off with its answers as control of the interviews shifted away from the researcher because she let the women talk about their soap operas in their own language and at their own pace.

Active Participant

Can researchers be active agents in the environment from which the evidence is to be gathered? This requires the researcher to be more than an observer; he or she must be a participant. According to J. A. Anderson (1987), in qualitative research, the researcher is always a participant in the action. Only by partici-pating (interviewing and actively observing) can adequate data be gathered. Lindlof (1991) agreed: "Some degree of active intervention by the investigator is needed to successfully generate these data" (p. 25).

The active research position in audience-focused research is characterized as going beyond simple observation or questioning and injecting a special treatment. For example, Morley (1980) showed a videotape of "Nationwide" to each of his focus groups, then ran a group discussion of that particular program. Liebes and Katz (1988, 1989) showed their subjects a tape of "Dallas," then stimulated a discussion of the program. Jhally and Lewis (1992) showed their focus groups an episode of "The Cosby Show," then asked questions about people's attitudes about race, gender, and class. Also, an active position is one where the researcher stimulates people to think about things they might never have thought about before. For example, Wolf (1987) had her seven research assistants participate in day-care activities and actively question 107 children about their media-use habits and reactions to shows.

Some institution-focused researchers are active. Altheide (1976), Elliott (1979), and Fishman (1988) said they were participant observers. But with the first two of these studies it is not clear what the "participation" meant other than they were given access to watch the media workers. With Fishman, it was made clear that he joined the staff of a newspaper and worked for 7 months as a reporter.

Active Observer

The middle position on identification allows participation but only to a limited extent and then with controls. For example, Denzin (1970) viewed the interview as an interaction of roles, where the interviewer must be careful what role he or she portrays, because that will influence the role that the subject plays: "The process of interaction creates attitudes and behaviors that did not exist before the interaction. Or if new attitudes are not created, old attitudes are reshaped" (p. 137). To provide researchers with guidelines to avoid disturbing the situation, Denzin took a strongly scientific view of qualitative research (primarily symbolic interactionism) by laying out rules for experiments and formal surveys in addi-tion to the more traditional qualitative methods of participant observation, life history, and unobtrusive measures.

In audience-focused research, this middle position of active observer is char-acterized by the researcher intruding into the lives of the respondents to some moderate degree, such as when the researcher enters the home or private environment of the people being observed. The researcher is active in gaining access, but then tries to be passive once inside the environment so as not to influence the naturally occurring behaviors and conversations. For example, Lull (1980) had students serve as participant observers in family households. He defined this participation as:

> Observers took part in the routines of the families for the duration of the observation period. They ate with the families, performed household chores with them, played with the children, and took part in group entertainment, particularly television watching. Families were told from the beginning that in no case should they change their routines in order to accommodate the observer. (p. 201)

Other examples of this nature are studies by Traudt and Lont (1987), who went to the homes of certain people to observe them watching television as a family for 15 hours; Pardun and Krugman (1994), who interviewed families, but they were only in each home for several hours and did not intrude on household activities; and Barrios (1988) whose data-gathering team was in the home for 16–46 hours and did not administer any special treatments.

In institution-focused research, Elliott (1979) was active in gaining access to a production crew but then tried to be a passive observer even to the point of "initially adopting a rule of not speaking until spoken to and then saying as little as possible consistent with not appearing rude or completely vacant" (p. 173). Auletta (1991) said "while gathering information for this book, I sought to be a fly on the wall, watching as CBS, NBC, and ABC tried to run their businesses. . . . My aspiration in writing was the one Flaubert set for his narrator: to be 'everywhere present and nowhere visible' " (p. 6).

SAMPLING

In quantitative research, the issue of sampling is the concern about how elements are selected from a population so that each element is given an equal chance of being selected, so that the patterns found in the sample can be generalized to the larger aggregate of the population. Under the qualitative approach, the issue of sampling is concerned more with gaining access to relevant evidence about the phenomenon. The two key words in this concern are *access*, which reflects a practical concern, and *relevant*, which reflects a validity concern.

With text- and institution-based research, access usually means getting permission to read, copy, and analyze, making findings public about certain documents. With audience-focused research, access usually means permission for physical presence in a data-gathering location. Once present, the observer must follow certain social rules so as to maintain access. This is especially true in relatively private settings where people do not want an outsider invading their communities to observe them. Bogdan and Taylor (1975) pointed out that although many different sites are usually equally acceptable for most studies, the criterion for selection is usually based on choosing the first site that permits access.

Although the issue of access addresses the "how," the issue of sampling is more concerned with the "why," that is, why the researcher selected the sample he or she did. There are two primary reasons for the why. First, the researcher might be primarily interested in efficiency—this results in a convenience sample. Here the researcher tries to get some evidence that is easily available so as to provide some substance to his or her arguments. For example, if the researcher is a college professor, she might ask the students in her classes to allow themselves to be interviewed. Or a researcher might go to community groups to which he belongs and observe the behaviors in those easily accessible groups. Or the researcher might use what is referred to as a "snowball" technique of interviewing those people who are available, then asking them to suggest others who might be willing to be interviewed. The researcher then uses each stage of referrals to expand the number of people being interviewed.

Second, the researcher might be guided predominantly by some formal purpose, such as representativeness, finding a critical case, finding a typical case, or looking for a set of cases that maximizes variation. With representativeness as a goal, the qualitative researcher uses the principles in quantitative reserach to articulate a complete sampling frame, then giving every element within that frame an equal chance of being selected. With looking for a critical case as a goal, the researcher rejects possible cases until he finds one that best captures the unique essence of what he wants to illustrate. This is a popular method in the analysis of television texts where many shows could be used for evidence, but where one or two shows are really good examples of an important point the researcher wants to make. When guided by looking for a typical case, the researcher looks for the evidence to exemplify the norm. And with the goal of maximizing variation, the researcher looks for cases that are as different from each other as possible.

The most often used argument is one of convenience (Lincoln & Guba, 1985); the researcher needs to collect some evidence and the people or texts that are most available provide the greatest convenience. For example, a professor might use some of her graduate students for a television-viewing study; the professor goes to the homes of these graduate students and observes them watching television. Or a researcher may call child day-care centers until he finds several that will allow him to observe the children during their viewing times.

There are a few examples where theoreticians advocate very careful sampling techniques. Hammersley and Atkinson (1983) offered guidelines for sampling of settings and cases as well as sampling within cases (in terms of time, people, and context). Also, Denzin (1970) devoted an entire chapter to it, and his treatment of it resembles the manner in which a quantitative methodology text outlines sampling rules to ensure the generalizability of results.

In contrast to these positions is Pauly (1991), who rebelled against the notion of sampling as addressed by quantitative researchers by saying that they "falsely assume that discourse is randomly scattered" (p. 12). In Pauly's view, it is pointless to select a sample randomly and expect it to be representative of something broader.

As can be seen from the preceding discussion, a reader of the qualitative research literature will see a range of positions exhibited on the issue of sampling. It is useful to illustrate four of them: no sampling information, some sampling information provided, argument for representative sample, and population study.

No Sampling Information

There are many examples in the qualitative literature where an author will provide the reader with no information about problems of access nor an argument for the relevance of the elements chosen. To illustrate, Cantor (1980) was careful to tell the reader that she limited her study to prime-time network entertainment programs and that her study is based on evidence gained through interviews with actors, directors, writers, and producers over a 10-year period. It is clear that actors, directors, writers, and producers are relevant *types* of sources of information, but she does not tell us who these people were and how they were selected.

Some Sampling Information Provided

Some scholars will foreground issues of sampling and provide the reader with a description about why they selected certain elements and how they achieved access. For example, with text-focused research, Haralovich (1992) explained that she selected the television series "Father Knows Best" and "Leave It to Beaver" to serve her purpose of illustrating how women were portrayed in 1950s sitcoms. Newcomb (1988) described his sample as "an entire night of prime-time television . . . aired on the three commercial networks on Thursday, October 3, 1985" (p. 90). A Thursday night was selected because this was the night the author liked to watch for 3 hours. His analysis focuses primarily on only 4 of the 11 programs aired that night; this subsampling was done so he could focus on those shows he watched most often. Quantitative scholars would find this sampling scheme and Newcomb's reasoning very unsatisfactory. But within the qualitative approach, his treatment of the issue of sampling is very positive for two reasons. First, he was clear about how and why he selected his elements for analysis. Second, the selection of his favorite shows highlights the personal nature of meaning making that is so fundamental to the approach.

Within audience-focused research, most scholars will assemble what is known as convenience samples because of the relative convenience in interacting with certain audience members. Sometimes convenience samples are called purposive in order to highlight the relevance characteristic (people were chosen with a purpose) over the efficiency characteristic (people who were available were chosen). In almost all instances the terms are synonyms, because purposive samples are chosen on convenience, and the people in convenience samples are chosen because they are relevant sources of evidence of the phenomenon.

Seiter et al. (1989a) talked about deriving their convenience sample, which was generated by an ad in a local newspaper. Each woman who responded was asked to invite her soap-opera-viewing friends to her home for a focus group interview. Tulloch (1989) laid out some problems he had in getting access to the elderly, and his resulting sample was composed of people who agreed to be interviewed. Barrios (1988) used a purposive sample of 13 families with at least two children. They were selected so as to have social and cultural differences among family groups. Rogge (1989) used a purposive sample in her analysis. She began by interviewing 420 families but did not say how those families were selected. During her analysis she constructed case studies, which relied on evidence from only a subset of her interviews, explaining that "the case studies have been selected out of a large number of families in order to illustrate typical trends" (p. 175).

A popular technique used in generating a convenience (or purposive) sample is called snowball. The snowball technique begins as a purposive sample where the researcher finds people to interview who could provide him or her with important insights. During the interview, the researcher asks for names of additional people to talk with—thereby expanding the initial list of interviewees. By using this technique, the interviewer starts out with a small list but gathers momentum and weight as the research proceeds. For example, Gitlin (1983) used a snowball technique that began with him contacting a few people in the television industry. Through a series of referrals, he ended up interviewing 200 producers, actors, writers, agents, and executives.

A bit more formal than a convenience sample is a quota sample where a researcher will select audience members in such a way as to fulfill a quota for different kinds of people. For example, Morley (1980) used a quota sample to get people from all strata of demographics (age, sex, race, and class) and cultural identifications (trade unions, political parties, sections of the educational system, etc.). Although the people for each strata were chosen by convenience (those who were available), Morley did not assemble a convenience sample because such a sample might not have had the variety of people he wanted. Also, Pardun and Krugman (1994) used a quota sample to get 20 families: 10 living in traditional homes and 10 living in transitional homes. As they selected families, they added households to the sample until the pattern in the results became iterative and no more households were needed to add insights.

There are some studies where the sample chose the researcher, such as with Ang (1985) who put an ad in a Dutch newspaper and asked for letters from viewers of "Dallas." The 42 letters she received were all included in her analysis. Of course, this was not the total set of all of the "Dallas" viewers in Holland; it was some subset and so it must be regarded as a sample.

Case for Representativeness

Some researchers attempt to make a case that their limited sample is representative of a much larger aggregate. Liebes and Katz (1988, 1989) used a purposive sample that they said was not randomly generated but that "one can make a good case that these are bona fide members of their respective subcultures" (p. 220). Also, Jhally and Lewis (1992) said they got the people for their 52 focus groups from Springfield, Massachusetts, which they argued was "a fairly typical small North American city. . . . Its 'ordinariness' indeed, was commented upon by journalist Bill Moyers, who in 1990 chose Springfield as the venue for a TV program because he felt it was a microcosm of national attitudes and opinions" (pp. 9–10).

Population Study

Several scholars seem to have conducted a population study; that is, they examine all of the data in the population and do not select a sample from it. We must be careful in defining populations, because almost any population is a subset of a still larger and more general population. However, we must let the researcher draw boundaries and tell us what he or she considers the phenomenon of interest; all evidence on that phenomenon then becomes the population (or totality of all available evidence). To illustrate this point, we can look at the study by Chesebro (1978) as not using a sample. If his population is all prime-time entertainment programs in two seasons, then he has included all elements in that set. Of course, the selection of two seasons out of the many seasons available indicates sampling if the population of interest were all television seasons. Also, he chose not to include nonentertainment programs as well as programs broadcast in non-prime-time hours. So it is important for researchers to define the phenomenon of interest; this translates into the full set of evidence that is the population.

In broad-scale studies of a complex social phenomenon, it is not always clear what the total set of evidence is. For example, Rowland (1983) presumably avoided sampling by trying to get all the information he could about the way research was used by policymakers concerned with violence on television. His set of evidence is the "hearings, records, and reports of the various congressional committees and national commissions involved in federal attempts to grapple with television and the question of its content. These records are examined for the patterns of argument advanced by the leading research spokesmen, industry representatives, public interest group leaders, and political figures" (p. 17). Sometimes it is difficult to tell whether research is a population study or not.

Also, Turow (1989) appears to have attempted a population study to learn as much as he could about the production decisions behind the 55 TV doctor series. Elliott (1979) observed the making of a series of seven programs for an adult education project entitled, "The Nature of Prejudice." His stated purpose was to conduct a case study of one television series, so the inclusion of all seven episodes of that series would make this seem to be a population study—he looked at all there was to look at. However, in his conclusions he talked about the larger issues of documentary film making. With the phenomenon of interest being all documentaries, the selection of only one documentary (even though all episodes of that documentary were analyzed) is clearly not a population study. Therefore, the key in determining sampling issues is to determine what the full set of units (population) is.

The issue of sampling is as important as it is complex. The importance lies in the trust the reader will develop for the researcher. If the researcher presents no information about how he or she collected the evidence, the reader will have less trust than if the researcher clearly articulates the scope of the phenomenon of interest, then describes the process of gaining access as well as the relevance of the set of units of evidence selected.

COLLABORATION

To what extent can qualitative researchers collaborate in gathering evidence? Some theoreticians say that qualitative research requires a high degree of subjective interpretation that makes it impossible for several people to work together and produce a report with a single set of findings that accurately reflects the various interpretations of all those involved. Lindlof and Meyer (1987) cautioned that interpretation "remains the province of the researcher, who will develop a case for what such findings mean and what is implied by them" (p. 17). Although it is possible for two scholars to agree on their interpretations (as is the case with Lindlof and Meyer who we must assume agree on the position expressed in the quote), it is rare for qualitative research reports (such as articles and book chapters) to be coauthored. Coauthorship shows up on a larger scale of books where the chapters have different authors. The edited volume then can be argued to be a coauthored production, because we are being presented with the thinking of a range of scholars within the covers of a single book. But in another sense, this is not collaboration because we do not see the interaction among those authors, unless they articulate the dialogue. Without the sharing of their dialogue, the reader cannot tell if the conclusions were written by one author or if they represent a higher order synthesis that could result from collaborators using their differing perspectives and talents to work through the problems inherent in any particular scholarly task.

However, there are examples of collaboration and these appear to be of three types. First, there is the sharing of analysis among researchers, or what I call *horizontal collaboration*. Second, there is collaboration of the researchers with the subjects being examined, or what I call *vertical collaboration*. Third, there is the collaboration among researchers, each of whom arrives at his or her conclusions independently and where those conclusions are presented together but unsynthe-sized across researchers. This third form I call *compartmentalized collaboration*.

Horizontal Collaboration

Horizontal collaboration is a research process where two or more researchers jointly plan a project, then together analyze the evidence. Insights are shared, synthesized, and refined so that it is not possible to say that a conclusion belongs to one of the researchers; all conclusions are a result of a genuine collaborative effort and all researchers are responsible for all conclusions.

According to Lindlof and Meyer (1987), "naturalistic observation rejects the idea of multiple observers producing a single interpretation" (p. 16), but "in qualitative inquiry, multiple observers can be used with some degree of reliability" (p. 17), especially when the focus is on the more concrete and overt behaviors.

Vertical Collaboration

Vertical collaboration focuses on the relationship between the researcher and the subjects being examined. Most typically, this becomes an issue in ethnog-raphies and reception studies where the researcher has a lot of contact with people in interview/observation situations. If the researcher simply interviews the subjects, then this is not collaboration. But if the researcher checks back with the subjects some time after the interview was completed, or if the re-searcher goes back to the interviewees to confirm some of his or her insights, then there may be collaboration between the researcher and the subjects. In order for true collaboration to take place, the researcher must regard a subject or subjects as equal partners in the analysis. I term this vertical because the two players (the researcher and the subject) are on two different levels in terms of power, expertise (of the phenomenon and of the qualitative approach), and motives. So the flow of discussion is across levels—not all on the same level as with horizontal collaboration.

Several theoreticians argue quite strongly for the importance of this type of collaboration. For example, Reason (1994) recommended that the researcher entering into a partnership with the subjects being studied. He called this "co-operative inquiry." With its roots in humanistic psychology, this type of inquiry breaks with orthodox methods that "exclude the human subjects from all the thinking and decision making that generates, designs, manages, and draws conclusions for the research" (p. 325). He said, "one can do research on persons in the full and proper sense of the term only if one addresses them as self determining, which means that what they do and what they experience as part of the research must be to some significant degree determined by them" (p. 326). Thus collaboration is required between researcher and the subjects.

Schensul and Schensul (1992) suggested another form of vertical collaboration—between researchers and the people who will consume the research. They viewed collaborative research as building "networks that link researchers, program developers, and members of the community or group under study with the explicit purpose of utilizing research as a tool for joint problem-solving and positive social change" (p. 162). According to them, collaboration is especially important when it is believed that "knowledge becomes useful only in the social context within which it is to be used—that is, it is the impact of the knowledge in effecting positive change that makes it useful" (p. 163).

Compartmentalized Collaboration

Compartmentalized collaboration is when two or more scholars are jointly responsible for a large project (such as a book), but undertake their duties separately from one another. For example, Jowett and Linton (1980) are coauthors on the book but they each wrote three chapters separately from one another. Dates and Barlow (1990) are coeditors, and each wrote his or her own chapters. Seiter et al. (1989a) worked together on a research team and coauthored a book chapter. Within that chapter, the various sections are labeled with the different authors' names to give the reader information about who worked on which parts.

Unknown Collaboration

When we see a research report with more than one author, we are signaled that there has been some sort of significant collaboration. But with many of these multiple-author reports, it is not clear what the nature of that collaboration was. For example, Liebes and Katz (1988, 1989) shared publication credit, but it is not made clear what the division of labor was or if they both were deeply involved in all facets of the process. Traudt and Lont (1987) presumably shared the observation duties but we are not told how. Pardun and Krugman (1994) were coauthors on their article, but it appeared that only one of them collected all the data. Altheide and Snow (1979) were coauthors but they did not explain how they split or shared duties. Ewen and Ewen (1992) are a husband and wife team that together authored the five essays in their book, but it is not made clear how the labor was divided, or even if it was.

Quasi-Collaboration

Sometimes researchers will acknowledge the help of others in the research project, but that help was not of a full-partner status. For example, Chesebro (1978) had 10 PhD students serve as coders of demographics of TV characters.

Although their help was acknowledged, they were not considered collaborators. Lewis (1991) acknowledged the help of four people who conducted the interviews on his study of "The Cosby Show." Wolf (1987) acknowledged using seven trained research assistants in gathering the data. Lull (1980) used students to gather data, but he was not clear about how many students, and none appear as coauthors. Barrios (1988) used a team of undergraduates, but we don't know how many or how.

When researchers do work with others, it does not appear that their collaboration is an equal partnership. For example, Fishman (1988) used the extensive fieldnotes of another sociologist who had observed in the newsroom several years earlier. However, he did not actually "work with" that other sociologist. Turow (1981) used two coders, but they did not analyze data or write up the report. Instead, they appeared to be employees or assistants. Cantor (1980) said she was accompanied by another person on most of her interviews, but we are not told what this other person did.

LENGTH OF DATA GATHERING

Jankowski and Wester (1991) argued that qualitative researchers must engage in long-term, firsthand observation, but they did not say for how long. Of course, providing a general rule to cover all types of situations is foolhardy. But how is a researcher to know how long is enough? Lull (1985) cautioned that the length of the observation period must be long enough "to insure that the behaviors observed are not staged for the researcher's benefit, thereby obscuring valid identification of concepts and relationships" (p. 82). As for observing the media usage patterns of families, he said that 7 days is the best.

Length of data gathering is an issue that is best regarded as having two components, because data gathering is usually not conducted in a continuous manner but instead in pulses. A researcher might say she made observations for a year, but what she might really mean is that over the course of a year, she made observations once a month for one afternoon each time. There are 12 pulses (once each month for a year) and 4 hours of observation during each pulse for a total of 48 hours. Let's say another researcher moved in with a family for 1 week and observed them during all their waking hours (over 100 hours). Who had the greater length of data gathering? The first researcher did, if our focus is on the span of time, but if our focus is on the number of contact hours, the second researcher experienced the greater length of data gathering. Both conceptions of time are important. Long periods of continuous contact allow the researcher to become sensitive to the micropatterns in the environment, and observation over a long time span of pulses puts the researcher in a position to see broad-scale patterns.

Among qualitative researchers, there is a general prescription that longer periods of contact and longer spans are better than shorter ones. The point is that the greater contact with the community or the evidence source, the better (more complete, more contextualized) will be the data. However, there is a point of diminishing returns beyond which the researcher risks the danger of losing his or her perspective to observe and becomes incorporated into the community, a condition referred to as "going native."

General rules of thumb for length of data gathering are dangerous to prescribe. In order to get a feeling for what the norm is in a particular research area, a scholar needs to read the literature and see how researchers have structured their contact, then make a judgment about how much contact is enough. If the reader of the research feels that the insights presented are too superficial or if the explanations lack a sufficient degree of contextualization, then there is reason to believe that the researcher might have had too little contact. Therefore, it is important that researchers address the issue of length of data gathering both in terms of span and degree of contact. This is a minimum requirement. Better still, researchers then need to present an argument justifying those decisions. This argument is clearest when addressed directly, that is, where the researcher explains why he or she cut off the contact at a certain point. But often this argument is made indirectly where the researcher demonstrates that he or she has indeed been able to uncover some interesting patterns and can justify them through adequate contextualization.

Among text-focused studies, length of the data gathering is never addressed; researchers never talk about how long they worked on viewing the texts. However, some of the authors provided information about the time span of the texts themselves. For example, Chesebro (1988) looked at television programs broadcast during the 1974–1975 and 1977–1978 seasons. D'Acci (1992) examined the run of "Cagney and Lacey," which was from 1982 to 1988. Deming (1992) looked at "Kate and Allie" from the 1984–1985 season. Flitterman-Lewis (1992) selected sequences in "General Hospital" broadcast in February 1986 and May 1987.

With audience-focused studies, there are some good examples of authors addressing this issue. Tulloch (1989) interviewed his 20 elderly subjects twice (one year apart) for 1–2 hours duration each time. Seiter et al. (1989a) collected all their data in focus groups within a 27-day period. Wolf (1987) observed children (4–12 years of age) at a day-care facility over a 10-month period; observations were for an average of 10 hours per week. She provided a lot of information about the phases of data gathering. Traudt and Lont (1987) spent 15 hours of in-home observation and interviewing within a 3-month period. Lull (1980) had his team of students visit the homes of more than 200 families from 2 to 7 days each. Each visit began at midafternoon and extended until bedtime. After the last session, each family member was intensively interviewed independently. Pardun and Krugman (1994) visited 20 homes once each for about 2 hours. Barrios' (1988) team spent between 16 and 46 hours in each of 13 homes. Radway (1984) conducted 60 hours in interviewing over an 8-month period.

With institution studies, the length of data gathering is rarely addressed, but there are exceptions to this. For example, Fishman (1988) said he gathered data in his target newspaper for 9 days, but this came after 7 months of working for a competing newspaper. He said, "the findings presented in this study are based on data which cover over six hundred hours observing six different reporters on the same news organization over two periods: 1964–1965 and 1973–1974" (p. 26). Altheide (1976) spent "more than three years in various news operations in a half dozen cities" (p. 198). Auletta (1991) said he interviewed people and wrote for 6 years. Tuchman (1978) observed in four locations over a 10-year period— about 1 day a week. Cantor (1980) said she interviewed industry people for 10 years. L. Brown (1971), as a working journalist, wrote about his observations about the TV business throughout 1970. Altschull (1984) said he was working on this project for 30 years—but not full time.

8

ISSUES OF DATA ANALYSIS

The task of analyzing qualitative evidence can appear to have a "black box" nature to it. Until recently, qualitative theoreticians and researchers have provided little guidance even of a general nature about how to conduct such analyses. To illustrate this point, Miles and Huberman (1984) observed that among those writing about the qualitative approach, "most attention went to issues such as gaining access and avoiding bias during data collection" (p. 16), but not to the details of the actual analysis. This lack of guidance about the details of the method, especially about how to conduct the analyses, did not begin to change until the late 1970s and early 1980s when several texts addressed this issue in more depth (e.g., Bogdan & Biklen, 1982; Guba & Lincoln, 1981; Spradley, 1981). The same lack of detailed guidance on methods was in evidence in the field of communication until the late 1980s when some extended methodological treatments were published (J. A. Anderson, 1987; Pauly, 1991).

This slow development of detail on analysis methods (when compared to the length of time detailed quantitative texts have been available) should not be taken as an indictment of the qualitative approach; instead, it should highlight the creative latitude the qualitative method provides researchers. Miles and Huberman (1984) asserted that "many qualitative researchers still consider analysis as 'art' and stress intuitive approaches to it" (p. 16). Of course, the downside is that qualitative researchers have a greater burden in demonstrating the nature and quality of their decisions, because their methods are not as routinized. Miles (1979) observed that researchers who are faced with qualitative data have very few guidelines for protection against self-delusion, let alone the presentation of unreliable or invalid conclusions.

Four issues of data analysis are presented in this chapter: expectations, process of analysis, conceptual leverage, and generalizability (see Table 8.1 for

TABLE 8.1
Template for Analysis Issues

Issue 1: Expectations

Key Question: To what extent do expectations for findings guide the selection of evidence?

Alternative Answers:
(1) A Priori Expectations: The researchers have set out a very clear goal for what data they need. With social science, theory and hypotheses are a clear guide. Also, ideologies serve as a priori guides.
(2) Emerging Expectations: No beginning expectations, but as researchers gather data, they become more focused on searching for certain data and ignoring other data.

Issue 2: Process of Analysis

Key Question: To what extent does the researcher illuminate the process of using the evidence to construct arguments/findings for the written report?

Alternative Answers:
(1) Authors describe the steps taken in analyzing the data, that is, the step between data gathering and presenting the report.
(2) Authors do *not* describe the steps used in analyzing their data.

Issue 3: Conceptual Leverage

Key Question: To what extent does the research extend his or her arguments/findings beyond reporting on the elements of evidence into a general conceptual level?

Alternative Answers:
(1) None: No attempt to move beyond describing the literal events in the data. The reporting is limited to description of the actual data themselves.
(2) Low Level: The researcher constructs patterns (through his or her own processes of inference) to make sense of the literal data.
(3) High Level: Inferring a connection to an a priori construction such as a theory or ideology.

Issue 4: Generalizability

Key Question: To what extent does the researcher attempt to use his or her evidence to generalize?

Alternative Answers:
(1) No Generalizations: Researchers only present data or patterns about their observed subjects during the times and places they were observed.
(2) Generalization: Researchers exhibit a large move from data to conclusion. The largeness in the degree can be due to the very small size of the sample or the very broad nature of the conclusions.

---

a template of these analysis issues). All qualitative researchers must address these issues regardless of the particular methods they employ and regardless of the methodology they choose.

EXPECTATIONS

After researchers have staked out a topic area, to what extent do expectations for the possible findings guide the selection of evidence? One way to deal with expectations is to make them a formal part of the research process; researchers can acknowledge their expectations and use them to guide the collection and analysis of evidence. This is the deductive process. With deduction, researchers begin with a preexisting theory or hypothesis and deduce a test of it. Deduction is the process of reasoning from general principles to specifics and requires the preexistence of general principles, such as those of a theory of human behavior. The deductive position is recommended by Miles and Huberman (1984), who argued that there is a place for confirmatory qualitative analysis where a theory is fairly well developed before going into the field. They suggested beginning with a conceptual framework that highlights the main variables and the expected relationships among them.

Another position to take with expectations is the inductive one. With induction, the research begins by making observations. The researcher then looks for patterns in the observations; the process moves from specifics (the observations) toward general statements (the explanations). The inductive position is characterized by a belief that everything within the topic area should be gathered as evidence and nothing should be ruled out. Once all the data that can be gathered have been gathered, the researcher leaves the observation site and begins to analyze the evidence. This inductive position is favored by Anderson, Pauly, as well as Lincoln and Guba. For example, J. A. Anderson (1987) maintained that qualitative researchers do not begin with a theory or hypotheses; instead they begin with a natural curiosity to learn more about the who, what, when, where, why, and how of something. In an even more radical position, Pauly (1991) criticized quantitative research for using hypotheses, saying that "research hypotheses cannot capture the meaning of the evidence, any more than a prose paraphrase can capture the meaning of a poem" (p. 7).

There is a middle ground between these two polar positions, one that blends induction with deduction in an iterative process. The researcher begins with no formal a priori expectations, however he or she necessarily must have some initial formulation of a problem in general terms (Bogdan & Taylor, 1975; Jankowski & Wester, 1991; Lincoln & Guba, 1985). This general formulation guides the direction of the investigation. Because the general formulation is not a theory, such as that used in traditional science, the formulation does not include theoretical propositions that can be used to generate operationalizations for testing. However, theoretical statements do emerge, but only as a product of the inquiry process. The idea of a general formulation is impossible to avoid in research. Miles and Huberman (1984) observed that "any researcher, no matter how unstructured or inductive, comes to fieldwork with *some* orienting ideas, foci, and tools" (p. 27). It is impossible not to have these.

Hammersley and Atkinson (1983) explained how this blending of induction and deduction works in ethnography. The first step is to pose a research question by foreshadowing a problem. The next step in the process—Hammersley and Atkinson argued—is very difficult to explain or to train someone to do, because the gathering of data is replete with the unexpected. When one is carrying out research in settings in which one has little power, and about which one has little previous knowledge, the research cannot be fully designed in the prefieldwork phase. Also, because ethnography is associated with naturalism, it consists of open-ended observation and description, and research design is thus almost superfluous. However, during the observation phase, the research forms tentative conclusions, which are then tested in subsequent observations.

Wolcott (1990) recommended writing a draft of a qualitative study even before beginning the study to establish a baseline for thinking: "You will have documented what you believe to be the case, making a matter of record certain biases and assumptions that otherwise might prove conveniently flexible and accommodating had they remained as abstractions" (p. 22).

A Priori Expectations

Some qualitative researchers exhibit formal expectations. One way to do this is to begin with a thesis to argue. For example, Kinder (1987) laid out her explanation for why music videos are popular. She presented the thesis that the music video genre forges "new codes that of spectator relations, or more accurately, it is making the codes that were already operative in television more transparent" (p. 230). Deming (1992), in his first paragraph, said his purpose is to show "that *Kate and Allie* participates in the displacement, containment and repression which fictions for women often undergo on television" (p. 203). Horowitz (1987), on her first page, set out the thesis that sitcoms have declined in popularity and this decline is due to the fact that structural changes have occurred in our society and sitcoms have not kept up. Also, Bird and Dardenne (1988), in their second paragraph, laid out their argument that the "pretense is maintained that every news story springs anew from the facts of the event being recorded" (p. 67), then presented evidence to show that myth is what structures the construction of news stories. Barker (1987) presented a clear thesis statement then set out to support it. His thesis is "the communicative ability of any television narrative is, in large part, a function of the production techniques utilized in its creation" (p. 179).

In institution-focused research, McChesney (1993) began with an argument that his interpretation is a better fit of the facts in the early development of the broadcasting industry. Innis (1950) argued for the thesis that each empire has its own form of communication that makes it cohesive and distinguishes it from other empires.

Other scholars overtly present an ideology. Haralovich (1992) clearly presented a feminist ideology early in her writing and used it to structure the presentation of her insights about "Father Knows Best" and "Leave it to Beaver." And Flitterman-Lewis (1992) began with the argument that soap operas are successful television because they display fragmented sequences and dispersed narrative elements. Lipsitz (1992) argued a Marxist thesis.

Critical scholars who focus on institutions usually begin with a clear articulation of their position. For example, Ang (1991) laid out her argument that the present conceptualizations of the media audience are faulty. Parenti (1986) argued that media do not meet their own standards of objectivity, informativeness, truthfulness, or independence. Dates and Barlow (1990) argued that the definition of control of African-American images in the mass media is determined by a hegemonic influence: "In American society, by reproducing the ideological hegemony of the dominant white culture, the mass media help to legitimate the inequalities in class and race relations" (p. 4). One way of doing this is through presenting stereotypes: "Stereotypes are especially effective in conveying ideological messages because they are so laden with ritual and myth, particularly in the case of African Americans" (p. 5).

Some researchers lay out hypotheses, such as Morley (1980). Similarly, Jhally and Lewis (1992) expected to find differences in reactions to "The Cosby Show" by race, gender, and class. Also, Traudt and Lont (1987) had a priori expectations to find what Altheide and Snow (1979) proposed in their book.

Some researchers begin with a question. Sometimes there is an implied answer to the question in the way it is presented at the beginning of the report. For example, Joyrich (1992) asked "has melodrama died? Or has it been subsumed into television, engulfing the medium as it engulfs its spectators and precluding its location as a separate category?" (p. 228). With questions posed like that, there can be little doubt about what the author has in mind for the answer. With other studies, researchers will pose the question in a simple, straightforward manner. For example, Chesebro (1988) began with a series of questions, such as: What patterns, types, or kinds of human relationships are portrayed in popular television series? and How have popular television series changed, particularly in the last 4 years? The way these questions were posed does not give the reader an indication of the political stance of the asker nor the way Chesebro planned to answer them.

Sometimes researchers will present other analytical guides such as templates (Wolf, 1987), an analytical scheme (Turow, 1989), or a model (Cantor, 1980).

Emerging Expectations

In institution-focused research, there are examples where scholars appear in the writing to have had expectations before beginning their studies; however, these expectations may have actually been developed during the data gathering

(Altheide, 1976, 1985; Altheide & Snow, 1979; Fishman, 1988; Turow, 1984). For example, Altheide (1976) presented his news perspective early as an explanation then used it to structure his book. But it appears that he did not begin his investigation that way; that is, the construct was developed over the course of the data gathering. Fishman said he began his study by reading 400 pages of field notes of a researcher who had previously observed that newsroom. These notes allowed him to "concentrate my time and efforts strategically" (p. 25). It is unclear whether this led him to any a priori conclusions or whether it merely directed him where to look.

Although Gitlin (1983) is critical of television production decision making, he did not seem to begin his investigation with a thesis or clear ideology. Instead, his critical points emerge throughout the narrative.

PROCESS

What is the process of analysis; that is, what are the steps of going from data to report? Jankowski and Wester (1991) observed that "it is striking" in media studies that "there is little or no indication of how the collected data were analyzed" (p. 63). For example, in his manual entitled, "A Beginner's Guide to Doing Qualitative Research in Mass Communication," Pauly (1991) said that the biggest problem is not in gathering the evidence but in sorting it all out. But unfortunately, he never provides a method for sorting. He argued that people must learn by emulating the work of others. This is sound advice, but how is one to know if he or she is doing it properly? It depends on readers' acceptance of the claims made by the qualitative researcher. How do readers make their judgments? They reason, according to Pauly, about whether the researcher has "read enough of the right kinds of materials" and whether the researcher has "interpreted those materials in a reasonable, useful, thoughtful, and imaginative way" (p. 19).

The interpretive nature of qualitative research does indeed present a real problem to scholars who attempt to explain the process. This is why most theoreticians do not explicate the process of analysis as a set of steps. Rather, they talk about the analysis process as an organic whole that begins in the data-gathering stage and does not end until the writing is completed. The process allows for multiple iterative passes back and forth from data gathering to writing and back to data gathering. According to Jensen (1991a), qualitative researchers follow the literary notion of exegesis or reading texts where analysis and interpretation are intertwined and "no firm line can be drawn between the analysis of data and the subsequent discussion of aggregated findings. The primary tool of research is the interpretive capacity of the scholar" (p. 31). But the process of analysis is unclear, because no rules exist for how a researcher takes the research subject's discourse and transforms it into the researcher's analytical discourse.

Lull (1985) said that after the researcher has completed the data gathering, he or she brings all the written notes, tapes, and transcripts together, then "with these materials at hand, the ethnographer organizes and writes a report" (p. 84). Nevertheless, Lull did not illuminate the process of analysis he uses to get to the final report. However open, flexible, and creative the analytical process, its amorphous nature can be frustrating to beginning researchers.

It is best to think of analysis as not being a discrete step in the research process. Instead, analysis begins in the prefieldwork phase, in the formulation and clarification of research problems, and continues into the process of writing the report. We can see evidence of analysis in the planning stage when the researcher formulates ideas, hunches, and procedures. Analysis should also take place in the field during data gathering—whether the field of data gathering be a person's home, a news organization, a library of texts and artifacts, and so on. Miles and Huberman (1984) claimed it a "serious mistake" to wait until the data are all gathered to begin the analysis, because this faulty procedure "rules out the possibility of collecting new data to fill in the gaps, or to test new hypotheses that emerge during analysis" (p. 49). Furthermore, delaying analysis until data gathering is complete prevents the researcher from dealing with rival hypotheses and puts him or her in the position of having to face the giant, overwhelming task of having to shift through all the data to find the trends after being removed from research setting.

In contrast, there are some theoreticians who have attempted to outline some generic steps to the method. For example, Marshall and Rossman (1989) said there are five types of analytic procedures: organizing the data; generating categories, themes, and patterns; testing the emergent hypotheses against the data; searching for alternative explanations of the data; and writing the report. "Each phase of data analysis entails *data reduction* as the reams of collected data are brought into manageable chunks and *interpretation* as the researcher brings meaning and insight to the words and acts of the participants in the study" (p. 114). Nevertheless, Marshall and Rossman admitted that the "interpretive act remains mysterious in both qualitative and quantitative data analysis" (p. 114).

Lofland and Lofland (1984) prescribed three basic steps in analysis. First, the researcher files and codes the field notes into organized patterns, either by people, places, organizations, documents, chronology, or analytical categories. Second, the researcher writes memos to himself or herself as he or she has insights about small pieces of the evidence and as he or she develops an overall structure for the report. Third, the researcher then undertakes the process of surrender and discipline, in which he or she surrenders to the evolving insights and proclivities revealed in the data. But discipline is also needed to keep the researcher focused on the more important insights and on completing the report.

Lindlof (1995) suggested that there are four general patterns in the process of qualitative analysis. First, there is the linear process that is often associated with hypothetico-deductive research. This means beginning with an explicit research framework and proceding one step at a time from beginning to end. Second, there is the funnel procedure, which begins with a wide pass through the topic area, then going back over the same material again and again, each time with a stronger focus and a tighter frame on the evidence. Third is a cycle where a researcher collects evidence then develps tentative conclusions. He or she then checks those tentative conclusions by collecting more evidence and revising them. And fourth is the expanding frame where the researcher begins with a tight focus on one element. When evidence is collected on this one element, it suggests new ways of considering the phenomenon, and these new perspectives force the researcher to widen the frame of the evidence in the analysis phase.

In an attempt to respect the view that qualitative analysis is a seamless process, but at the same time trying to recognize the essential steps in the procedure, I regard the overall process of analysis as having three primary components: (a) recording field notes, (b) analysis of notes, and (c) moving toward the product.

Recording Field Notes. Field notes are key to the analysis process (J. A. Anderson, 1987; Bogdan & Taylor, 1975; Hammersley & Atkinson, 1983; Lancy, 1993). Notes need not be in written form but may also include recordings (audio and video), transcriptions, photography, sketches, objects, and so forth (J. A. Anderson, 1987). However, when the field notes are in written form "the goal is not to record everything . . . but to carefully note those critical moments when some meaning of the social action was revealed . . . to the researcher" (p. 258). For this reason they are recorded once the researcher has had time to reflect, because the notes are not descriptions of the event but the researcher's interpretation of the event. Other theoreticians present a different view. For example, Bogdan and Taylor argued that field notes should be comprehensive and contain every detail.

The notes should be written as soon as possible to prevent the forgetting of details (Hammersley & Atkinson, 1983). During data gathering, the field notes are usually organized in chronological fashion, but once the analysis begins, notes are reorganized in terms of topics and themes.

Analysis of Notes. Most theoreticians view analysis not as a separate process but as an activity taking place during all phases of the research project. The focus of the analysis is "to formally identify themes and to construct hypotheses (ideas) as they are suggested by data and an attempt to demonstrate support for those themes and hypotheses" (Bogdan & Taylor, 1975, p. 79). The working hypotheses are propositional statements about what is taking place, which are continually modified. Analyzing data is difficult and time consuming because the qualitative researcher "has relatively little idea at the outset how to partition this continuous mass (of observations) into discrete, perhaps even countable, categories" (Lancy,

1993, p. 20). This is why the observer should be the analyzer so that he or she has some sense of the criteria used in coding certain statements and behaviors as supportive or nonsupportive evidence of some hypotheses and not others.

J. A. Anderson (1987) said that after the field notes are recorded, the next step is "composing the episode" where the episode is "the written descriptive interpretation of an event of the social action under study" (p. 258). These are narrative stories of part of the social action. They weave together the empirical facts of the event.

When dealing with the facet of people, the qualitative researcher must develop a composite picture about how people think about things. Each person's belief may be different because people focus their attention on different things and interpret the same things differently. Also, their beliefs change over time. The researcher must make sense out of all of this seemingly conflicting information. The researcher must try to examine why there are differences in meanings. "The analytical task is to show the meaningful coherence of these expressions, as it is experienced by the people who are studied" (Lindlof, 1991, p. 25).

Moving Toward the Product. The steps of moving toward the product depend on what the purpose of the research is—description, interpretation, explanation, or action. At the most elementary level is description where "there is relatively little analysis per se" (Lancy, 1993, p. 21). The field notes (descriptions of fundamental terms various events, situations, and actions that occur in a particular social setting) are then developed into case studies of social phenomena (Jankowski & Wester, 1991).

When the goal is explanation, researchers break "the data into the smallest pieces possible," systematically code and collate "all the lower level (grounded) categories," and then move upward "to seek meaningful, larger aggregates" (Lancy, 1993, p. 21). In attempting explanation, the data are particularistic and local and placed in a larger context by emphasizing holism, historicity, and process. The goal is to construct theoretical propositions.

The process of analysis is rarely addressed explicitly in the research literature. Instead, authors seem to use two strategies to finesse the need to present a clear articulation of how the analysis was conducted. One strategy is the argument; a scholar will lay out a thesis or ideological position then assemble the best evidence to support the argument for the position. The second strategy is for the researcher to present the evidence as if the evidence was speaking for itself. This is especially popular where the author makes it seem that the conclusions were emerging from the mass of collected evidence—as if the data arranged themselves into patterns and the researcher is simply presenting a descriptive photograph of them.

However, there are examples of researchers who open the door for readers and invite them into the process the author undertook in the analysis. For example, Newcomb (1988) explained that he took the total text of each show and broke them down into "strips," which is an individual's pattern of viewing throughout the night. Using what he called dialogic analysis, he first describes what happens in a program then pointed out some rhetorical devices, ideological exchanges, and stylistic characteristics. He brought in some semiological tools (dichronic, synchronic, syntagmatic, paradigmatic); then, while developing his conclusions, he showed the reader how he made his analytical decisions.

Another example of an author providing details of the analysis is Chesebro (1987), who carefully described his four lines of analysis that structure his study. First, he developed a classification system for TV shows out of a theory of logical types, which consists of five perspectives that can be used to look at TV series: ironic, mimetic, leader centered, romantic, and mythical. Next he chose television shows to illustrate each of these five types. He then classified all shows in two different seasons (3 years apart) as a way of showing differences across time. Finally, he profiled television characters in terms of their marital status, gender, race, size of city, occupations, and members in their household.

In audience-focused research, Wolf (1987) addressed the issue of analysis in great detail. She provided a clear description of each step in the data-gathering and analysis stages. In the first step of data analysis, notes were recorded in daily summaries of significant events of the day's observations. Also, a profile was developed on each child. In the second stage, a card was written for each observation of a child using cognitive skills to negotiate mediated content. Those cards were grouped by cognitive ability: coding processes, language acquisition, memory, and social-cognitive development. The cards were then regrouped according to program interest areas. However, she said, "it is impossible to duplicate the procedures used in this study because they emerged in vivo, as parts of a holistic process" (p. 91). So she was not presenting her procedure as a model for others to follow as much as an explication for the reader who must decide the value of her interpretations.

Jhally and Lewis (1992) explained that the analysis was designed to reduce the voluminous data they gathered and also to make judgments about those data. They recorded the comments of the focus groups and transcribed those comments. The transcriptions were analyzed in a process where the researchers regarded themselves as a "prudent jury, we must use our knowledge and skill to interpret what people tell us rather than accept all testimony at face value" (p. 9). They did not discuss the criteria they used to make those judgments, preferring instead to say "we will not try the reader's patience by detailing it completely" (p. 9).

Lewis (1991) performed a semiological analysis on the transcriptions of the interviews and talked in detail about his four-step procedure. First, he broke down the transcripts into analytical units of meaning (lexias). Second, he looked at the sequence of lexias and the connections among them. Third, the topography of meaning was examined to determine what is the overall meaning in an interview, that which cannot be reduced to lexias. And fourth, he sought to connect the meanings (ideologies or discourses) in the interviews with the meanings in the texts of the TV shows.

Morley (1980) clearly articulated his three-level strategy for analyzing the "complex, informal discourse" (p. 34) he used as evidence in his study. First, he used the lexical repertoires of the different groups to separate them by their overall perspectives on the show. Second, he focused on how the different groups constructed their arguments and used evidence. And third, he looked at the underlying cognitive and ideological premises that structured those arguments.

Pardun and Krugman (1994) analyzed their transcripts of interviews in a three-step procedure. First was the step of open coding, which was a line-by-line examination to identify potential categories to guide subsequent steps. Second was axial coding, a procedure of fitting data to the eight main themes identified in the first step. Third was selective coding that focuses on identifying an overarching core concept for the study.

In institution-focused research, Cantor (1980) explained how she partitioned the industry into concentric circles of influence and began with the smallest then moved out, extending "the meaning of the word 'social' to include political and economic aspects of social life as well as the organizational, symbolic, and cultural" (p. 15); within each section she combined historical and contextual analyses.

Perhaps the most detailed explanation of the process of analysis in this set was offered by Elliott (1979). First he took notes in which he tried "to record both the substance of discussion and behaviour and the patterns of interaction and relationships involved in it" (p. 172) and to regard nothing as irrelevant. At the end of each day, he transferred his notes onto "sheets summarizing who had done what with whom" (p. 172) so as to begin organizing the observations according to the role each person played in the production process. Then "propositions began to emerge concentrating on the process and its social setting more than on the individuals involved" (p. 173) and these propositions became more and more obvious as his contact with the project continued. He then wrote an initial report of over 200,000 words and he conducted several rewrites each of which "became progressively less descriptive, sharpening up the analysis and cutting down the length" (p. 174).

These preceding examples illustrate that it is possible for researchers of relatively short articles to devote some of their limited space to describing their analytical procedures to readers. Also, researchers who undertake very involved and complicated projects are able to clarify their procedures for readers. The variety of those examples highlight the need for flexibility in analysis. There is not one superior method or set of methods. Each research project is unique and requires the researcher to construct a procedure to allow him or her to extract the most insightful meaning from the evidence. However, this flexibility comes with a price; it is essential that authors describe the key elements of their procedures so that authors can have a context in which to appreciate their conclusions.

CONCEPTUAL LEVERAGE

Conceptually, how far does the researcher move from the data? Does the researcher stay close to the data and simply describe them? Or does the researcher leverage the reader up off the data and into the more general, abstract realm of argumentation and explanation?

At first, conceptual leverage might appear to be the same thing as generalization, but there is an important difference. Generalization is the inferring that the findings found in the sample of one study can be stretched to apply to other samples or other settings. In contrast, conceptual leverage is the moving from concrete observations to explanations at a higher level of abstraction. The abstract statements can be in the form of models, an explanatory inference, or a construction of a pattern. For example, if an ethnographer interviews one individual and uses the conclusions from that one interview to talk about how all people in the culture behave, that is generalization (from one to many). In contrast, if the ethnographer looked at how the people in a culture constantly change their posture, bite their fingernails, and always stutter when they talk to strangers then moved from these concrete observations to infer a pattern of communication anxiety among strangers, that is conceptual leverage (from the concrete to the general).

A study by Lull (1980) is a good example of the difference between conceptual leverage and generalizability. He had a very high degree of conceptual leverage with his induced typology of social uses of television. However, he did not generalize; that is, he did not say that a certain percentage of families are in each component of the typology. The observations suggest the structure of a typology, but he did not use his sample to reflect on all families.

In order to achieve a relatively high-level inference, researchers must use either deduction or induction. But the process of deduction does not fit well with the qualitative assumption of phenomenology, which abhors a priori conceptions. However, qualitative researchers can use the methods of grounded theory and analytic induction. Grounded theory is the building of general statements from the individual observations made in the data gathering. It is a system of explanation that results from an inductive process; it follows rather than precedes data gathering (Lincoln & Guba, 1985). It is broader than analytical induction, because it includes definitional work, but is not limited to it; it also deals with creating statements of patterns among several terms.

An important issue in the area of high-level inference is causality. Among those theoreticians who call for a high level of inference, one might wonder if they allow for qualitative researchers to make statements about deterministic influence, probabilistic influence, or no influence? Lindlof and Meyer (1987) are theoreticians who allow for the development of causal statements: "The analytic induction procedure represents a way to arrive at causal explanation through the progressive analysis of negative cases and modification of theoretical propositions until a universal relationship can be posited" (p. 11). Jankowski and Wester (1991) also hold this position in favor of exploring causality.

A high degree of conceptual leverage is not regarded as a desirable thing by more than a few qualitative theoreticians. For example, Manning (1982a) asserted that "a commitment of many, if not most, qualitative researchers is to low-level abstraction and persistent resistance to building models, totalistic logics, or theories that are all-encompassing" (p. 8). Also, there are many, such as Bogdan and Taylor (1975), who reject the idea of causality. Hammersley and Atkinson (1983) argued that the social world cannot be understood in terms of causal relationships or by subsuming social events under universal laws. The search for universal laws is rejected in favor of detailed descriptions of the concrete experience of life within a particular culture and of the social rules or patterns that constitute it. This is because naturalistic researchers assume that the social world cannot be understood in terms of causal relationships; instead human actions are based on social meanings in the form of intentions, motives, attitudes, and beliefs.

The examples that follow show that there is a range of practices from concrete description, through low-level inference, to high-level inference.

Concrete Description

The research in this category stays at a basic descriptive level and does not attempt explanation. The authors let the evidence speak for itself as they try to be faithful scribes, not expert theoreticians. For example, Wolf (1987) described her results and did not infer to larger principles—in fact, she rejected the larger principles such as Piagetian developmental stages as a good explanation of children's understanding of television. Hobson (1989) presented her results as quotations from the interviewees arranged as answers to sets of questions.

Low-Level Inference

Low-level inference was exhibited in numerous studies. For example, Flitterman-Lewis (1992) examined two wedding narratives within "General Hospital" and said that these illustrate some characteristics about how soap opera narratives are structured. She did not attempt to present a model for or a typology of soap opera narratives. Also, Rogge (1989) presented case studies that establish "qualitative links between day-to-day life and a family's use of the media" (p. 175). She did not attempt to make general predictions nor did she "make statistically relevant statements about the relationships between media-related actions and the various aspects of people's everyday worlds" (p. 175). When Bodroghkozy (1992) analyzed letters sent to the producers of "Julia," she attempted some conceptualization in her inferring motives behind some of the comments. For example, she said that "perhaps these viewers engaged in a denial of the 'otherness' of African-American people in an attempt to reduce white anxiety about racial difference" (p. 149). However, this is more speculation than it is an attempt to create new constructs or explanations.

In institution studies, Gitlin (1983) presented his interpretations as a tentative look, not as a definitive statement about how decision makers select images for television.

High-Level Inference

An example of high-level inference is the study by Chesebro (1978), who attempted to link his examples of television programs to his scheme of logical types. Bird and Dardenne (1988) presented high-level inference in their argument that all television news stories are examples of a myth perspective. Barker (1987) wrote his article as an argument supporting his thesis. Rowland (1983) inferred patterns of behavior among policymakers concerning their decisions and action about violence on television. Lipsitz (1992) interpreted 1950s working-class sitcoms in terms of the economic, political, and cultural environment of the time. This is a high degree of leverage to project patterns on the entire society over two decades. Also, Mann (1992) made some high-level statements about the use of Hollywood stars and why they are used the way they are. She cited some portrayals, but did not interview the stars or the producers of the shows so she had to infer the motives of the writers, producer, and industry in general. And Deming (1992) interpreted "Kate and Allie" as a text (did not focus on particular shows as much as the entire program itself). But then he used this as an example to demonstrate that shows present the opportunity to elicit multiple readings saying, "the work of ideological, format, and female-character containment continues to be carried out through a proliferation of points of view, a scrambling of codes, and a multiplication of means whereby a spectator is given access to knowledge through a variety of contradictory social positions" (p. 203).

In audience studies, a high-level inference was exhibited by scholars who take the general principles of other scholars and seek to test them on their own areas or attempt to extend those principles. In either case, the focus of the article is much more on the conceptual issues than on the words of the interviewees. For example, Hoover (1988) sought to extend Turner's concept of luminality. Traudt and Lont (1987) exhibited a high degree of conceptual leverage by taking some propositions from the work of Altheide and Snow (1978) and testing them in their one-family case study. Some scholars exhibit a high degree by building their analysis around an ideology (Ang, 1985; Rakow, 1992). Also, some scholars use grounded theory to develop their own general principles, and this exhibits a high degree of conceptual leverage (Barrios, 1988; Liebes & Katz, 1988, 1989; Lull, 1980; Pardun & Krugman, 1994; Rogge, 1989; Turkle, 1984). For example, Turkle provided grounded theory. She arranged her data to examine ideal types and showed the deviations. Also she categorized people's use of the computer into three modes of relating to the computer: metaphysical, mastery, and identity. Pardun and Krugman also exhibited a high degree with their core concept of hub viewing (magnet and retreat homes) as a way of explaining family viewing behaviors. And Lull (1980) also exhibited a high degree of conceptual leverage with his development of a typology.

Some institution-focused scholars provide a relatively high-level inference where they try to link up their study with broad-scale explanations such as theories or ideologies. For example, Turow (1984) presented a very broad and very general model as an explanation of how the mass media industries work. Broad-scale models were also developed by Altschull (1984), Cantor (1980), and Jowett and Linton (1980). And broad-scale explanations are provided by Altheide (1976, 1985), Altheide and Snow (1979), Berman (1981), Elliott (1979), Fishman (1988), Innis (1950), Litman (1990), Snow (1983), and Tuchman (1978). For example, Altheide attempted a high level of conceptual leverage by trying, like a social scientist, to provide an explanation for the form of the mass media and how that form influences content and the subsequent effects on people in general. And Fishman argued that his observations show a news ideology:

> routine journalism communicates an ideological view of the world. What news-workers end up reporting is not what actually happens, not what is actually experienced by participants or by observers of news events. Instead, the journalist winds up weaving a story around hard data, which means the bureaucratic categories and bureaucratically defined events that agency officials mean to happen and need to happen. (p. 155)

Critical scholars usually use a high level of inference (Allen, 1985; Ang, 1991; Bagdikian, 1972, 1987; Bernhard, 1993; Collins, 1989; Dates & Barlow, 1990; Gandy, 1982; Gitlin, 1980, 1987; Kellner, 1987; Mander, 1978; McChesney, 1993; Meehan, 1993; Parenti, 1986; Schiller, 1989). For example, Mander laid out some evidence of negative effects of television, then argued that all of television is bad as he called for its total elimination. Schiller argued for broad changes in culture as a result of corporate control of media. Meehan argued that all of broadcast and cable views audiences solely as commodities and that the only commodity that is of interest to them is the consumer one. She also said the industries are not producing entertainment messages, but instead produce "artifacts" that are designed solely "to assemble the consumerist cast for measurement and sale" (p. 217).

The key to appreciating conceptual leverage in qualitative research is not to require it to be maximized in all research studies. The design of many studies does not warrant more than low-level leveraging. Instead, the key is to think about the appropriate level of conceptual leverage for each particular study. With some studies, we should expect authors to give us more conceptual insight from their work. With other studies, authors may go too far, as is the case when we, the readers, feel that the evidence they present is not strong enough to warrant their conclusions. Overleveraged results are a weakness as are under-leveraged results. Good conceptual leverage lies in the correspondence between evidence and conclusions.

GENERALIZABILITY

Are qualitative researchers limited to describing the people observed? Can they generalize to a larger subgroup? Or can they generalize to all humans or texts?

A key to understanding the issue of generalizability lies with sampling (see chapter 7). From a scientific perspective, generalizability is only possible when the elements in the sample are representative of the population (the totality of all elements of interest). One can never be absolutely sure that the selected elements are truly representative unless the researcher goes to the trouble of gathering all elements in the population and compares the patterns in the population with the patterns in the selected sample. To avoid this task, scientists make an assumption. That crucial assumption is that if all elements in the population are given an equal chance of being selected, then the resulting sample will be a microcosm of the population; that is the sample will truly represent the population. And if the sample is truly representative, then the research need only look for patterns in the sample and know that they reflect accurately the patterns in the population. The practice of talking about those patterns in the sample as if they were occurring in the population is known as generalization.

Some qualitative scholars accept this scientific perspective on generalization. But others do not, hence there is a debate. On the side against generalizability is Pauly (1991), who argued that discourse is not randomly distributed, so sampling in any scientific manner is not possible. Without a random sample, it is not possible to generalize in a scientific manner. He took the burden of generalizability away from the researcher and placed it with the reader when he said "qualitative research is also generalizable to the extent that some community of readers considers a particular study representative of a wider set of concerns" (p. 11).

M. L. Smith (1987) rejected the notion of generalization on different grounds. He argued that because objectivity is not possible, different scholars will make different interpretations of the evidence. Therefore, there can never be a universal, context-free generalization.

On the opposite side of this issue are scholars such as Jankowski and Wester (1991), who allow for generalizable statements in the form of grounded theory. Also, Miles and Huberman (1984) argued for the importance of researchers checking the representativeness of their findings. Manning (1982a) regarded generalization as enumerative induction, a process in which the researcher gathers information on a sample of cases that are chosen to represent a larger population. The use of statistics tells the researcher the degree to which he or she can have confidence that the patterns found in the sample are good estimates of the inferred patterns in the population.

Many qualitative theoreticians take a middle view on the issue of generalizability. This middle view includes a variety of definitions for how we should define generalization. For example, Christians and Carey (1981) allowed for what they called "naturalistic generalizations," which "combine a scientific need for precision with the necessity to represent complex culture accurately" (p. 357). Fortner and Christians (1981) said that qualitative researchers must be careful when generalizing to other situations. "The more densely textured our specifics, the more we can maintain external validity" (p. 365). "The objective is representative rather than anecdotal (i.e., spectacular but idiosyncratic) cases" (p. 366).

Some scholars accept the notion of generalization, but only under certain conditions. Bogdan and Taylor (1975) did not rule out the possibility that many people might hold the same interpretations (i.e., that shared meanings might exist), but they claimed that:

> all settings and subjects are similar while retaining their uniquenesses. This means that qualitative researchers can study certain general social processes in any single setting or through any single subject. They hope to observe and understand these general processes as they occur under specific circumstances. In a sense, then, all settings and subjects are representative of all others. (p. 12)

This range of options is fully in evidence in the research literature as is seen in the sections that follow.

No Generalization

With text-based research, there are many examples of researchers examining one or a small set of television shows then limiting their conclusions to those particular shows. For example, Schwichtenberg (1987) analyzed one program ("Love Boat") and did not generalize to other programs. Haralovich (1992) analyzed the elements in 1950s sitcoms, especially "Father Knows Best" and "Leave it to Beaver," and did not generalize. And Newcomb (1988) explicitly discussed this point by saying that his interpretations are subjective and that everyone else will have their own reading of their strips of viewing.

An interesting example of no generalizing but still providing a high degree of conceptual leverage is the study by Bird and Dardenne (1988). They talked about news in general and do not refer to individual shows as examples. Without individual examples, there is no need to generalize from the chosen examples to news in general. With their text as news in general, they argued their case on the same level as their conclusions.

Also, scholars who conduct population studies have no opportunity to generalize. For example, Chesebro (1988) did not generalize, because he classified all prime-time programs during two seasons. In short, he did not sample, but instead conducted an analysis on the total set of shows in his population of interest.

Several qualitative researchers make a point of cautioning the reader that they will not generalize (Ang, 1985; Bodroghkozy, 1992; Lindlof, 1987; Morley, 1980; Wolf, 1987). For example, Wolf avoided generalizing, saying "the goal here is not to make generalizations about all children. It is to be able to talk about *these* children in the context of knowing them as they revealed themselves through the course of the study" (p. 94). Bodroghkozy did not try to generalize, cautioning against doing so by saying that the documents she analyzed were not a representative sample of the viewers of "Julia"; instead, she was cautious to say that the letters contain "traces, clues, parts of a larger whole to which we have no access. Indeed like all histories of audience reception, this one presents partial knowledge, pieces of the past that we must interpret in a qualified manner" (p. 148).

In institution research, Altheide (1976) stuck fairly close to his data and did not generalize to all news workers. Elliott (1979) talked about making generalizations, but these are really summary statements of his data or conceptual insights; in either case, they are limited to reflecting on his study. At the end of his chapter on "preparing programme outlines and scripts" he said:

> Two generalizations may be drawn—on the one hand there was an unwillingness to commit the programmes to any particular view; on the other hand, views were allowed to emerge as a consequence of decisions influenced by presentation or audience attention. In the course of this study a distinction needs to be drawn between *communication*, attempts to transmit particular meanings to an audience, and *attention*, judging the level of audience satisfaction. (p. 84)

These are more insights about his data than they are generalizations.

Generalization

Some qualitative researchers do generalize. An example in text research is a study by Horowitz (1987), who speculated about the health of all TV sitcoms from her analysis of a few programs. Kinder (1987) examined some rock videos on MTV and argued that the elements she uncovered in those videos influence all of television narratives.

In audience research, Rogge (1989) as well Traudt and Lont (1987) concluded their studies with a series of generalizations about how all families use television. Liebes and Katz (1988, 1989) also exhibited a high degree of generalizing. Their sample consisted of a handful of purposively chosen people in focus groups. They used the information gained there to talk about all people of a culture or a country. Jhally and Lewis (1992) also showed a high degree of generalization by casting their conclusions from their focus groups as if the findings applied to all viewers of "The Cosby Show."

In institution research, Cantor (1980) limited her analysis to prime-time programs on three commercial networks but generalized her explanations to television production in general.

Fishman (1988) admitted "the generality of my findings can be questioned" (p. 19). He did generalize and defended this by saying:

> the news organization chosen for study is fairly typical of American newspapers in terms of its internal structure, monopoly over the local news market, and position in the community. Most importantly, the routine news practices I found on this newspaper closely correspond with journalists' practices mentioned by a variety of independent sources: biographies, autobiographies, and other reports by journalists, as well as empirical studies of news practices on other newspapers. (p. 19)

Like with the issue of conceptual leverage, the key to appreciating generalizability is in looking for correspondence between evidence and conclusions. Whether generalization should be permissible or not within the qualitative approach is a debate that will not likely be resolved given the strongly held beliefs of the scholars on each side. So it is best to accept the range of beliefs. However, once a scholar establishes his or her position, we as readers can check to make sure that their beliefs as reflected in their design support the level of generalization in their research.

CHAPTER

9

METHODS OF ANALYSIS

There is a wide selection of methods of analysis available to qualitative researchers. These methods can be used separately, but more likely they are used in combinations created by the researcher to fulfill a particular purpose. A good illustration of this is the study by Wolf (1987), who selected several analytical methods and assembled them into a procedure that "essentially grew out of our natural responses to the situations at hand: we were continually confronted with 'puzzles' to be solved" (p. 91). She said her team was not locked into any one procedure and this kept them flexible, which "allowed us to experiment with our guesses of how to solve the puzzles and then adapt our efforts to achieve maximal results" (p. 91). Further "it is impossible to duplicate the procedures used in this study because they emerged in vivo, as parts of a holistic process" (p. 91). This is typical of most qualitative research projects.

What analytical methods are available to qualitative researchers? In this chapter, I illuminate 20 of them; there may be more, but these are the ones used most often. For presentation, these 20 methods of analysis are grouped into four categories: orienting methods, deductive methods of construction, inductive methods of construction, and other methods of construction.

ORIENTING METHODS

When confronted with their phenomenon, what do qualitative researchers look *at*? What guides the researcher to select and assemble certain evidence? Six of the most prevalently used techniques are: semiotics/semiology, discourse analysis, narrative analysis, genre analysis, dialogic analysis, and historical analysis.

Recognizing the complexity of each of these methods, I present only a brief introduction here to give a sense of the range of options available. Readers who want more information should go to the cited writings of theoreticians as well as the examples of research where these methods are used.

Semiotics/Semiology

With this method, the researcher focuses on the analysis of signs and their functions. It is concerned primarily with how meaning is generated in "texts" (films, television programs, music, letters, body language, etc.), the way signs communicate, and the rules that govern the use of those signs. Of course, it is a very important method in textual analysis, but it can also be useful in institution- and audience-focused research.

Semiotics is very different from traditional criticism, in that its first order of business is interpretation of an aesthetic object or text in terms of its immanent meaning: "Semiotics first asks *how* meaning is created, rather than *what* the meaning is" (Seiter, 1987, p. 17).

Semiotics was developed in the 19th century by Charles Saunders Peirce (1839–1914) and Ferdinand de Saussure (1857–1913). Saussure argued that a sign has two components: signifier (sign as symbol) and the signified (object of the sign), whereas Pierce said it has three: representament (sign), object (signified), and interpretant (the sign that we use to translate the first sign). Peirce looked at three characteristics of signs: symbolic, in which the relationship between the signifier and the signified is arbitrary (as with words); iconic, which is a structural representation such as a picture or drawing; and indexical, in which the meaning of the symbol must be inferred (from red spots on a child's face we may infer the child is suffering from measles).

Signs are arbitrary. We need the interpretant in order to derive the meaning of the sign. If we change the interpretant of a particular sign, its meaning changes. Interpretants are nested; that is, in order for us to use a particular interpretant to derive the meaning of a sign, we first need to know the meaning of the interpretant, which requires a more foundational interpretant to use as context.

Several scholars have attempted to extend and adapt semiotics to the study of the media. For example, Barthes (1972) showed that the media require the researcher to make a distinction between denotative and connotative meaning. With denotation, the signifier is the image on camera (picture of a person) and the signified is the object (the person who picture was taken by the camera). In contrast, connotation, which is a second-order signifying system, uses the denoted sign and attaches another meaning to it. Another important distinction is that symbols can be studied synchronically (analytically, i.e., the relationships that exist among the elements) or diachronically (historically, i.e., the way the narrative evolves).

Fiske and Hartley (1978) provided a semiotic-based method of analysis for critically reading television that follows Barthes' ideas. But, they argued, the role of television is different from other media in the sense that television presents messages with preferred meanings that coincide with the perceptions of the dominant sections of society, yet television also allows viewers to arrive at their own meanings, because TV presents such a variety of messages, many of which are contradictory.

Semiological analysis now gives less priority to the reality behind the sign and focuses more on how the sign creates reality. A proponent of this newer position is Bennett (1982) who provided three examples: As his first example, he pointed to the research on the propaganda function of the press as newspapers are no longer regarded as being objective sources of information. Each newspaper has a particular political philosophy and it sells this political definition in the way it reports events. This is not limited to the editorial page, but is also in the articles, headlines, pictures, and layout. A second set of studies focuses on the signifying behavior of "outsiders" (such as drug users and criminals), the people who threaten the cohesiveness of the dominant social norms. A third set of studies examines culture as a reflection of consensus politics. These studies look for implicit norms governing the selection of television news. In all three of these examples, the power of interpretation rests with people rather than on the signs themselves.

Fry and Fry (1986) took these ideas to develop a semiotic model for the study of mass communication. They grounded their model on three postulates: First, mass media messages are textual resources capable of engendering multiple levels of potential meanings. Second, texts are made meaningful through a process of audience signification. And third, textual meaning is constituted by the interaction between textual and extratextual factors. When extratextual factors come into play, there is a chance for interpretations that deviate from the intended meaning.

Other scholars are concerned about the usefulness of employing semiotics to study the media. For example, Seiter (1987) said "semiotics is extremely useful in its attempt to describe precisely how television produces meaning, and in its insistence on the conventionality of all signs" (p. 29). But she was bothered by its limitations, saying that one of the "gravest shortcomings of semiotics" is "the tendency to ignore change, to divorce the sign from its referent, and to exclude the sender and receiver. These characteristics limit the usefulness of semiotics in the study of television" (p. 29). She cited Barthes' idea of connotation as a troubling example of the problem with semiotics. In order to establish a connotative meaning, the researcher should look at changes in television signs, but semiotics does not allow for a change perspective in the analysis. She identified another problem as the implied uniformity in interpretation of texts:

> Semiotics frequently speaks of a text as though it were understood in precisely the same way by everyone. At worst, it operates as though all meanings were

translatable and predictable through the work of a gifted semiotician. Such an approach is nowhere more deficient than in television criticism, where the text is ephemeral but the audience remains a central preoccupation. (p. 38)

Semiotics/semiology was used by several scholars in conducting audience-focused research. Fiske (1991) used it in his search for meaning in a scene from "Hart to Hart." Condit (1991) used it in her analysis of reactions of Jack and Jill in their very different readings of one abortion episode of "Cagney and Lacey." Lewis (1991) performed a semiological analysis on the transcriptions of the interviews. Radway (1984) said she used a semiotic analysis "in the sense that it focuses on the various ways human beings actively *make* sense of their surrounding world" (p. 8).

Discourse Analysis

A researcher using this method orients toward finding the social and ideological dimensions of language or some other language-like system of representation, such as films and television programs. With its roots in the textual scholarship of philosophy, theology, and other humanities, discourse studies are conducted in a variety of different disciplines with different research traditions, and there is no overarching theory common to all types of discourse analysis. However, all discourse analysis rests on three principles (Gee, Michaels, & O'Conner, 1994). First, human discourse is internally structured and governed by rules. Second, it is produced by speakers who are submerged in an environment where cultural, political, economic, social, and personal realities shape the discourse. And third, the discourse conveys information about the speaker's environment (socio-historical matrix).

A primary figure in discourse analysis is Michel Foucault, who in the 1960s used the term *discourse* to refer to the relationship between language and social institutions. Discourse is a foundational code that people use to perceive schemas, language, and knowledge. He argued that social institutions established rules for the way language was used, and these rules influenced how people attached meaning to the institutions. Institutions engaged in this process in order to accumulate and maintain power.

What is a discourse? From linguistics, the term discourse refers to a system of related or linked sequential utterances beyond the level of the sentence (Fiske, 1987; Orr, 1991). In discourse analysis, scholars look for complete units of language longer than a sentence, such as the scene, the story, the episode, or the film. Discourse analysis also extends the idea of language beyond words to include nonverbal communication and production techniques.

Where does a discourse originate? A human being may say something and have that communication regarded as an example of a discourse, but we should not regard the person as having created that discourse. Individuals cannot create discourses. Instead, discourses exist at the social level; they are sets of meaning that societies attach to certain symbols. In this way society circulates meanings about how people should communicate (or think) about topics. When a set of meanings is accepted in a society, that set becomes regarded as common sense and is not questioned. At this point the discourse has become institutionalized. The media are primary tools in the circulation of discourses because of the repeated use of certain symbols that viewers habitually interpret in a certain way.

What is discourse *analysis*? When scholars look at an act of communication and examine the symbols in order to make inferences about the sets of meanings circulating about them, they are conducting a discourse analysis. Any account of a discourse or a discursive practice should include its topic area, its social origin, and its ideological work (Fiske, 1987). Therefore, it is a mistake to think about a discourse of economics or of gender; instead, we should think of a capitalist (or socialist) discourse of economics or the patriarchal (or feminist) discourse of gender.

Gee, Michaels, and O'Conner (1994) argued that discourses can be studied in two ways. First, they are sometimes studied for their own sake. For example, scholars can study structures of grammar, poems, conversations, and so on, to identify the discourses. Questions of this type include: What forms do mythic narratives take across cultures?, What are the recurring patterns that constitute cooperation within a group?, and How does the use of grammatical morphemes reveal the structure of a narrative?

Second, discourses can be studied in terms of how they relate to other social, cognitive, political processes and outcomes. Questions of this type include: Can we tell about children's literacy development by comparing their spoken and written words?, How do the stories adolescents tell about sex influence their experiences?, and Can the structures of conversations about people tell us how subordinates negotiate successfully with superordinates?

Discourses can be studied both in their encoding phase by institutions and in their decoding phase by individuals. Hall (1980) pointed out that media organizations must encode a message before sending it, and this encoding must apply the "discursive rules of language for its product to be 'realized' " (p. 130) and that "before a message can have an 'effect,' satisfy a 'need,' or be put to a 'use,' it must first be appropriated as a meaningful discourse and be meaningfully decoded" (p. 130). This encoding is done on a denotative level where "the televisual sign is fixed by certain, very complex (but limited or 'closed') codes" as well as on the connotative level which "is more open, subject to more active transformations" (p. 134). As for the decoding of the meaning by individuals, Hall said that messages are open to more than one meaning; that is, the codes in media messages are polysemic. However, he does not believe the codes are "pluralistic"; in order for a code to be pluralistic, all readings must be given equal status. Hall argued that there is one dominant reading of a code; this is usually the reading that is preferred by the encoder of the message. There are also oppositional and negotiated readings possible. An oppositional reading is one in contrast to the dominant one, and a negotiated reading is one that is created when a reader constructs a new interpretation somewhere between the writer's intention and the reader's natural position.

Discourse analysis was used by Morley (1980) when he listened to his audio-tapes of the viewers of the "Nationwide" television program. He tried to infer the patterns of meaning in the way those viewers interpreted the show. Turkle (1984) used discourse analysis although it is not her primary method. She got children talking about whether they believe computers to be alive, then she looked for discourses about what it means to be alive. Seiter et al. (1989a) also used discourse analysis to identify the themes underlying the statements expressed by the women they interviewed.

There are also examples of discourse analysis in text-focused research (D'Acci, 1992; Deming, 1992; Haralovich, 1992; Rowland, 1983) and institution-focused research (Gitlin, 1980, 1983, 1987; Kellner, 1987; Spigel, 1992, 1993). For example, Gitlin (1980, 1987) and Kellner looked at the discourses in the use of hegemony as an explanation by critical scholars. Spigel looked at discourses in the popular press.

Narrative Analysis

Narrative analysis is an analytical technique that seeks to fit messages into a pattern of storytelling. The storyteller uses characters and events as symbols to tell his or her interpretations about how things in the world behave and change over time. This method was popularized in the late 1920s by Vladimir Propp and was later influenced by the ideas of Kenneth Burke and Wayne Brokriede, among others. "It has since been fed by studies of a diverse, inter-national group of linguists, anthropologists, folklorists, literary critics, semiologists, and film theorists" (Kozloff, 1987, p. 42).

Scholars who use narrative analysis make the assumption that all messages follow the conventions of a story. It is the task of the researcher to find the story and illuminate its structure. The analysis is usually conducted along two dimensions: syntagmatic and paradigmatic. A syntagmatic analysis is the examination of signs in sequence; it focuses on looking for the sequence of events and establishing individual links between events until the overall structure is illuminated. The paradigmatic part focuses on the meaning behind the use of people and places. It is assumed that characters and settings were not chosen randomly—they are symbols for particular meanings. So the paradigmatic analysis examines elements (camera shots on the microlevel to types of programs or genres on the macrolevel) and putting all like examples in the same paradigm.

Within this view is the assumption that when we use formal logic to understand communication, we get into trouble. Therefore, scholars should not give technical discourse a higher status than rhetorical or poetic discourse. Instead, scholars are asked to recognize that people use a more informal rationality in telling stories, so scholars should use a "narrative rationality" in order to understand communication. This narrative logic is based on the principles of coherence and fidelity. Coherence means the consistency of characters and actions (a kind of internal validity), whereas fidelity is a matter of truth (analogous to external validity; i.e., does the story ring true to the listener's own experiences in real life and provide a reliable guide to our own beliefs, attitudes, values, and actions?).

The narrative method of analysis offers two alternative ways of proceeding: top-down or bottom-up (Manning & Cullum-Swan, 1994). In the top-down approach, the investigator begins with a set of rules and principles then seeks to exhaust the meaning of a text using those rules and principles. In contrast, researchers using the bottom-up approach, which is popular in ethnography, look for contextual units and builds those units into an argument for the interpretation of the text.

Kozloff (1987) observed three parts to narrative analysis of television programs—examination of story, discourse, and schedule. The story is the sequence of events that reveals what happens to whom. The discourse is how the story is told. The schedule is a larger discourse about how the story is programmed within the station's overall sequence of stories. Not all narrative elements are equally important; some are kernels (important events in the progression of the story) and others are satellites (routine or minor elements) (Chatman, 1978). Notice that the narrative and discourse methods can be used to work together; this possibility for combinations is not unique to these two methods but can be tried with any pair or even trio of methods.

Narrative analysis is also linked with myth analysis, although not as often as in the past. Fisher (1987) complained that the idea of myth was stripped out of narrative analysis when film scholars began using narrative analysis to examine television, and he argued that this is an important loss. "Human communication in all its forms is imbued with mythos—ideas that cannot be verified or proved in any absolute way. Such ideas arise in metaphor, values, gestures, and so on" (p. 19). "The most compelling, persuasive stories are mythic in form, stories reflective of 'public dreams' that give meaning and significance to life" (p. 76). Also, Kozloff (1987) pointed out that "it is inescapably 'formalist' and largely unconcerned with questions about 'content' and thus with political or ideological judgments" because of its focus on narrative structure (pp. 42–43). Further, according to Kozloff:

> because narrative theory concentrates on the text itself, it leaves to other critical methods questions about where the story comes from (for instance, the history, organization, and regulation of the broadcast industry, the intentions of the networks or of individual professionals) and the myriad effects (psychological or sociological) that the narrative has upon its audience. (p. 43)

But despite the criticism, narrative analysis remains a popular analytical technique, especially in text-focused research (C. Anderson, 1987; Barker, 1987; Douglas, 1993; Flitterman-Lewis, 1992; Kinder, 1987).

Genre Analysis

This method focuses on what makes certain types of messages similar. Scholars examine texts for their form of composition to determine the conventions that unify certain sets of texts while distinguishing them from other types. According to Jensen (1991a), the focus is on the form of composition and the conventional subject matter of various genres. Genres are defined by formal composition, appropriate subject matter, and mode of address. "Addressing their readers, genres imply both a subject position from which they may be interpreted and a set of appropriate social uses of the contents" (p. 36).

How does the genre analysis method work? Researchers first construct categories by: (a) identifying and describing basic structural similarities (such as dialogue, settings, themes, tone, point of view, characters, camerawork, etc.) among groups of texts, and (b) looking at the evolutions of genres in terms of historical, technological, ideological, and aesthetic factors (Vande Berg & Wenner, 1991).

There are three approaches—the aesthetic, the ritual, and the ideological—that can be used in constructing genres and in justifying the classifications of examples into genres (Feurer, 1987). The aesthetic approach attempts to define a genre as a system of conventions about artistic expression, especially in terms of individual authorship; it assesses whether an individual work fits or transcends the genre. The ideological approach regards genre as an instrument of control. Genres build certain types of audiences, which then assure certain advertisers of a quality audience. The ritualistic approach regards the industry and audiences in negotiation with one another to define culture. These studies focus on (a) systems of production of shows, (b) analyses of the structures of texts, and (c) how audiences as interpretive communities receive the shows.

An example of the genre analysis method is in the work of Morley (1989), who argued that looking at genres was a good starting place for reception analysis. He said that genres are better than particular programs. However, even within a genre, there should be a wide variety of readings.

Dialogic Analysis

Dialogic analysis focuses on how "conversations" among various ideological systems are woven into a narrative. The characters in these conversations are the embodiment of an ideological language through their social positions. Scholars analyze the characters and actions to determine the hegemonic intention of the author (Vande Berg & Wenner, 1991). The most influential theorist here is M. M. Bakhtin.

Lipsitz (1992) employed dialogic analysis in his examination of 1950s television dramas. He began with the thesis that the working-class sitcoms "evoked the experiences of the past to lend legitimacy to the dominant ideology of the present

... and served important social and cultural functions" (pp. 72–73). He then examined television programs to find the ideologies that were conversing there. He found several points of view; among them were economic messages growing out of the depression in the 1940s and into a shift to large-scale production of consumer products, political messages reflecting a shift to a welfare state and big-government involvement in a world war, and consumerism messages, not just with ads, but with the values presented in the fictional programming.

Historical Analysis

This method is perhaps the most difficult to describe, because it can be regarded as a qualitative or quantitative method, as a part of either the humanities or a social science, and as focusing on either idiographic description or on generalizations. Nord (1989) said, "scholars with strikingly different goals and methods work within the catch-all category. All are historians" (p. 291).

However, we can identify some essential characteristics of historical analysis. First, it is relatively safe to say that historical analysis has an interest in the past. Marshall and Rossman (1989) simply stated that historical analysis is "a method of discovering, from records and accounts, what happened in the past" (p. 95). Second, historical analysis is empirical. Historians rely on primary sources (such as oral testimony of eyewitnesses, documents, records, and relics) and secondary sources (such as reports of persons who relate the accounts of eyewitnesses). And third, although historical analysis has an interest in the unique, the particular, and the local, historians must do more than simply tell a story about those particulars. Instead, "there is a pressure for synthesis and meaning" and a "demand for definite principles of historical judgment" (Stern, 1956, p. 23). This means that historical analysis must use "various levels of generalization to describe, interpret or explain collections of data" (Nord, 1989, p. 291). It is not the simple reporting of facts and occurrences that happened in the past. Even with a focus on idiographic description, historians usually provide a link to some wider context or deeper interpretation.

Nord (1989) made a distinction between two ideal types: the humanist historian and the social science historian. He said the humanist "is interested primarily in unique events and sequences, seeks to understand an event by understanding its context in a particular place and time ... and the mode of description and explanation is often, though not always, narration" (p. 294). The social science historian in contrast is more interested in testing preexisting theories primarily through quantitative analyses.

The accepted definition of history has changed over the course of this century (Tuchman, 1994). In the 1920s, the prevailing definition saw history as the documenting of concrete events as they actually occurred in time and place; history sought to find out what actually happened and how the events occurred. It was more concerned with the people in power and the elites than with the common folk. In its contemporary definition, history is much more concerned with providing interpretations about why certain things occurred given the prevailing culture of the time; it is now focused more on exploring meaning than on documenting occurrences.

Historical analysis has been applied in the area of media studies. For example, it has been used to examine television criticism where it attempts "to assess the roles that technological, economic, political, legal, regulatory, and aesthetic factors have played in the creation, reception, and impact of television texts in a particular society" (Vande Berg & Wenner, 1991, p. 31). Also, it has been applied to journalism where, according to Stevens and Garcia (1980), there are three types of historical analysis: descriptive, explanatory, and exploratory. The descriptive type lists salient features of its subject over time; it is focused on describing the nature, growth, and evolution of media. Examples include Barnouw's (1975) *Tube of Plenty* as well as *Broadcasting in America* by Head and Sterling (1990). The explanatory (or interpretive) type, which usually focuses on content, addresses the reasons behind the salient features. They say that a popular form of this type is the "great man" approach where specific individuals are shown as shaping the development of the media. But other forms focus on how certain developments (such as press freedoms or movie production) evolve out of the climate of the times. An example is Jowett's (1976) *Film, The Democratic Art.* Exploratory studies examine the literature to identify gaps and shortcomings.

METHODS OF CONSTRUCTION: DEDUCTION

Deduction is the process of starting with general principles, then constructing an argument showing that the evidence supports those general principles. The general principles need not be a formal theory from which tests are deduced; they can also be a scheme, model, or an ideological position. For example, Cantor (1980) conducted a study to show how various forces influence the production of prime-time television programs. She developed a model early in her book then arrays her evidence in order to illustrate and show support for the model. Altheide (1985) presented his thesis about how journalists construct the news, then followed with his observations to demonstrate support for his thesis.

In the sections that follow, I present six frequently used analytical methods of deductive construction: Marxist analysis, feminist analysis, psychoanalytical analysis, postmodern analysis, myth analysis, and hypothesis testing. This section culminates by contrasting how thesis-based methods and hypothesis-based methods differ in the way they build their arguments.

Marxist Analysis

This ideology has spawned a very complex research tradition, and Marxism has now come to mean different things to different people. The original ideas of Marx focus attention on materialism, the belief that a person's economic and social condition determines his or her consciousness. The economic system produces a "superstructure" of values and institutions (such as the legal system, religion, philosophy, ideas, art, culture) within each society. Those in control of the economic system (the wealthy) create a "false consciousness" in order to control the masses and thereby protect their position by maintaining the status quo; thus a false consciousness is planted and maintained in the minds of the working class of people who are employed in narrow job functions as they mass produce products within a capitalist society. This false consciousness alienates them from one another and makes them feel satisfied with their existence.

In the early 1920s, Marxist thought began to spawn some subgroups, the most influential of which was known as the Frankfurt School. In 1923, some young German intellectuals (Adorno, Marcuse, and Horkheimer) were strongly influenced by: (a) a disappointment that the Russian revolution did not spread to western Europe in 1917, (b) a shock over German fascism, and (c) the inexplicable political stability that occurred after the First World War. Members of the Frankfurt School tried to show that American culture was debased, because it was under the monopoly of capitalism, which was particularly repressive. Their primary objection to capitalism was that it supported a mass culture that fostered a totalitarian state that took away freedoms from individuals.

Throughout the 1940s, there was a widespread, popular belief that the media exerted a powerful effect on a mass audience of atomized, anomic individuals—an idea introduced at the turn of the century by the influential sociologist Durkheim. The Frankfurt School rejected the idea of the mass society. It was also at this time that American social science demonstrated that there was no mass society and that the media's effect on society was very small or nonexistent. The Frankfurt School also rejected social science research, saying that it was uninteresting, because it ignored the notion of the media as ideological agencies that play a central role in maintaining class domination.

Marxist thought ran into a problem when television became the dominant medium of information and entertainment. Marx's position was that people were unaware of the effect the society had on them—that is, people suffered from a false consciousness. This false consciousness was a belief that the "ordinary person" would never be able to change his or her lot in life, so he or she should be happy in their powerless condition. Marx believed that once this false consciousness was revealed to people, they would became aware of the negative effects of capitalism and would rebel against the apparatus that keeps the false consciousness in place, thereby changing their lives for the better. But Marxism fails to explain *why* people find TV so enjoyable (White, 1987). If television is what keeps the false consciousness in place and is the constant reminder of oppression, why do viewers find it so enjoyable?

As a way around this problem, Gramsci introduced the idea of hegemony, which substantially enlarged the concept of domination by saying that ideology is not just psychological or moralistic, but also structural and epistemological.

Hegemony is supported by the assumption that all societies are composed of complex forces and conflicting interests, so there is not a consistent false consciousness manufactured by the ruling elite. Instead, all the cultural forces balance out into a single prevailing view—this is the "commonsense view of things" that most people in the society accept without question. When people are exposed to messages in the media, they decode symbols according to the preferred reading as indicated by the prevailing view in the culture. Often codes will not be read in a "perfect" way—according to the hegemonic meaning—but will be negotiated, resulting in a mixed meaning, a combination of the prevailing ideology filtered through the person's own experience.

Another major extension or refinement of Marx was provided by Althusser, a French philosopher. He reasoned that the elements that support the false consciousness are subject to uneven development. "Social formation" is a complex process of influence from economic, political, and ideological elements, which are sometimes in conflict and in which the dominant economy determines all other practices. With television, people are regarded as a commodity to be sold to advertisers, but television's effects are not unidimensional. Television's messages reflect a fragmented and dispersed system of representation, without a clearly "dominant" ideology. People are regarded as interacting with other factors in the social formation, so people both construct and are constructed by systems of representation such as the media. Althusser's ideas lend themselves to media analysis, especially in the form of text-oriented ideological criticism.

Another refinement was advanced by Fiske (1987), whose perspective is essentially Marxist in that he started with the belief that meanings and the making of them are indivisibly linked to the social structure and only explained in terms of that structure and history. These constructed meanings are what maintain the social structure. Fiske also assumed that capitalist societies are divided societies; but whereas Marx focused the division on social class, Fiske argued that the divisions are along the lines of gender, race, nation, age group, religion, occupation, political allegiance, and so on. Society then is composed of many groups, each of which has a different power relationship with the dominant classes. The "have-nots" struggle to get power. In the domain of culture, the struggle is for meaning, where the dominant classes attempt to neutralize the meanings that serve their interests into the "common sense" of the society as a whole, whereas the subordinate classes resist this process by attempting to construct meanings that serve their interests.

Fiske (1987) differed with Marx in one important respect. Marx said that the powerful class creates a false consciousness that it forces on the powerless and makes them believe something that helps the powerful maintain that power. Fiske argued there is no such thing as a false consciousness, that it is not possible because there is no such thing as an objective empirical truth. Consciousness is never the product of truth or reality, but rather of culture, society, and history. As support for this position Fiske cited Althusser's theory of over-determinism, which states that ideology is not a static set of ideas but a dynamic process that is constantly reproduced and reconstituted in practice. The relationship between ideology and culture is not determined solely by economics but is also strongly influenced by the ideological state apparatuses, which are social institutions such as the family, the education system, language, the media, the political system, and so on. These social norms are not neutral or objective. They have been developed in the interests of those with social power, who work to maintain their sites of power by naturalizing them into the common sense.

Feminist Analysis

Like Marxism, feminism is multifaceted. Feminists caution that their approach is very difficult to define. For example, Bowen and Wyatt (1993) took the position that there is no single definition of *feminism* or *feminist* precisely because it is the nature of feminism and feminist thought and inquiry to resist definitive statements. And Olesen (1994) asserted that there are many feminisms.

However, there are some commonalities across the types of feminism. In general, feminism assumes an imbalance of power between men and women at all levels of society and that this imbalance influences our perceptions about what is important in the world. The purpose of feminist criticism is not to provide a reading of a work "but the mapping and changing of attitudes and conditions and the reformulation of a new language which is woman-centered and free of patriarchal constraints and oppression" (Orr, 1991, p. 134). Thus feminism is oriented toward changing people's perceptions and attitudes about women. It is also oriented toward changing power structures (Olesen, 1994) by taking an oppositional position to the existing power structures (Bowen & Wyatt, 1993). Finally, feminists examine the ways in which knowledge is generated and how it is used selectively to legitimate certain types of people.

By the 1980s, the feminist approach to film and television criticism had become multifaceted and had taken several different forms. Feminist scholars have different views on how this research is organized. I present three of those organizations next. Notice how each of these organizational schemes focuses on how the feminist method is linked with other methods.

Lont (1993) perceived three types of feminist research. First, there is the tradition of content analysis with its descriptions of the frequency of representation of women in the media. Second, since the early 1970s, there have been historical narratives of individual women as processes of the media. And, there is the feminist critical analysis of media and society. This criticism grows out of the Marxist interpretation of power.

Olesen (1994) also saw three models for feminists' research (standpoint, empiricism, and postmodern), but her scheme is very different from that of Lont. The standpoint model for research embodies women with a special perspective on any given situation because of their unique experiences. The empiricist model is used by feminists who consciously avoid research standards in their field, because they believe those standards codify rules that lead to androcentric findings. Instead feminists "self-consciously try to create new, but rigorous, research practices" (p. 163) that will allow them to document their own perspective. Feminist research conducted in a postmodern model regards truth as "a destructive illusion. The endless play of signs, the shifting sands of interpretation, language that obscures—all promote these feminists to view the world as endless stories or texts" (p. 164).

Kaplan (1987) identified four stages in the evolution of feminist research. First, there was bourgeois feminism concerned with women's quest to obtain equal rights and freedoms within the capitalist system. Second, there was Marxist feminism, which attempted to link specific oppressions of women to the larger structure of capitalism. It also linked the oppression of women to the oppressions of other groups such as gays, minorities, and the working class. The third stage was radical feminism, which focused on establishing separate female communities (apart from men) in order to achieve the specific needs and desires of women. In the fourth wave, there is poststructural feminism, which is concerned with examining how language treats women differently than men. Kaplan also pointed out that the first three of these stages are an "essentialist" feminism, based on the assumption that women are essentially (biologically) different from men in the sense that they "embody a more humane, moral mode of being, which, once brought to light, could help change society in beneficial directions. Female values become a standard for critiquing the harsh, competitive, and individualistic 'male' values that govern society" (p. 217). The antiessentialists, on the other hand, seek to understand how female subjectivity is constructed in a society. Gender criticism looks at how story elements (such as language, character, settings, narrative structure, camerawork, etc.) maintain or deconstruct existing cultural definitions of gender (Vande Berg & Wenner, 1991).

Psychoanalytical Analysis

This method of analysis begins with an a priori template of Freudian psychological principles and applies them in the examination of human behaviors or texts. It has been characterized as "a form of applied psychoanalysis, a science concerned with the 'interaction of conscious and unconscious processes' and with the laws of mental functioning" (Berger, 1982, p. 68).

Psychoanalytical criticism is based on Freud's idea of the unconscious mind. The barrier that prevents us from understanding more of our unconscious mind is our own mechanism of repression or other defense mechanisms that are controlled by the ego. These defense mechanisms include ambivalence, avoidance, denial, fixation, identification, projection, reaction formation, repression, suppression, rationalization, and regression. Humans strive toward maturity by repressing the drive toward gratification (the pleasure principle) and replacing it with conscious activities (the reality principle). There is then a split between the rational conscious (ego or self) and the unconscious. Within the realm of the unconscious are repressed instinctual drives, illogical and contradictory, yet yearning for gratification. These yearnings are played out in dreams, which are the symbolic fulfillments of our unconscious yearnings.

When studying people, the psychoanalyst looks for symbols in order to interpret what is happening in the unconscious mind. Psychoanalysis is a process of discovering the way humans develop their personalities and sexual identities as a product of unconscious mechanisms of resistance, repression, sexuality, and the Oedipus complex (Flitterman-Lewis, 1987).

When studying the media, scholars who use this Freudian perspective focus their attention on certain symbols in the media messages then speculate on how specific individuals and audiences will react to those messages. Although this approach has been frequently used to analyze films, because of film's ability to present the fantasy of dreams (Metz, 1982), some scholars have also found it useful for analyzing television. For example, Flitterman-Lewis (1987) argued that this approach has value in understanding television audiences even though television is a very different medium because of its "blurring the categories of fiction and nonfiction, embedding distraction in its very core, instilling a desire for continual consumption (not only of its programs but of the products that it sells)," and "trading on the powerful sense of immediacy that it creates" (p. 204). This psychoanalytical perspective has also been applied to analyzing media symbols and interpreting what is going on with the producer of the media messages in particular or with the culture in general.

A refinement of psychoanalysis into a more powerful tool for examining the media was developed by Lacan. His perspective takes us back to the time of infancy, when we do not make a distinction between self and other—where our world is a mass of sensory experience. The process of making meaning of this sensory data begins when the child starts to understand the "other" and enters into that meaning system where he or she learns how to process the symbols there. Children develop an image of who they are, and when they look in a mirror, they see this imaginary self along with the real one. When they are able to close the gap between the two, they feel pleasure. Television viewers also gain pleasure when they see characters that conform closely to their image of their ideal self.

Postmodernism Analysis

As characterized by scholars such as Baudrillard, De Man, and Derrida, postmodernism refers to the current state of affairs in "late capitalist" society in which manufacturers are greatly outproducing consumers' needs and thus bombarding us with advertising messages to change the way we act with others, ourselves, and the world—and ultimately to increase our desire to consume. These messages from the media are believed to have destabalized the ideological processes that socialize us. As a result we bounce back and forth between the two poles of our existence. On the one side, we feel we are in control of our lives and that our opportunities are limitless. On the other side, we feel hopelessly lost in a chaotic tidal wave of conflicting messages that fragment our existence into isolated experiences.

To understand the characteristics of postmodernism, it is helpful to contrast it with modernism, as Harvey (1989) did. Modernism is rationalistic; exhibits a belief in linear progress, absolute truths, and rational planning of ideal social orders; and believes in the standardization of knowledge and production. In contrast, postmodernism seeks a heterogeneity of culture as evidenced by fragmentation of messages and a distrust of all meta narratives—large-scale discourses that are purported to apply universally.

As Richardson (1994) put it:

> [The] core of postmodernism is the *doubt* that any method or theory, discourse or genre, tradition or novelty, has a universal and general claim as the "right" or the privileged form of authoritative knowledge, Postmodernism *suspects* all truth claims of masking and serving particular interests in local, cultural, and political struggles. But postmodernism does not automatically reject conventional methods of knowing and telling as false or archaic. Rather, it opens those standard methods to inquiry and introduces new methods, which are also, then subject to critique. (pp. 517–518)

In its rejection of the notion of universal truths, one might think postmodernism does not provide a basis for scholarship, for if scholars are distrustful of all knowledge claims and if our culture is fragmenting into isolated pockets of idiosyncratic perceptions, how can scholars operate? Richardson (1994) replied that "a postmodernist position does allow us to know 'something' without claiming to know everything. Having a partial, local, historical knowledge is still knowing" (p. 518).

Many scholars have found the postmodern method of analysis useful in examining the media. As explained by Seiter et al. (1989b), "broadcast television has been seen as embodying postmodern aesthetics, with its relentless intertextuality, its reworking of popular culture, its effacement of history. As a theory of aesthetics, postmodernism offers the possibility—yet unrealized—of dissolving the rigid distinctions between high and low art so characteristic of modernism" (p. 9).

Myth Analysis

Mythic analysis focuses on the elements in narratives (such as characters, plots, settings, etc.) that serve to reaffirm the values and identities in a culture (Vande Berg & Wenner, 1991). This analysis is related to semiotics (especially with Barthes) where myth is regarded as a second-order sign, that is, a sign that goes beyond representational and iconic meaning to present cultural meaning.

Barthes (1980) defined myth as "a type of speech. Myth cannot possibly be an object, a concept, or an idea; it is a mode of signification, a form. Because myth is a type of speech, everything can be a myth provided it is conveyed by a discourse. Myth is not defined by the object of the message, but by the way it utters this message: there are formal limits to myth, there are no 'substantial' ones" (p. 109).

Breen and Corcoran (1986) followed up with an operational definition that includes the following characteristics: A myth is dreamlike, and involves a romantic quest. It is accepted unknowingly. It is language based and takes a narrative structure. It is concerned with the religious instinct, and it forms the basic models of society.

Myth analysis has been used by a few scholars in media studies. Bird and Dardenne (1988) used myth analysis in their exploration of the difference between the reality of events and the symbols that are used to construct stories about that reality within news texts. They argued that news follows a mythological narrative that is ritualistic, communal, and orienting. Myth does not reflect objective reality, but instead builds a world of its own in order to explain baffling or frightening phenomena. "News is a particular kind of mythological narrative with its own symbolic codes that are recognized by its audience" (pp. 71–72). Journalists are governed by the grammar of their culture. If we study the models of news narratives, we can learn about the values and symbols of a given culture.

Himmelstein (1984) used myth analysis as a critical strategy in locating the meanings in television programs and ads. His goal was to demythologize the ideology in TV messages so as to reveal the constructed nature of the reality presented by television. He then suggested alternative realities that are "representations rejected outright or coopted by the dominant television apparatus" (p. 7).

Hypothesis Testing

Hypothesis testing is a deductive method used by those scholars more on the scientific end of the qualitative approach. The researcher will begin with some sort of general proposition such as a theory or a model, then construct a test of that proposition. This general proposition usually expresses the relationship between two or more concepts. For example, the researcher might begin with a belief that children who talk with each other a lot about scary media portrayals will be less frightened by them than will other children. The researcher could then design a reception study to test a hypothesis that 4-year-olds in Happy Valley Playschool who talk the most about snakes and spiders will be the least scared when they are shown a TV program about snakes and spiders. The hypothesis is less general than the proposition so that it can be tested. In the proposition the people are all children, whereas in the hypothesis they are 4-year-olds in Happy Valley Playschool. Also, in the proposition, the stimulus material is media portrayals, whereas in the hypothesis it is a TV program about snakes and spiders.

Building an Argument

The essential task of all deductively structured research is the building of a solid argument. The form of the argument is different with thesis-based and hypothesis-based research. Let's compare and contrast the two. The deductive structure is the same with hypothesis testing as it is with a scholarly thesis (such as Marxism, feminism, etc.). Both begin with a general explanatory statement, both present relevant evidence reflecting on the explanatory strength of that statement, and both present conclusions about the correspondence of that evidence with the position expressed in the general statement. However, there is an important difference in the purpose the researcher has for using deduction. Researchers who begin with a scholarly thesis are almost always overt advocates of their position, so their purpose is to persuade the reader to accept their thesis. They assemble purposively gathered evidence in such a way as to provide maximum support for that thesis. In contrast, scholars who test a hypothesis regard the hypothesis as a tentative guess. They seek to gather a wide range of evidence; some of it may support the hypothesis and some may not. When they present their conclusions, it is not in an overtly persuasive mode; but instead, it is in a mode that acknowledges evidence counter to the hypothesis and seeks to balance it with evidence that supports the thesis so that a reasonable conclusion can be drawn about the degree to which the hypothesis has been supported as well as the manner in which the general proposition can be reformulated so as to be a more accurate explanation of the phenomenon.

The reader is the key arbiter of the effectiveness of the argument. Readers who are persuaded that the evidence strongly supports a thesis will accept the thesis. With hypothesis-based work, the reader must be convinced that the researcher gathered enough evidence to provide a good test of the hypothesis and that the preponderance of the evidence supports the researcher's conclusion (either support for the hypothesis or rejection of the hypothesis).

METHODS OF CONSTRUCTION: INDUCTION

There are five inductive methods to guide researchers from data to conclusions: grounded theory, triangulation, maximum comparisons, sensitized concepts, and thick description. This section ends with an examination of how the inductive methods are used in drawing conclusions.

Grounded Theory

This is an analytical technique that directs researchers to look for patterns in data so they can make general statements about the phenomenon they examined. The process follows inductive reasoning—looking for patterns across individual observations then arguing for those patterns as having the status of general explanatory statements.

Grounded theory was developed by scholars attempting to provide techniques to overcome the criticism that qualitative research findings never amount to much, because they cannot be generalized. In 1967, Glaser and Strauss published a book entitled *The Discovery of Grounded Theory*, in which they provided a rationale and method for moving beyond data description to making general statements about phenomena. They argued for using induction for building theory from qualitative data.

With grounded theory, researchers do not begin with a theory and deduce hypotheses to be tested. Instead, researchers begin with an area of study, then make observations within that area. After observations are made, the researcher looks for patterns and explanations to emerge. The resulting theory then "is one that is inductively derived from the study of the phenomenon it represents. That is, it is discovered, developed, and provisionally verified through systematic data collection and analysis of data pertaining to that phenomenon. Therefore, data collection, analysis, and theory stand in reciprocal relationship with each other" (Strauss & Corbin, 1990, p. 23). In essence, it is a constant comparative analysis, because it focuses on the interplay between analysis and data collection. In this way, new theories can be generated or existing theories can be elaborated through a process of modification as new observations are meticulously compared to the explanations evolving out of perceived patterns from previous sets of observations.

With this technique, the analysis includes two tasks: explication of the meaning systems and building theory. The researcher studies the data then "builds an argument for the symbolic alignments that motivate or inform overt behaviors" (Lindlof & Meyer, 1987, p. 9). Theory is built when researchers "interleave concept formation, data collection, and hypothesis testing throughout many phases of the project" (p. 10). Inductively derived theories look more like descriptive typologies and dynamic models than they look like formal scientific theories composed of general propositions from which tests can be deduced.

There are several good examples of grounded theory in the media qualitative literature. Lull (1980) made many observations of the punk culture in San Francisco, then arranged those observations into a social uses of television typology that was composed of two major components: structural and relational. The structural component included environmental use (background noise, companionship, and entertainment) and regulative use (punctuation of time and activity and talk patterns). The relational component had four subcomponents: communication facilitation (agenda for talk, experience illustration), affiliation/avoidance (relationship maintenance, family solidarity), social learning (behavior modeling, legitimization, substitute schooling), and competence/dominance (role reinforcement, argument facilitation). Liebes and Katz (1988, 1989) interviewed people in focus groups about why they watched "Dallas" and what they got out of the program. The researchers sifted through all the comments of the participants, looking for a pattern. In order to express that pattern, the authors developed the concepts of primordiality and seriality as explanations about why the viewing of "Dallas" was so important to people. Rogge (1989) interviewed members of German families to determine the importance media had for them in their everyday lives. She built to generalizations that make an interesting distinction between objective and subjective media reality. Objective media reality has a formative influence on lifestyles and patterns of communication. Subjective media reality deals with "people's everyday knowledge about the media, the patterns of behavior adopted" (p. 178). Several authors specifically cited the grounded theory guidelines laid out by Strauss and Corbin (1990), then applied those procedures in their work (Barrios, 1988; Pardun & Krugman, 1994).

Triangulation

An author who argues that his or her conclusions are derived from many different kinds of people across many different situations will be more convincing than another author whose conclusions are based on observations of one person in one setting. The method of strengthening of one's argument by building in many different dimensions is called triangulation. When researchers find a common perspective expressed among many different kinds of people in a community, it lends credibility that the insight exists in the community (Lincoln & Guba, 1985).

When using this method, researchers add dimensions to their data gathering by increasing their sources of data (across time, space, and analytical level), increasing the number and types of investigators (multidisciplinary team), increasing exposure to different theories (applying concepts and perspectives from diverse theories and disciplines), and increasing the variety of methods used (Denzin, 1978; Jankowski & Wester, 1991).

Oftentimes a researcher will encounter conflicting evidence and must decide which set of evidence has the higher degree of credibility. Triangulation is a valuable method to use in dealing with this common problem of reconciling facts obtained during data collection (Lindlof & Meyer, 1987). There are two views on reconciling facts. The convergent view uses triangulation to demonstrate that all the observations conform to one interpretation. With the convergence of observations from many different sources, settings, and investigators, the researcher can make a powerful argument that the interpretation is indeed robust, that the interpretation is not sensitive to differences across people, settings, or investigators. In contrast, there is a view that looks for divergence. Researchers holding this view want to document the differences across people, settings, and investigators, so they triangulate in order to uncover the conditions in which differences emerge.

A good procedure is to incorporate both the convergent and divergent techniques into the same research design so as to use the full power of the method. Triangulation is a such an important method, because it provides researchers with a means to distinguish between the idiosyncratic (focusing on the differences) and the representative (focusing on the convergences) (Fortner & Christians, 1981).

Maximum Comparisons /

Maximum comparisons is another useful method of analysis. When employing this technique, researchers need to focus on pairs—people, texts, or events—so as to maximize the differences between them. This results in clearer contrasts that can improve the substance and explanatory power of the interpretations. Thus, cases are not chosen randomly; instead, they are chosen to clarify gross features and thus make conceptual categories more precise (Christians & Carey, 1989).

Sensitized Concepts

Qualitative researchers sometimes use metaphors and analogies to capture the meaning of some event or behavior. As an example, television viewing could be referred to as a religion where viewers are the worshipers, and the messages are the religious parables. Viewers engage in certain rituals to demonstrate their worship, and television producers and programmers are the priests who carefully tailor messages to convert people to their way of thinking. The concept of religion is used metaphorically to illuminate the meaning of television viewing:

> Whether by initiating special metaphors, creating analogies, or using direct expressions, the qualitative researcher maps out territories by finding seminal ideas that become permanent intellectual contributions while unveiling the inner character of events or situations. Interpretive research seeks to capture original meanings validly, yet explicate them on a level that gives the results maximum impact. (Christians & Carey, 1989, p. 370)

Further, according to Christians and Carey (1989), a sensitized concept can also be a "portrait, illustrative story, or description of ritual behavior that crystallizes sentiment and life style" (p. 370). These are "categories that are meaningful to the people themselves, yet sufficiently powerful to explain large domains of social experience" (p. 369). The analogies and metaphors should not be regarded literally as explanations, only as a means of increasing understanding.

Thick Description

Thick description is an explication "of the layers of meaning that lend the events their significance for social actors" (Lindlof & Meyer, 1987, p. 8). It is through thick description that researchers convey the layers of context that are used by the social actors as they construct meaning. In order for the reader of the qualitative research report to understand how those actors constructed their meaning, the researcher must provide enough description.

Drawing Conclusions

The product of the inductive procedure is the presentation of general conclusions, which is regarded by many as theory construction. The process of constructing a theory is essentially a research argument in which the claims about the phenomenon are analyzed and advanced. Within the qualitative approach, the "contribution to theory comes in the form of a dialectic between the researcher's understanding of the social action as presented in the ethnographic text and the theoretical framework which is used to interpret the text for others" (J. A. Anderson, 1987, p. 264). This ethnographic text is part of a dialectical (interactive) analysis of the terms and constructs of theory.

In this view, the process of analysis begins at the beginning of a research project and continues until the writing is done. However, because analysis is pervasive, researchers must not take their analytical decisions for granted. Instead, they should illuminate for the reader the key elements in their decisions, especially when context is an important determinant of meaning. For the reader of a qualitative research report, the context *is* the author's illumination of the key decisions.

How can researchers structure their arguments when they draw their conclusions? According to J. A. Anderson (1987), there are three forms of argument or analysis: narrative form, inductive exemplar, and models/types. The narrative form, the most common form of qualitative argument, is an extension of the episode and as such it overarches the individual episodes by attempting to provide a coherent descriptive framework that ties together the individual episodes. No attempt is made to link the case under study to higher abstractions in a theory. The inductive exemplar highlights a construct (such as social action or marriage). The researcher selects a construct, displays its categories, shows that the texts fit into the categories, and uses this pattern to argue that the construct exists in this situation. Models/types provide for a high degree of generality.

Within the overall task of drawing conclusions, there are many techniques that have proved very useful. Miles and Huberman (1984) listed 12 of these techniques for drawing conclusions (generating meaning) from qualitative data: counting, noting patterns or themes, seeing plausibility, clustering, making metaphors, splitting variables, subsuming particulars into the general, factoring, noting relations between variables, finding intervening variables, building a logical chain of evidence, and making conceptual/theoretical coherence. When researchers select from among these techniques, they need to be guided by the types of evidence they have available for analysis as well as the kinds of conclusions they want to construct.

OTHER CONSTRUCTIONS

There are several other analytical methods that exhibit features of both induction and deduction. They are: analytical induction, negative case analysis, and retroduction.

Analytical Induction

Analytical induction is a process of exhaustive examination of cases in order to prove universal, causal generalizations. The analysis is a cyclic process of refining insights to build theory (Jankowski & Wester, 1991). In practice the method is: definition, tentative explanation, possible reformulation, and generalization. The procedure is to look at one case and construct a generalization, and to look at the next case, to determine if it fits the generalization, if it does not, the generalization must be adjusted, and so on.

The goal of analytic induction is "to develop *universal* statements containing the *essential features* of a phenomenon, or those things that are always found to *cause* or lie behind the existence of a social occurrence" (Manning, 1982a, p. 277). This is essentially the definitional task of continually redefining and reconceptualizing the phenomenon.

Among the benefits of using inductive analysis, as Lincoln and Guba (1985) pointed out, is that it is more likely to identify the multiple realities to be found in the data. It is also used because such analysis is more likely to make the investigator–respondent interaction explicit, and it provides a better description of context, which increases transferability to other settings; finally, inductive analysis makes values a more explicit part of the analytical structure.

Analytical induction appears very similar to grounded theory. Both utilize a process of induction resulting in general explanations of the individual data. The difference is that analytical induction requires many iterations to test the fit of new cases to the general explanation. With grounded theory, a researcher can conduct one study, examine the observations, and speculate as to a general explanation. That explanation is a theory grounded in the data—but only the data of that one study. Over a series of studies, scholars will continually test the fit of new cases to the explanation—this is the process of analytical induction. This raises the issue that this method may be misnamed, because it seems to rely as much, if not more, on deduction. The first study in a line of research may be predominately inductive, but once a general explanation is introduced and used to guide subsequent studies (or iterations), those additional tests should be deduced from the initial general explanation.

Negative Case Analysis

Negative case analysis is a useful analytical method when dealing with hypotheses. Lincoln and Guba (1985) called it the "process of revising hypotheses with hindsight" (p. 309), because this process begins after the data have been collected. The researcher looks for instances in the data where the hypothesis does not hold. When exceptions to the hypothesis are found, the research examines the characteristics of those cases and rewrites the hypothesis so that it excludes them. For example, we might start with a hypothesis that all television viewers change their opinion of the realism of televised violence after they see the warnings placed at the beginning of violent shows. We collect data from observations and interviews with 60 people and find this hypothesis to hold only with 40 of those people. We examine the 20 exceptions and discover that all 20 are children, whereas the remaining 40 are all over the age of 12 years. So we rewrite the hypothesis by limiting its application to the positive cases: Television viewers over the age of 12 change their opinion of the realism of televised violence after they see the warnings placed at the beginning of violent shows.

Retroduction

Turow (1984) used a method of retroduction, which is very similar to deduction. He explained that retroduction "is the activity of deductively applying ideas from certain bodies of knowledge and emerging frameworks to case studies and then inducing from findings of the case studies the extent to which (and the manner in which) the bodies of knowledge and emerging frameworks should be altered" (p. 71). He began with a belief that his starting point should be an explicit exposition of the relationships between organizations, resources, and power in order to build toward a many-leveled understanding of the production of mass media materials. He started with two theoretical perspectives of resource dependency approach (of Howard Aldrich) and the power role scheme (by George Gerbner). His book is then the fitting of data and insights into this scheme. Later, he (Turow, 1989) tested his scheme in examining TV doctor shows.

SUMMARY

There are many alternative methods of analysis available to qualitative researchers. Twenty of these methods of analysis were presented in four groupings: orienting methods, deductive methods of construction, inductive methods of construction, and other methods of construction (see Table 9.1 for the template of these methods of analysis). None of these methods is superior to the others in general. Methods are tools, and they acquire their value according to how useful they are in helping the researcher move from evidence to conclusions. Typically the methods are used in combinations so that the weaknesses of one can be balanced by the strengths of another.

TABLE 9.1

The Template for Methods of Analysis

Orienting Methods

---

1. Semiotics/semiology
2. Discourse analysis
3. Narrative analysis
4. Genre analysis
5. Dialogic analysis
6. Historical analysis

Construction Methods: Deductive

---

1. Marxist analysis
2. Feminist analysis
3. Psychoanalytical analysis
4. Postmodern analysis
5. Myth analysis
6. Hypothesis testing

Construction Methods: Inductive

---

1. Grounded theory
2. Triangulation
3. Maximizing comparisons
4. Sensitized concepts
5. Thick description

Other Methods of Construction

---

1. Analytical induction
2. Negative case analysis
3. Retroduction

10

WRITING PURPOSE

Scholars who undertake a qualitative research project have the goal of increasing our understanding about how humans construct and share meaning. When the project is finished, the scholar will share the findings in a research report, such as an article, book, monograph, and so forth. In writing the report, how much interpretation should be allowed—or required? On this matter, there is much debate (Strauss & Corbin, 1990). Several scholars have observed three alternatives to this issue: simple description, interpretation (focus on the emergence of concepts through data analysis), and explanation (theory building) (Burgess, 1984; Strauss & Corbin, 1990). To these three parts, I add criticism and action advocacy. Each of these five writing purposes is examined in the sections that follow. (See Table 10.1 for a synopsis of these purposes.)

DESCRIPTION

Qualitative research can be simply descriptive when its purpose is to preserve the form, content, and context of social phenomena and analyze their qualities, rather than separate them from historical and institutional surroundings (Lindlof, 1991). Description is evidenced when a scholar displays the facts of a situation in a relatively straightforward manner. Employing a journalistic form of analysis and reporting, these descriptions presume that the researcher can be objective and that facts can speak for themselves. In this view, facts are paramount; the writer is merely the objective (if he or she is properly trained) mechanism of gathering and assembling them.

We must acknowledge that interpretation cannot be removed from writing, even when the goal is description. Authors who attempt to achieve this descrip-

TABLE 10.1
Issues of Purpose and Standards of Quality

Issue: Purpose

Key Question: What is the author's view about the purpose of qualitative research?

Alternative Answers:
1. Description: The researcher is limited to describing occurrences without making any inferences.
2. Interpretation: The researcher moves beyond literal description and groups occurrences (of behaviors or textual elements) into patterns. These patterns are the researcher's interpretations; they are created to make sense or organize the individual points of data. In this interpretive process, the researcher develops contexts for interpretation.
3. Explanation: The researcher constructs general explanations about human behavior or cultural development. In this explanation, the researcher moves beyond the data to talk about more general patterns.
4. Criticism: The researcher develops a central, predominant judgment concerning the value of some media work or concerning the value of some controlling mechanism in society that determines the production and meaning of its messages. In the first case, the research usually follows the conventions of literary criticism; in the second case, an ideology is usually used to frame the arguments.
5. Action Advocacy: The researcher argues that there is a problem that needs a remedy; he or she advocates a course of action to remedy the identified problem.

tive goal must make decisions about the selection of facts and the sequencing of those facts in their presentations. This requires interpretation from the writer. But description-oriented writers would argue that the decisions they make, although personal, are not idiosyncratic. Using a rationalist perspective, they would argue that anyone shown the same mass of facts would make the same selections and would assemble those facts into essentially the same narrative structure. Thus they are saying that their interpretation is not special to them; they are simply describing the interpretation that anyone would have given access to the same information.

There is a good amount of support for this descriptive purpose among qualitative theoreticians (Bogdan & Taylor, 1975; Garfinkel, 1967; Hammersley & Atkinson, 1983; Lancy, 1993; Marshall & Rossman, 1989; Strauss & Corbin, 1990; Vidich & Lyman, 1994; Wolcott, 1990). For example, Wolcott argued that "description is the foundation upon which qualitative research is built. Unless you prove to be a gifted conceptualizer or interpreter, the descriptive account is likely to constitute the most important contribution you have to make" (pp. 27–28).

How can the descriptive purpose be achieved? Strauss and Corbin (1990) said that researchers should:

> gather the data and present them in such a manner that "the informants speak for themselves." The aim is to give an honest account with little or no interpretation of—or interference with—those spoken words or of the observations made by the

researcher. . . . The philosophical principle underlying this approach is that by presenting this faithful account, the researcher's biases and presence will not intrude upon the data. (p. 21)

Qualitative researchers who pursue the descriptive purpose must be careful not to inject their own thoughts into the writing. Garfinkel (1967) observed that people are often nonrational in their meaning making, and it is a mistake of the researcher to impose rationality on the data even though scientists are trained to look for rational explanations. Instead, researchers need to document the irrationality without making a value judgment about it and without exposing it as being irrational. Making value judgments destroys the descriptive nature of the research. Therefore the researcher's task within analysis and writing is description rather than the interpretation of observation. Lancy (1993) argued that the researcher must tell a story but at the same time remain descriptive. He said, "because of the enormous importance of description and context, as well as the growing importance of describing in very personal terms the researcher's history vis-à-vis this particular topic, the qualitative research report is written as a story" (p. 22).

Some theoreticians argue that description may include analysis. For example, qualitative researchers are not limited to describing broad social practices, but they can break those practices down into components through analysis and then describe those components. An example of this is when qualitative researchers focus on the models people use to guide their thoughts and actions. Christians and Carey (1989) asserted that the purpose of qualitative research is to analyze what those models are and thereby illuminate the categories we use to think. But the presentation style can still be descriptive, rather than interpretive or explanatory.

Also, according to Garfinkel (1967), the purpose is to discover the formal properties of commonplace, practical, commonsense actions from within actual settings. These tasks of highlighting categories and commonsense actions can be accomplished on a descriptive level if the researcher conveys them in the words of the subjects themselves. If, however, the researcher adds his or her interpretation to the words of the subjects, then the presentation moves beyond description to interpretation.

The qualitative research literature displays many examples of a descriptive purpose in the writing. In audience-focused research, Hobson (1982) interviewed viewers of the British television series "Crossroads" to find out why they watched and what they got out of the program. Her report is primarily descriptive as she reported the meanings articulated by the people she interviewed; she added very little interpretation to those meanings. In a later article, Hobson (1989) again stayed at a fairly descriptive level—presenting many passages of transcriptions of conversations with very little interpretation or analysis of them.

In institution-focused research, there are examples of writers acting like journalists (or who are journalists) and providing purely descriptive treatments of the media industries. For example, L. Brown (1971) is a journalist who applied his trade to looking at the business of television during 1970. Auletta (1991) focused on the actions of the three commercial TV networks in the later 1980s. Some of the journalistic descriptive pieces take an historical perspective; that is, a context is developed by either showing the reader the cultural forces of a different time or by showing how cultural influences change over time. For example, Barnouw (1975) told the story of the development of American broadcasting from the invention of photography in the late 1870s through 1975. Metz (1975) focused on CBS from its beginning to the mid-1970s.

INTERPRETATION

Many qualitative theoreticians argue that description is not a purpose of the qualitative approach, that no writer can ever seriously believe that the facts speak for themselves. Facts are not objective, enduring truths that are discovered by writers and recognized uniformly by readers. Instead, all writers have an interpretive stance from which they select and weigh observations to construct their own narratives.

Interpretation places the focus of qualitative research on illuminating a series of subjective decisions made about the phenomenon of interest from the particular scholar's point of view. Rather than hiding the decision-making process, researchers foreground it so that readers can understand the process and use it as a context for understanding the scholarship.

Interpretation differs from description in several important ways. First, interpretation reveals a self-consciousness by authors who acknowledge that their findings are not objective facts but rather products of his or her subjective decisions. In this self-reflexive posture, an author may, for instance, relate to the problems and limitations of the data gathering. Another important feature of interpretive writing is the careful and detailed illumination of the contexts of the observations and conclusions so that the reader can see the basis for the subjective decisions the researcher made in moving through the research process. Third, interpretive scholars operate from a perspective of *verstehen,* which directs them to become sensitive to the meaning that others (not the researcher) ascribe to their social situations and activities. In short, the interpretive research report interweaves the researcher's interpretive decisions with elements about the phenomenon itself.

Many theoreticians argue for interpretation as the primary purpose of qualitative research (J. A. Anderson, 1987; Christians & Carey, 1989; Jankowski & Wester, 1991; Jensen, 1991a; Lindlof & Meyer, 1987; Pauly, 1991; J. K. Smith, 1983; Strauss & Corbin, 1990). For example, Jankowski and Wester insist that the qualitative researcher's purpose is primarily to reconstruct, through interpretation, the perspective of the acts in naturalistic situations. "First among the fundamental concepts of qualitative research is the axiom that the study of human life is an interpretive science" (J. A. Anderson, 1987, p. 244).

How does a researcher achieve the purpose of interpretation? Strauss and Corbin (1990) focused on the decision-making process. They pointed out that researchers cannot present all their data, so they must decide how to screen, reduce, and order their materials for selection and interpretation. In their view, interpretation is inherent in the writing process as researchers "typically intersperse their own interpretive comments in and around long descriptive passages and the quotations from interview fieldnotes" (p. 22). For Christians and Carey (1989), the key to interpretation is context, because the meaning of actions can only been interpreted in the "linkages among various units on a broader scale" (p. 363) such as cultural and historical contexts. For J. A. Anderson (1987), the key to interpretation is in the interactions between the analyst and the observational text; vary the text or the analyst, and the interpretation will vary.

Some qualitative scholars see the task of interpretation as akin to moving into a scientific form of explanation. Although Lindlof and Meyer (1987) saw qualitative research primarily in the interpretive mode, they also included inference as part of interpretation, because the task of interpretive research is not simply the "re-creations of the actors' subjective constructions" (p. 5). They also argued that the products of the research are not "exempt from the rules of inference traditionally employed by the social sciences" (p. 5).

There are many examples of an interpretive purpose in the qualitative research literature. In text-focused research, the most popular perspective is the interpretive one. For example, Newcomb (1988) conveyed his personal interpretation in his "reading" of television shows and argued that programs can be interpreted in a variety of ways. In an article of almost pure interpretation with very little factual support or scholarly acknowledgment, Horowitz (1987) selected a few sitcoms to fit her interpretation that sitcoms are losing viewership and must adapt in order to survive. And Rowland (1983) examined the relationship between the media research community and policymakers concerned with violence on television. His interpretation of the events over several decades characterizes the social science research as sterile and unresponsive to the debate over violence on television; he also characterized politicians as being more interested in appearing to do something about a social problem than in actually doing anything.

In audience-focused writings, Morley (1980) interpreted the data from his focus groups to show that there is a range of decodings (dominant, oppositional, and negotiated) and that this follows demographic and cultural identity lines, but still affords individuals the freedom for their own interpretations. Morley's scheme is an interpretive one, but his presentation of evidence is very descriptive as he presented lists of direct quotes from those he interviewed. Also, Rogge (1989) conducted a reception study focusing on how German families use media in their everyday lives. She said her purpose was "to subject linguistic utterances and observed behavior to interpretation in order to arrive at general statements about the structures of everyday behavior" (p. 174).

In institutional research, Altheide (1976) developed his news perspective construct, then interpreted a wide variety of behaviors in the newsroom according to this perspective. Because of the development of his news perspective construct, it is more than simple description. The focus is on the patterns organized around the news perspective rather than on the actual happenings in the newsroom. Turow (1984) developed an interpretive framework built from the theoretical perspectives of the resource dependency approach (of Howard Aldrich) and the power role scheme (by George Gerbner).

Historical scholarship can also be interpretation, especially when it is revisionist, that is where a scholar seeks to reinterpret an event and thus alter the commonly held version of the event. For example, Baughman (1990) argued that the belief that the film industry was at first antagonistic toward television is not an accurate reading of the evidence. He traced ABC's rise to prominence in the early 1950s and showed that this was made possible with the help of film production companies. And Bodroghkozy (1992) examined the controversy surrounding the television show "Julia." She accessed a set of data that was 24 years old when she began analyzing it (letters viewers of the show wrote to the producers). To this she added a historical context that was richer because of the passage of time, thus allowing her to show long-term patterns of television programming and more clearly present a fairly good historical context for understanding the social and political forces in existence in 1968.

EXPLANATION

Some theoreticians think that qualitative research can serve an explanatory purpose. For Christians and Carey (1989), the aim of qualitative studies is a "well rounded and parsimonious explanation" (p. 354) about the underlying regularities in the natural structure of the social world. They argued for placing some, but not all, qualitative research within science. They said the purpose of qualitative research is to study the creative process of humans making meaning, which is the central focus of any social science. They cautioned that social science is not objective but an active intervention in social life that can be studied in a scientific, systematic manner leading to explanations. Bogdan and Taylor (1975) argued for explanation as qualitative research's purpose by placing some qualitative research within the scientific tradition.

Some theoreticians make a distinction between short-term and long-term explanation. For example, Bogdan and Taylor (1975) acknowledged that the purpose of a qualitative report is for the researcher to present his or her writing as an interpretation, because each researcher's perspective is different. But over time when multiple reports are available, true explanation will arrive. "Truth then emerges not as one objective view but rather as the composite picture of how people think about the institution and each other" (p. 11). In short, individual research reports are interpretive, but the overall purpose of the field is explanation, which can be achieved through the accumulation of individual interpretive reports.

The idea of explanation suggests theory, and many qualitative theoreticians argue strongly for the building of theory (Jankowski & Wester, 1991; Lancy, 1993; Strauss & Corbin, 1990). But theory within the qualitative approach is different from the formal scientific theories that are built and tested in the quantitative approach. According to Strauss and Corbin, qualitative theory "is discovered, developed, and provisionally verified through systematic data collection and analysis of data pertaining to that phenomenon.... Therefore, data collection, analysis, and theory stand in reciprocal relationship with each other. One does not begin with theory, then prove it. Rather, one begins with an area of study and what is relevant to that area is allowed to emerge" (p. 23). Lindlof and Meyer (1987) argued that theory might be a typology, such as emic and etic. An emic typology tries to represent natural categories of the native's point of view and relies on the natural language of the people being studied. In contrast, the etic typology relies on observations of the investigator who is trying to build structural, cross-cultural explanations of systems of objective behavior. The emerging categories are entirely those of the researcher (e.g., Piaget).

In contrast to the position supporting explanation as a purpose, some theoreticians argue vigorously that qualitative research can never be explanatory. For example, J. A. Anderson (1987) asserted that qualitative research can never provide explanation, because meaning making is dynamic and changeable across humans and even across time within a human; meaning making is also complex, idiosyncratic—so beyond the normal rational ability of a researcher to find consistent or systematic explanations for it, that it is possible to construct explanations only for individual behaviors within particular narrow contexts, not for classes of behaviors. J. K. Smith (1983) said the purpose is not to search for a series of overarching causal laws, because of the complexity of the social world, changes over time, and cultural differences. And, according to Pauly (1991), qualitative research cannot fulfill an explanatory purpose even in the long run, because it is not progressive; no one set of findings is better than any other, and therefore there is no need for newer research to build on and advance the thinking in earlier research. He argued that qualitative researchers should not seek causal explanations, operationalize, or use hypothetical statements. He said, "Qualitative research hopes only to arrange a forum in which different styles of imagination can meet and debate" unlike quantitative research, which "hopes to rewrite others' results into a single theoretical tale" (p. 8).

The qualitative literature includes some examples of writing exhibiting an explanatory purpose. For example, Chesebro (1978) developed an analytical scheme to classify TV shows then categorized them; this is bordering on social science. Barker (1987) sought to explain "the relationship between narrative structure and production techniques, as it is manifested in entertainment television" (p. 179). His explanation focuses on how different television shows have different ways of encoding (using camera space and performer space) their narratives.

Within audience-focused research, there are many examples of studies using an explanation purpose when analyzing audience behavior (Barrios, 1988; Liebes & Katz, 1988, 1989; Lull, 1980; Pardun & Krugman, 1994; Traudt & Lont, 1987; Wolf, 1987). For example, Liebes and Katz appear to follow scientific conventions in attempting to develop an analytical scheme to explain viewers' differing reactions to "Dallas."

The grounded theory technique is a clear signal of an author's desire to provide an explanation. Lull (1980) conducted a process of grounded theory in developing a typology for the social uses of television. This typology was composed of two major components: structural and relational. The structural component included environmental use (background noise, companionship, and entertainment) and regulative use (punctuation of time and activity and talk patterns). The relational component had four subcomponents of communication facilitation (agenda for talk, experience illustration), affiliation/avoidance (relationship maintenance, family solidarity), social learning (behavior modeling, legitimazation, substitute schooling), and competence/dominance (role reinforcement, argument facilitation). Pardun and Krugman (1994) took a grounded theory approach as they built toward an overarching core concept that families regard the TV either as a magnet or as a retreat. Families who live in transitional-style homes treat the TV as a common hearth for family gatherings. In contrast, families who live in traditional-style homes treat the TV as a retreat; that is, individuals use the TV to get away from the family.

Several studies sought to apply the explanatory schemes of other scholars. For example, Traudt and Lont (1987) wanted to explain how people make sense out of television by using the media logic propositions laid out by Altheide and Snow (1979) and to provide support through an empirical test. Also, Wolf (1987) provided an explanation about how children negotiate television. She drew from previous schemes, especially the work of Applebee, which lays out the conventions children use in making sense of fictional narratives (story frameworks, theme, fantasy/reality, and ways of constructing reactions to stories).

Several institution-focused scholars appear to move beyond interpretation and into explanation (Altheide, 1979, 1985; Jowett & Linton, 1980; Litman, 1990; Turow, 1989). For example, Altheide (1985) appears to be interpretive but his purpose is more in line with social science when he said "my goal, then, is to suggest some features of the major media that transcend specific content . . . so I will use mass media information and procedures to make some theoretical points about another approach to understanding communication" and "I believe that it is important for social science to have a perspective on communication that transcends political and ideological inputs; we want to know what is more basic, perhaps even invariant, to the look, form, and process of communication in our lives" (p. 12). Turow used his interpretive scheme, which he developed in an earlier writing (Turow, 1984), to explain how production decisions are made on TV doctor shows.

CRITICISM

A writer focusing on criticism will foreground value judgments. Scholars pursuing a purpose of interpretation also make judgments, but those judgments are less a focus of the research than they are a means to decide what evidence gets collected, how the observations get weighted in the analysis, and how the conclusions get presented. With criticism as a purpose, the development of a central, predominant judgment is the focus. The judgment can be about the value of some media work or it can be about the value of some controlling mechanism in society that determines the production and meaning of its messages.

Although all qualitative research should exhibit self-reflexivity, this is especially important with criticism, as Ang (1989) argued. This self-reflexive perspective is demonstrated by scholars when they show they are conscious of the social, discursive, and political nature of any research practice. With every decision in the research process, scholars need to reflect on the ways in which their research contributes to our understanding of the world.

Criticism has its foundation in two traditions: literary criticism and the structuralist linguistics or semiotics that developed out of it. Within these two traditions, four assumptions underlie current critical work in media studies. First, the media are believed to be one of a number of complex sign systems through which we experience and come to know the world. Second, the focus is not on an independent piece of work (one TV show or one scene), but on the symbolic structures and the systems of relationships among those symbols that create meaning. Third, the traditional notion of author or artist as the source of meaning is changed, because the mass media involve so many people in the production of messages. And fourth, no particular representation of reality is recognized as being shared, because programs are products of people's imagination and also because words acquire meaning by virtue of their positions with a conceptual system of similarity and difference.

These four broad assumptions support a wide range of scholarly activity. Several scholars have provided organizational schemes to identify the types of critical purposes in media studies. For example, Curran, Gurevitch, and Woollacott (1982) observed three types: cultural studies, political economy, and structuralist textual analysis, which draws from semiotics, linguistics, psychanalysis, and anthropology. Becker (1985) posited four types: rhetorical or literary examinations of media texts; cultural studies; evaluation of media practices compared against social, political, or economic change; and examinations of the political economy institutional infrastructures of media and information in a capitalistic society. Seiter et al. (1989b) pointed to four bases of criticism in media studies: literary criticism, ideology, opposition to science, and taking a moral stance against the media. In this view, a variety of definitions for the term *critical* are offered. First, critical "may simply mean pertaining to the practice of criticism" (p. 6) by professional critics who "produce textual analyses of the media from a vantage point of high culture, especially literary theory" (p. 6). Second, critical refers to the work emanating from "the Frankfurt School tradition by combining psychoanalytic and Marxist theories into a broad social critique" (p. 6). Third, and more contemporary, critical "refers broadly to those philosophical traditions which mistrust empiricism and positivism and insist on the relationship between knowledge and power" (p. 6).

After analyzing the typologies of critical studies, Real (1986) concluded that it is simplest to use a two-part division as follows: (a) political-economic critical research, and (b) philosophical-epistemological research. The first is conducted by political economists engaged in uncovering the size, organization, and influence of current media monopolies and cartels on the level of tangible historical and economic data; political economists critique the role of transnational and domestic institutions as communication infrastructures and as manufacturers of public consciousness. In contrast, the second type of research is conducted by intellectual historians, philosophers, and epistemologists who scrutinize the ideological and theoretical implications of communication—a group that goes by the name of cultural studies, which is not the same as critical studies. Cultural studies is an umbrella term for an innovative and powerful form of critical theory (Real, 1986). Its primary proponents are Carey and Hall, who argued against the limitations of conventional research, claiming it is too reductionistic, narrow, and epistemologically naive.

Synthesizing across the ideas just presented, it appears that the most significant difference is reflected in the division between ideologically based critical work and critical work that follows a literary form. There are other important differences but these other differences are subordinate to the ideological-literary one. This is illustrated in the next sections.

Types of Ideological Criticism

Ideological criticism is a form of analysis in which the scholar begins with an a priori ideology. The purpose of the research is to gather and present data to support this position and to persuade the reader that some form of action is required.

Within the field of communication, ideologically based research has been characterized as "public communication in reference to economic and political forces and the exercise of power, with attention given to social, historical and ideological contexts" (Real, 1986, p. 460). There is also a "skeptical scrutiny of concentrations of power and a willingness to consider change and alternatives" (Real, 1986, p. 460). It has been defined in opposition to what has been called "administrative" research, which is a view of research that is "carefully delimited experimental behaviorism which examines variables and relationships isolated from context" (Real, 1986, p. 461).

Morley (1981) expanded the idea of ideology: "Ideology is not a collection of discrete falsehoods, but a matrix of thought firmly grounded in the forms of our social life and organised within a set of interdependent categories, which constitute a network of established 'given' meanings embedded in the 'assignment' of events to the 'relevant' contexts within these pre-established cultural 'maps of meaning' " (p. 371).

There are four major types of ideologically based, critical scholarship in communication studies: Marxism, feminism, psychoanalysis, and postmodernism (see chapter 9 for their definitions).

Types of Literary Criticism

The literary critic applies artistic or aesthetic perspectives or standards to some object, such as a book, a film, a television commercial, a genre, a speech, and so on. His or her purpose is to make judgments about the object's quality. Carey (1977) extended this idea by saying that the critic has a ritualistic function of showing the "representation of shared beliefs" (p. 412).

It is very important to make a clear distinction between traditional forms of criticism and a current approach that goes by many names such as *contemporary criticism* or *critical studies*. Traditional criticism, as Vande Berg and Wenner (1991) pointed out, conceives of its object of study as a unified "work." In contrast, contemporary criticism takes as its object of study the text, that is, the site of intersection for a complex web of codes and conventions. Traditional criticism looks to great art to reveal enduring truths about the world; contemporary criticism considers the worlds constructed within texts. Traditional criticism is artist centered; contemporary criticism foregrounds the contexts within which authorship occurs and the forces that circumscribe it. Traditional criticism conceives of meaning as a property of an artwork; contemporary criticism views meaning as the product of the engagement of a text by a reader or by groups of readers. Traditional criticism functions to establish a work's meaning, to arbitrate tastes and artistic standards, and to erect a hierarchy of greatness among works. Contemporary criticism examines the criteria by which those in a position to define literature make such determinations and expands the scope of literary studies to include both "nonliterature" and critical discourse about texts. In summary, contemporary criticism is a set of approaches that share the same assumptions, but differ in terms of (a) the goals of criticism, (b) the critic's role in that project, (c) the nature of the thing criticism hopes to illuminate, and (d) the kind of knowledge that might be produced by the critical act.

Examples of Criticism

With the critical approach, the author argues that there is a problem with the media. Here a distinction is made between critical and action oriented. Criticism focuses on or foregrounds a problem; action orientation calls for a particular solution. Bird and Dardenne (1988) provided a critical interpretation of television news, saying that journalists can never be objective despite the fact that journalists argue that they are. In this essay the problem is the focus. The authors provided no particular solution to the problem, thus leaving the reader with the feeling that the identification of the problem is enough to inform news viewers to beware.

Criticism usually follows an ideological perspective held by the author, such as feminism (Ang, 1985; Radway, 1984; Rakow, 1992; Seiter et al., 1989a) or a psychoanalytical perspective (Rogge & Jensen, 1988). Although critical, these studies do not go so far as to call for specific changes. For example, Haralovich (1992) criticized 1950s sitcoms, especially "Father Knows Best" and "Leave it to Beaver," from a feminist perspective. This is evident in a sentence such as "By defining access to property and home ownership within the values of the conventionalized suburban family, women and minorities were guaranteed economic and social inequality" (p. 112). Lipsitz (1992) provided a Marxist analysis when he said that the producers of working-class situation comedies in the 1950s "evoked the experiences of the past to lend legitimacy to the dominant ideology of the present" (pp. 72–73). Gandy (1982) argued from a political economy perspective that government decisions are politically grounded and result in economic consequences, such as a widening of the information gap.

Often when an ideology is at the base of the interpretation, its effect is subtle. For example, Mann (1992) examined 1950s variety shows, but did not use an overly ideological approach, although at the very end of her article she said, "these television tributes to Hollywood served both the interests of the network hegemony and consumer culture by diverting viewer skepticism away from the anonymous corporate institutions" (p. 64). Also, Lipsitz (1992) interpreted 1950s working-class sitcoms in terms of the economic, political, and cultural environment of the time. He used a capitalistic ideology to explain the reason for the content and portrayals in those programs. Despite the ideology, he was not overtly critical and did not call for any direct change. On the last page, he presented a perspective that knowledge can free us from our pain of ignorance— which in a way is a criticism of what television has done to the society and a call for change in the minds of readers.

Other critical scholars do not use a clearly identified ideology, but there is a clear point of view from which the criticism is made. For example, Bagdikian (1972) criticized press coverage, and Barnouw (1978) criticized broadcast advertising.

ACTION ADVOCACY

Some theoreticians see the purpose of the qualitative approach as not merely criticism. For them it is not sufficient to articulate value judgments about what is wrong with media and the meanings they impose. Instead, these scholars employ criticism to develop an awareness of a societal problem, but they also advocate social change to resolve the problem. It is one thing to write an essay condemning action/adventure programs on television as being inferior works of art, but to write an essay calling for the elimination of this genre from television is an argument for doing something specific to resolve the problem. In the first case, the author is making a value judgment about the degree to which entertainment genres live up to artistic standards. In the second case, the author is advocating a particular change in the way the media present their fare.

The action-oriented purpose is especially popular with those scholars using a Marxist or feminist ideology. However, this is not to say that the use of one of these ideologies automatically translates into action advocacy. For example, a feminist might focus on criticism without ever advocating specific changes. Action advocacy is implied in all of criticism, but many critical scholars do not bring that implication to the surface by recommending specific changes.

Some qualitative theoreticians are uncomfortable with action advocacy. Bogdan and Taylor (1975) argued that qualitative research should not go beyond description to the point of calling for some sort of action. They said "the researcher seeks not truth and morality, but rather, understanding" (p. 9). Also, it is clear that Pauly (1991) eschewed action advocacy when he asserted, "The purpose of qualitative research is not to control others' behavior with our bromides . . . nor to rev the engines of public opinion, but simply to know our cultural habitat" (p. 23).

In text-focused research, a few scholars exhibit an action advocacy purpose, mainly from an ideological critical approach such as Marxism or feminism. For example, Schwichtenberg (1987) was critical in her analysis of the "Love Boat." According to her, the show presents an ideology *a la* Althusser where ideology is defined as "a system of representations such as images, myths, ideas or concepts which represent the imaginary relationship of individuals to their real conditions or existence" (p. 139) and she called for action—sink the boat. Also, Esslin (1987) looked at TV ads in terms of dramatic structure and myth. On the last page he hoped for "a more rational regulation" of ads from viewers who are more literate about the structure of those ads. He argued that if ads were placed between shows rather than within shows, the programs might ascend to "a higher intellectual, artistic, and moral level" and the ads might then also increase their "own level of intelligence and rationality" (p. 317). Himmelstein (1984) used a critical perspective from a literary, not ideological manner. He argued for the demythologization of television in his analysis of eight types of programming.

Several institution-focused studies present an argument for a solution to the problem being criticized. Mander (1978) argued for the total elimination of television. Bagdikian (1987) called for regulation of the media to prevent concentration of power that comes from cross-ownership. Schiller (1989) called for some changes in the way corporations deal with mass media. Dates and Barlow (1990) used an ethnic-based ideology in analyzing the media and called for a change in the way African Americans are treated by the industry.

Several scholars argue that there is a problem with the way scholarship is conducted. They present their view to bring about a solution. For example, Ang (1991) criticized the industry's emphasis on decontextualized quantitative data and recommended ethnographic work instead. Collins (1989) was critical of critical scholarship that relies on the concepts of "mass culture" and "dominance." He argued for a postmodern interpretation that regards culture as a complex of conflictive power relations, not just one. Kellner (1987) was also critical of some critical scholarship. He argued that there is not one dominant ideology, but that "hegemonic ideology is saturated with contradictions" and that "Many radical theories of ideology have neglected the role of mass-media images and messages in the production and transmission of ideology" (p. 471). Also, Browne (1987) criticized the use of an aesthetic analysis of television texts; instead, he said, the megatext of television should only be analyzed from a political economic point of view. And Corcoran (1987) argued against the use of both positivist and film criticism approaches to analyzing television.

CONCLUSIONS

There are five basic purposes that qualitative researchers can exhibit when writing up their reports: description, interpretation, explanation, criticism, and action advocacy. Authors almost always exhibit more than one of these types in their writing, but there is usually one that predominates and indicates to the reader the researcher's primary purpose in writing the report. Scholars who have strongly held ideologies will likely exhibit criticism and action advocacy. In contrast, journalists and researchers with a more scientific perspective will favor description and explanation. The purpose of interpretation is most likely the mainstream purpose of qualitative writing. Interpretation is a part of all aspects of qualitative research; however, when we talk about interpretation as a purpose signaled in the writing, we expect to see a high degree of self-reflexivity where the author illuminates the decision points in the interpretive process.

This is an area where the practices of the quantitative researchers clearly diverge from the practices of the qualitative researchers. A major characteristic of the quantitative approach is that of progression from specific observations to general patterns as well as a progression from a base of what is known to a useful contribution. Therefore, quantitative researchers place a premium on explanation, and their exposition is very formulaic to build on recognizable research traditions. In this sense, quantitative research can be viewed as a vertical movement from specifics to abstract explanations. In contrast, the qualitative approach is much more horizontal—that is, a premium is placed on examining a wider range of meaning making and the exceptions to the norm. Therefore, qualitative researchers require a wider range of expressive tools in order to help them capture the greater variety in the phenomenon and to communicate this in such a way as to make it interesting and useful to the readers.

11

ISSUES OF WRITING

How do qualitative researchers go about writing up their research? This chapter presents four issues that authors must confront in the writing process: form of expression, locus of argument, contextualization, and degree of self-reflexivity.

Before we get into these four issues, it must be made clear that although writing might seem like a task separate from the other tasks (such as data gathering and analysis) in the qualitative research process, it is not. Richardson (1990) considered writing itself as a method of inquiry:

> . . . a way of finding out about yourself and your topic. Although we usually think about writing as a mode of "telling" about the social world, writing is not just a mopping-up activity at the end of a research project. Writing is also a way of "knowing"—a method of discovery and analysis. By writing in different ways, we discover new aspects of our topic and our relationship to it. Form and content are inseparable. (p. 516)

The presentation of the topics of form of expression, locus of argument, contextualization, and degree of self-reflexivity in this chapter on writing is not meant to imply that these four begin only after all the analysis is finished. To the contrary all of these (especially the later two) might arguably be presented in one of the previous chapters on analysis. The reason they are grouped together and presented in a chapter on writing is because they illuminate the essential decisions a researcher must make when he or she shifts into the author mode, regardless of whether that shift is made once at the end of the analysis or whether it is made repeatedly while working on other tasks throughout the qualitative research process. (For a template of analysis issues, see Table 11.1.)

TABLE 11.1
The Template for Analysis Issues

Issue 1: Form of Expression

Key Question: What does the researcher use as a form of expression?

Alternative Answers:
(1) Interpretive realist tale: The author exhibits interpretive omnipotence, which is a no-nonsense manner of presenting representations and accounts as the final word about how the culture is to be interpreted.
(2) Mainstream realist tale: Using a journalistic style, the author tries to stay out of the way and let the multiple voices of the subjects speak for themselves.
(3) Critical tale: The author shows a problem and argues for a particular solution.
(4) Confessional tale: The focus is far more on the researcher than on the culture studied. This tale uses the first person where events are presented intimately from the fieldworker's point of view, and mistakes are related as well as successes.
(5) Literary tale: A novelist's sense of narration brings alive the culture in its concrete characterizations and dramatic tension in the flow of events. The author is trying to show what happened rather than tell about it.

Issue 2: Locus of Argument

Key Question: Where does the researcher place the locus of his or her argument?

Alternative Answers:
(1) Ethos: The authority or expertise of the author/researcher. ("You should believe these findings because I say so.")
(2) Logos: The logic of the argument or presentation. The focus is on structuring the facts in an orderly manner to convince the reader that this interpretation is the best explanation. There is the use of logic, if–then statements, syllogisms, and so on.
(3) Evidence: The focus is on the facts themselves. ("Look: The instances speak for themselves; I just need to show you what I saw.")
(4) Pathos: The presentation is designed to appeal primarily to the emotions, especially anger. ("The cultural elite are very selfish and this is causing problems that you should be upset about.") These articles have the feel of a sermon or lecture of a parent to a child (designed to make us feel guilty, angry, etc., and want to do something to change).

Issue 3: Contextualization

Key Question: To what extent does the researcher contextualize the evidence?

Alternative Answers:
(1) Strong contextualization: Authors provide a great deal of description of the context of the phenomenon about which they are writing; this context is then illuminated as the basis for their interpretations of meaning.
(2) Low degree of contextualization: Authors provide some description of contexts, however there are some obvious contexts ignored or the author's interpretations/conclusions are not well grounded in the descriptions of context provided.
(3) No contextualization.

(Continued)

TABLE 11.1
(Continued)

Issue 4: Self-Reflexivity

Key Question:

Alternative Answers:
(1) None: The author presents no self-reflexivity. This would be characterized by no disclosure about the decisions he or she made.
(2) Low level of self-reflexivity: The author describes some of the basic decisions such as selection of some evidence or the shortcomings of the data.
(3) High level of self-reflexivity: The author opens up the whole process of decision making for view by the reader. The author presents shortcomings and second thoughts.

FORM OF EXPRESSION

Although qualitative researchers spend a great deal of time and effort writing field notes and making tapes, the notes and tapes do not constitute the findings. "Rather, as part of our research agenda, we fashion these accounts into a prose piece; we transform biographical interviews and fieldnotes into a sociological text. Although this stage of the research process requires complex decision-making, there is little in the literature about the issues and their resolutions" (Richardson, 1990, p. 116).

What are the options for presenting the information? Hammersley and Atkinson (1983) suggested some alternatives. One way is to write the natural history of the research project. A second way is the chronology, that is, to follow the developmental cycle of the organization or the moral career of the individuals. Third is to use an hourglass image: beginning with general statements, then gradually narrowing the focus to individual events, and finally moving back to general statements. Fourth is to separate narration and analysis; this allows the data to speak for themselves unencumbered by the author; later the author interprets the data. A fifth form of presentation is thematic organization in which each part of the typology is dealt with in order.

But writing a research report is more than just presenting the information. Richardson (1994) criticized much of the qualitative writing as being boring, because many qualitative writers attempt to emulate a scientific form of presentation that "requires writers to silence their own voices and to view themselves as contaminants" (p. 517). She suggested that qualitative researchers write narratives, because the narrative form "displays the goals and intentions of human actors; it makes individuals, cultures, societies, and historical epochs comprehensible as wholes; it humanizes time; and it allows us to contemplate the effects of our actions, and to alter the directions of our lives" (Richardson, 1990, p. 117). Denzin (1994) amplified this point by urging qualitative researchers to write vital texts, because "a vital text is not boring. It grips the reader (and the writer). A vital text invites readers to engage the author's subject matter"

(p. 504). To accomplish this vitality, Denzin called for thick description. Other techniques can also contribute to vital texts, techniques such as metaphor, figurative allusions, semantic devices, decorative phrasing, plain speaking, and varying the textual organization (Van Maanen, 1988).

What writing style should be used? Pauly (1991) said qualitative researchers should tell their stories in a literary style. Christians and Carey (1989) called for a poetic style to capture the resonance of native interpretation.

The most extensive treatment of writing style for qualitative researchers was developed by Van Maanen (1988), who suggested that qualitative researchers should remember they are telling a tale, especially realist, confessional, and impressionistic tales. The realist tale is told from the point of view of the subjects of the study, who "provide a rather direct, matter-of-fact portrait of a studied culture, unclouded by much concern for how the fieldworker produced such a portrait" (p. 7). This is "by far the most prominent, familiar, prevalent, popular, and recognized form of ethnographic writing" (p. 45). The four important characteristics of the realist tale are: experiential authority (complete absence of the author from the text), typical forms (documentary style focusing on minute details of everyday life), native's point of view, and interpretive omnipotence (no-nonsense manner of presenting representations and accounts as the final word about how the culture is to be interpreted). The confessional tale focuses more on the researcher than on the culture studied. This tale is determined by three characteristics: personalized authority (first-person intimacy conveying war stories), fieldworker's point of view (the fieldworker shows how his or her perceptions changed as he or she moved from an outsider to a native), and naturalness (the researcher admits that there are flaws and limitations, but he or she concludes that he or she "got it right"). The impressionist tale is a personalized account of fleeting moments of fieldwork cast in dramatic form. There are four characteristics of impressionist tales: textual identity (transparency and concreteness give the tale a power to appeal to readers who must make their own interpretations), fragmented knowledge (reads like a novel with its unfolding of event by event), characterization (the fieldworker becomes a feeling character in the tale), and dramatic control (artistic nerve is required to build tension in the narrative; literary conventions are followed over scientific ones).

There are also four other less used types of tales: critical (social structures as seen through the eyes of disadvantaged groups from economic, political, or symbolic means), formal (focus on building theory such as is done with ethnomethodology, semiotics, symbolic interactionism, and conversational analysis), literary (mainly journalists with a novelist's sense of narration), and jointly told tales (the fieldworker and a native write a dialogue together) (Van Maanen, 1988).

In his experience with qualitative writing, Denzin (1994) observed that it is mainly realistic, and that there are three forms of realism: mainstream, interpretive, and descriptive. He characterized mainstream realist writing as single-voiced, objective accounts of events, persons, and experiences conveyed through thin and thick description. Realist writers use "experience-distance concepts," which appear to be hypothetical constructs (such as kinship structure, TV viewing habits) developed to explain the human behavior. Interpretive realist texts are those in which the author inserts his or her personal interpretations. Descriptive realist texts, journalistic in nature, are those in which the author tries to stay out of the way and let the multiple voices of the subjects speak for themselves.

My own reading of the qualitative literature leads me to agree with Denzin (1994); almost all of the literature is realistic, especially interpretive realistic. However, there are some examples of the more interesting styles suggested by Van Maanen (1988).

The Interpretive Realist Tale

The most popular form of realist tale is the interpretive one among audience-focused research (Ang, 1985; Bodroghkozy, 1992; Hobson, 1982, 1989; Hoover, 1988; Liebes & Katz, 1988, 1989; Lull, 1980; Radway, 1984; Rogge, 1989; Rogge & Jensen, 1988; Seiter et al., 1989a; Traudt & Lont, 1987; Tulloch, 1989), institution-focused research (Allen, 1985; Bagdikian, 1972; Baughman, 1990; Berman, 1981; Bernhard, 1993; Collins, 1989; Douglas, 1993; Ewen & Ewen, 1992; Gandy, 1982; Gitlin, 1983; McChesney, 1993; Pauly, 1988; Reeves, 1988; Spigel, 1992, 1993; Wajcman, 1991), and text-focused research (C. Anderson, 1987; Flitterman-Lewis, 1992; Joyrich, 1992; Newcomb, 1988; Schulze, 1990).

In the interpretive realist tale, the author assumes a kind of interpretive omnipotence. The omnipotence is apparent in the practice of authors not citing other interpretations that conflict with their own. An example of this is C. Anderson (1987), who began his essay with a highly personal statement that leaves the reader feeling that he is sharing his opinion in a burst of excited self-disclosure: "One of the great achievements of twentieth-century culture beams into our living rooms every Thursday night. Offered to us by the only household appliance that really cares about Western civilization, it has insinuated itself into the fabric of American society with a subtlety that would confound Iago. And Karl Marx. And Ronald Reagan. Its name is *Magnum, P.I.*" (p. 112). There are few citations of scholarly work, and there is no acknowledgment of other published opinions on the show. Likewise Flitterman-Lewis (1992) provided her personal interpretation of some events in soap operas; she included very few citations of scholarly foundation pieces and she never acknowledged the possibility of other interpretations.

Mainstream Realist Tale

The mainstream realist tale is a research report primarily concerned with presenting conclusions and building theory such as is done with ethnomethodology, semiotics, symbolic interactionism, and conversational analysis. There are many examples among institution-focused research (Altheide, 1985; Altheide & Snow, 1979; Altschull, 1984; Browne, 1987; Cantor, 1980; Gitlin, 1987; Innis, 1950; Jowett & Linton, 1980; Snow, 1983; Turow, 1978, 1984, 1989).

In audience-focused research, a mainstream realist tale was exhibited by Jhally and Lewis (1992) and Wolf (1987). For example, the study by Wolf in some ways exhibited the characteristics of a social science study with its attention to conveying lots of information about methods and its structure of presentation. This made the article seem rather like a mainstream realist tale, but still there were more elements that made it seem like an interpretive realist tale.

In text-based research, the mainstream realist tale is approximated by Deming (1992), who argued that there are many ways to read "Kate and Allie." She did not say which one way is best or which way she chose to read it. Instead, her purpose is to demonstrate to the reader what that range is. Other examples include the work of Mann (1992) and Rowland (1983). In some of these writings, the authors seek to build theory (Barker, 1987; Chesebro, 1988). All of these examples "approximate" the mainstream realist tale, which is the primary mode of expression with quantitative research.

Critical Tale

The critical tale is a style of presentation where the author points out a problem and argues for some change. It is frequently used in institutional research (Ang, 1991; Bagdikian, 1972, 1987; Barnouw, 1978; Corcoran, 1987; Dates & Barlow, 1990; Kellner, 1987; Mander, 1978; Meehen, 1993; Parenti, 1986; Schiller, 1989). However, in text-based research, there are no examples of the critical tale as indicated when the author clearly articulates a problem then argues for a particular solution. But when we look for more subtle articulation of problems and solutions, we can see that there are several examples of the critical tale. Several authors begin with a clear position that is counter to conventional wisdom or practices and seek to inform readers about the validity of their position (D'Acci, 1992; Himmelstein, 1984; Lipsitz, 1992). Schwichtenberg (1987) was also critical but from a literary, not ideological, stance.

Confessional Tale

The confessional tale tells the story about how the researcher made observations and saw patterns in the field. There are some good examples of the confessional tale in institution-focused research (Altheide, 1976; Elliott, 1979; Fishman, 1988; Gitlin, 1980, 1983; Tuchman, 1978). In audience-focused research, Rakow (1992) presented some elements of a confessional tale. In her ethnomethodology about how various women in a small town make meaning of the telephone in their everyday lives, she had an opportunity to focus attention on herself in the research process. However, Rakow kept the focus on the women she was studying, with few exceptions. One of these exceptions is her confessional narrative concerning the problems of identifying the women to study and how to gain access and acceptance.

Literary Tale

The literary tale is written with a novelist's sense of narration and is usually attempted only by professional writers such as journalists (Auletta, 1991; Barnouw, 1975; Brown, 1971, 1978; Clark, 1988; Metz, 1975). Sometimes a scholar (as differentiated from full-time journalists) will attempt this style in part, but the attempt usually lacks some of the elements of a full literary tale. For example, Lull (1987) described the San Francisco punk subculture, and Turkle (1984) described the computer culture. Sections of their descriptions read like a novel, but their writings lack an overall plot structure as well as the development of specific, concrete characters.

LOCUS OF ARGUMENT

On what basis does the researcher expect readers to be persuaded that his or her interpretations (descriptions, explanations, or arguments) are useful or accurate? This characteristic is very important where the interpretations of various researchers are at odds, and the reader must decide which interpretation is the most meaningful. There are four loci that writers can use to focus their writing: ethos (the author), logos (the argument), evidence (the data themselves), and pathos (appeal to the emotions).

The key word in analyzing the research on this issue is *locus*. Most of the individual writings exhibit a combination of the elements of argument, evidence, and researcher reputation. However, each writing has its own locus—that is the characteristic of having one tone dominate.

Ethos

Ethos refers to an argument resting on the reputation of the author. The author is a key figure, and his or her personal interpretation is what is illuminated. The author needs to have a respected reputation (developed through previous work or status in the field) or needs to exhibit a compelling style of writing in order for the reader to be persuaded by the author's personal interpretation.

Ethos appears to be a popular locus of the argument among text-focused research (C. Anderson, 1987; Deming, 1992; Douglas, 1993; Esslin, 1987; Flitterman-Lewis, 1992; Himmelstein, 1984; Horowitz, 1987; Joyrich, 1992; Kinder, 1987; Mann, 1992; Newcomb, 1988; Rowland, 1983; Schulze, 1990; Schwichtenberg, 1987; Zynda, 1988), institution-focused research (Allen, 1985; Ang, 1991; Bagdikian, 1972, 1987;

Baughman, 1990; Berman, 1981; Bernhard, 1993; Clark, 1988; Collins, 1989; Corcoran, 1987; Dates & Barlow, 1990; Douglas, 1993; Ewen & Ewen, 1992; Gandy, 1982; Gitlin, 1980, 1987; Kellner, 1987; Mander, 1978; McChesney, 1993; Meehan, 1993; Parenti, 1986; Pauly, 1988; Reeves, 1988; Schiller, 1989; Spigel, 1992, 1993; Wajcman, 1991), and audience-focused studies (Ang, 1985; Lull, 1980, 1987; Radway, 1984; Rogge, 1989; Rogge & Jensen, 1988; Traudt & Lont, 1987; Tulloch, 1989).

In text-focused research, C. Anderson's (1987) personal interpretation of "Magnum, P.I." is a good example of ethos. Also, when Kinder (1987) explored the issue of how music videos are developing new codes, her article is less an argument of a particular position or set of conclusions than it is her personal interpretation of how she makes sense out of the phenomenon of music videos.

In institution-focused studies, Ang (1991) laid out her argument that the present conceptualizations of the media audience are faulty. Parenti (1986) presented his belief that media do not meet their own standards of objectivity, informativeness, truthfulness, or independence. Dates and Barlow (1990) argued that the definition of control of African-American images in the mass media is determined by a hegemonic influence.

Logos

Logos focuses on the logic of the argument. Researchers who frame their presentations on logos carefully construct an argument on the systematic selection or sequencing of key points. But the evidence is less important than the structure of the argument. If the author presents an ideological position (or thesis position) and keeps the focus on the analytical process that moves the reader to the inevitable conclusion; if the author does not shift the focus to him or herself; and if the author does not shift the focus to the evidence itself; then logos is the locus of the writing. Ideological essays are a good example of this logos logic, as long as the author avoids foregrounding him or herself. Also, research of a scientific nature where there is a systematic structure for analyzing previous literature or where the author is inducing a grounded theory are likely to exhibit a strong logos locus.

Logos is a popular form in text-based research (Barker, 1987; Bird & Dardenne, 1988; Cheseboro, 1978; D'Acci, 1992). These studies differ from ethos in their foregrounding of an argument that has existed apart from the author's own interpretation. For example, Bird and Dardenne placed the emphasis on myth analysis and argued that it applied to news. D'Acci foregrounded feminism and argued that feminist characteristics are strong in "Cagney and Lacey" and this was why the show was popular and controversial. Chesebro used logos to set up his categorization scheme, but then took a social science approach to categorizing shows and profiling the demographics of TV characters; therefore, this is an example of data as the locus of argument. In contrast, some scholars present personal views where the work of other scholars is backgrounded whereas their own opinions are foregrounded (C. Anderson, 1987; Esslin, 1987). For example, Esslin placed his logic at the heart of his argument, ignoring types of ads that do not fit his conception of a dramaturgical analysis.

Logos is the locus when an argument for a hypothesis or a model is the primary focus (Bodroghkozy, 1992; Hoover, 1988; Liebes & Katz, 1988, 1989; Pardun & Krugman, 1994; Seiter et al., 1989a; Wolf, 1987). For example, Bodrogh-kozy backgrounded her data to illustrate the argument that the show "Julia" elicited a range of reactions. Hoover argued that Turner's concept of luminality can be used to explain the change in religion in our culture. Seiter et al. argued that "soap opera texts are the products not of individual and isolated readings but of collective constructions—collaborative readings, as it were, of small social groups such as families, friends, and neighbors, or people sharing an apartment" (p. 233).

In institution-focused research, there are logos studies that sought to build a model, test a hypothesis, or developed grounded theory (Altheide, 1976, 1985; Altheide & Snow, 1979; Altschull, 1984; Fishman, 1988; Innis, 1950; Jowett & Linton, 1980; Snow, 1983; Tuchman, 1978; Turow, 1984, 1989).

Evidence

With evidence as the focal point of the research, the author treats the observations or quotations as if they had the power to convey the meaning of the situation. The author makes it appear that he or she was not to be part of the analysis, preferring instead to hold up the facts as if they were free of his or her interpretive processes.

With some text-focused writings, the data seem to dominate over the argument. For example, Haralovich (1992) analyzed the elements in 1950s sitcoms, especially "Father Knows Best" and "Leave it to Beaver," and has a feminist perspective. But surprisingly, there is no heat to this argument. Rather than using ethos or pathos, she clearly relied on the data to carry the weight of the argument—she seemed to be saying to the reader "I know you'll come to the same conclusion as I have after you see my evidence." This also seems to be the case in the examination of the visual images (performance, narrative, and dreamlike) in MTV rock videos conducted by Kinder (1987).

In audience-based research, many studies place their focus primarily on the evidence (Barrios, 1988; Hobson, 1989; Jhally & Lewis, 1992; Lewis, 1991; Lindlof, 1987; Morley, 1980). For example, Morley presented an overwhelming number of quotes. This is not to say that he did not also present an argument and conclusion; however, the evidence, perhaps because it is so voluminously presented, is clearly the center of attention. Hobson also is very descriptive in her presentation of lots of quotations from people she interviewed.

Some institutional scholars focus on the evidence as the locus. These examples are from journalists (Auletta, 1991; Metz, 1975), and historians (Barnouw, 1975; L.

Brown, 1971). Elliott (1979) in his ethnography of the production of a television series remained at a fairly descriptive level in his attempt to bring the reader into the experience. Fishman (1988) did the same in his ethnography of newspapers as did Cantor (1988) with her interviewing of television producers.

Pathos

Pathos is an appeal to the emotions of the reader. This is very rare in the published qualitative research. The closest example of pathos is by Barnouw (1978), who began as a descriptive history but then shifted into an appeal to the emotions as his criticism became strong. Also, Lipsitz (1992) interpreted 1950s working-class sitcoms in terms of the economic, political, and cultural environment of the time. His argument seems to be the locus until the last page where pathos takes over—telling the readers to free themselves from false consciousness through knowledge of television's ideology. He said, "the unfinished dialogue of history can also be what helps, what takes us back into the past in order to break its hold on the present. By addressing the hurt, and finding out how it came to be, we begin to grasp ways of understanding the past, and ending the pain" (p. 105).

CONTEXTUALIZATION

To what degree is the context of the phenomenon highlighted in the writing? Under the qualitative approach, individual behaviors and texts acquire their meaning through their position in the historical and situational contexts within which they are embedded (Lindlof & Meyer, 1987). For example, let's say a researcher observes a mother grabbing a remote control device away from her young son. How are we to interpret this action? We must begin by putting this action in context. If the mother performed the action as she walked in the door from work, then sat down in front of the TV and proceeded to watch her shows while she ignored her son's hurt cries, the action would be interpreted as a cruel exercise in power to serve her selfish needs. If instead, the mother performed the action after asking her son calmly several times to switch the channel away from a violent horror movie she did not want her son to see, the action would be interpreted as an exercise in discipline oriented toward the benefit of the child. Thus the behavior of snatching the remote control device acquires its meaning for the mother, the child, and the researcher through the context of surrounding events and motives.

The preceding example illustrates the importance of context when trying to derive meaning from a situation—that is, when the analysis is one of induction. However, contextualization is also important in deductive types of analyses where authors begin with a premise, a thesis, or a point of view then present their evidence in support of it. If the evidence is thin, the argument is weak; but if the evidence is richly contextualized, the reader develops a greater understanding of the phenomenon and is likely to give the evidence more weight.

How is contextuality achieved? Lindlof and Meyer (1987) asserted that it can be implemented by means of *in-situ* observation, the employment of multiple data sources, and continuous reference to emergent explanations of observed events. This allows thick description of the layers of meaning for the various social actors in a situation. Lindlof (1991) listed the major characteristics of good contextualization as a focus on the local and particularistic and an "emphasis on holism, historicity, and process" (p. 25).

Contextualization is a major point used by theoreticians to differentiate the quantitative and qualitative approaches. J. A. Anderson (1987) illustrated this with two arguments. First, he claimed that qualitative research is not conducted to build grand theory, because this is impossible; it is conducted to add to the library of discourse on human life, which in turn might lead to midrange theory. In order to add to this library of discourse, contextualization is essential. Anderson's second argument is an hermeneutic one. By his account, the qualitative researcher must understand the totality of what is being examined before the meaning of the parts becomes apparent. The parts do not speak for themselves. Instead, the researcher must give the data a perspective, and this requires contextualization.

Strong Contextualization

Good contextualization, as characterized by Clifford Geertz, requires taking each element and, through thick description, showing how it fits into a context. The context then provides meaning for the element. There are many good examples of contextualization through thick description in institution-focused research (Altheide, 1976, 1985; Altheide & Snow, 1979; Auletta, 1991; L. Brown, 1971; Cantor, 1980; Collins, 1989; Elliott, 1979; Fishman, 1988; Gitlin, 1983; McChesney, 1993; Metz, 1975; Snow, 1983; Tuchman, 1978; Turow, 1989).

With text-focused research, the issue of contextualization is important to most authors (C. Anderson, 1987; Barker, 1987; Bird & Dardenne, 1988; Himmelstein, 1984; Mann, 1992; Newcomb, 1988; Rowland, 1983; Schulze, 1990; Zynda, 1988). In particular, contextualization is a strong element in the work of Lipsitz (1992). His interpretation of 1950s working-class sitcoms is based on literary criticism, cultural studies, and a sociological perspective (especially ideas about how capitalist cultures legitimate themselves). He used these contexts to draw his interpretations in the economic, political, and cultural areas. Like Lipsitz, Deming (1992) presented a strong contextualization, but Deming was focusing on what happens in the developing of one particular program, "Kate and Allie." However, unlike Lipsitz, he looked at the economic and political forces; however, these are played out on a microlevel (within a network) rather than on the macrolevel (the culture throughout the country). D'Acci (1992) also provided a good deal of context about the development of "Cagney and Lacey" and how those developments influenced the portrayals of the characters and themes. Focusing on the types of visual images (performance, narrative, and dreamlike), Kinder (1987) examined issues of whether a spectator is present in the video, presence of TV receivers, structural discontinuity, and decentering. And Haralovich (1992) analyzed the elements in 1950s sitcoms, especially "Father Knows Best" and "Leave it to Beaver," and presented a good deal of context in the development of a good explication of the social history of the time (political, family patterns, architecture of homes, neighborhood distinctions, etc.).

Much audience-focused research also displays strong contextualization (Barrios, 1988; Bodroghkozy, 1992; Hobson, 1989; Lull, 1987; Morley, 1980; Pardun & Krugman, 1994; Radway, 1984; Rakow, 1992; Rogge & Jensen, 1988; Seiter et al., 1989a; Traudt & Lont, 1987; Turkle, 1984). For example, Morley presented his interpretation in terms of the variables of demographics (age, gender, race, and class) and cultural identifications (trade unions, political parties, sections of the educational system, etc.). Lull provided a high degree of description about the punk subculture in San Francisco, then linked these contextual elements with his interpretations. Barrios presented a good deal of contextualization by talking about life in Venezuela, its family structures, its economy, its television systems, TV programs, and history of television audience research. Bodroghkozy contextualized the show through thick description of both the program (its sets, music, characters, etc.) and of the historical period; but she did not contextualize the viewers, whom she "knows" only through their letters to the show's producer. Pardun and Krugman provided a good deal of contextualization in their examination of household architectural styles.

Low Degree of Contextualization

In contrast to the studies just illuminated (studies with a high degree of contextualization), there is a set of qualitative studies that present a much lower degree of contextualization. In these low-degree studies, authors provide some description of contexts, however there are some obvious contexts ignored. For example, Lindlof (1987) attempted to contextualize the quotes he collected from his interviews with prisoners concerning their media use habits. However, because his contact with the prisoners was so limited, and because he was not permitted to observe them using media, he was able to provide very little contextual information to the reader.

Another facet of this problem is exhibited by Wolf (1987) in her ethnography of how children understand the characters and stories of television entertainment. It is ironic that although her study clearly demonstrated the importance of context for children in making sense of the media, she largely ignored the context of her ethnography in her making sense of the phenomenon for her readers. This is not to say that her conclusions are not interesting; those con-clusions have a lot to say about what children do with television messages and how they make sense of them. However, she could have increased the level of insight in the findings had she developed more of a context (social interactions, parental values, etc.) for her interpretations. Also, in audience research, Ang (1989) argued strongly that it is contextualization that essentially distinguishes qualitative from quantitative research and makes qualitative more useful. She argued against "dissecting 'audience activity' into variables and categories in order to be able to study them one by one," arguing instead for "a more historicized insight into the ways in which 'audience activity' is related to social and political structures and processes" (p. 101). But in her study of viewers of "Dallas" (Ang, 1985), she relied on letters and is therefore partitioned from her sources and unable to assemble the evidence needed to provide strong contex-tualization of her evidence.

Another characteristic of a low degree of contextualization is when an author's interpretations or conclusions are not well grounded in the descriptions of context provided—the reader feels something is missing and cannot understand how the author arrived at a particular interpretation. For example, Horowitz (1987) ana-lyzed some episodes of "Kate and Allie" and concluded that sitcoms are dying as a genre. She ignored the context of programming (what is scheduled against sitcoms on competing channels) and the cyclical nature of their popularity (by tracing trends over years). She speculated near the end of the article that there may be an upswing, but she did not develop that point, which would have been an important contextual element. Also, she did not discuss where the audiences are going when they leave sitcoms; this would be important context to understand the changes in the popularity of genres. Also, Hobson (1982) provided a lot of description about what people say, and there is some context expressed by some of the interviewees. But she did not build contextualization of her own by laying in background of the interviewees or some other form of interpretive context. Instead, she simply let the interviewees speak for themselves.

No Contextualization

Examples of no contextualization are rare in qualitative research, but there are some. One example is Turow (1978), who looked at the diversity of programming for children over three decades, but he did not place his analysis of programs in a context of historical developments in the industry, education, or the culture. Another example is the reception study of how family members use television for social purposes in their homes by Lull (1980). It appears from his method of participant observation in 200 homes that he had a great deal of contextual information. However, in his article he placed the focus on building an explanatory typology that sorted all motives into two groups (structural and relational). The structural component included environmental use (background noise, companionship, and entertainment) and regulative use (punctuation of time and activity and talk patterns). The relational component had four subcomponents: communication facilitation (agenda for talk, experience illustration), affiliation/avoidance (relationship maintenance, family solidarity), social learning (behavior modeling, legitimazation, substitute schooling), and competence/dominance (role reinforcement, argument facilitation). Each of these subcomponents presented an opportunity for a great deal of contextualization, but the author chose not to provide any. This example illustrates that authors with a limited amount of space must make trade-offs, and because good contextualization requires much description, an author cannot do justice to context if he or she is keeping the focus on higher level explanation that has many components.

DEGREE OF SELF-REFLEXIVITY

Because qualitative researchers cannot remove themselves from the situations they study, they need to be able to reflect on the progression of their decisions in the research process and illuminate this for their readers. By doing so, they are revealing their scholarly perspective and thus providing readers with an important context to understand the research. Reason (1994) referred to this as critical subjectivity, which "means that we do not suppress our primary subjective experience, that we accept that our knowing is from a perspective; it also means that we are aware of that perspective and of its bias, and we articulate it in our communications. Critical subjectivity involves a self-reflexive attention to the ground on which one is standing" (p. 327).

Despite the premium placed on this characteristic, there is a great deal of qualitative research that demonstrates very little self-reflexivity in text-based research (C. Anderson, 1987; Barker, 1987; Chesebro, 1988; D'Acci, 1992; Deming, 1992; Flitterman-Lewis, 1992; Himmelstein, 1984; Horowitz, 1987; Joyrich, 1992; Kinder, 1987; Lipsitz, 1992; Mann, 1992; Rowland, 1984; Schwichtenberg, 1987; Schulze, 1990; Zynda, 1988) and in audience-focused research (Barrios, 1988; Hoover, 1988; Lull, 1987; Rogge & Jensen, 1988; Traudt & Lont, 1987). These authors present their evidence with total authority and do not question either their evidence itself or the decisions they made in selecting and sequencing that evidence. Altschull (1984) even went so far as to say that his interpretations are better than other people's by stating, "the interpretations of historical developments are sometimes at variance with traditional points of view. These shifts in interpretation support my view that traditional journalism history is faulty in its adherence to the folklore of progressive, Great Man views that cannot provide adequate explanations of the direction of the history of journalism" (p. xii), but he did not reflect on how he made his interpretations so that the reader could follow those decision-making processes.

The lack of self-reflexivity is ironic among researchers who argue so strongly for a conscious awareness that interpretations are subjective and contextualization is essential for understanding. These are important features to apply to the research process when scholars try to make sense of the phenomenon they are studying. But this is equally important to apply to the writing when scholars attempt to convey their insights to readers who need to see a high degree of self-reflexivity in order to understand how the decisions of analysis were made. An example of this irony is evident in a book chapter authored by Bird and Dardenne (1988), who spent a good deal of effort criticizing journalists who believe the myth that news stories are objective reflections of reality. The authors argued that if journalists were more aware of what they did, they would realize that news stories are creations produced by subjective processes. However, Bird and Dardenne appear unaware that their chapter is also a construction produced by their subjective processes, not an objective reflection of truth. Had they exhibited some self-reflexivity, they would have been holding themselves to the same standard to which they were holding journalists.

There seem to be three techniques for exhibiting self-reflexivity. At the minimum level, the author illuminates the key details of the research process to the reader. This would include the setting, key contextual characteristics, the researcher's self-presentation to the research subjects, major events in the gathering of data. Altheide and Johnson (1994) observed that "the traditional problems of entree or access to a setting, personal relations with the members in a setting, how field research data were conceived and recorded, and a host of other pragmatic issues" (p. 486) can influence the results in important ways, so researchers need to be self-reflexive in their writings so readers can understand the context of the work. This level of self-reflexivity is advocated by Lancy (1993) who called for authors to make their framework explicit to the reader by reporting on the methodology, data gathering, and data analysis. Hammersley and Atkinson (1983) said the reflexive researcher must remain as self-conscious as an author as he or she has been in planning the research, gathering the data, and the analysis. In this view, it is impossible to be totally objective, and there is no natural language. The biggest challenge is to present the material in a linear manner, but the phenomenon is never linear.

A second technique for presenting self-reflection is where a researcher consciously reflects on the nature of the methods he or she used and displays a concern about the value of the data and his or her interpretations. The third technique of self-reflexivity is demonstrated when a scholar lays out his or her biases, as biases, so that the reader can be forewarned about the author's perspective. At the higher levels of self-reflexivity, the reader is given the invitation to share insights about why decisions were made the way they were.

Articulating Decisions

A minimal level of self-reflexivity is demonstrated when the author chooses to describe many of the decisions he or she made in conducting the research, such as gaining access, establishing credibility, and so forth. For example, Altheide

(1976) said, "I do not believe that the reader should 'take my word,' or uncritically accept the analysis without knowing a little more about the way the study was done" (p. 198). He then provided a 20-page methodological appendix where he described his three settings, gaining entree, gaining trust, nature of data, and verification. Fishman (1988) talked about gaining access, establishing credibility, and so on. Gitlin (1983) presented information about his method and continued to illuminate the elements of data gathering and analysis throughout his narrative. Turkle (1984) added an appendix to her book, which gave her an opportunity to be very self-reflexive. Wolf (1987) presented 12 pages (about one third of the article) in talking about sampling, data gathering, and a plan for analysis. Jhally and Lewis (1992) said:

> establishing connections between attitudes and perceptions is technically difficult and demanding. It is a little like a trial in which the jury can only reconstruct events from evidence and testimony presented to it after the fact. So it is with this kind of investigative audience research inasmuch as we cannot perch inside people's brains and watch ideas and opinions forming. Like the prudent jury, we must use our knowledge and skill to interpret what people tell us rather than accept all testimony at face value. (p. 9)

In audience-focused research, Hobson (1989) talked about the setting for the interviewing and how she seemed to lose control of the interview as the women went off on tangents and often talked among themselves. Lull (1980) presented a fair amount of detail about the data gathering and showed some concern for testing the internal validity of the observations by asking those observed to read and react to the reports of those observations. Jhally and Lewis (1992) talked about the difficulty of linking perceptions to attitudes and the need for their judgment in order to separate good data from bad. Several scholars talk about the limits to their sample (Bodroghkozy, 1992), their methods (Morley, 1980), their data (Ang, 1985), or their study itself (Pardun & Krugman, 1994).

In text-based research, Newcomb (1988) illustrated some self-reflexivity when he said, "my own reading, of course, is also personalized, but the persona is that of the critic attempting to 'see more' than other individualized viewers" (p. 91).

Conscious Reflection

A second kind of self-reflexivity is where the researcher consciously reflects on the nature of the methods he or she used and worries about the value of the data and his or her interpretations. Altheide (1976) also exhibited this kind of self-reflexivity in his appendix, where he made numerous statements reflecting on what he did and questioning his decisions and the quality of evidence he was gathering. He presented a section on "mistakes, misconceptions, and surprises" (p. 207). Elliott (1979) also presented a high degree of reflexivity by carefully describing the decisions he made when choosing his method and by questioning the limitations of his method saying, "One drawback to the partici-pant observation as a method of research is that the situation observed and the account recorded may have been arranged for the benefit of the researcher" (p. 7). Reeves (1988) talked about how other research on this topic has been limited so he chose a cultural approach that is superior; therefore, he was reflexive about his choice of method but not about its limitations. Seiter et al. (1989a) were very self-reflexive in talking in detail about the setup of their study and its limitations as an ethnography and in terms of not interviewing any people of color.

Illuminating Biases

The third kind of self-reflexivity is demonstrated when a scholar lays out his or her biases, as biases, so that the reader can be forewarned about the author's perspective. A good example is in the introduction to Innis' (1950) book where he acknowledges his analytical perspective and the influence of bias on it. Innis also has a tentative and self-effacing manner of writing at times; this too con-tributes to the reader gaining a sense of who the author is and how he may be less sure of some insights than others.

Other examples of a high degree of self-reflexivity is when an author raises deep philosophical concerns about the nature of knowing. For example, Metz (1975), although making a journalistic presentation, worried (on the very first page of his preface) about what is truth (which he regards as a properly bal-anced presentation of information) and can it ever be presented. Fishman (1988) raised philosophical issues about the nature of knowing and what it means to construct knowledge.

Tuchman (1978) presented a high degree in her last two chapters where she examined the arguments about science, social science and the limits to knowing. But she laid out these arguments in a rather distant and scholarly way—not putting herself into the picture, so we do not know if she was writing a history of this thinking or if it is her personal belief system. It is much more a description of the issues than an argument as support for her work. The ideas themselves give this piece a high degree of reflexivity, but ironically, we see very little of Tuchman revealed here.

CONCLUSIONS

In this chapter, writing is treated as a task separate from data gathering and analysis. This should not be interpreted to mean that the three tasks (gathering, analysis, writing) are a linear process where one step must be completed before the researcher is able to move onto the next one; instead, the three are inter-leaved. However, when scholars are performing their authorship tasks, they become concerned with four issues simultaneously. First, they must decide what form of expression to use to match their purpose and to most cleanly communicate to the reader not only their findings but also their research perspective (as a realist, an interpreter, a critic, etc.). Second, they must nest their argument within a particular locus, such as themselves as authority, logic, the evidence itself, or an appeal to the emotions. Third, they need to decide how much contextualization to reveal and how to present those elements so as to maximally convey the meaning of the parts of the phenomenon examined by the researchers. And fourth, they must decide to present a certain degree of self-reflexivity in order to help readers understand the meaning of the research project and its report.

12

STANDARDS

This chapter addresses three major questions: Is it possible to prescribe meaningful standards for judging the quality of qualitative research; if so, what do theoreticians suggest as general standards? How can qualitative researchers establish internal validity? How can qualitative researchers argue their case for external validity?

ARE STANDARDS POSSIBLE?

The issue of research standards—especially whether standards are meaningful in an endeavor based on the supremacy of individual interpretation—is one of the most contested debates in all of qualitative thinking. This debate has been vigorously waged for over a decade and shows no signs of resolution.

On one side of the debate are scholars who take the position that quality standards can never be developed for qualitative research. For example, J. K. Smith (1984) contended that qualitative research is built on an idealist foundation in which the human mind subjectively constructs reality. From this fundamental belief, it follows that as individuals construct their own reality there will be important differences in the interpretations across people. Meaning making is always subjective. Because there is no objectivity, we should not expect all qualitative researchers to see the same thing (reliability) in the phenomenon. And if no one's perception of truth is any better than any one else's, then there can be no truth standard for judging validity.

On the other side of the debate are scholars who believe that it is not only possible but essential to establish standards for qualitative research (Altheide

& Johnson, 1994; J. A. Anderson, 1987; Fortner & Christians, 1981; Howe & Eisenhart, 1990; Lancy, 1993; Lincoln & Guba, 1986, 1990; Marshall & Rossman, 1989; Penman, 1988). These theoreticians argue that they are part of a scholarly community and that there are accepted practices that define membership in that community. Without common ground, their practices and the research they produce would have no meaning that is shared among them. For example, Altheide and Johnson defended the need for standards saying "as long as we strive to base our claims and interpretations of social life on data of any kind, we must have a logic for assessing and communicating the interactive process through which the investigator acquired the research experience and information" (p. 485).

Both sides of the debate present a trap. The pro side (those who argue for standards) need to avoid the trap of defending standards and at the same time espousing the belief that meaning making is necessarily a subjective process where different researchers can have different interpretations, each of which is equally good, because there is no objective basis from which to determine that one subjective interpretation is better than another. We can see J. A. Anderson (1987) struggling with this trap when he argued that "validity is set in time and place" (p. 78), meaning that reality changes and that there are multiple realities so one cannot compare a research claim to one standard to determine how accurate the claim is. In the measurement realm, he said, "objective measurement is rejected; interpretation is valorized" (p. 78). Yet he still proposed criteria saying that it is possible for different researchers to agree on a single interpretation, thus the criterion of intersubjectivity.

The con side has its own trap. The scholars holding this position argue to "put aside the desire to be foundational" (J. K. Smith, 1984, p. 390) because there is no common basis upon which to establish criteria. Mere understanding through interpretation is enough, and all interpretations are equally good. If they genuinely believe this, then they must be prepared to allow any interpretation to be published in their books and journals; there is no basis for excluding or even criticizing another's work as not being good enough. There can be no review process for their students' thesis, dissertations, or term papers, because there is no basis from which they can give advice for students to improve their work. And there is no basis for criticizing the work of quantitative researchers. The interpretations of all researchers regardless of approach or degree of training are equally valuable.

Overview of Standards

There are many schemes for judging the quality of qualitative research. In order to demonstrate the variety of thinking about standards, eight of these schemes are presented here. The first few present clear lists of criteria that contain elements that are analogues of quantitative research; these scholars parallel the criteria traditionally used in quantitative research. The later examples shift the base of making judgments away from quality and toward morality, and the lists of criteria that follow from those bases are very different.

1. J. A. Anderson (1987) suggested six criteria, which are oriented more toward readers, rather than researchers. Those six criteria are: (a) explanatory purpose, which means that the explanation must include an interpretation of the meaning that the actions have for the actors, not the researcher, (b) source of information, which means that the researcher must have participated in the situations but still been detached enough to make good observations, (c) evidence of a committed study, which Anderson measured as number of days in the field, length of record, number of interviews conducted, and so on, (d) completeness, which Anderson operationalized as utility (i.e., does it work?) and that is accomplished by looking at the number of layers of meaning in which the actions are interpreted from the minute details to higher levels of explanatory abstraction, (e) generalizability, which is the degree to which the researcher moves beyond specific acts to patterns of actions to the larger construct of social action, and (f) propriety of the argument, which relates to how well the research supports the claims with relevant arguments. On this last point Anderson said that it is unfair to criticize qualitative researchers for a "lack of objectivity, random sampling, statistical measures of reliability, deductive logic and the like" because such elements are not part of the method (p. 355).

2. Howe and Eisenhart (1990) advocated five criteria; they are targeted more for the researcher than the reader. First, they called for a fit between research questions, data collection, and analysis techniques; they urged researchers to select questions of value then choose the appropriate method. Second, they called for an effective application of specific data collection and analysis techniques, which once chosen, must be applied competently. However, they did not specify what it means to apply different methods competently. Third, they called for an alertness to and coherence of background assumptions on the part of the researcher. Because "studies must be judged against a background of existent knowledge" (p. 7), the literature should be reviewed so that contradictions can be explained. Their fourth criterion is "overall warrant" or internal validity, which "encompasses responding to and balancing the first three standards discussed as well as going beyond them, to include such things as being alert to and being able to employ knowledge from outside the particular perspective and tradition within which one is working, and being able to apply general principles for evaluating arguments" (p. 7). The fifth criterion established by Howe and Eisenhart is value constraints, which have external and internal components. External value constraints raise the "So what?" question. The internal value constraints focus on ethics, that is, the way research subjects are treated. For each of these five criteria, they were careful to lay out what they

called a nonpositivist foundation; that is, they tried to avoid modeling their criteria after those used in quantitative approach.

3. Lincoln and Guba (1990) said the central criterion for judging the quality of the research process is trustworthiness, which is defined indirectly as having four major aspects: credibility (as an analog to internal validity), transferability (external validity), dependability (reliability), and confirmability (objectivity). To increase the credibility of qualitative research they suggested the use of techniques such as prolonged engagement with the phenomenon, persistent observation, triangulation, peer debriefing, negative case analysis, and member checks (showing the researcher's interpretations to the research subjects). For transferability, they suggested the use of thick description of data. For dependability and confirmability they suggested an external audit.

They also argued that authenticity is a major criterion. Their subdimensions of authenticity are fairness, ontological authentication, educative authentication, catalytic authentication, and tactical authentication.

4. Marshall and Rossman (1989) agreed with the position of Lincoln and Guba (1990) when they said "all research must respond to canons that stand as criteria against which the trustworthiness of the project can be evaluated" (p. 144). Although they recognized four subdimensions of trustworthiness, these are different than the four of Lincoln and Guba. The first subdimension is truth value, which addresses the question of how accurate are the particular findings of the study? This is similar to credibility in qualitative terms or internal validity in quantitative terms. Second is applicability, which addresses the question of how generalizable are these findings to another setting or group of people? This is similar to transferability or external validity. Third is consistency, which poses the question about how can we be reasonably sure that the findings would be replicated if the study were conducted with the same participants in the same context? Synonyms of this are dependability and reliability. Fourth is neutrality, which raises the question of how can we be sure that the findings are reflective of the subjects and the inquiry itself rather than the product of the researcher's biases or prejudices? This relates to confirmability or objectivity.

5. Lincoln and Guba (1990) also presented four criteria for judging the case report or the product of qualitative research. These criteria are resonance, rhetoric, empowerment, and applicability. Resonance refers to the degree of fit between the report and the nonpositivist position. The report should present the multiple realities of the research subjects, avoid a priori expectations and formal theories, reject generalizability, account for value influences that impinge the inquiry, and reflect the investigator's subjective involvement in the project. Rhetorical criteria refer to the form, structure, and presentational characteristics of the report. Empowerment refers to the report's ability to "evoke and facilitate action on the part of readers" (p. 57), and applicability refers to the ability of the report to facilitate "the drawing of inferences by the reader that may have applicability in his or her own context and situation" (p. 57).

6. Denzin (1970) argued for reliability, validity, and generalizability as the major standards of qualitative work—thus borrowing the standards unaltered from the quantitative approach. He reminded qualitative researchers of the eight threats to internal validity (history, maturation, testing, instrumentation, statistical regression, selection, experimental mortality, selection-maturation interaction) and the four threats to external validity (interaction effect of testing, interaction between selection and the experimental variable, reactive effects of experimental arrangements, and multiple-treatment interference) developed by Campbell (1963) for quantitative research. However, in later writings (especially Denzin, 1994) he showed a change in his thinking by arguing that the traditionally quantitative standards he previously espoused be replaced by postmodern standards, which are more local, personal, and political; nevertheless, Denzin maintained his concern that qualitative researchers achieve legitimation and quality.

7. Penman (1992) argued for shifting the goal of research from the seeking of some truth to the highlighting of morality. With such a shift in the goal, there must be a change in criteria. She listed four such criteria. First, constitutiveness addresses the concern that "both our meanings and our knowledge are socially constituted within the communication process" (p. 243). Second, contextualness is the recognition that social knowledge is historically embedded. Third, diversity is the caution that there is a great variety to communication and our interpretations. And fourth, incompleteness is the "recognition that neither communication nor the meanings generated are ever complete or even ever finishable" (p. 246).

8. Altheide and Johnson (1994) observed that many qualitative scholars will advocate the abandonment of validity altogether or else go to a new form of determining validity such as validity-as-culture, validity-as-ideology, validity-as-gender, validity-as-language, validity-as-relevance/advocacy, validity-as-standards, or validity-as-reflexive-accounting. For example, the validity-as-culture argument is based on the belief that researchers attempt to interpret the points of view of others so as to construct a vision of culture; the more points of view accounted for, the more valid the interpretation of the researcher. The validity-as-relevance/advocacy argument is also based on the belief that qualitative research should affect change. Therefore, the more a research report is able to uplift those groups of relatively powerless people, the greater the validity. They seemed to favor the validity-as-reflexive-accounting which "places the researcher, the topic, and the sense-making process in interaction" (p. 489). The more a researcher can explicate the interaction of these elements in the research process, the greater the validity: "Good ethnographies show the hand of the ethnographer. The effort may not always be successful, but there should be clear 'tracks' indicating the attempt has been made" (p. 493). Finally, they argued that if the researcher is reflexive, then it is possible for the researcher to have "superior authority over all knowers" (p. 497); quality research is not producing just another interpretation among many, but a superior one.

In addition to the general schemes illuminated in the preceding list, there have been some more specific criteria suggested by qualitative theoreticians and methodologists. These suggestions are presented next in two sets. The first set deals with the internal criteria—those that are focused on the decisions made in the evidence gathering and analysis. The second set deals with external criteria—those that are focused on the claims made about the generalizability and application of the findings. (See Table 12.1 for a breakdown of the issues of internal and external quality.)

INTERNAL QUALITY

Internal quality refers to the value of the evidence that is gathered. In quantitative research, scholars seek to establish a case for the reliability, validity, and usefulness of their data. Reliability means the consistency and stability of the measures. Validity means the accuracy (or the truthfulness) of the data. And usefulness refers to the appropriateness of the data for the purpose they were gathered.

Some qualitative theoreticians seem to find the criteria used by quantitative researchers acceptable. For example, Lindlof and Meyer (1987) appeared to take a scientific perspective when they said there is a need for interobserver reliability, which is "consensus among multiple observers of the same phenomenon" (p. 16). This is desirable because of the assumption "that there are common

TABLE 12.1
Issues of Purpose and Standards of Quality

Issue: Internal Quality

Key Question: What, if anything, does the researcher do to convince the reader of the internal quality, that is, the quality of the evidence and analysis?

Alternative Answers:
(1) Researchers talk about confirming their data or conclusions by remeasuring people or triangulation, and so on.
(2) Eschews the need for validity. The concept of validity is alien to the idea of this type of research.
(3) No attention to making a case for internal quality.

Issue: External Quality

Key Question: What, if anything, does the researcher do to convince the reader of the external quality, that is, the quality of the argument/findings?

Alternative Answers:
(1) Researchers attempt to make a case for the quality of their conclusions by justifying their constructions and/or generalizations.
(2) Eschews the need for validity. The concept of validity is alien to the idea of this type of research.
(3) No attention to making a case for external quality.

---

interpretations of phenomena if observers are carefully trained in what to look for and how to recognize various displays of behavior" (p. 16). However, they showed their ambivalence on this point in the next paragraph when they said, "for the most part, naturalistic observation rejects the idea of multiple observers producing a single interpretation" (p. 16).

Other qualitative theoreticians try to translate these quantitative criteria into a useful form to use in judging the different nature of qualitative research. For example, Hammersley and Atkinson (1983) accepted the quantitative idea of validity and suggested a translation into qualitative thinking by proposing two techniques to establish the validity of qualitative data. The first method is respondent validation in which subjects are shown the report and asked if it corresponds with their perceptions of their own beliefs and practices. Second is triangulation, a process of gathering data from several different sources to determine if all accounts conform. This technique of triangulation is favored by many qualitative theoreticians (Jankowski & Wester, 1991; Jick, 1979; Lindlof & Meyer, 1987). When researchers conduct within-method triangulation, they are examining reliability of the data gained through that method by cross-checking observations for internal consistency. In contrast, between-method triangulation is done to establish external validity. Lindlof and Meyer called triangulation the "qualitative researcher's most effect defense against the charge of being subjective" (p. 20). However, Jankowski and Wester cautioned that "triangulation does not absolve qualitative researchers of interpretive work. Indeed, when findings derived from different methods conflict or fail to corroborate each other (as well as when they support each other), this signals not the end of the study, but the beginning of a phase of theoretical analysis examining the nature of agreements and disagreements" (p. 63).

Several theoreticians focus on the notion of openness when translating quantitative criteria into the qualitative approach. These theoreticians argue that when researchers openly present the steps in their process of data generation, readers come to feel that the evidence is of higher quality. For example, Bogdan and Taylor (1975) asserted that findings are "credible and fully understandable only to the extent that your techniques are open to the scrutiny of readers" (p. 142), so it is necessary to explain the process that was used to collect and interpret the data. They also said that researchers should explain the checks they use on determining their subjects' truthfulness, but they did not suggest what such checks are. Wolcott (1990) held a similar position saying that:

> readers must be informed about the nature and extent of your data base. When, exactly, did you conduct the fieldwork? How extensive was your involvement? To what extent do interviews constitute part of your data base, and what constituted an interview? Are you claiming to triangulate your data? Under what circumstances was information cross-checked, and how are data reported that were not so checked? (p. 27)

If this is not done, readers will not be able to have confidence in the data.

Fortner and Christians (1981) also reminded qualitative researchers of the importance of making the case that their evidence is of high quality when they said, "observations must reflect the genuine features of the situation under study" (p. 366), which requires a faithful account of people's own words. In order to do this, researchers need to immerse themselves deeply enough to be able to establish the principal aspects of the event being studied and to distinguish the main features from the digressions. "If true interiority has occurred, that is, if data accurately reflect the natural circumstances, those data are valid and reliable even though not based upon randomization, repeated and controlled observation, measurement, and statistical inference" (p. 366). They said that exegetics, or the reading of situations or documents with precision, is also very important. This requires cultivation in the environment so that the context of events can be understood fully. Lull (1985) argued that validity and reliability checks on specific observations, concepts, behavioral rules, or theory are important and can be accomplished through final interviews with research subjects.

Miles and Huberman (1984) presented 12 tactics researchers should use to ensure the internal quality of their research: checking for representativeness, checking for researcher effects, triangulating, weighting evidence (some data are better than others), making contrasts/comparisons, checking the meaning of outliers, using extreme cases, ruling out spurious relations, replicating a finding, checking out rival explanations, looking for negative evidence, and getting feedback from informants. They offered these tactics to help researchers avoid what they referred to as the three archetypical sources of bias: the holistic fallacy (ignoring outliers and exceptions to find patterns), elite bias (overweighting data from high-status informants), and going native (losing one's perspective [bracketing ability] as a researcher).

Silverstone (1988) argued "that although meaning is theoretically unlimited, it is empirically limited. It is perfectly possible to imagine as many readings as there are readers ... but in practice only some will be socially significant" (p. 30). So how do we know which will be more significant? He said that we must examine each reading in context of "the intersecting and competing discourses which both the text and reader are placed" (pp. 30–31). He has attempted to create a model of textual analysis and explained that as he develops it, it grows "more complex, [and] it is hoped also more sophisticated, more adequate, and more useful" (p. 31); therefore, it appears that the goals of his effort are sophistication, adequacy, and utility, and those then are the standards upon which he feels the model should be judged.

It is useful to summarize by illuminating three general positions on the issue of internal validity. First, researchers can take the position of presenting some sort of an argument for the quality of their measures. This can be done by checking observations with subjects, triangulating measures of some other technique to seek out information about the accuracy of the observations or texts. Second, researchers can present an argument for *not* making a case for the internal validity, saying that this issue has no meaning in qualitative research. And third, re-searchers can simply ignore the case for quality of measures. This third position is the most troublesome, because the reader cannot tell if the researcher is concerned with quality but does not know how (or neglects) to demonstrate it *or* if the researcher is opposed to standards. This is an important difference. If a researcher does not reveal his or her position on this issue, the reader lacks an important piece of context to use in interpreting the research report.

Much of the qualitative research is of the third type, where authors do not make a salient argument for the quality of their evidence and of their analysis of it. However, there are some good examples where authors do. In his audi-ence-focused research, Lull (1980) had participant observers write a report about their observations of each family. "Following the writing of the reports, family members were asked to read and confirm the validity of the observations" (p. 200). Jhally and Lewis (1992) raised the issue of internal validity when they said they regarded themselves as a "prudent jury ... must use our knowledge and skill to interpret what people tell us rather than accept all testimony at face value" (p. 9). However, they did not discuss the criteria they used to make those judgments, preferring instead to say "we will not try the reader's patience by detailing it completely" (p. 9).

With institution-focused research, Altheide (1976) used an internal process of verification; that is, he checked his observations from one station with what was happening at another station to see if his perceptions of a pattern held up. Also, he checked what he heard with what he saw. Also, Turow (1981) trained coders to analyze the characteristics of children's television. To demonstrate that the resulting coded data were good he reported the results of a test of intercoder reliability. Elliott (1979) told the reader about the importance of plausibility as a criterion when he said, "The important test to apply to the analysis of participant observation data seems to me not to be simply how many other cases is this likely to be true for ... but how plausible is the posited relationship between belief, behaviour and situation in the light of possible alternative explanations?" (p. 174).

Altheide (1976) argued that building a case for the internal validity is possible, but that it "cannot be done through rhetoric or assertions of 'scientific training.' Nor can it be done by making claims about how extensive one's notes are. The final test of worthwhile field studies is the researcher's explication of the way the study was carried out, including oversights, errors, uncertainties, etc." (p. 198). So his warrant for validity is sharing methodological decisions and limita-tions of the study, which is what he did.

EXTERNAL QUALITY

Much of the theorizing on the issue of external validity can be summarized by J. K. Smith and Heshusius (1986), who said that "valid" is a label applied to an interpretation or description with which one agrees. It is simply a matter of what the reader believes. Having said that, we must realize that the issue grows more complex as we look at it more closely.

External quality raises the issues of generalizability and conceptual leverage. Generalizability is the concern about the degree to which the researcher can generalize his or her findings to other texts, people, or institutions. Conceptual leverage is the concern about the degree to which the researcher can extend his or her results from the concrete evidence to more abstract explanations. In chapter 8, we examined these two issues from the perspective of whether or not qualitative researchers generalized and leveraged their findings conceptually. It was found that many qualitative researchers did. In this chapter, the view on these issues is from the perspective of whether authors who engage in these practices make a clear argument for doing so in their writings.

Those theoreticians who allow for generalization caution that researchers should make a clear argument why their results can be generalized. For example, Lindlof and Meyer (1987) said the case for generalizability needs to be made in the research report itself. They argued that "although the scope of the resulting claims is normally idiographic, the evidence used to advance them is subject to evaluations of their completeness and adequacy that are not solipsistic" (p. 6). Jensen (1991a) placed the focus on the reputation of the researchers, saying "rather the validity of an interpretation depends on a more universal confidence in the scholar's expertise and sensitivity, his/her legitimacy and authority, or perhaps an appreciation of the interpretation as original and stimulating" (pp. 31–32).

Strauss and Corbin (1990) presented two detailed schemes for achieving and arguing for conceptual leverage as evidenced in grounded theory. Their first list contains four criteria as follows: (a) fit (the theory must be faithful to the everyday reality of the substantive area and carefully induced from diverse data), (b) understanding (it should be comprehensible and make sense both to the persons who were studied and to those practicing in the area), (c) generality (should be conceptually broad and abstract enough and include sufficient variation to make it applicable to a variety of contexts related to that phenomenon, and (d) control (theory can guide action). Then at the end of the book, they presented seven more criteria for the empirical grounding of the study:

1. Are there concepts generated?
2. Are the concepts systematically related?
3. Is there conceptual density; that is, are there well-developed categories and are there many conceptual linkages?
4. Is there a lot of variation built into the theory (lots of conditions under which the phenomenon appears and a wide range of consequences)?
5. Are broader conditions that affect the phenomenon built into its explanation; that is, are their broader cultural trends linked to the phenomenon?
6. Has process been taken into account, that is, fluidity of the phenomenon over time?

7. To what extent are the theoretical findings significant (needs imagination and insight)?

   Denzin (1994) focused on the writing phase, because it is the research report that must make the case for the value of the author's findings. He said that authors must create a voice that conveys the legitimacy of the author's claims through thick description that "gives the context of an experience, states the intentions and meanings that organized the experience, and reveals the experience as a process. Out of this process arises a text's claims for truth, or its verisimilitude" (p. 505). Even if a writer follows all these rules, Denzin argued that "a text's and an author's authority can always be challenged" (p. 506) for three reasons. First, there are always other ways to tell the story. Second, all writing is biased in some way because of the perspective of the writer. And third, the interpretive logic that the author uses in assembling the elements of his or her story can be questioned. On this last point, we can question how the author selected certain elements, how the author injected himself or herself into the text through voice, and how the author interpreted the subjects' intentions.

   In summary, on the issue of external validity, there appear to be three positions. First, researchers present an argument for the quality of their findings/conclusions. They present some sort of justification that other researchers would have arrived at the same conclusions or that their findings are useful in some way. Second, researchers present an argument for *not* making a case for the external validity, saying that this issue has no meaning in qualitative research. And third, researchers ignore the case for quality of findings/conclusions. As with the issue of internal validity, this third position is the most troublesome.

   Examples of authors making a clear argument for external validity are rare, but there are some examples where authors present a case for generalizability. Within audience-focused research, Liebes and Katz (1988, 1989) used a purposive sample that they said was not randomly generated, but that "one can make a good case that these are bona fide members of their respective subcultures" (p. 220). Barrios (1988) used a convenience sample of 13 families with at least two children. They were selected so as to have social and cultural differences among family groups. Jhally and Lewis (1992) said they got the people for their 52 focus groups from Springfield, Massachusetts, which they argued was "a fairly typical small North American city. . . . Its 'ordinariness' indeed, was commented upon by journalist Bill Moyers, who in 1990 chose Springfield as the venue for a TV program because he felt it was a microcosm of national attitudes and opinions" (pp. 9–10).

   Some qualitative authors avoid the issue of external validity by saying that they will not generalize their findings to other groups of people (Ang, 1985; Bodroghkozy, 1992; Lindlof, 1987; Morley, 1980; Wolf, 1987). For example, Wolf avoided generalizing, saying "the goal here is not to make generalizations about all children. It is to be able to talk about *these* children in the context of knowing them as they revealed themselves through the course of the study" (p. 94). Bodroghkozy did not try to generalize, cautioning against doing so by saying that the documents she analyzed are not a representative sample of the viewers of "Julia"; instead, she was cautious to say that the letters contain "traces, clues, parts of a larger whole to which we have no access. Indeed like all histories of audience reception, this one presents partial knowledge, pieces of the past that we must interpret in a qualified manner" (p. 148).

Finally, Altheide (1976) presented an explicit argument on the point of external validity, but ironically, his argument said that it is beyond the scope of the author to make the validity case. He said that his 3 years of observing and interviewing reports and editors in news rooms "does not guarantee validity. Only assessments of the findings and conclusions by other media researchers and journalists will uncover oversights and errors" (p. 198).

ILLUSTRATIONS OF DECISION MAKING

13

AN ILLUSTRATION OF
DECISION MAKING IN A
QUANTITATIVE ANALYSIS

Throughout the seven chapters in the previous section we explored the issues qualitative researchers must deal with in designing, executing, and writing up their research studies. In this chapter I show that many of these same issues are important to scholars in designing, executing, and writing up quantitative research.

This chapter and the next are similar in form; both illuminate the decisions that were made in the design and execution of a single research study. However, the studies examined are different. This chapter attempts to illuminate the decisions about a quantitative research study and the next chapter focuses on a qualitative study.

The illustration in this chapter is based on a quantitative research study that I conducted with four graduate students several years ago. Our purpose was to determine how much qualitative research appeared in the major journals of mass media scholarship. We also wanted to determine the prevalence of certain characteristics in that published literature. Because we were primarily interested in prevalence, we used the quantitative approach, and because we wanted to examine the content of texts, we chose the content analysis methodology.

This chapter illuminates the decision making that guided that project. The form of presentation here does not follow the usual organization of quantitative research reports (introduction, review of the literature, methods, results, and discussion). Instead of focusing on the results of the study, in this chapter I shift the focus to the decision making. The purpose of this chapter is to illustrate how we made decisions about the major methodological areas of data gathering, analysis, writing, and standards.

DATA GATHERING

The key data-gathering issues of the content analysis methodology are sampling, variables, and procedures.

Sampling

Within the quantitative approach, researchers make an important distinction among the terms *population, sampling frame,* and *sample.* The population is the total set of all units of interest to the researcher. The sampling frame is the list of all units in the population. The sample is the set of units selected for analysis from the sampling frame. If all units of the sampling frame are used in the analysis, the research is regarded as a population study; if a subset (a sample) of units is used, then some form of selection must take place.

In order for a sample to have high utility to a quantitative researcher, two criteria must be met. First, there must be correspondence between the population of interest and the sampling frame. Second, the units within the sampling frame must be given an equal chance of being selected for the sample. When the second criterion is met, the results in the sample are considered representative of the sampling frame and can be generalized to that frame. When both criteria are met, the results found in the sample can be generalized to the larger population of interest to the researcher.

In this study, we began with an interest in a population of all qualitative articles published in the major mass media journals. This conception of the population caused some problems in translating it into a sampling frame, because it was too general—that is, there were no time limits. To correct this problem we needed to limit the time span, so we decided to focus on only those articles published in the years just prior to our study—1987 to 1991.

We also needed to define the key terms (such as *article* and *major journals*) in an operational manner. We decided to define an article as only those full reports of research studies (not research in brief or book reports). And in order to be considered major, a journal had to be affiliated with a scholarly society, have a minimum circulation of 2,000, and exhibit very high standards as evidenced by a blind review process resulting in an acceptance rate under 20%. The journals of five professional associations of mass media scholars were selected for an analysis of their qualitative articles. Those associations along with the seven journals are: Association for Education in Journalism and Mass Communication (*Journalism Quarterly*), Broadcast Education Association (*Journal of Broadcasting & Electronic Media*), International Communication Association (*Journal of Communication*), Popular Culture Association (*Journal of Popular Culture*), and Speech Communication Association (*Communication Monographs, Communication Quarterly,* and *Critical Studies in Mass Communication*).

The clarifying of the population through limiting the time span and operationalizing the key ideas of article and major journals resulted in a workable sampling frame. However, this changed our population by making it more limited. This is the trade-off in sampling; the techniques that are used to make the sampling frame more clear and operational also serve to make the population less general and more limited. The limitation of including only those articles published in seven journals results in a clear depiction of all elements in the population of interest, but it excludes many potentially interesting examples such as books, book chapters, monographs, articles published in other journals, and nonpublished material. Other populations exist, such as all qualitative books produced by certain publishers, all papers read at a certain scholarly convention, and so forth. By selecting only one of these populations of texts for this study, we were not advocating that the other populations should be ignored; to the contrary, they too should be analyzed in future research studies.

We sampled within our sampling frame. Instead of examining all qualitative articles published in those seven journals from 1987 to 1991, we selected three (1987, 1989, 1991) of those 5 years. If this selection were done in a purely random manner, we would have needed to engage in some procedure, such as putting five slips of paper into a hat where each slip of paper would have written on it one of the 5 years. A drawing of three of those pieces of paper out of the hat would have given all 5 years an equal chance of being selected. However, we instead reasoned that given the stability of selection of types of articles during an editor's term and the long lead times for publication, the nonselected years of 1988 and 1990 would have patterns very similar to their contiguous years. For example, if we sampled all 5 years, the patterns found in the 1988 journals would be the average of the patterns in the 1987 and 1989 journals so that 1988 would be redundant. Therefore, to use coding time more efficiently, we regarded the project as assessing patterns over 5 years although we were only analyzing articles from 3 years, feeling that the 3 years selected could represent well the 5-year span.

When we did our initial pass through the articles in the seven journals over the 3 years (1987, 1989, and 1991), we counted 906 articles in total, but only 185 of these were qualitative studies of media. For purposes of this study, "qualitative" was defined in a very broad manner; that is, any study that did not focus primarily on quantitative analyses was regarded as qualitative. A quantitative focus required the use of enumeration (translating concepts or properties into numerals) and the subsequent use of statistical analysis to arrive at the study's main conclusions. Mass media studies were defined as those that focused on the transmission of messages through a mediated channel to an audience that was primarily anonymous to the sender. The focus on mass media ruled out interpersonal or other forms of communication that did not deal with mass media. Legal and policy-type articles were also excluded.

Our population of interest, which was originally all qualitative articles published in major media journals, is now all qualitative articles (not research in brief or book reports) that focus on media analysis published in 1987, 1989, and 1991 in the seven scholarly journals of major communication organizations.

Variables

Now that we had our 185 articles, what did we look for in the articles? We (the research team of four graduate students and myself) began with a list of variables that I had developed in my reading, and we met weekly for 4 months to develop a final list of 22 variables, which were well defined in an a priori manner so that all coders could be trained to look for the same things.

Of the total set of 22 variables, 2 were considered independent variables (year of publication and methodology used) and 20 were dependent variables (mention of axioms, nature of the phenomenon, ontology, epistemology, purpose of research, nature of evidence, use of numbers, expectations for data, researcher identification, researcher activity during data gathering, collaboration, length of data gathering, analysis process, conceptual leverage, generalizability, product, contextualization, locus of argument, making a case for internal quality, and making a case for external quality). We made this distinction to guide the analysis. The patterns in the 20 independent variables were to be examined in the context of time and methodology—the independent variables. We reasoned that the patterns in the 20 variables would be dependent on the passage of time and would vary across methodologies. Beyond this general expectation, we formulated no hypotheses.

Independent Variables. Each article in the sample was coded for year and methodology. Methodology had seven categories as follows: ecological psychology (culturally and environmentally patterned behavior), symbolic interactionism (meanings people ascribe to interactions), ethnomethodology (*how* people make sense out of *everyday life*), ethnography (the creation and maintenance of communities), reception studies (the meaning readers construct from texts), textual analysis (texts from a literary point of view), and cultural studies.

Dependent Variables. The list of dependent variables as well as their definitions were based closely on the analytical templates used in the previous chapters. However, there are some minor deviations. Because this analysis was conducted before the book was written, the variables used in this analysis represent a forerunner of the template issues presented in this book.

The first five dependent variables deal with foundational issues: mention of axioms, nature of the phenomenon, ontology, epistemology, and purpose of research. Coders scanned the articles to see if any of the five *axiomatic beliefs* were mentioned. These were: phenomenology, interpretive, hermeneutics, naturalism, and humanistic studies. The *nature of the phenomenon* variable had four values: focus on symbols of communication, focus on how people create meaning from everyday experiences, focus on how people create meaning from the messages of institutions and the media, and focus on the production of culture. The *ontology* variable had four values: solipsism, idiographic, ordered reality, and radical materialism. The *epistemology* variable had three values: purely subjective, inter-subjectivity, and objectivity. The *purpose* variable had four values: report on observables, description about how people construct meaning, inferring patterns about observables, and making inferences about how people construct meaning.

The remaining 15 dependent variables were oriented toward practices used by the qualitative researchers. These variables are grouped into four concerns: evidence (nature of evidence and use of numbers), data-gathering issues (expectations for data, researcher identification, researcher activity during data gathering, collaboration, and length of data gathering), analysis (process, conceptual leverage, generalizability, product, contextualization, and locus of argument), and making a case for quality (internal and external). Each is defined in detail in the remainder of this section.

Concerning the nature of evidence used in qualitative research, the variable of *nature of evidence* had three values as follows: (a) The phenomenon of interest is unknowable through empirical means so all research must be a creative construction; (b) there are tangible, material artifacts that reflect the phenomenon of interest, but this reflection is very fractured and inaccurate; the artifacts can be a starting place to suggest what the phenomenon is like, but they require much interpretation; and (c) artifacts are relatively accurate reflections of the phenomenon, some more so than others; the key act of research then is to make judgments about which artifacts to use and which to discard; and when the proper selection is made, little interpretation is needed in the analysis. The *numerical evidence* variable had four levels as follows: (a) no enumeration was used, (b) some numbers were used but are citations from other sources, (c) numerical data are generated and simple statistics used, and (d) numerical data are generated for use in inferential statistical tests.

Concerning the practices used in the gathering of data, the *expectations for data* variable had five values: (a) no a priori expectations, (b) funnel procedure (no beginning expectations, but as researchers gather data, they become more focused on searching for certain data and ignoring other data), (c) informal expectations, (d) formal a priori expectations (such as hypotheses), and (e) ideology drives selection of data. The *researcher identification* variable had five values: (a) no contact made with people; data are texts and the like, (b) unidentified (no one in the situation knows the researcher is there to gather data), (c) identified as a member of the group, (d) identified as a researcher, and (e) identified as a group member and a researcher. The *researcher activity* variable had seven values as follows: (a) passive observer, (b) active observer, (c) active participant, (d) researcher gathers data mostly from people but also uses some documents, (e) researcher gathers an equal amount of data from people and documents, (f) researcher relies primarily on documents, but also gets some information from people, and (g) researcher gathers information from documents only. The *collaboration* issue posed the question: Is this research the product of one person, or were there others involved in the data gathering? The *length of data gathering* was included in the analysis to determine if researchers provided information about how long they had contact with the phenomenon they were studying.

Concerning the practices used in the analyses of data, the *process of analysis* issue posed the question: Do authors describe the process of analysis; that is, what are the steps of going from data to report? Coders determined whether this issue was addressed or not (yes or no). The *conceptual leverage* variable focuses on how far does the researcher move conceptually: (a) no attempt to move beyond describing the literal events in the data, (b) reasoning of patterns but limited to data points, (c) researcher infers how other people construct meaning, and (d) inferring a connection to an a priori construction such as a theory or an ideology. The *generalizability* variable poses the question: Are qualitative researchers limited to describing the people (or units) observed or do they generalize? Values include: (a) no generalizability, (b) informal generalizations, and (c) formal, explicit generalizations. The *product* variable poses the question: What is the end point of the analysis? This variable has four values: (a) provide a clear description of the data, (b) provide an interpretation of the data, (c) provide a test of a theory (or operationalized hypothesis), and (d) support an ideological position. The *contextualization* variable poses the question: How is context used in the analysis? This variable has three values: (a) no contextualization, (b) context described only to provide a background or the details of the methodology, and (c) context used as an important element in the analyses. The *locus of argument* variable poses the question: On what basis does the researcher expect the reader to be persuaded that his or her interpretations are useful or accurate? This variable has four values: (a) ethos (authority or expertise of the author/researcher), (b) data, (c) logos (logic of the argument or presentation), and (d) pathos (appeal primarily to the emotions).

Concerning the issue of setting out criteria for quality, the variable of *internal quality of data* had three values: (a) researchers talk about confirming their data or conclusions by remeasuring people or triangulation, (b) no attention to making a case for internal quality, and (c) eschews the need for validity. The variable of determining the *external quality* of the research posed the question: Do researchers explicitly make a case for the quality of the findings generated by the analysis? Coders decided whether or not (yes or no) this concern was addressed in the article.

Coding Procedures

The coding team consisted of myself and four students in the telecommunications graduate program at Indiana University. We worked for 3 months in pilot testing the list of variables, their definitions, their values, the coding form, and coding procedures. We conducted several rounds of reading articles and pilot testing to determine if we should add (or subtract) variables from our set, whether we should alter definitions of variables, and whether we should add to (or subtract from) the list of alternative values that could be coded for each variable.

After 3 months, our weekly discussions ceased to uncover any changes we felt were important to make to our coding scheme. The four graduate students then independently coded the 185 articles; each student coded from 32 to 85 of the articles. For each variable they decided which value most accurately characterized that article and wrote the number of that value in the proper column of the coding sheet. For each article then there was a line of numbers, one number for each of the variables.

I randomly selected 30 of those articles and coded them independently from the graduate students. I then compared my coding decisions with theirs to compute the percentages of times we agreed. Those percentages of agreement for the variables are as follows: .87 for methodology, .87 for nature of the phenomenon; .90, ontology; .83, epistemology; .87, purpose of research; .93 for nature of the evidence; .96, numerical evidence; .80, expectations for data; .96, researcher identification; .87, researcher activity; .80, process; .77, conceptual leverage; .80, generalizability; .83, product of analysis; .87, contextualization; .83, locus of argument; .96, internal quality; and .83, external quality. These percentages compare favorably with those reported by other scholars conducting content analyses. We concluded that our codings were conducted in a reliable manner—that is, there was good consistency in our coding.

The data were entered into a computer for statistical analysis. I conducted cross-checks to ensure that the keypunching was done accurately and it reflected (with no errors) the numbers recorded on the coding sheets.

ANALYSIS

Our first interest was to find out how prevalent the qualitative approach was in the published literature. We kept a count of total articles (906) that we scanned through to get our sample of 185. Therefore, the percentage of articles that were qualitative was 20.4%. In order to provide some meaning for this figure, we cited the figures from another content analysis study as context. This other study (Cooper, Potter, & Dupagne, 1994) found that the prevalence of qualitative research had declined from 50.0% in 1965 and 59.3% in 1968 to lower levels of 30.2% in 1986 and 28.1% in 1989. The results of the two analyses are not directly comparable, because the definitions of qualitative research are slightly different and the compositions of the samples are also slightly different. The Cooper et al. study included legal, policy, and regulation articles as qualitative research, whereas the study on which this chapter is based did not. Also, the two studies shared six journals in their samples, but the Cooper et al. study included two other journals (*Communication Research* and *Human Communication Research*) in its set of eight, whereas this study included one unique journal (*Journal of Popular Culture*) in its set of seven.

Our second purpose for conducting this study was to determine the prevalence of certain characteristics (our 20 dependent variables) in the literature and to see if these characteristics varied by year and methodology (our two independent variables). Year of publication was an easy variable to code and use in the analysis. However, methodology turned out not to be a useful independent variable, because there were so few examples of certain methodologies. There were only eight reception studies, four symbolic interaction studies, four ethnomethodologies, one ethnography, and one ecological psychology study. This meant that five of the seven methodologies accounted for about 10% of the entire sample of 185 studies. The most prevalent methodologies were cultural studies, which accounted for 56.9% of all the coded studies, and textual analysis, which accounted for 33.1%.

Because of the extreme imbalance, methodology was not regarded as a useful independent variable. Two other variables (source of data and type of study) were developed to take its place in the analyses. Source of data had three values: people, archives, and texts. Of the total of 185 articles, 20 (10.8%) were categorized as using people as the primary source of data, 61 (33.0%) used archives, and the remaining 104 (56.2%) used texts. However, determining the type of study was both much more difficult and interesting as is explained in the following paragraph.

What are the types of qualitative research? Lindlof (1991) offered an interesting scheme based on five groups: social-phenomenological, communication rules, cultural studies, reception study, and feminist research. When we compare the results of this content analysis of journal articles to Lindlof's scheme, we find at least one article in each of his five groups. But there are only four articles that used a feminist ideology and only one that could be called an audience reception study. Of course, Lindlof's conceptualization applies to all of mass media qualitative research, not just to journal articles.

We decided to construct our own variable of type in such a way as to have a relatively small number of types (four to seven) that would be conceptually meaningful and that would provide a relatively balanced typology of the different kinds of qualitative studies in the published literature. The coding scheme we developed for type of study was a bit more involved than had been the coding for methodology. Coders were given a list of key terms and for each article checked those terms that applied. The terms included: descriptive/journalistic, ethnography, ethnomethodology, genre analysis, historical, ideographic case study, ideological, literary analysis, semiotic, social science, symbolic interaction, and textual analysis. When the key terms were used as a basis for constructing types of qualitative articles, a five-part scheme emerged. This scheme includes the categories of texts, history, social science/ethnography, discourse, and ideology. The text group includes approaches that focus on tangible symbols of communication (such as scripts, television shows, books, etc.) and relies on key terms like textual analysis, genre analysis, literary analysis, and semiotics. The history group includes those articles that focused on trends or changes over time. The social science and ethnography group is composed of articles that provide description and explanation based on an objective or intersubjective approach. The discourse group includes studies that provided analyses of certain kinds of messages across media; that is, the focus was primarily on the message, not the symbols or the medium. And the ideology group is composed of essays that were argued from a clearly labeled philosophical position, such as Marxism, feminism, structuralism, postmodernism, and psychoanalytic theory. When the coding was completed, the ideological category contained 16 articles; text-based analyses, 69; historical, 52; discourse focused, 22; and social science/ethnography, 26.

Looking for Patterns

When we look across types of qualitative articles in Table 13.1, the numbers change as we read across the lines (showing differences across years) and as we read down the columns (showing differences among types of research). One thing that is obvious is that there are more qualitative articles from 1991 than either of the 2 previous years. Also, there are more qualitative articles in the types of text and history. The prevalence of articles in 1991 is generally consistent across all types of research and the prevalence of the text and history types are prevalent across all 3 years. However, there are some exceptions to this general pattern; for example, the history type of research seems to decrease over time. This raises the question: Is there an interaction between type and year? Within the quantitative approach, we can use a statistical test to provide

TABLE 13.1
Type of Article by Year of Publication

	1987	*1989*	*1991*	*Total*
Texts	17	17	35	69
	(33.3)	(32.7)	(42.7)	(37.3)
History	19	17	16	52
	(37.3)	(32.7)	(19.5)	(28.1)
Social Science/Ethnography	8	3	15	26
	(15.7)	(5.8)	(18.3)	(14.1)
Discourse	4	9	9	22
	(7.8)	(17.3)	(11.0)	(11.9)
Ideological	3	6	7	16
	(5.9)	(11.5)	(8.5)	(8.6)
Total Articles	51	52	82	185

Note. Numbers in parentheses are column percentages.

an answer. Given this type of question and the type of data (nominal) an appropriate statistical test is the chi-square, which compares the observed pattern of numbers to expected patterns. In this case, the expected pattern is that all numbers in the 1991 column should be much higher than numbers in the other 2 years and that the numbers in the text and history rows should be much higher than the numbers in the other rows. If there are large differences between the expected and observed, then the chi-square statistic will be very large and we can conclude that there is an interaction; that is, there are important differences across columns and rows that do not match the general pattern. When we run the chi-square test on the data displayed in Table 13.1, we get a chi-square of 8.8; in order for us to interpret this, we need some context. The statistical context is the probability that we could have gotten a number this large through error means; if not, we can have confidence that the number is indeed large and that the pattern is an interaction. The probability associated with this chi-square in this table is .36, which means that 36 times out of 100 we could get a chi-square this large or larger by chance alone. Statisticians are usually very conservative and are willing to accept only about a 5% chance of error. Therefore by usual statistical standards, this error risk is much too high, and we would conclude that we are *not* willing to conclude that any deviations from the general pattern are statistically significant.

If the chi-square procedure tells us that the results are significant, it means only *statistical* significance; that is, the deviation from the expected pattern is not likely to have occurred because of error variations. We must then look at the patterns and find the meaning of them—this is the task of finding substantive significance. Substantive significance is much more important than statistical significance, which is only used as a guide to tell us where to look. However, it is usually not productive to look for substantive significance if we do not first see evidence of statistical significance.

Now, let's look at the patterns produced by the 20 dependent variables.

Mention of Axioms. Very few authors consciously addressed any of the foundational axioms. Only eight (4.3%) even mentioned interpretation, three (1.6%) hermeneutics, two (1.1%) each mentioned naturalism or phenomenology, and none mentioned humanistic studies.

The Phenomenon. Of the 185 articles examined, the majority (58.2%) focused on symbols (see Table 13.2). Of least frequency was a focus on the meaning people ascribe to the symbols, rather than the symbols themselves.

There was a significant difference among the types in terms of the assumptions made about the phenomenon (chi-square = 49.3, $df = 12$, $p < .001$). As should be expected, the text group focused on symbols. The ideological group focused in the areas of the production of culture, institutions, and art as well as *how* people derive meaning from the messages of institutions and the media.

TABLE 13.2
Four Foundation Issues by Type of Article

	S.S./Et	History	Ideol.	Disc.	Texts	Total
The Phenomenon						
Symbols of communication	42.3	59.6	12.5	36.4	80.9	58.2
Meaning—everyday experience	19.2	9.6	–	9.1	–	6.5
Meaning—institutions	11.5	15.4	43.8	27.3	10.3	16.8
Production of culture	26.9	15.4	43.8	27.3	8.8	18.5
Ontology						
Solipsism	–	–	–	–	–	–
Idiographic	7.7	1.9	31.3	22.7	10.1	10.8
Ordered reality	92.3	98.1	68.8	77.3	89.9	89.2
Radical materialism	–	–	–	–	–	–
Epistemology						
Subjective	–	–	6.3	9.1	2.9	2.7
Intersubjective	46.2	59.6	93.8	86.4	49.3	60.0
Objective	53.8	40.4	–	4.5	47.8	37.3
Purpose						
Describe observables	48.0	50.0	–	9.1	15.9	27.7
Describe meaning construction	4.0	3.8	–	4.5	4.3	3.8
Infer patterns	24.0	25.0	12.5	36.4	49.3	34.2
Explain meaning construction	24.0	21.2	87.5	50.0	30.4	34.2

Note. All numbers are column percentages within their groups. For example, the first number, 42.3, means that of all the articles coded as Social Science/Ethnography, 42.3% were placed in the "Symbols of Communication" value for the group of Phenomenon.

Ontology. No examples were found for the extreme positions of solipsism or radical materialism. Among the two middle positions, ordered reality was clearly the more popular (89.2%). Ontology was related to the type of qualitative research (chi-square = 14.7, $df = 4$, $p = .005$). Studies in the ideological group were more likely to show an idiographic conception of the nature of reality, whereas history, social science/ethnography, and texts were almost exclusively based on an ordered reality.

Epistemology. In only five (2.7%) of the articles was there a clear exhibition of a belief that knowledge was purely subjective. Instead, the majority of articles (60.0%) took an intersubjective perspective.

Epistemology was related to the type of qualitative research (chi-square = 30.3, $df = 8$, $p < .001$). Research in the ideological and discourse groups was almost purely intersubjective, whereas research in the other three groups was distributed between intersubjective and objective.

Purpose. When the first two categories of purpose are collapsed, there is an almost equal split among description, interpretation, and explanation.

The purpose is related to type of research (chi-square = 51.7, $df = 12$, $p < .001$). The lowest level task of describing observables is fairly prevalent in social science/ethnography and history. Research in the categories of discourse and text focus much more strongly on inference about observables as well as explanation actors interpret their own meaning.

Nature of Evidence. The researchers in about two thirds (66.8%) of the articles exhibited a great deal of confidence in their evidence (see Table 13.3). These articles were strongly empirical with the belief that it is possible to gather data as a relatively accurate reflection of the phenomenon, and that little interpretation is needed in the analysis. This characteristic was especially prevalent among articles in the archives category (85.2%). In contrast, researchers in 32.9% of the articles exhibited a belief that there are tangible, material artifacts that reflect the phenomenon of interest, but this reflection is very fractured and inaccurate. In only two articles (1.1%) was there a belief exhibited that the phenomenon of interest is unknowable through empirical means.

Numerical Evidence. Not surprisingly, the majority (62.9%) of the sample did not use any ennumeration. When numbers were used, it was primarily to cite figures gathered by others. But there were some examples of researchers gathering data and reporting either descriptive statistics (13.0%) or even inferential statistics (2.7%).

Expectations for Data. The most prevalent characteristic is informal (53.6%), which means that most authors lay out a direction for their research, but do not begin with formal hypotheses or carefully delineated research questions. There is a significant difference (chi-square = 30.0, $df = 8$, $p < .001$). Archive-based research seemed to be more likely (than the other two) to present formal expectations, whereas text-based research was more likely to be ideologically driven.

Researcher Identification. This unexpectedly became an unimportant characteristic, because over 89% of the articles reported on studies where the researcher had no contact with humans and therefore had no opportunity to reveal their identity in the data-gathering situation. With people-based research, the authors were most likely to identify themselves as researchers (61.1%) to their subjects. Very seldom did they join the groups they were measuring. This pattern shows up again in the third variable of researcher activity, where the active observer was the most prevalent (52.6%) among the people-based research. In only two people-based studies (10.5%) was there an active participant.

Researcher Activity. In most of the studies (88.6%), the researcher did not have direct contact with people. Even in the first column of Table 13.3 where people were the primary source of data, there were many examples where the

TABLE 13.3
Differences in Methodological Features Compared by
Primary Source of Data: Data-Gathering Issues

	Source of Data			
	People	*Archives*	*Texts*	*Total*
Nature of Evidence				
Unknowable Through Empiricism	10.5%	—	—	1.1%
Material Artifacts—Fragmented	31.6	14.8	42.3	32.1
Material Artifacts—Stable	57.9	85.2	57.7	66.8
	(*n* = 19)	(*n* = 61)	(*n* = 104)	(*n* = 184)
Numerical Evidence				
No Enumeration	40.0%	65.8%	65.4%	62.7%
Citation of Numbers	30.0	29.5	15.4	21.6
Descriptive Statistics	25.0	13.9	15.4	13.0
Inferential Statistics	5.0	—	3.8	2.7
	(*n* = 20)	(*n* = 61)	(*n* = 104)	(*n* = 185)
Expectations for Data				
No a Priori Expectations	15.0%	—	1.9%	2.7%
Funnel Procedure	5.0	13.6	1.9	6.0
Informal Expectations	65.0	52.5	51.9	53.6
Formal a Priori	5.0	23.7	19.2	19.1
Ideology Driven	10.0	10.2	25.0	18.6
	(*n* = 20)	(*n* = 59)	(*n* = 104)	(*n* = 183)
Researcher Identification				
No Contact With People	27.8%	95.1%	96.2%	89.1%
Unidentified	—	—	—	—
Identified—Member of Group	5.6	—	—	0.5
Identified—As Researcher	61.1	4.9	3.8	9.8
Identified—Both	5.6	—	—	0.5
	(*n* = 18)	(*n* = 61)	(*n* = 104)	(*n* = 183)
Researcher Activity				
No Direct Contact With People	26.3%	95.1%	96.1%	88.6%
Passive Observer	10.5	—	—	1.1
Active Observer	52.6	4.9	2.9	8.7
Active Participant	10.5	—	1.0	1.6
	(*n* = 19)	(*n* = 61)	(*n* = 104)	(*n* = 184)
Collaboration				
Not Indicated	31.6%	75.4%	60.6%	62.5%
Collaboration in Data Gathering	42.1	4.9	21.2	17.9
Cannot Tell	26.3	19.7	18.3	19.6
	(*n* = 19)	(*n* = 61)	(*n* = 102)	(*n* = 183)

(Continued)

TABLE 13.3
(Continued)

	Source of Data			
	People	*Archives*	*Texts*	*Total*
	Length of Data Gathering			
Span: Mentioned	30.0%	11.5%	17.3%	16.8%
Not Mentioned	70.0	88.5	82.7	83.2
	($n = 19$)	($n = 61$)	($n = 102$)	($n = 183$)
Contact: Mentioned	15.0	—	3.8	3.8
Not Mentioned	85.0	100.0	96.2	96.2
	($n = 19$)	($n = 61$)	($n = 102$)	($n = 183$)

researcher did not have direct (but instead indirect such as through the mail) contact.

Collaboration. In most of the studies (62.5%) it was clear that the researcher acted alone in gathering all the data, and in another 19.6% it was unclear if there were multiple people involved in the data gathering. That leaves a small percentage (17.9%) where there was collaboration. This collaboration was most popular where the primary source of data was people and least popular where archives were the source of data. The differences in collaboration over type of source were statistically significant (chi-square = 17.7, $df = 4$, $p < .001$).

Length of Data Gathering. This variable was measured in two ways. First, the coders looked for an indication for the span of time (in days) the phenomenon was examined. Then the coders looked for an indication of how long (in hours) the researcher had contact with the phenomenon. For example, in an ethnography a community may have been studied over the course of a year during which the researcher would have visited it for 2 hours each week. In this case the span would be 365 days and the contact would be 104 hours (2 hours per week for 52 weeks).

The majority of articles (83.2%) did not give any indication about the span of the examination. The studies that used people as source of information were more likely to mention the span, but this difference was not statistically significant (chi-square = 3.8, $df = 2$, $p = .15$). Among the 29 articles that did mention a span, the range was from 2 days to 30 years with a median of 2 years. Ten of these studies had a span of 6 weeks or less, whereas 15 had a span of over 5 years.

A very small percentage of articles (3.8%) mentioned the degree of contact the researcher had with the phenomenon of study. The studies that used people as source of information were more likely to mention the degree of contact (chi-square = 9.8, $df = 2$, $p < .01$). Among the eight articles that did mention a degree of contact, the range was from 6 hours to 154 hours with a median of 45 hours.

Process of Analysis. Do authors describe the process of analysis; that is, what are the steps of moving from the raw data to the final report? From Table 13.4, it can be seen that authors seldom (13.6%) provide a description about how they conducted their analysis. There appears to be a difference across the three types of research (chi-square = 9.4, $df = 6$, $p = .009$) with people-based research the most likely to provide such a description and archives-based the least likely.

Conceptual Leverage. How far does the researcher move conceptually in the analysis? If the four values of this coding scheme can be regarded as a hierarchy, it appears that the overall median level is pattern construction. A small percentage (23.8%) remain at a low level of description, but about a third (31.9%) attempt to connect their results to a theory or ideology. This pattern differs across the three types (chi-square = 32.9, $df = 6$, $p < .001$) with text-based articles more likely to have a higher degree of conceptual leverage.

Generalizability. Related to conceptual leverage is the topic of generalizability. Almost 60% engage in generalization in an informal manner. Again there are differences across types of data (chi-square = 16.5, $df = 4$, $p = .002$) with archive-based research exhibiting this the least.

Product. The most prevalent product is interpretation of data (45.4%), but this varies across data types (chi-square = 25.8, $df = 6$, $p < .001$). Archive-based studies are more likely to be descriptive; providing an argument for an ideology is more likely among text-based research.

Contextualization. This was found to be an important element in the analysis in 57.3% of the research. This varies in importance across type of data (chi-square = 12.5, $df = 4$, $p = .014$), with archive-based research giving it the highest priority.

Locus of Argument. It is logical argument (43.2%) and the data themselves (40.5%) that are given the task of making the authors' cases, but this varies across research type (chi-square = 18.2, $df = 6$, $p = .006$). The data are almost twice as prevalent an element compared to logic in people-based research, but this is the opposite in text-based research. Pathos is very minor in all forms of research, but ethos is fairly prevalent in archive- and text-based research.

Internal Quality. Almost 80% of qualitative articles ignore the point of making a case for the accuracy of their evidence. There seems to be a difference across the three groups (chi-square = 19.5, $df = 4$, $p < .001$) with people-based

TABLE 13.4
Differences in Methodological Features Compared by
Primary Source of Data: Issues of Analysis

	Source of Data			
	People	*Archives*	*Texts*	*Total*
Process of Analysis				
Describe Steps in Analysis	26.3%	3.3%	17.3%	13.6%
No Description	73.7	96.7	82.7	86.4
	($n = 19$)	($n = 61$)	($n = 104$)	($n = 184$)
Conceptual Leverage				
Literal Description of Data	30.0%	45.9%	9.6%	23.8%
Pattern Construction	30.0	27.9	32.7	30.8
Inferences–Other's Constructions	20.0	9.8	14.4	13.5
Connection to Theory or Ideology	20.0	16.4	43.3	31.9
	($n = 20$)	($n = 61$)	($n = 104$)	($n = 184$)
Generalizability				
None	30.0%	57.4%	27.9%	37.8%
Informal	70.0	41.0	66.3	58.4%
Formal, Explicit	–	1.6	5.8	3.8
	($n = 20$)	($n = 61$)	($n = 104$)	($n = 184$)
Product				
Description of Data	30.0%	42.6%	9.6%	22.7%
Interpretation of Data	45.0	37.7	50.0	45.4
Test of Theory	10.0	8.2	15.4	12.4
Support for Ideology	15.0	11.5	25.0	19.5
	($n = 20$)	($n = 61$)	($n = 104$)	($n = 185$)
Contextualization				
None	15.0%	–	2.9%	3.2%
Uses as Background	40.0	34.4	42.3	39.5
Important Element in Analysis	45.0	65.6	54.8	57.3
	($n = 20$)	($n = 61$)	($n = 104$)	($n = 185$)
Locus of Argument				
Ethos	5.0%	11.5%	16.3%	13.5%
Data	60.0	55.7	27.9	40.5
Logos	30.0	29.5	53.8	43.2
Pathos	5.0	3.3	1.9	2.7
	($n = 19$)	($n = 61$)	($n = 104$)	($n = 185$)

(Continued)

TABLE 13.4
(Continued)

	Source of Data			
	People	*Archives*	*Texts*	*Total*
Internal Quality				
Makes Case	30.0%	6.6%	17.6%	15.3%
Ignores	55.0	93.4	79.4	81.4
Eschews Need	15.0	—	2.9	2.9
	($n = 20$)	($n = 61$)	($n = 102$)	($n = 183$)
External Quality				
Explicit Case	36.8%	10.0%	24.0%	20.8%
No Case	63.2	90.0	76.0	79.2
	($n = 19$)	($n = 50$)	($n = 104$)	($n = 183$)

research either making a clear case (30.0%) or arguing that there is no need to make a case (15.0%).

External Quality.   Only a small percentage (20.8%) of the research makes a case for the external quality of the findings. This also differs across research types (chi-square = 7.9, $df = 2$, $p = .019$) with people-based research showing the most prevalence for this characteristic.

WRITING

When writing the report of the research study, a scholar must make decisions about what to say and how to say it. With quantitative scholarship, the decision making is much more concerned with the what. The how is usually not much of an issue, because the conventions governing expression are fairly strong and are very limited in terms of options. The writing purpose is almost always either description or explanation; almost never criticism or action advocacy. Sometimes quantitative scholars adopt an interpretive stance at the end of their article when they write a section entitled "Discussion" where they engage in some self-reflection and interpret the meaning of their results within the progression of the research literature given the limitations of their methods. Our contextualization for the importance of the study as well as the variables we selected was established through a review of two literatures. One of these was the thinking of qualitative theoreticians who wrote about what the approach should include. The other literature was composed of quantitative content analyses of research reports.

In writing up the results of this study (see Potter, Troiano, Riggs, & Robinson, 1993), we used a primarily descriptive tone. Our locus was the data and our form of expression was realism. These are typical choices for quantitative researchers. To provide an illustration of the product of these decisions about writing, I present next a section of that report. This example of the writing displays what we thought were the five major conclusions of our social scientific analysis of the qualitative literature in mainstream media journals.

1. The Qualitative Literature Displays a Family of Methodologies

The central finding of this analysis confirms what is sometimes suggested—that there is no one qualitative methodology. Lindlof (1991) said that there are five and we argue that there are seven. All of these were found in this analysis, however some are much more prevalent than others in the mainstream journals.

Another way of looking at the variety of forms of qualitative research is to look at the results of the five-part scheme developed in this study. This five-part scheme derives its usefulness as a profiling device from its attention to the assumptions underlying the qualitative research as well as to the practices displayed. This scheme includes the categories of texts (37.3%), history (28.1%), social science/ethnography (14.1%), discourse (11.9%), and ideology (8.6%). The research in each of these five categories is profiled next.

Texts. Text-based research is the most prevalent type of qualitative research found in this analysis. It focuses on the symbols of mass communication and is based on the ontological assumption of an ordered reality where people can give the texts an intersubjective or even an apparently objective reading. The assumption that each person is a unique individual with a special reading is *not* very prevalent (only 2 articles out of 66). The purpose of this research moves well beyond description with researchers providing inferences about patterns and explanations about how meaning is constructed for those exposed to these texts.

History. The historical research is similar to textual research in a relatively strong focus on symbols, its ontological assumption of an ordered reality, and its belief in an intersubjective or objective reality. However, it differs from textual analysis primarily in terms of its purpose, which focuses on describing observables and to a lesser extent providing inferences or explanations.

Social Science/Ethnography. This group resembles the History research in terms of the ontological, epistemological, and purpose assumptions. The difference is in the nature of the phenomenon where there are examples at all levels of this assumption, and no sharp pattern is observable as with other research types.

Discourse. This group of articles differs substantially from the three types presented thus far. It spreads its attention across symbols, the meaning constructed from symbols, and the creation of culture from these symbols. It virtually ignores the way people attribute meaning in their everyday lives. More than the other types, these researchers exhibit an assumption that there is an idiographic reality; that is, there is a nonmaterial world but that it is not ordered and does not follow regular patterns. It does allow for intersubjectivity, but objectivity is seldom possible. Its view of purpose is interpretation and explanation.

Ideological. This group resembles the Discourse group in terms of ontology and epistemology. However, it is much more oriented toward explanation of meaning construction as a purpose and more strongly focused on the phenomenon as an interaction of people with culture or institutions.

This content analysis of the qualitative literature also revealed a key difference across articles in terms of their primary source of data: people, archives, or texts. Because the data in each of these categories are very different, it follows that the methods to gather the data and the ways to analyze them also will differ. This is what was found, and these findings are profiled next.

People-based studies resemble quantitative research the most closely. In contrast to the other two types, people-based studies are more likely to assume stable data, use statistics, provide descriptions of analytical steps, make an explicit case for external validity, and focus their results on the data themselves. This pattern seems to reflect the ethnographic tradition; but lest we equate the two, a more complete comparison is needed to show that some elements are incompatible with ethnographic research. For example, very little of people-based research is free of beginning expectations, and seldom is the researcher an active participant (or even a member) in the group being studied. Also, less than half of this research uses context as a major element in the analysis.

Archive-based research is essentially historical where scholars gather data from existing sources and almost never have contact with people as data sources. They take an objectivist approach to their data, accepting them as they are without making a case for their validity. They will use numbers from secondary sources but merely cite them or provide descriptive statistics and will rarely generate any numerical data. They almost never explain the steps in their analyses, perhaps because they are often likely not to analyze, but simply frame facts on a descriptive level within an explicit context.

Text-based research is more likely to exhibit a distrust of empirical data as a focus of the scholarship. Instead, interpretation is required, mainly through logical argument and sometimes simply through the reputation of the authors.

This practice is based on a belief that data are fragmented elements reflecting culture and that they are open to many different interpretations. More than other research, this is ideologically driven, but the majority (over 70%) of these studies is guided by expectations that are not linked to an ideology. Like archive-based research, text-based is likely to ignore the need to establish a case for the quality of the data and for the validity of their findings. Also, they are not likely to provide a description of the process of analysis.

Individual scholars are often prescriptive in their beliefs about what qualitative research *should* be. But these prescriptions are often conflicting, and this is one of the reasons why it is difficult to understand qualitative research. It is really a family of methodologies (and perspectives) that were developed independently and later incorporated into a group, which is then presented in opposition to other (primarily quantitative) research practices.

2. Foundational Issues Are Rarely Discussed in the Empirical Literature

Fewer than 5% of the studies even mentioned *any* of the five major axioms of qualitative research. Also, very few studies made a clear statement about the phenomenon they were examining or about their purpose (description, interpretation, explanation, or call for action). And almost none dealt explicitly with ontological or epistemological issues. This statement is not meant as a criticism of the qualitative empirical literature, because there is no expectation that the empirical literature *should* deal explicitly with any of these issues (with the possible exceptions of phenomenon or purpose). Articles are always truncated reports of research, because space is so limited in the journals. Foundational issues must be reduced to assumptions; that is, authors must make certain assumptions about the expectations, beliefs, and level of knowledge about their readers. Looking at the patterns in the published research, it is clear that these issues are regarded as fundamental assumptions that the reader must hold and the author need not address.

3. When the Assumptions Behind the Empirical Work Are Inferred, It Appears That Many of the Assumptions Are Very Similar to the Assumptions Underlying Studies That Use the Quantitative Approach

This conclusion, which will be regarded as very controversial, is supported by the ontological and epistemological assumptions. For example, in only about 11% of the articles was there exhibited a belief that the world was ideographic; the remaining 89% exhibited a clear belief that the world contained ordered reality. And from an epistemological point of view, less than 3% of the articles had a clearly subjective perspective where the authors presented their findings in the context of them being only one among many equally useful interpretations. Instead, 60% of the articles presented a perspective of intersubjectivity where some subjective observations are presented as "better" than others, where better means the observations or conclusions are a more accurate fit of the phenomenon. And another 37% exhibited an objective perspective on knowing.

It is indeed surprising that so few of the articles displayed a belief in a subjective epistemology. It is understandable that social science/ethnography and history researchers would exhibit an assumption of intersubjectivity or objectivity, but researchers in the other three groups should be expected to have the freedom to exercise much more subjectivity in their interpretations. However, they too favored these less subjective positions. In only five (2.9%) of the articles was there clearly exhibited a belief that knowledge was purely subjective. Instead the majority of articles (57.8%) were written from an apparently intersubjective perspective and another 39.3% exhibited a perspective that meaning was derived in an objective fashion.

This conclusion may be more of a reflection of a limitation of this study, rather than a reflection of qualitative research in general. Because this study focused on research published in journals (most of which have a strong quantitative perspective), most of the authors who were successful shared the same perspective of intersubjectivity and objectivity that is prevalent among quantitative researchers.

However, the interpretation advanced as a result of this analysis is that the qualitative empirical literature closely resembles what many qualitative theoreticians criticize about the quantitative literature, that is, that the quantitative approach is defective in its assumption of an ordered reality and a belief that there is an objective process of knowing that reality. Why should this be so? Two possible explanations come to mind. First, perhaps only those qualitative researchers with less subjective positions are able to get their work published in these journals—most of which have a strong quantitative history. A second and related explanation is that perhaps qualitative scholars really do hold a subjective position on epistemology but mask their subjective interpretations in the hope that this will make their work more acceptable to the mainstream journals. However, neither of these would explain why the pattern holds even in the research published in the *Journal of Popular Culture*.

4. On Many Points, the Practices of Qualitative Researchers Closely Resemble the Practices of Quantitative Researchers

This conclusion is supported on the points of level of evidence, expectations for data, generalizability, and locus of the argument. In about two thirds (66.8%) of the articles, authors exhibited a great deal of confidence in their evidence; that is, there was a belief that it is possible to gather data as a relatively accurate reflection of the phenomenon and that little interpretation is needed in the analysis. This characteristic was especially prevalent among articles in the archives category (85.2%).

As for generalization, only about 38% of the articles avoided presenting their results as a reflection of something beyond the limited data they examined. Almost 60% engaged in some form of generalization when presenting the results. As for locus of the argument, over 40% focused on the data themselves.

The pattern with generalizability is an especially curious one. To provide a careful analysis on this point, the important distinction between conceptual leverage and generalizability is again highlighted. Conceptual leverage means moving from the literal findings to broader systems of explanation, such as those provided by theories or ideologies. In contrast, generalization refers to the expansion of conclusions beyond the limits of the data, such as to other samples, populations, situations, contexts, and time. Generalization can be formally conducted through the use of inferential statistics (which is very rare in qualitative research) or in carefully weaving in the results of a particular study with the results of other studies reported in the literature so that the author can make broad statements about when and with whom the results hold. Given these definitions of conceptual leverage and generalization, the research with the greatest utility would be that which exhibits a high degree of leverage (such as connecting one's results to theories or ideologies) and formal generalization. However, in this analysis of the qualitative literature, only 34.5% exhibited such leverage, whereas almost 64% made generalizations. Most of this generalizing was done in an informal manner (exhibited by 59.8% of studies) where authors push their findings beyond their limits without providing explicit arguments why this is warranted. On this issue, the observations of J. A. Anderson (1987) appear to be right on the mark. According to Anderson, "Little of what is currently available in the communication journals approaches this ideal form" (p. 253) of what qualitative theoreticians prescribe. Qualitative researchers frequently give the appearance of generalizing their results to wider groups of people, situations, and times. Not only is this a mistake (without the methodological design to allow them to do this), but it is not warranted given the "blueprints" of qualitative research, most of which purposely prescribe against generalization. It is sufficient to provide a subjective interpretation of observations, and it is therefore a mistake to regard the data as representative of anything but themselves.

5. Seldom Did Authors of Journal Articles Address Issues of Internal or External Quality

Whether or not researchers should attempt to make a case for the quality of their data and their results is a matter of longstanding debate among qualitative theoreticians (see chapter 12). If the empirical research is an arbiter of this debate, it appears that the negative side is winning. Only 15% of the studies make any case for the quality of their data, and about 21% make a case for the usefulness of their results.

It is surprising that researchers paid so little attention to the internal quality of data; over 80% totally ignore the point of making a case for the quality of their evidence. Theoreticians have laid out at least three forms of establishing credibility: triangulation, rechecking data with sources, and interobserver reliability. But seldom are any of these methods in evidence in the writings. Of course, these methods are presented primarily for researchers who observe people, but they have applicability to archive- and text-based research. Scholars who examine archival material need to recheck sources for accuracy and triangulate their data so that inaccurate facts or quotes can be eliminated. Scholars who examine texts often take the position that the interpretations are much more important than the texts themselves. This position would remove the concern over making a case for the internal validity of data. However, textual scholars were no more likely to ignore this concern than other types of scholars. Furthermore, none of the textual scholars made a case for the supremacy of interpretation over data, and more than a quarter of them focused their articles on the data rather than the interpretation of the text.

If qualitative researchers were too much influenced by a rationalistic perspective, we should expect to see a pattern of *over*checking the data for internal validity, that is, putting too much credibility in the data and not enough on interpretation and context. Clearly this is not the case. The rationalistic perspective cannot be blamed for the deviation from an "ideal" form of qualitative research.

Self-Reflection

The Discussion section of our article contains some elements of a self-reflective nature in the form of expressing the limitations of the study. First, the study's database contained only those articles published in certain journals and ignores other journals, for example, non-American publications. Also excluded were monographs and books. Because of the history of the editorial foci of these journals, certain types of qualitative research may have been systematically excluded. Perhaps it has been difficult for ideological research to be accepted in journals, and authors find a more sanguine outlet in books. Some types of qualitative research (such as extended ethnographies) require a longer form treatment than a journal would allow.

Second, the time frame is limited. Perhaps certain kinds of qualitative research (such as audience reception studies) were almost nonexistent in our study, because this type of research was on a down cycle during the 5-year span we examined. If this study were extended for a longer time frame and a wider range of publication outlets, it is likely that the five-category structure would change. The most troublesome category in our scheme is social science/ethnography, which ended up as more a miscellaneous collection, and this may obscure the essential characteristics of the articles categorized there. Additional content analyses might show that this group can be split into two or three clear research traditions.

Finally, it must be remembered that this is a quantitative analysis of qualitative research. There are scholars who will object to this. But this analysis is not presented as a definitive study on qualitative research. Instead, it is presented as a tool that is used only to generate some interesting findings about the prevalence of qualitative research and its characteristics. Because the pattern of results diverges from the prescriptions of qualitative scholars, these findings should raise some intriguing questions about what nonquantitative research is being published. The answers to these questions will move us a step closer toward providing a clearer, broad-based understanding about the typology of assumptions underlying the family of methods currently gathered under the single "unifying" title of qualitative research.

STANDARDS FOR JUDGING QUALITY

The traditional standards for judging the quality of quantitative research are reliability, validity, and utility. Reliability refers to the consistency and stability in the data. Here the data were the coders' decisions. When I compared my codings to their codings, I was able to assess the degree of agreement, and it was found to be fairly high given the typical benchmarks of at least 70% agreement used in studies of this type. So we were able to present evidence for good reliability.

Validity has two components: internal and external. Internal validity is the concern with the accuracy of what is being examined and measured. We purported to examine the qualitative literature. By laying out our rules for selecting certain articles and ruling out others, we present a case that our focus does in fact include qualitative research articles and excludes other types. As for measurement, in the research report, we present a review of the literature to show how other scholars have defined certain characteristics as being essential ingredients in the qualitative approach. By citing those scholars and by using their definitions for the variables, we present a case that our measures do in fact get at the essence of qualitative research.

External validity is the issue of whether the researchers can generalize from the results of their study. In our study, we are careful not to generalize. We can make a good case that our patterns can be generalized to the sampling frame of all mass media qualitative research published in seven journals in the years 1987, 1989, and 1991; but this is not a particularly interesting sampling frame. It would be much more interesting if we were able to generalize our patterns to make claims about all qualitative research. But there is reason to believe that qualitative research has changed in these journals over time. Also, there is reason to believe that qualitative research published in other journals as well as in books and monographs may be very different.

Finally, there is the criterion of utility; that is: How useful will scholars find the examination of qualitative research? and How useful were our methods in generating interesting insights on such a topic? This criterion of utility is where we expect to find the most trouble. To illustrate our reasoning, dyed-in-the-wool quantitative researchers would not find our purpose of examining qualitative research at all useful. Our patterns, no matter what they are, would not matter to such scholars. Also, many quantitative scholars are very theoretically oriented; they would want to see an acknowledgment of some sociopsychological theory, the deduction of hypotheses, and the argument for supporting (or reshaping) the theory. Other types of research would have low utility for them.

Also, qualitative researchers might find our study of questionable utility. They might ask: Isn't the quantitative approach antithetical to the qualitative approach? How can a quantitative approach, which is based on assumptions that are not sensitive to the purpose of qualitative research, be a useful tool for this task? And isn't this really a political statement about the author's regard for the two approaches? These are legitimate concerns raised by these questions. We could answer these concerns in several ways. We could argue that if a researcher is interested primarily in interpreting the meaning of something, then the qualitative approach is generally superior to the quantitative one. The primary contribution of the qualitative approach using interpretive analysis is to provide illustrations of the important elements of the literature in a useful context so the reader can realize a deeper meaning about the nature of certain procedures. However, if a researcher is instead interested in the prevalence of certain characteristics, the quantitative approach is the superior one. Each of the approaches has its different strengths. When the two are used together, it makes it possible to examine more of the phenomenon well, and the resulting sets of findings provide a combination of insights that lead to a more complete understanding of the phenomenon.

Or we could argue that there is a lot of rhetoric about the two approaches being antithetical. Much of this writing serves to illuminate the differences in their purposes. It is most useful to think of the two approaches as tools. To illustrate, a hammer and a saw should not be used for the same purpose; that is, the task of cutting wood is not suited for a hammer. When viewed in this way, the two tools are antithetical. However, a saw can be used to cut a new handle for a hammer, and a hammer can be used to nail a new handle on a saw. When viewed this way, the two tools can be seen as providing a useful service for the other. In this chapter, the quantitative methodology of content analysis is used as a tool to make quantitative assessments of prevalence—it is being used for the purpose for which it was designed.

But as for utility (and to a lesser extent the criteria of reliability and validity), judgments about standards must take place in the mind of the reader. Readers must make their own assessment about the degree to which a researcher has provided a convincing argument that the data are relevant and good, that the analyses were done correctly, that the results have merit as an accurate reflection of the phenomenon being examined, and that the study has something useful to say.

14

AN ILLUSTRATION
OF DECISION MAKING
IN A QUALITATIVE ANALYSIS

How are the decisions made by a qualitative researcher different than the decisions that a quantitative researcher makes? This chapter answers that question by representing a contrast with the previous chapter. Both this and the previous chapter are similar in form; that is, both illuminate the decisions that were made in the design and execution of a research study designed to examine the qualitative literature. However, the study illuminated in chapter 13 took a quantitative approach and the study in this chapter took a qualitative approach.

What is the study illuminated in this chapter? It is the research that was undertaken to produce this book. I explicate the series of decisions I made that have defined a path over which this book took shape. I address the issues in the template, which were illuminated in the previous section of this book, in the following order: (a) Why begin this project?, (b) the formal start, (c) analytical decisions, (d) writing, (e) examining my axiomatic beliefs, and (f) standards.

WHY BEGIN THIS PROJECT?

I first heard the term *qualitative* almost 20 years ago and my first impression was that it was a kind of umbrella term for many different tools of research. I was a graduate student at the time, and I became intrigued with the idea of making sense of these "new" methods. I later found out that many of these methods were not at all new. I had used textual analysis and criticism while I was an undergraduate English literature major, where we grappled with questions such as: What makes a novel, play, or poem great? Why do different readers have different reactions to the same book or movie? Why do I have different reactions to certain books each time I read them? Also, I worked as a journalist for several years where I relied on the methods of observation and interview. I was using qualitative methods even though I had never heard the term. But in graduate school I heard the term all the time, but it seemed to allow for all sorts of meanings. I thought that if I had more experience with the approach, its meaning would become more clear. So I undertook many different kinds of qualitative projects. I wrote a dissertation using an interpretative analysis. As a graduate student and then as a full-time consultant on a major faculty development grant, I conducted several ethnographic projects. But I still felt unclear about how to integrate all the meanings of qualitative.

The more I used qualitative methods, the more I valued them. However, I also realized that they had their limitations. I felt that if I were able to use quantitative methods, I would be able to overcome the limitations of the qualitative ones. So I went back to graduate school to learn about quantitative analysis and research, and spent about a decade working primarily with these methods. During that time, I still read the qualitative research, although much of my research appeared to be highly quantitative.

Then in the early 1990s, two things happened to push my curiosity about qualitative thinking to the fore and make it a high priority for me. First, some graduate students at Indiana became interested in alternative methods to the quantitative approach; so we formulated a reading group, which soon changed into a research team that conducted a careful analysis of some of the qualitative literature (see chapter 13 for details). Second, in 1991 when I became the editor of the *Journal of Broadcasting & Electronic Media*, I wanted to expand the scope of the journal, so I needed to strengthen my understanding of various "nontraditional" topics and forms of research. As I read more widely across many types of research, I saw the term qualitative appear all the time, sometimes in very unexpected places. My curiosity was piqued again. So I started taking field notes of my journeys through the literature produced by the qualitative theoreticians in the mass media and related scholarly fields. At first these notes consisted primarily of questions I was asking along with some quotations of particularly interesting expressions of the authors I was reading. As my reading continued, I found my note taking organizing itself around what had become important issues for me, such as definitions for qualitative, assumptions underlying it, and prescribed practices. The more I read, the more I wanted to read, and think, and write about this approach.

BEGINNINGS OF FORMAL PROJECT

In early 1993, I began organizing my notes in earnest to try to make sense of all the jottings I has amassed over the years. It was not sufficient for me to simply arrange the notes in order or in an outline; I wanted a narrative that told the story of qualitative approach to me—one that I could share with my students. When I had written it all out, I had about half a dozen chapters that were primarily critical (especially of jargon, multiple definitions, and fuzzy axioms) and descriptive (of what methods books said about the approach).

I noticed that there were a lot of perspectives written by qualitative scholars talking about the approach. So I went through some major reorganizations to formulate what I thought was the key set of issues that one should orient to when reading any qualitative research piece. The more I read of the ideas of qualitative theoreticians, the more I tinkered with this set, which I came to refer to as a template. In this hermeneutic process, I would add issues, redefine some, and reorganize others as I learned more about the variety of perspectives.

After many reorganizations of the template, I began reading the qualitative research literature to test it. I wanted to see if the set of issues in the template really did orient me to the valuable aspects of many different kinds of qualitative research. The hermeneutic process continued as I found that new issues needed to be added (notable here was purpose of writing) and some needed to be redefined (especially with the foundational issues). The more I learned through reading the research literature, the better context I had for understanding the positions of various theoreticians; and as I reread the theoreticians, the better context I developed for understanding how certain decisions were made in the research literature.

Guiding this hermeneutic process was my quest to answer the central question: What does qualitative mean? As I got well into the process, the question shifted to: What do scholars who write about qualitative mean; that is, what do they say it is? I expected to see some diversity, but I believed that the more I read the more of a consensus would emerge. This did not happen in the way I expected (see chapters 15, 16, and 17 for a full treatment of how my expectations were met).

At a relatively recent point in the analysis, when I began feeling confident in the template, I wanted to share my interpretations. My initial purpose for writing was predominantly critical. I saw many problems with the approach. For example, it seemed that communication was very poor between qualitative and quantitative types—that is, neither had a good idea of what the other did. This false information resulted in unfair criticisms from both sides. I feared that students who were introduced to the qualitative approach through these contentious writings would be led to put too much trust (or too little) in the approach. I was also bothered by the seeming lack of correspondence between what qualitative theoreticians prescribed and what practicing qualitative researchers did.

With rewrites, I mellowed from a critical perspective to an interpretive one, realizing that my intentions would not be best served with a critical tone. Many quantitative researchers were already critical of the qualitative approach, and more criticism would calcify their existing views rather than serve to open up new interpretations for them. And qualitative researchers who might read the book would see this as yet another politically motivated attempt to marginalize their efforts. Because of the sensitive nature of the topic and the history of the rhetoric on this issue, I realized that a critical treatment would add much more heat than light to the area. So I tried to adopt a predominantly interpretive tone throughout the book, until chapters 15 and 16, which are critical and action oriented in tone.

Several major revisions were made at the end of the process (from summer 1993 to spring 1995) after I signed a contract with Lawrence Erlbaum Associates. I received several rounds of editorial feedback from Hollis Heimbouch, a senior acquisitions editor at Erlbaum, as well as very detailed and critical reviews from two reviewers. This feedback forced me to rethink some of the positions I had taken. The critiques also indicated that the reviewers misunderstood what I was trying to do—I had misled them somehow. These problems were very difficult to correct and required the hardest thinking in the rewriting process. Finally, I was fortunate to have a group of articulate graduate students at University of California at Santa Barbara, who enrolled in a seminar where this book was pilot tested. Some of these students had considerable background in qualitative thinking whereas others had very little. Their feedback gave me a great deal of insight into how various readers would react to my descriptions and arguments.

ANALYTICAL DECISIONS

The hermeneutic process underlies all the analysis that was used to produce this book. Right from the beginning, the only way I could make sense of an element in my notes was to view the total set as context for each element, then that element would have new and enriched meaning for me. But that new meaning often served to change the entire context, which then forced a reevaluation of each of the other elements. As each element was reinterpreted the context changed yet again. After several iterations (sometimes a dozen) through the entire set of elements, I would have a significant conceptual breakthrough that would force me to radically change my view of the project. These break-throughs were stimulated by the addition of much new information (such as the addition of the analysis of the research literature), of substantial criticism (such as the comments of the reviewers), or of my muse suddenly waking up and showing me a new perspective on a particular structure of information.

In this section I illuminate the series of decisions I made in continually sorting through my notes, trying different forms of organization, looking for patterns, and moving to insights. I try to highlight those decisions in five areas: evidence, generalizations, conceptual leverage, orienting methods, and analytical methods.

Evidence

What should be considered evidence of the phenomenon, which in this case is qualitative thinking and research? At first this might seem like a simple question, but that is deceptive. To provide a good answer to this question, I must begin with the distinction between emic and etic evidence. When I searched for expressions from theoreticians and researchers, I was looking for how they express their meaning; this is emic evidence. Evidence is emic when it is composed of the expressions in the categories and meanings of the object—that is, the person being studied. However once I selected some quotes or an expression of their point of view, I used that evidence to construct my arguments, and this then transforms the evidence into the etic realm. When a researcher uses expressions in his or her own language or from his or her own perspective, the evidence is etic.

My view of the emic evidence is one of subjective valuing; that is, I believe that there are tangible, material artifacts that reflect the phenomenon of interest, which in this case are the printed expressions of qualitative thinkers and researchers. I did not make the assumption that the emic evidence was a pure construction of the qualitative scholars, but rather they themselves were building on their own evidence in formulating their insights.

As for broadness of evidence, I gathered evidence on the research literature one study at a time, so this was the individual level. Also, when looking at the writings of theoreticians, I gathered evidence one writing at a time but these writings were themselves syntheses of sets of research literatures.

No enumeration was used in this book. Even in chapter 13 where I use the quantitative methodology of content analysis, there is no enumeration. Although there are many numbers presented, these numbers are percentages so they indicate real mathematical properties. In other words, I did not translate qualitative concepts into numbers, such as having coders rate (on a 5-point scale) the degree to which an author provided contextualization, for example.

But I did use inferential statistical tests to determine the degree to which the patterns could have occurred by chance alone. This is a key characteristic that distinguishes quantitative from qualitative analysis. Quantitative researchers accept the assumptions behind inferential tests such as chi-square and therefore find it a valuable tool to determine if fluctuations in the aggregate should be regarded as evidence of random variation (error) or of substantive patterns.

All of my evidence was gathered through document examination. I decided not to interview qualitative scholars or to observe them at their tasks. Instead, I limited my examination to the texts they produced for two reasons. First, the texts are the stable, enduring records of their thought. Because the records are enduring, they are what is most available to students and scholars. Second, I reasoned that qualitative thinkers and researchers would be more careful in their writings than in the spoken words so that the writings would be an more accurate portrayal of their thoughts. In the future, I would like to interview and observe qualitative scholars; the evidence from such methods would be suitable to focus on how their thinking changes when they are confronted with different research tasks and how they negotiate those differences (if there are differences) between their thinking about the approach and the practices they employ.

Because of my exclusive focus on texts, the concerns of researcher identification and researcher activity were not issues for me as they are for those who interview and/or observe people.

As for sampling, I primarily used a snowball technique guided by the purpose of trying to uncover as broad a range of thinking about qualitative approach as possible within the areas of media studies. With theoreticians, I began with the mass media and communication methodology books and worked out from their reference lists to try to identify all theoreticians within media studies and then also to include major thinkers from contiguous fields of education, sociology, and anthropology.

As for the sample of studies used in the analyses of the research literature, I wanted to use a population of research examples different from those used in the quantitative study referred to in chapter 13. I stayed away from the journals used in the content analysis and looked at other journals, but mainly focused on longer form treatments of projects such as books. A combination of selection procedures was used. I asked qualitative researchers what they were reading and selected many of those writings. I browsed the shelves in the Indiana University library to identify other writings. And I used a snowball technique to identify writings that were familiar to many researchers. My guiding principle was to read as widely and as much as possible within media studies. From that set of readings I selected for analysis those studies that either (a) served as a good example of some analytical point (the template issues that structure chapters 6 through 12), and/or (b) served to expand the set of examples by showing a variation on the points that had already been well documented in my set of writings in the sample up to that point. That set of writings is displayed in annotated bibliographic form in the Appendix. When you browse through the Appendix, you will notice that it is organized by facet (audience, institution, and text) and within facet by methodology. Some methodologies have many more examples than others. This was because it is very easy to find certain examples (such as cultural studies of institutions or reception studies of texts), whereas others were very rare. In the areas were there were many examples, I made a distinction among subtypes and kept the numerous examples to illuminate the great variety within that type.

As for collaboration, I alone am responsible for the interpretations in this book. However, that is not to say that I did not have considerable help from scholars (Walter Gantz, Ellen Seiter, Tom Lindlof, Dan Berkowitz) who critiqued my interpretations, and they provided considerable challenges to my thinking in many areas. On many points I modified my interpretations, but in many other places I did not. Their advice is invaluable but the interpretations are still mine, and if you, the reader, disagree with them then I alone am to blame.

Generalization

I tried to avoid generalizing with one exception. I talk about the insights from the theoreticians as if they were all qualitative theoreticians; this is because I believe I have uncovered all the points of view among the mass media qualitative theoreticians.

At times it may appear that I am generalizing beyond the limits of the population (or sampling frame) to all of published qualitative research. If I have given that impression at times, I did not intend to. It is not my purpose in chapters 6 through 12 to make claims about the prevalence of qualitative research or about its key characteristics. The examples I use are intended to show what exists, not how often they exist. The "big picture" of what the qualitative approach is on both the theoretical and practical levels is for each individual reader to decide. What I hope to provide is a way of looking at the literature so that you can construct your own conclusions about the enterprise in general.

The underlying theme of this book is that this is my interpretation of the selection of evidence to which I have been exposed and under the purposes that I operated. Change the set of evidence, the purpose, or the interpretive process, and the findings most likely will also change. Therefore, I do not make a claim that these findings hold under all conditions and this restriction is the barrier to generalization.

Conceptual Leverage

In contrast to a minimalist view on generalization, I hope to achieve a much more ambitious goal concerning conceptual leverage in three areas. If you, the reader, find my template of issues useful in reading a wide range of qualitative research, then my insights exist at a high enough level of abstraction to be broadly applied. In order to achieve this, I have tried to keep the focus on the patterns rather than on individual examples.

Also, I hope that you will find the insights I present in the first five chapters a useful perspective on the problem of understanding the qualitative approach. To the extent that these insights useful, I will have provided some conceptual leverage by moving the focus beyond the examples of individual problems and into the more abstract conceptual realm of thinking about the patterns of barriers, their causes, and the implications they have on the structure of the approach.

A third area in which I have tried to present some strong conceptual leverage is in the three concluding chapters. The first two of these are critical of some elements in the thinking and practices within the approach; the last chapter develops a position on synthesis. If these chapters are to have value, they should stimulate a debate, not over my individual interpretations themselves as much as over the larger issues of the definition of the approach, the extent to which prescriptions can be followed, the desirability of standards, and the extent to which qualitative researchers share many of the same practices and perspectives of quantitative researchers.

Orienting Methods

My primary orienting method in this research was discourse analysis where I tried to uncover the ideological dimensions underlying the writings of the theoreticians. This can be seen in the way that I looked at how qualitative theoreticians characterized themselves and the researchers operating under the quantitative approach so as to understand their rules of expression. Then I examined the research produced by qualitative scholars to try to understand how they responded to the scholarly environment set up by the discourse of the theoreticians.

Analytical Methods

My analytical perspective was primarily inductive. I did not begin with any formal hypotheses. Instead, I began with (and was continually driven by) a desire to answer a question: What is qualitative? Within the inductive perspective, I followed the model of grounded theory, by trying to find patterns across individual writings and build up to concepts that could explain those patterns. My template provides many examples of my interpretation of the patterns of concerns I saw theoreticians express time and again.

In checking my interpretations, I used triangulation. Once I put forth an interpretation, I would try to read the work of scholars holding a differing opinion to see if my tentative conclusion could be expanded to include differing points of view. Hence, my interpretations are more reflective of an inventory of thinking than of my own personal positions. For example, each item on the analytical template is a different position espoused by qualitative theoreticians. The number of positions on a given issue grew as I read more and thus needed to acknowledge additional positions. Sometimes, I needed to change the name or definition of the issue to be able to include all the positions.

In building the template, I relied on examples to illustrate the various positions on each issue. The method of maximum comparisons was very useful here to make the illustrations sharper. Also, I developed some sensitized concepts to extend my explanations. For example, I constructed conceptual leverage as a term to contrast with generalization, so as to separate out the two distinct ideas, which are usually confounded. Making this distinction is very important in qualitative research to show that a research study does not need to generalize in order to make a powerful conceptual contribution. Also, in chapter 16, I create some distinctions between balanced and focused evidence, and I argue for understanding practices as being influenced by the essential tension supported by a pair of diametrically opposed themes. One tension is the pull between the themes of fluidity and order. The second tension is the pull between the themes of reflection and transformation.

WRITING

Form of Expression

I have used several forms of expression, but the predominant one is the interpretive realist tale. My arguments are my own interpretations of things outside me that have a material realism, such as the words of qualitative theoreticians and the products of qualitative researchers. My evidence exists apart from my interpretation of it. However, my interpretation is required to infer the meaning about how practitioners made their decisions, what options were available to them, and why they chose the course they did.

Some chapters exhibit a different form of expression. For example, I use the descriptive realist tale in chapter 2 where I use a journalistic form of presentation in laying out all the different definitions for qualitative and let those multiple voices speak for themselves.

This chapter is a confessional tale. The focus here is far more on the researcher than on the culture studied. This should be illustrated in my use of the first person as I take you through the process I used in writing this book. In the following two chapters, I shift into a critical tale as I illuminate my personal biases as a foundation for recognizing problems.

Locus of Argument

I would characterize my predominant locus as logos, which is logic of the argument or presentation. My focus is on structuring the facts in an orderly manner to convince you, the reader, that this interpretation is interesting and useful. To do this, I use logic, if–then statements, and syllogisms. However, I also use data as a focus in many chapters and sections—especially the second halves of chapters 6 through 13 where I present examples.

Contextualization

I have tried to provide a high degree of contextualization—first, by presenting the foundational chapters to provide a basis for the information; second, by revealing my own interpretive stance in the Preface, chapter 1, and this chapter.

Self-Reflexivity

This chapter and the previous chapter are the clearest examples of self-reflexivity in the book, although this characteristic shows up in other areas also. In the Preface I explain my motivation for writing the book. Also, in chapters 6 through 12 I show the range of thinking and analyze the issues before providing a synthesis of template points.

REALIZING MY AXIOMATIC BELIEFS

This research process turned out to be an important exercise in self-realization. I had held certain attitudes about the qualitative approach, but they operated largely at a subconscious level. In the 1980s, I had been socialized into the quantitative approach and came to accept the assumptions underlying that approach. However, I was still curious about the qualitative approach, so when I began this project, I had to dredge up many assumptions and confront them. As I brought many of these assumptions to the surface, some of my beliefs changed under the close scrutiny. In this section, I explain what those beliefs were and are now. I hope this discussion illustrates two things. First, I hope readers are given an insight to understand the perspective from which I wrote this book. And second, I hope this illustrates that belief changes are possible under certain conditions.

I address axioms at two levels: (a) philosophical issues of ontology and epistemology and (b) the five fundamental axioms of the qualitative approach. I begin by reminding you of four premises I presented in the Preface. These are my fundamental assumptions about the world and about human knowing; they did not change when I switched from qualitative to quantitative approaches in graduate school, and they have not changed as my interest in the qualitative approach has been rekindled. Those premises are as follows:

Premise 1: There is a material reality that exists apart from our interpretation of it.

Premise 2: We, as humans, can never experience the phenomenon directly or completely, because: (a) Our conduits of information (the five senses) are limited, and (b) the way we make meaning from the raw sense data is subjective. For these reasons, there will always be a range of interpretations about physical phenomena (such as the movement of electrons, chemical reactions, nature of living cells, etc.) and an even wider range of interpretations about social phenomena (human conversations, meaning of texts, construction of institutions and cultural artifacts).

Premise 3: All scholarship necessarily is composed of the components of speculation and empiricism. In the speculation phase, the scholar constructs an interpretation of the phenomenon. In the empirical phase the scholar cites observed characteristics about the phenomenon to illustrate and support the interpretation.

Premise 4: Among the various interpretations of a phenomenon, some are better than others; that is, all are not equally useful. In all research communities, scholars have developed norms for what constitutes acceptable research and what does not. These norms are often difficult to discern (because they consist of multiple elements, the elements vary in importance, and some elements are unwritten; that is, they are only observable in the practices), but they still exist. Underlying these norms is the idea of utility. Useful scholarship accounts for what is known and either (a) extends the reader's knowledge of the topic, and/or (b) presents the reader with some intriguing new way to look at the phenomenon.

What has changed is my perspective on scholarly activity in general. Operating under the quantitative perspective socializes one to believe in objective standards that should be applied consistently across all work. Fundamental to these standards is the idea that you are doing the work of others; that is, you are conducting a study in such a way that had others done the same study, they would have made the same decisions and generated the same results. I used to hold these beliefs in general and apply them to all scholarship, but now I apply them only to the domain of quantitative approach.

Within qualitative research, I no longer look for replicability. Instead, I am more concerned with the degree to which a research report stimulates my thinking to consider important phenomena from various interesting points of view. If an author presents a really intriguing perspective on media use, then I value that work for presenting me with something new to think about, even if I am incapable of replicating that work myself.

As for ontology, my perspective is that of actional idealism; I believe that humans are active agents who possess goals and have the capacity to choose goal-maximizing actions. Humans are regarded as being subject to situational and social forces that they cannot control, but they are also subject to their own choice-making behavior. I do not believe in a mechanistic world determined purely by physical forces outside of one's control; but neither do I believe in a strong idealist position that the meaning making is so complex and dynamic that we will never be able to get a grasp of it in a way that scholars can share that meaning. In order for there to be even low-level communication, we must have some sharing of meaning. Of course, the sharing of meaning cannot never be complete; there are often differences between the message sent by one person and the meaning received by another. This is a matter of asking if the glass is half full or half empty. I believe that the glass is more than half full with shared meaning. And in formal areas of scholarship, the level of shared meaning is most likely quite a bit higher than it is in the general population, because scholars in those areas have engaged in formal and directed study in order to learn the traditions of meaning making among the community of scholars they wish to join.

This project rests on all five axioms of qualitative research. Phenomenology is defined by researchers not having preconceived notions about the phenomenon, but keeping themselves open to the experience fully. As I articulated earlier, I did have a thesis, but this thesis is now pushed far into the background. I tried to stay focused on the phenomenon (of qualitative thinking and research) and changed my interpretations when evidence of the phenomenon did not conform to my working interpretations that I held at the time. In short, I did not use the thesis as a screen for filtering out discrepant information.

The interpretive axiom says the researchers should strive to see the situation from the perspective of the other. My other is less the qualitative thinker than the student new to the approach. I tried to create interpretations that would be useful for those people.

The naturalism axiom says that researchers need to go to the phenomenon and experience it in its natural, undisturbed state. Here I need to be careful in articulating what the phenomenon is. Is it the theoreticians and the researchers or is it their writings? These may not be the same thing. In deciding to make a choice between the two, I selected the writings, because this is the record of thought that would be available to students and scholars. I also assumed that qualitative thinkers and researchers would be more careful in their writings than in the spoken words so that the writings would be a more accurate portrayal of their thoughts. However, thoughts change, and it would be of value to conduct interviews with thinkers and researchers in future analyses.

Humanism is also an important foundation for this study. Throughout the process I have tried to keep the focus on language as a demonstration of meaning. The quotes and examples have been interpreted in the widest possible content of thought about the qualitative approach.

The hermeneutic axiom states that research is a never-ending process of observing an instance and interpreting it in terms of a context that is itself a construction of instances. This is perhaps the strongest axiom underlying this research project. Even now, I do not feel the work is finished. As you, the reader, react and share those reactions, you provide more with more context within which to regard my interpretations and this requires me to see those interpretations differently.

STANDARDS

I do believe standards are essential. This belief is axiomatic in me. It comes from my experience of being a university teacher where I must continually evaluate the work of students in short quizzes, major essay exams, group projects, creative writing/productions, as well as scholarly theses and dissertations. I realize that all of these products are constructions from idiosyncratic individuals. However, to me the purpose of teaching is to bring students into the community of the educated by making them aware of certain knowledge and skills. They can reject these by selecting a different major (but other majors also have their sets of content and skills, although they may be different than the standards of media studies) or by not enrolling in college. However, when someone enrolls in college, they are asking to be admitted into certain communities.

Members of a community need to know how well aspirants are assimilating, and that is why someone must observe their performance and test them. Implied in the evaluation of every test is a standard of performance. If there is no standard, then there can be no evaluation.

I have also served as a reviewer of convention papers and journal articles as well as a journal editor. The process of review requires a set of standards. Without a shared set of standards, all this activity would be pointless. How many times have you heard someone say of the review process "Those reviewers were terrible; they didn't understand what I was trying to do!" or "The reviewers wanted me to write another article, not the one I sent them; it is so unfair." Reactions such as these indicate that standards are often not shared to a high enough degree that reviewers are able to communicate their feedback well.

So what are the standards by which I would like this book to be judged? For me, the three major criteria should be completeness of the evidence, resonance of the insights, and heuristic value.

As for completeness of the evidence, it is important for readers to ask whether I have included all the major mass media qualitative thinkers and have I included their main ideas. I may have overlooked some. However, if I have, I would hope that the criticism on this point were done with a sense of proportion. Let's say that a reader feels that I have missed two major ideas. If I only dealt with three major ideas in the book, then this would be a shortcoming to a degree that the overall warrant of the book would greatly suffer. If however, I dealt with 95 major ideas, then in proportion this weakness is not so dominant.

Resonance of insights: Does the reader feel the same problems as I do? When I point out problems does the reader say "Yes, that has bothered me too"? Also, when I make a point and present examples, does the reader feel a sense of identity that he or she not only follows what I say but feels a spark of recognition of an experience.

Heuristic value: Does the reader learn something from this? This learning can be triggered in two broad ways. One way is to show the reader something that he or she will be able to use. For example, I hope the list of issues is a useful contribution—a tool that readers will adopt when reading the literature on their own. A second way for readers to learn from what I have said in this book is to disagree with an insight and become involved in that disagreement to a point where they will learn more about their axiomatic beliefs as well as the nature of the qualitative approach. This does not mean that their initial disagreement melts into embarrassment as they begin to agree with me after learning more about the approach. That, however, would give me a warm feeling knowing that everyone who disagrees with me is at a lower level of learning and all they need to do is read more and think about it more and they will be able to reach up to my level of "getting it right." Although I sometimes dream of having such power, I know that this book is a construction, and there are likely to be elements that other scholars can construct better. When these other scholars see these shortcomings and think through why their constructions are superior to mine, this book is also exerting some heuristic power. In order for me to receive back from them some of that power, I hope they will share their constructions with me. In this way, a significant dialogue can be initiated; such a dialogue if conducted positively can set up an environment of synergy where we both learn much more than the sum that either of us could learn separately.

CRITICAL INSIGHTS

15

EXTERNAL CRITIQUE OF QUALITATIVE THEORY FOUNDATIONAL ISSUES

This chapter presents a critical analysis of the writings of the qualitative theoreticians and highlights six barriers to entry that new scholars and quantitative scholars would find to their understanding of the qualitative approach. In short, these issues identify problems that the qualitative theoreticians exhibit in presenting the approach to others.

In my critique, I do not argue that any of these problems is a fundamental flaw; all are subject to amelioration. I present this critique in a constructive manner in the hope that through critical analysis, you, the reader, will be able to work past some initial barriers and more quickly achieve a useful understanding of the approach. Also, many of these problems are necessary characteristics of an approach going through the growing pains of self-definition. In time, many of these issues will cease to be problems. However, at this point in time, they serve as conditions that frustrate those scholars wanting to understand the qualitative approach more fully.

First, I examine the problem of determining what the qualitative approach is. Is there a community where meaning is shared? Second, I show that there is much misunderstanding about the quantitative approach. Third, I examine the faulty arguments theoreticians make when trying to highlight their method. Fourth, I analyze the problem of differing assumptions about reality and knowing. Fifth, I highlight the problem about a lack of guidance on specific methods. And sixth, I explore the issue of how qualitative theoreticians form the locus of value for the research.

SENSE OF COMMUNITY

The examination of this issue begins with the question: To what extent is there a community among scholars who write about the qualitative approach? Once this question is answered, a second question becomes important: What are the barriers to entry?

Community

By community, I mean a place where scholars share meaning and in this sharing develop a sense of identity with one another. This does not mean that everyone in the community is the same. Instead, there can be many different people with differing talents, perspectives, and goals. However, despite the many differences, there must be a shared sense that there are important and salient commonalities that tie them together into this community. The concept of community allows for diversity, but it also requires a certain commonality. Both characteristics can coexist—this is why the concept of community is so useful in understanding the essence of the qualitative approach.

Communities are nested; that is, different kinds of communities can exist simultaneously in a hierarchy. For example, an analogy is the political divisions in this country. There is the community of our town, which is part of a larger community of our state, which is part of a larger community of the United States. There are certain things about our own town that make us a part of everyone else living in our town and at the same time make us different from those living in other towns. There are local traditions, high school athletic rivalries, shopping loyalties, local leaders we elect, and the like. We may have rivalries with surrounding towns, but these local rivalries disappear when we think about being part of our state community. Likewise, state rivalries disappear and differences among states appear trivial when we think about being part of our country community. The community concept works only as long as people feel a sense of identity with these communities; that is, if we know what it means to be part of each community. If people do not have much in common with each other in a particular town and/or if they feel they have as much or more in common with people in their surrounding towns, then they will not feel a sense of community at the town level, but they could still feel a sense of community at the state and national levels.

If the scholars operating under the qualitative approach all share a sense of the same community, then it would be a relatively easy task to identify what those commonalities are and use them to define the community. But this does not seem to be the case. Some scholars operating under the qualitative approach seem to exhibit commonalities more in subcommunities, such as to methods (participant observation, case study, grounded theory, etc.), and they also have a higher level identity at the "state" level to methodologies, such as ethnography, textual analysis, cultural studies, experiment, survey, and so forth. But it is less clear what commonalities they hold that would tie them together into a still higher level "national" identity of the qualitative approach.

Theoreticians' Views of Qualitative. When we take a look across theoreticians to see how they have used language to construct a meaning for the qualitative approach, there appears to be very little agreement. In chapter 2, I presented the variety of meanings by displaying the wide range of synonyms and definitions. But the differences appear even more profound than what was exhibited there; that is, theoreticians even disagree about whether it is a method, a paradigm, or a set of techniques (Lancy, 1993). Lindlof and Meyer (1987) used the term "interpretive paradigm." But they also said that it is not monolithic "and indeed there are many varieties" (p. 5) of which they included ethnomethodology, ecological psychology, and symbolic interactionism. They said further that whereas these varieties all have one thing in common, "empirically studying meaning systems" (p. 5), they each have important uniquenesses. Some scholars point out that the qualitative paradigm is distinct from the quantitative paradigm—that is, they each deal with more than methods. If it is a paradigm, then more is needed than simply distinguishing it from another set of beliefs—a task these writers are successful in doing. However, they are *not* successful in showing that the research activity that takes place within the paradigm is uniform to an extent that it is useful to regard that activity as a set in some way.

One of the practices that seem to add to this fragmentation is that theoreticians rarely build on each other's work in a systematic manner that would lead to a shared definition. Because of the independent nature of the contributions, each new definition has added more to the clutter than to an integration. If the scholars who identify with the term qualitative are to show that they have formed a community, then they need to show some conceptual cohesiveness. If they are unwilling to do this, which is a legitimate alternative, then their identities are to methods and methodologies, and any groupings done at a higher level of abstraction, such as with approach, hold very little meaning.

Another way to view this situation is to say that the qualitative approach is so amorphous that it is and always will be, undefinable. There appear to be three reasons for arguing for the amorphous nature, but none of these can be taken to the extreme that the approach will always be undefinable. First, it could be argued that no one has the ultimate definition of qualitative research, so why should a particular theoretician be required to come up with one? But we could reply to this question by pointing out that when someone addresses one of these ideas as a scholar, he or she has an obligation to inform readers what his or her perspective is so that readers can follow the line of argument. Second, it could be argued that qualitative is a primitive term and therefore can never been adequately defined. It is like *chair* where we all know what it means but it is impossible to write a clear definition of it. The response to this is that qualitative is a construct, not a primitive term. Each theoretician constructs a meaning to be useful for his or her purpose. Because it is a theoretician's construction, each theoretician should communicate that definition so that readers are clear on the starting place in the argument. Third, some theoreticians argue that the thinking that the approach is too complex to define. For example, Lincoln and Guba (1985) made a point of resisting a simple definition. In the preface to their long book, they warned readers that they will not find a simple direct definition. They said "it is not possible to provide a simple definition. . . . Instead a proper impression . . . can be gleaned only as an overall perspective" (p. 8). Also, Marshall and Rossman (1989) wrote a book on qualitative methods without defining *qualitative*. Instead they said, "throughout the text we refer to *qualitative research* and *qualitative methods* as if these were one agreed-upon set that everyone understands. We intend no such implication" (p. 9).

But if the thinking is so complex, then either (a) no one has yet been able to discern the similarities within all the complexity, or (b) there truly are no similarities across all this thinking. If the first is the case, then there is reason to call for more analysis and synthesis. If the second is the case, then it would seem pointless to group all the methods and methodologies together in a group that has to conceptual coherence; what would be the point of doing so?

Semantic Problems.   The argument that communities are more likely to be local than national shows up in the meaning given to key terms, especially when there are several meanings for the same term, such as naturalism and empiricism as was argued in chapter 1. When multiple meanings arise for the same term, this is an indication of fragmentation within a community; that is, scholars are unwilling to share the same meaning. Or perhaps they are unaware of changes in meaning by other scholars; if this is the case, the condition can most likely be traced to a lack of clarity in writing. If a scholar does not define his or her terms clearly in the text, readers will construct their own meanings, and these meanings do not always conform to the meanings intended by the writer.

There should be no expectation that once a term is coined, everyone must hold precisely the same definition for it. There should be a variety of connotated meaning that grows as different kinds of people develop experience with the term. However, over time, we can look at the meanings across scholars and see where the sharing of definitions exists. When it is found that several scholars hold the same meaning for a term, this can be taken as evidence that on this point there is communication. We can observe shifts in meanings for key terms across scholars to see patterns in communities. The previous examples (and there are many more) illustrate a pattern that there are many communities at methods and/or methodological levels, but that there is less sharing of meaning at the approach level.

Is it really important for a shared sense of meaning at the most general level? It is possible to answer no; the communities of shared meaning might exist at the less general level of methodologies or methods. But if this is the case, what is the purpose for having a general level labeled qualitative? It is a finding of the analysis in this book that very little of a shared perspective exists at the general level of meaning for qualitative. And it is the purpose of this book to show where the commonalities are and to fill in some of the gaps in the hope that qualitative scholars will move toward a greater sharing of meaning. This is not to say that all qualitative scholars should conform to a standard of thinking alike; there is still plenty of diversity available through identifications with various subcommunities. However, it would also seem beneficial that there should evolve a greater sense of general community.

There is also another possible explanation for why there does not appear to be a community at the general level. It is, of course, possible that scholars could feel an emotional attachment to the qualitative community even though they cannot construct that attachment into a cognitive language that can be communicated with others. This could account for the strong attachments exhibited in a literature that does not have a corresponding strong sharing of definitions and language. If the community exists at the general level, it may be felt emotionally rather than understood intellectually. But this would add to the barriers of entry by making the area even more inexplicable to those who wanted to learn about it.

Barriers to Entry

Assuming that there is a community of scholars who have shared meanings at some level, the next concern becomes: To what extent are there barriers to entry? Low barriers indicate a scholarly area that welcomes thinkers and researchers from all areas to come in and contribute. High barriers tell scholars that they must invest a great deal of effort to learn the special perspectives and terms used in that community. High barriers should not be interpreted to mean that the scholars in the community have erected unreasonably high rites of initiation so as to keep others out and thus foster an elite status among themselves. There are constructive reasons for high barriers. In some communities, neophytes must be shown that there are precise ways of doing things that must be learned before they can enter. Neophytes must learn the specialized languages consisting of technical terms that are the tools that scholars use to access the ideas that are important to the area. However, some languages exhibit characteristics that make them more difficult than others.

Technical Terms. Technical terms are essential to scholarship. When a theoretician or researcher creates a construct that lacks an existing word, then a new technical term is required. For example, when Gramsci wanted to introduce a new explanation for how media messages exert an influence on people, there was no existing word that would serve as an adequate label for his new construct so he invented the technical term *hegemonic* and constructed a definition.

But there appears to be a practice in qualitative research of the inventing of technical terms where there are already well understood common terms that could be used. For example, in narrative analysis, voice-overs at the beginning of television shows have been called homodiegetic (Captain Kirk who is also a character in the program) and heterodiegetic (such as Walter Winchell who provided the initial voice-overs on the "Untouchables") (Kozloff, 1987). Why not simply call one "narration by characters" and the other "noncharacter voice-overs"? Diachronic means occurring over time. Why not just say continuous or sequential? Another example is the sentence "Our knowledge about television audiencehood has been colonized by what I want to call the institutional point of view" (Ang, 1991, p. 2).

The area of semiotics is especially dense to some readers, particularly because of the technical terms. Pierce had his representamen (which is a symbol) and the object (the thing to which the representamen represents). Saussure called the symbol the signifier (sign as symbol) and the object behind the symbol the signified. Metz (1974) employed semiotics in the study of films, and extended it by adding two new concepts of paradigmatic and syntagmatic. Why not just call them genre and sequence? But if he must use a special term, why did he use *paradigmatic*, which has another well-established meaning totally alien from how Metz was defining it. This is another example where an author, who is attempting to clarify meaning of some phenomenon, ironically obscures his meaning for readers.

The criticism here is not that we should do away with technical terms. Quite the contrary, I am arguing that technical terms are essential to scholarship; they make it possible for us to talk about creative, new explanations in an efficient manner. When they are used properly, they allow for greater precision in thinking. However, if they are not defined clearly, then the goal of explanation is not achieved. Therefore, scholars must pay a price when using technical terms. They must provide careful definitions that clearly illuminate the meaning of each technical term and how its meaning differs from common language. If scholars are unwilling to do this, then they are only increasing the complexity, not the degree of insight.

Providing definitions of key words and concepts should be done in each piece of qualitative scholarship, because with many terms there is no established common usage of technical terms with the field. Even with apparently common terms, there is a wide variety of meaning in use. For example, Seiter et al. (1989a) pointed out that even with a relatively common term such as *critical*, there is a variety of definitions. First, critical "may simply mean pertaining to the practice of criticism" (p. 6) by professional critics who "produce textual analyses of the media from a vantage point of high culture, especially literary theory" (p. 6). Second, critical refers to the work emanating from "the Frankfurt School tradition by combining psychoanalytic and Marxist theories into a broad social critique" (p. 6). Third, and more current, critical "refers broadly to those philosophical traditions which mistrust empiricism and positivism and insist on the relationship between knowledge and power" (p. 6).

Understanding Writers' Meanings. In some writings the writer's ideas are very accessible. In other writings (such as those of Derrida, Foucault, Saussare), it is very difficult for the reader to penetrate the membrane of the writing; that is, to get into the writer's world and access his or her meaning. I am not going to argue that writings that are difficult to read automatically make them bad. Some ideas are very difficult to comprehend, and writers who try to express that type of idea will necessarily produce some difficult to read passages. However, some writing is difficult to understand, because the author has not expressed the ideas as clear or as interesting as they could be. Richardson (1994) said that qualitative research "could be reaching wide and diverse audiences, not just devotees of the topic or the author. It seems foolish at best, and narcissistic and wholly self-absorbed at worst, to spend months or years doing research that ends up not being read and not making a difference to anything but the author's career" (p. 517). She called most of qualitative research boring to read because most authors suppress their voice to a scientific style of writing.

What makes writing good? Certainly, it should be interesting, as Richardson (1994) argued. But it should also be clear. Clarity again speaks to the accessibility of the author's ideas. There are many examples of unclear writing in the published qualitative literature. The following example, unfortunately, is not a rare case:

> Whatever the qualitative research style, and whether or not self-consciously defined as feminist, these many voices share the outlook that it is important to center and make problematic women's diverse situations and the institutions and frames that influence those situations, and then to refer the examination of that problematic to theoretical, policy, or action frameworks in the interest of realizing social justice for women. (Olesen, 1994, p. 158)

Appearing in the second paragraph of her chapter on "feminisms and models of qualitative research," it really serves to confuse the reader. If you read this sentence several times, you realize that the individual ideas expressed in that sentence are not very difficult. With difficult ideas, authors often have to present difficult sentences to convey that idea adequately. But that is not the case here. The ideas are relatively simple (and important), but the author has introduced the difficulty needlessly.

With truly difficult writing, readers should not try "to storm the gates," but instead find a guide, such as secondary sources where scholars write about their ideas and seek to digest those writings. The advantage of using guides is the reader will reduce the chance of getting lost and make more efficient use of his or her time. However, there is also a problem with using guides. Because

guides are secondary sources, they are once removed from the original "difficult" ideas. This means the path set out by the guide is influenced by the guide's
own interpretations of those ideas. If the interpretations are not well grounded
in the original ideas and if they are not insightful, then the guide can contribute
to the reader getting lost. Also, two guides might disagree about how to navigate
through the typology of ideas. For these reasons, a scholar should not stop after
reading a guide but should move on to the original writings in order to complete
the journal of making one's own interpretation.

The publishing of scholarly thinking would seem to be primarily an act of
communication. Unless scholars want to limit their readers to the few initiated
elite, they need to be more forthcoming with the specialized definitions. They
should also be more consistent in the use of the terms by acknowledging the
intellectual traditions that have created and supported certain meanings. When
scholars create new terms, which is a very important part of the creativity
inherent in qualitative theorizing, they need to be sure there are not already in
existence common terms that are more accessible to readers. If common terms
do not exist, then there is a compelling need for a new term, but the new term
should be presented with its specialized meaning highlighted. These prescriptions are especially important with the amorphous qualitative approach, which
is striving to establish its identity.

It is indeed ironic that researchers who focus on language are not more
careful in their use of it. They also focus on context, but then neglect to build
a complete context for their own interpretations of meaning. This would not be
a problem if they were obviously willing to allow readers to formulate their own
meaning. But there is a clear perspective in their writings that they want to have
their thoughts understood for what they are, and therefore *their* meaning is what
is presented as important, not the readers' interpretations.

This leaves us with a question about why there is a lack of clarity within and
across writings. There seem to be three possible reasons for this: (a) Qualitative
theoreticians are not sure about what their community is, so they cannot be
clear when writing in a state of ambiguity, (b) qualitative theoreticians are clear
about their community, but they prefer to write for the members who have been
initiated, and they do not mind raising the barriers to entry for others, and (c)
qualitative theoreticians have not figured out which communities their alle-
giances are to, so their writings wobble around through different communities,
each with its own meanings for key terms. Perhaps the best answer to the
question is a combination of all three reasons.

What Level Community?

What can we say about the communities in qualitative research? Is there reason
to believe that there is something like a *national* identity with the qualitative
approach? It appears that there is a sense of identity felt by scholars, even

though they have a difficult time consistently showing the meaning of what they identify with.

A good explanation at this national level was offered by Denzin and Lincoln (1994b), who said that:

> Qualitative research is multimethod in focus, involving an interpretive, naturalistic approach to its subject matter. This means that qualitative researchers study things in their natural settings, attempting to make sense of, or interpret, phenomena in terms of the meanings people bring to them. Qualitative research involves the studied use and collection of a variety of empirical materials—case study, personal experience, introspective, life story, interview, observational, historical, interactional, and visual texts—that describe routine and problematic moments and meanings in individuals' lives. Accordingly, qualitative researchers deploy a wide range of interconnected methods, hoping always to get a better fix on the subject matter at hand. (p. 2)

My definition of the qualitative approach is that it is a perspective on research that it is composed largely of seven methodologies: ethnography, ethnomethodology, reception studies, ecological psychology, symbolic interactionism, cultural studies, and textual analysis. Each of the methodologies relies on a variety of data-gathering methods, analytical methods, and forms of expression in the writing to achieve a purpose that can be descriptive, interpretive, historical, critical, explanatory, action oriented, or any combination of the preceding. But most important, scholars using these seven methodologies share a common basis of five axioms: (a) Researchers should have relatively few preconceived notions about the phenomenon so as to keep themselves as open to the experience as possible and not limit their examination to testing a few a priori expectations, (b) researchers should strive to see the situation from the perspective of the other rather than from predominantly their own perspective, (c) research is a never-ending process of observing an instance and interpreting it in terms of a context that is itself a construction of instances, (d) researchers need to go to the phenomenon and attempt to experience it in its natural, undisturbed state as much as possible, and (e) researchers focus on language (in its broadest sense) as a demonstration of meaning, and this language must be interpreted in cultural and historical contexts. These assumptions are less prescriptions than they are ideal goals that qualitative researchers value—goals that distinguish them from quantitative researchers.

Both of these definitions are very broad; that is, they both define a community encompassing enough to be considered at a high enough level of generality to include all scholars who regard themselves as qualitative. However, the existence of these definitions by themselves is not enough to insure the existence of such a community.

At this time, there is very little reason to believe that there is a national or broad-level community in media studies. Instead, it appears that there are some regional and some local communities where meaning is more commonly shared. Although scholars with local identities may also feel some sense of identity with a larger national community of qualitative, the way these scholars write about what that national level is, makes it clear that there is very little shared meaning. The condition resembles a confederation of unique city-states, such as reception study, feminist criticism, symbolic interactionists, cultural historians, and the like. Each has its own band of adherents. Although the scholars in each city-state think in terms of some national identity, this is with a nebulous recollection that they all belong to some line of thinkers who have served as ancestors to those who now populate the broad intellectual territory surrounding where they call home. So scholars feel a much stronger identity to their city-state within whose walls they do their work.

MISUNDERSTANDINGS ABOUT THE QUANTITATIVE APPROACH

Often qualitative theoreticians will argue that their approach is a better one than the quantitative approach. In making their contrasting argument, they need to describe the characteristics of the quantitative approach. If this is done well, it can be a convincing argument to quantitative researchers; but when it is done poorly, the argument is very dangerous. The danger is not to quantitative researchers who know when the argument is based on a false premise; rather the argument is dangerous to students and to qualitative researchers who are led to believe that either a distinction exists where there really is no distinction, or they are presented with a distinction that is mischaracterized. There are many examples of both of these problems as is exemplified in the sections that follow.

Sampling

There seems to be a misunderstanding about the nature of samples used by quantitative researchers. For example, Lewis (1991) said:

> The statistical accuracy of a survey, as a representation of a more general population, may depend upon the size of the sample. The preference for quantity rather than quality is sometimes based on the rather more amorphous idea that the bigger the sample, the more "scientific" or "objective" the survey. Consequently, the qualitative survey, because it is based upon too small a sample to be "representative," is seen as of little value. Suffice to say that if the quality of information is suspect, the merits of a large sample are fairly dubious. (pp. 74–75)

For quantitative researchers, the key to a good sample is its ability to represent the population from which it was drawn and to which researchers want to generalize their conclusions. A representative sample allows social scientists to work parsimoniously—that is, to limit the expense of gathering data but still being able to generalize the conclusions.

How does one ensure representativeness of the sample? Some researchers will use a quota procedure to select a certain number of males and females, a certain number of people in each age category, a certain number of people of each social class, and so on, so as to construct a sample that reflects the proportion of each type of person in the population. But there is a problem with this quota procedure. The problem is that quantitative researchers know that humans are very complex beings, and their complexity derives from their possessing an almost infinite number of traits, attitudes, values, motives, physical properties, and so forth. It is impossible to ensure that any sample will reflect the population on all these characteristics, so it is impossible to derive a quota for all these variables. Instead, social scientists use a random selection procedure. To social scientists, *random* does not mean haphazard or "take what you can get." A random selection procedure means giving everyone in the population of interest an equal chance of being selected to the sample. If everyone is given an equal chance, the resulting sample is regarded as being representative of the population.

Although the key to sampling for social scientists is representativeness, there is also a secondary concern with sample size. For example, if social scientists were interested in the population of the entire country and selected only one person, we would not argue that the one person in the sample can represent all 260 million citizens, even if that person were selected randomly. If the person selected were a teenage girl, then both the male point of view and the adult point of view would be excluded and the results from the teenage girl could not be generalized to the entire population of the country.

Lewis (1991) was correct that social scientists have a concern with sample size, but the concern is traceable to the idea of representativeness, not to sample size per se. For example, let's say a qualitative researcher conducts an ethnography of four families in an effort to describe how they use the VCR and the television. The ethnographer provides rich description about the four families and their viewing behaviors. In this study, there is no generalization to a larger population, and a social scientist would not criticize the sample for being "too small." Instead, let's say the ethnographer infers some patterns of power and control of the technology from these four families, then talks about these patterns as if they exist in all families. This is a case of generalizing. The social scientist would likely level a criticism of such conclusions. But the criticism would be over the degree to which these four families can represent all families, not primarily because there were only four.

Experimental Research

Seiter et al. (1989b) characterized "mainstream mass communications research" as the use of "white middle-class college students (in their role as experimental subjects) as the universe of media audiences" (p. 3). This characterization is misleading. Less than 16% of quantitative research examining media issues published in the past 25 years uses an experimental approach (Cooper et al., 1994), and within this set there is no requirement that researchers must use only White, middle-class college students as subjects. Granted, a large number of these experimental studies use convenience samples, and because most of the researchers are university professors, they have found it convenient to use college undergraduates. But social science does not *require* researchers to use these weak samples. The fallacy with this criticism is that it appears to be criticizing the design of social science, but the problem is really one of faulty execution.

Operationalization

Pauly (1991) said that "quantitative researchers operationally define their key terms of analysis, in order to make possible a consistent, valid coding system, which, in turn, makes possible the application of appropriate statistical techniques" (p. 6). Without operationalization no empirical research is possible. Unless theoretical concepts are operationalized, they remain general abstract terms with no link to the real world. The process of operationalization is the clarification of how the researcher (quantitative or qualitative) is to decide what constitutes examples of the concepts he or she is examining in the research.

Pauly (1991) also argued that operationalization "troubles the qualitative researcher, for it deliberatively distances the researcher's language of analysis from the subject's language of experience" (p. 6). Again, this shows a lack of understanding about what operationalization means to quantitative researchers who regard the subject's language of experience to be the operationalized manifestations of the concepts. Quantitative researchers are often criticized for creating data where they did not exist. For example, quantitative researchers might ask people about a concept they had never thought about before, thus forcing people to respond with some opinion. Although this does happen, it is not a requirement of operationalization; instead, it is a negative by-product when operationalization is not done well.

If researchers (quantitative as well as qualitative) deal with both the conceptual and empirical levels, they must operationalize; that is, they must make connections of their empirical examples with their general concepts. If they cannot demonstrate correspondence between their measures and their conceptualizations, the examples are poor. So the issue is not one of operationalization per se; if it is, then the only way to avoid it is for researchers to stay on one level, either the conceptual/theoretical level or the empirical level. The issue is the quality of the operationalization.

When Pauly (1991) reacted against operationalization, he was really saying that qualitative researchers need to stay on the empirical level only and not attempt to generalize to higher order explanation. Whenever a qualitative researcher (like a quantitative researcher) develops an abstract conceptual point then uses an observation as a concrete example to illustrate it, he or she is arguing that the example (datum) is an empirical operationalization of the concept.

Reductionism

Fiske and Hartley (1978) in *Reading Television* criticized quantitative content analysis as being too reductionistic in its focus. "It does not help us with matters of interpretation nor with how we respond to the complex significance and subtleties of the television text" (p. 36). "That sort of reading of television requires that we move beyond the strictly objective and quantitative methods of content analysis and into the newer and less well explored discipline of semiotics" (p. 36).

Like many critical scholars, Thornburn (1988) criticized content analyses that use reductive analysis and thereby provide only superficial or wrong readings of television texts. As an example, he singled out Barnouw's (1975) *Tube of Plenty* as treating six spy TV shows in the 1960s as representing television entertainment that was supporting an ideology of Cold War propaganda—America being the good guys fighting the Communist bad guys and leading to a mentality that supported escalation in the Vietnam war. He said that if Barnouw had looked at the aesthetic character of the individual shows, such as tone and atmosphere, it would have been obvious to him that some of these were satires, especially "Get Smart," and that they were not examples of an imperialist ideology.

Granted there are some poor quantitative content analyses in the literature. There are simple "bean counts" of the number of women on different shows, the number of families, the number of sexual references, and the most popular—the number of acts of violence. The things that can be clearly defined and counted usually result in uninteresting conclusions. And the things that are much more interesting, such as violence, are very difficult to define and hence count. Most definitions do not have much ecological validity; that is, most readers would not accept the definition, because it does not fit their understanding of what violence is.

Also, there is the problem that quantitative researchers have of relating their counts of certain instances with effects on viewers. Let's take violence for example. Suppose a quantitative study found that there were an average of five acts of violence (given their definition, of course) broadcast every hour. The authors conclude that this prevalence of violence has negative effects on viewers. Qualitative researchers would criticize such a conclusion saying that much of the violence might have been humorous, such as in cartoons, so why would that have a negative effect? Also, much of the violence might have been punished, so the viewer is constantly seeing simple morality plays. This should lead to viewers developing an aversion to violence. In short, the context of the portrayals is more important than the frequency. Simple bean counts can be very misleading.

This type of criticism, although very legitimate, is really a criticism of simple-minded research, not a criticism of the quantitative approach to content analysis. This content analysis method can be used to focus on the contexts as well as the acts themselves. For example, I conducted several of these studies of antisocial as well as prosocial behavior on television and looked at the contextual variables of justification for the acts, punishment, type of perpetrator (hero, villain, or neutral), and remorse (Potter & Ware, 1987a, 1987b, 1989). I have recently begun another project looking at aggression on television using many more contextual variables: covert/overt, presentation style, intention of perpetrator, motive of perpetrator, justification, remorse, consequences, type of harm, selection of victim, degree of realism, humor, portrayal of perpetrator, profile of perpetrator (number, type, gender, race, and age), profile of victim (number, type, gender, race, and age), and relationship of perpetrator to the victim. The statistical analysis of the resulting database allows for strong contextualization by examining the propensities of certain characteristics (such as lack of justification and remorse) to be associated with certain portrayals (such as when powerless people are victimized by serious physical violence).

Critics of the content analysis method characterize it as simple bean counting and say that it does not matter how many variables are included in the design—it is still bean counting. However, this criticism serves to put simple and sophisticated, poorly designed and well-designed content analyses all in the same category, and this is wrong. A content analysis that is well designed to examine contextual variables may still be gathering beans; but, to extend this analogy, when different variables are used then different colors of beans are collected, and when multivariate analyses are conducted, we can see the big picture in the aggregate of beans. Saying that a content analysis is limited to revealing only those findings that are counts of how many beans are in each row or column is the same as saying that a television screen is limited to showing rows of colored dots and not a picture. Of course, some content analyses are nothing more than counts of beans, but others are able to situate the focus on the big picture. I am not arguing that the grain of that picture is not as fine as that produced by qualitative analysis. But I am arguing that it is a serious underestimation of the content analysis method to say that it is limited to counting beans and that it can never show patterns or pictures within context.

One Variable Limitation

At times qualitative theoreticians complain that quantitative researchers report that their findings on one variable will explain all of human behavior (or a large part of it). For example, Lewis (1991) argued that human behavior is very complex and requires rich description about each individual, so using a variable like gender or age to explain a person's behavior greatly reduces the person to a stereotype and is a very inaccurate finding. There have been many univariate studies done by quantitative researchers, especially before the popular use of computers, which make multivariate analysis easier. Also, there are quantitative researchers who conduct multivariate studies, but still report the results of one variable at a time.

Humans are very complex beings, so why do quantitative researchers try to simplify so drastically? A good answer to this question can be inferred surprisingly from a critical scholar. In his book *Channels of Discourse*, Allen (1985) talked about how readers of texts fill in the gaps in their reading, and in so doing ends up making a strong statement about why holistic analysis is not possible. He said:

> The cat sitting on my lap at the moment is not just any cat, but *this* small, purring four-year-old, female tabby named Dorothy. Still, however, I can only perceive a few of the manifold aspects of this particular cat at any given moment. Looking down at her now, I see her as a rather indistinctly shaped mass of fur with no face, feet, or tail. I can pick her up and thus reveal these hidden aspects, but in doing so I necessarily obscure others. Nothing can be perceived in all its aspects at once, and we constantly make sense of the world by extrapolating from a small number of qualities to a whole thing. (p. 78)

Quantitative researchers are not trying to explain all of human behavior with one variable; instead they are trying to assess the degree to which each variable (one at a time) has value in explaining a large class of behaviors. Social scientists see research as a linear process, just as writing is a linear process; that is, you must address one topic at a time. Even with multivariate analysis, the mathematical algorithm controls the analysis so as to show the researcher the influence that one variable has on other individual and sets of variables.

In the practice of quantitative research, we focus on one variable at a time. But the goal of quantitative research is to be able to provide explanations of the total phenomenon. In order to reach such a goal, we must determine how each variable works by itself, then in combination with another variable, then in combination with all other variables, and finally how all variables work in combination. To get started on such a task we must begin with what appears to be a reductionistic approach, but that is more the nature of getting started in the analysis than it is a reflection on the aims of the quantitative approach.

Effects

There seems to be a misunderstanding about the effects focus of quantitative research. Some qualitative theoreticians seem to think that quantitative researchers are focused only on documenting whether an effect occurs and that they are not interested in exploring why the effects occur or what factors bring those effects about. For example, Seiter et al. (1989b) observed that "the field of mass communications has given us the stimulus-response, or 'hypodermic needle,' theory of the mass media, with its simplistic notion of direct effects" (p. 2). Their solution to this problem was to present research that focuses on "the way that audiences' interpretations of television programs are influenced by race, nationality, class, age, and gender" (p. 2). A reading of the media effects literature will show that quantitative researchers almost always take these demographic variables into consideration. However, sometimes their importance is relegated to a background role, but scientists still consider these variables an important part of the understanding of the effects process. For example, let's say a scientist is interested in seeing if the long-term viewing of violence on television has an effect on viewers' perceptions of the world. This researcher will gather information on viewing exposure and perceptions, but he or she will most likely also gather lots of other information about the viewers (their demographics, motivations for viewing, use of other media, interpersonal relationships, etc.). This other information will then be used as "contextual" information in a multivariate statistical analysis that will foreground the key relationship of interest (exposure influencing perceptions). This foregrounding of a central relationship should not be interpreted to mean that the researcher is only interested in this relationship, nor should it be interpreted as an indication that the researcher believes that the relationship is evidence of a direct, simple effect.

Reliability and Validity

There is also a misunderstanding of the meaning of the technical terms *reliability* and *validity*. For example, Altheide and Johnson (1994) stated that "positivism answered the validity question in terms of reliability: Reliable (repeatable, generalizable) methods and findings were valid ones" (p. 487). This is a wrong statement on several counts. First, the term *generalizable* is not a synonym for *reliable*; instead it is a synonym for a particular kind of validity; that is, external validity. Second, although the two concepts of reliability and validity in social science are related, they are related in an asymmetrical manner. A test cannot be valid unless it is reliable, but it can be reliable without being valid. A simple example of this is a bathroom scale. If we repeatedly put a bag of rocks on the scale and it reads 10 pounds each time, we can say the scale is reliable; that is, it is consistent and stable in giving us the same reading. But this does not mean the scale is valid. Perhaps the bag of rocks weighs 12 pounds on all other scales. Although our scale is consistent—it is consistently wrong. Therefore the scale is reliable (consistent) but not valid (accurate).

Uses and Gratifications

The uses and gratification theory has been both praised and attacked by qualitative theoreticians. For example, Morley (1989) said the uses and gratifications perspective was a positive factor that moved the debate forward with its recognition that audiences were actively engaged with the media. He stated, "clearly, uses and gratifications does represent a significant advance on effects theory, in so far as it opens up the question of differential interpretation" (p. 17). In contrast, Ang (1989) criticized the uses and gratifications approach for being limited. She said, "rather than the classification of differences and varieties in all sorts of typologies, which is a major preoccupation of a lot of uses and gratifications work, cultural studies would be oriented toward a detailed understanding of how and why varieties in experience occur" (pp. 107–108).

The praise and criticism highlighted in the preceding paragraph shows that the writers are misunderstanding the nature of quantitative approach. Let's take a closer look. Morley's (1989) quote that "clearly, uses and gratifications does represent a significant advance on effects theory, in so far as it opens up the question of differential interpretation" (p. 17) raises a concern about what he meant by differential interpretation. It appears that he was saying that effects research up to that point was looking at nondifferential interpretation; that is, making the assumption that all people interpreted the media messages the same way. If this is what he was saying, then his perspective is that the quantitative approach was limiting itself to dealing only with constants, not variables, until uses and gratifications came along. But this would be wrong. Of course effects research used variables, and this use resulted in findings that always showed a variation in response. Even reading one study would show that clearly. However, in science there is a goal of providing a high degree of conceptual leverage—that is, seeking higher level abstractions to explain broader and broader sets of phenomena. So our focus is on commonalities among people. When social scientists talk about regularities of behavior, they are not saying that everyone behaves the same way; instead they are saying that they are reporting what seems to be a pattern within the otherwise chaotic mass of behavioral elements.

Ang (1989) saw the uses and gratifications approach as limited. She said, "rather than the classification of differences and varieties in all sorts of typologies, which is a major preoccupation of a lot of uses and gratifications work, cultural studies would be oriented toward a detailed understanding of how and why varieties in experience occur" (pp. 107–108). This is a more accurate description of uses and gratifications, because it recognizes that the approach not only allows for, but also focuses on, differences. However, it is still inaccurate to say that uses and gratifications does not seek an understanding of the how and why of the differences.

Understanding Philosophy of Science

Much of the way qualitative theoreticians characterize science is with a 19th-century vision of it. This vision sees scientists as looking for another planet or going into the jungle to discover the existence of another type of plant or insect. With the quantitative approach, they characterize researchers as people who believe that there are simple, direct effects lying out there in the social arena and who see their job as discovering what those effects are. This vision sees scientists as adventurers who explore unknown terrains to find the treasure—the existence of things that have been lying around for years waiting to be discovered.

There are probably some scientists who operate like this, but their numbers are very small and growing smaller each year as there are fewer and fewer obvious physical phenomena left to be discovered. This does not mean that science is dying, only that this vision of it is finally changing; the actual practices of scientists have changed long ago.

In social science, almost no scientist has a vision for his or her activity anywhere near this 19th-century explorer/adventurer one. This vision was briefly popular among some social scientists at the turn of the century who considered themselves positivists. The term *positivist* was coined by Comte who used it to refer to a strict form of empiricism. "The positivist maintains that only those knowledge claims which are founded directly on experience are genuine" (H. I. Brown, 1977, p. 21). Positivism meant that claims for truth had to be verified empirically. If something cannot be verified, it is non-sense by definition. Positivism is best regarded as a reaction to those scholars who based their research on pure speculation or mentalism. The primary contribution of this positivist position was in reminding scientists of the importance of checking their speculations in the world. However, the early positivists fixated on the empirical component of science and virtually ignored the theorizing/speculation component. Almost immediately, the strict positivists were criticized for being exclusively empirical just as the positivists were criticizing the mentalists for being too speculative. A group of scholars who called themselves logical positivists sought a synthesis of the two extremes in order to get the two essential components of science (speculation and empiricism) back in balance.

These two components of speculation and observation had been essential parts of scientific thinking for centuries. Ever since the Renaissance and the development of the procedure known as "the scientific method" of induction, the procedure of science has been to construct explanations about the material world, then to check those constructions with observations.

The ideas of the philosophers of the Vienna Circle changed thinking about science in the early 20th century, when they called into question the status of scientific findings. "Scientific truth was found not be absolute, enduring, and ontologically basic, but rather to be contingent upon the frames of references, the constructions, the conceptual premises that give to the scientific argument its unique possibility" (Turner, 1965, p. 105). In physics, Einstein and Mach made corrections to Newton's mechanics and in so doing revealed that a change in assumptions requires a change in theory and explanation. Their new theories were found to be more useful than Newton's theory, because they could explain the same phenomenon that Newton explained (mechanics on earth) along with additional phenomena (mechanics in the universe) and do so more parsimoniously. Science was shifting to the newer criterion of utility, and in so doing was becoming more vital and more creative.

They abandoned claims of truth, reasoning that humans have limited perceptions and will never be able to perceive natural phenomena in an unfiltered completely accurate manner. Instead, they set out a criterion of utility, reasoning that it is possible for scientists to improve their explanations. Improved explanations are those that more clearly and more parsimoniously accounted for broader phenomena.

Today, scientists are guided by a purpose of providing useful explanations about phenomena. In the construction of these explanations they make observations, but this empirical component serves as a check on their explanations; it does not take the place of explanations. These constructions are judged according to their utility. Scientists do not see themselves as "discovering" reality.

This current thinking among scientists is very similar to what many qualitative theoreticians espouse for their approach, and it has been this way for a long time despite the fact that many qualitative types are still drawing a major distinction. To illustrate this point, Toulmin (1983) explained that when Dilthey drew a "sharp distinction between scientific explanation and hermeneutic interpretation" (p. 100) a century ago, that distinction might have held at the time but that it certainly does not hold now with postmodern science. However, many people still subscribe to this distinction. He said, "It is a pity then for scholars working in the humanities to continue shaping their critical attitudes and theories by relying on a contrast with a modern science that—among scientists themselves—no longer even *seems* to exist" (p. 101). He pointed out that significant changes have occurred in scientific thinking. During the "classical" period from the mid-17th century until around 1920, scientists were regarded as pure spectators as if looking at the universe from outside it somehow. However, this perspective broke down when "the scope of investigation was extended to include systems and subjects whose behavior may be changed by the very fact that they are being investigated" (p. 102). This was clearly the case when investigating human behavior, but it also applies to subatomic particles.

In support of this argument of only minor differences between the quantitative and qualitative approaches, Toulmin (1983) presented several principles. First, he asserted that "the doctrines of the natural sciences are critical interpretations of their subject matter, no less than those of the humanities" (p. 101). He also observed that scientists are enculturated into their professional community and once they are fully inside that community their work takes on the same interpretive processes as others in that community. He also tried to debunk the belief that interpretation is always personal and idiosyncratic. He argued that scholars in well-defined disciplines draw from the accumulated experience of other scholars, so their own interpretations conform to those of the community and are therefore not purely personal or arbitrary. The community standard then determines what is the correct interpretation. This does not rule out alternative interpretations within a community, but each alternative interpretation has its own scope and justification. He said, "In sciences and humanities alike, we must be prepared to consider the products of human imagination and creation—whether ideas or artifacts, poems or theories—from a variety of different points of view" (p. 110). Second, he argued that both employ a hermeneutic process of discovery. On the science side, he observed that people give too much credence to the position that science is objective and rational. He stated that physics, for example, "has always asked its participants to adopt an interpretive standpoint" (p. 100). This interpretive standpoint is used to construct reality. He asserted that "the supposed contrast between the scientists' claim to rational objectivity (which requires no interpretation) and the humanists' rival claim to subjective sensibility (in which interpretation is all) shows *on its face* its essential irrelevance to the actual work of art and science. At most, there is a difference of balance or emphasis" (p. 111).

Toulmin (1983) further argued, "We should ask scholars to pay more attention to the elements of interpretation—even of hermeneutics—that have nowadays become essential to both the natural and human sciences and to base their comparisons between the sciences and humanities not on the assumed *absence* of hermeneutic interpretation from natural science but rather on the different *modes* of interpretation characteristic of the two general fields" (p. 101).

Physical scientists who are concerned with explaining the behavior of the universe, its origin, the composition of matter and energy are certainly operating as scholars focused on constructing explanations that are judged on the criterion of utility not truth. Social scientists, who are dealing with even more complex phenomena of human thought and behavior are also focused on constructing explanations that are judged on the criterion of utility not truth. Philosophers established this criterion about a century ago, and any scholar who has carefully worked through a scientific project knows this to be the goal of science.

However, many nonscientists, especially many who seek to criticize science, are still clinging to a 19th-century view of the scientist as discoverer, and they steadfastly characterize science as positivism. Fortunately, some of these non-scientists are realizing their mischaracterization. For example, for years Lincoln and Guba (1985) were criticizing social science for being positivistic, but more recently Lincoln has seen that this form of science is long since passed. And Denzin and Lincoln (1994a) talked about a postpositivist approach. However, physical scientists have long since left positivism, and it is doubtful if many social scientists (with the exception of strict behaviorists within experimental psychology) have ever seriously operated under a belief in positivism.

FAULTY ARGUMENTS

Straw Man Arguments

The adversarial nature of much of the writing by theoreticians depends on making clear distinctions between qualitative and quantitative approaches. The theoreticians have no difficulty in setting up the distinctions clearly. Instead, the problem is in characterizing the quantitative approach accurately. In their quest to emphasize differences, they caricaturize science. These caricatures are straw men, which they can easily destroy with their arguments. Many of these straw man characteristics are attributable to a misunderstanding of the purpose and practices of the quantitative approach (see the previous section). But there are also some other examples, the most pronounced of which is the characterization of media research by social scientists as being guided by a hypodermic needle view of the media. Morley (1989) asserted that "the hypodermic model of media influence" represents the tradition of media effect studies for the past 45 years (p. 16). Also, Seiter et al. (1989b) said, "the field of mass communications has given us the stimulus-response, or 'hypodermic needle,' theory of the mass media, with its simplistic notion of direct effects" (p. 2).

There are two reasons to consider this a straw man argument. First, this characterization is inaccurate. Some authors talk about science (at least in the early years, but some still maintain this to be the case even today) as being dominated by a perspective that the audience is helpless and that the media have a "magic bullet" or hypodermic needle effect. This is nonsense. Gerbner (1983) explained:

> No responsible communication researcher ever advanced a theory of helpless receivers falling under a hail of media bullets. That construction was advanced more to caricature exaggerated popular beliefs in the uniform efficacy of wartime (and other) propaganda and to call attention to research findings showing the greater complexity of the persuasion process. But it was elevated, with assistance from broadcasting industry funds, publications, and researchers, to the stature of scientific ideology relating to media influence in general and not just to specific types of campaigns. (p. 359)

Second, the qualitative scholars who characterize social science as being fixated on a hypodermic needle model of the media offer no attribution for this perception. So where do they get this idea?

It is interesting to note that no qualitative author who uses one of these misconceptions of science ever acknowledges the perspective to a scholar who created the perspective. It is an idea that is just there without an author. Perhaps the idea is an inference from the many studies that appeared to look for direct effects of mediated material on individuals—there were many of these studies in the 1930s to 1950s. But making such an inference (that social scientists believed in a magic bullet) would be wrong. The design of these studies should not be taken to indicate that those researchers believed in direct effects; instead, it is a process of science to ask the simplest questions first, then go on to the more complex questions. Also, the experimental method, which was very popular at the time, required the controlling of as many as possible of all factors but one. That isolated factor is then systematically varied so its single effect can be assessed. As the research matured and more advanced tools of analysis (such as high-speed computers) were available, it became more easy to assess the effects (individually and in combination) of multiple factors. But that does not mean that science has changed its fundamental perspective, only that it is further down the road conceptually and methodologically.

Another example of this straw man argument was presented by Reinharz (1992) who observed in her book *Feminist Methods in Social Research* that "quantitative research defines itself as hard, firm, real ... and strong" whereas qualitative research is "soft, mushy, fuzzy, and weak" (p. 295). Where does she get this? There are no citations or examples. If this is indeed a stereotype, it is kept alive by qualitative writers much more than by quantitative writers.

Also, Altheide and Johnson (1994) talked about a shift in criticism "from the traditional enemies, the positivists who fault qualitative research for its failure to meet some or all of the usual positivistic criteria of truth" (p. 485), but nowhere do they cite who these critiques are.

This leads the reader to believe that qualitative researchers feel this general free-floating persecution that cannot be pinned down to any particular critics. It is as if the qualitative theoreticians have drawn the wagons together in a tight circle, then sit around their protected campfire and tell stories about ghosts that only appear in their minds. Over time, the telling of these stories sustains a myth that social science is brute empiricism oriented toward narrowly defined data points stripped of context and that it has generated a useless body of faulty facts. Like a myth, the story has no acknowledged source; it belongs to everyone in the circle. It is kept alive only in the retelling. This myth still appears today. For example, in an historical overview of approaches to communication research, Lindlof (1995) said that "until recently, the work produced by practitioners of qualitative social science was burdened by a reputation of softness. It seemed too imprecise, value laden, and particularistic to be of much use in generating general or causal explanations of communication behavior" (p. 10). Lindlof clearly illuminated this perspective over several pages of text, but he did not present any sources for this view nor acknowledge any scholars who espouse this perspective.

False Dichotomy

Sometimes the comparison between the two approaches leads to a *false dichotomy*. To illustrate, Allen (1985) observed, "the battles against exclusively quantitative analysis, the presumed objectivity of the investigator, and appropriateness of research models based on the natural sciences for the study of cultural phenomena, and other tenets of empiricism are no longer being fought; the war is over, and the antiempiricists now occupy the field" (p. 5). This statement most clearly displays a combatant nature rather than a cooperative perspective on understanding the phenomenon. Also, it shows an elitism that his position is superior and beyond question. This attitude with the attendant misapplication of terms is not constructive. It is also wrong. Gerbner (1983) clearly showed why this false dichotomy of qualitative-quantitative is very misleading:

> Qualitative distinctions and judgments (as in labeling or classifying) are prereq-uisites to quantitative measurements; the two are inseparable. To say that one can only measure what exists and, therefore, quantitative efforts can only support the status quo, is sophistry. The careful observation of existing conditions is necessary to support any judgment of or strategy for change, and judgment is not hurt by some attempt at precision. . . . Qualitative change cannot be understood, let alone achieved, without noting the accumulation of quantities. Add heat (quantity) to water and it changes to steam (quality). To consider quantification only mindless counting or number crunching is both a philosophical and strategic fallacy. (p. 361)

The criticism of this qualitative-quantitative dichotomy cuts both ways. Quantitative researchers who characterize qualitative methods as not being rigorous are also creating a false distinction. Rosengren (1989) argued that qualitative methods are no less rigorous than quantitative methods: "The most 'humanistic' of activities, the interpretation of texts, may be carried out in a very systematic and rigorous way" (p. 26).

Rising Dominance Myth

Another misleading argument is that there is an emergent new interpretive paradigm that is not only gaining acceptance, but is replacing the older, "bankrupt paradigm" of magic bullet that dominated media research in the past.

Within media studies, Gitlin (1978) was one of the early scholars to express dissatisfaction with what he called the dominant paradigm of media sociology or quantitative work with its focus on effects of:

> broadcast programming in a specifically behaviorist fashion, defining "effects" so narrowly, microscopically, and directly as to make it very likely that survey studies could show only slight effects at most. It has enshrined short-run "effects" as "measures" of "importance" largely because these "effects" are measurable in a strict, replicable behavioral sense, thereby deflecting attention from larger social meanings of mass media production. (p. 206)

He predicted the decomposition of the "administrative" approach, which poses "questions from the vantage of the command-posts of institutions that seek to improve or rationalize their control over social sectors in social functions" (p. 225). Several years later, Corcoran (1984) observed that since the mid-1970s, there "has been a major shift of interest away from the positivist emphasis of the dominant Anglo-American paradigm" to a "textual, anti-empiricist paradigm" (p. 533). Allen (1985) called "empiricist methods usually employed by American media researchers to study fictional programming" a "now thoroughly discredited research philosophy" (p. 5). Lewis (1991) said that by the 1960s, "the 'effects' approach to the TV audience was, to all intents and purposes, abandoned" (pp. 6–7). He wrote: "The 1970s marked a turning point in the study of television. . . . By the end of the decade, with the possible exception of some cultivation studies in the United States, audience research was in grave danger of becoming an almost moribund area of media studies" (p. 23). Where do they get these ideas?

We could speculate about what types of research are waxing and waning, or we could employ a methodology that would tell us about what the patterns in the research literature are. Or we could do both—speculate then put the speculations to the test. When we do put those speculations to a test, we do get some results (albeit an intersubjectively derived estimate) that finds Lewis' (1991) subjective opinion to be way off the mark, rendering it a very misleading characterization of media research. In a content analysis of the media research in mainstream media journals from 1965 to 1989, about 22% of all research focused on the topic of effects of media on individuals (ranking it as the most popular single topic) and almost all of these studies were conducted within the social science paradigm (Potter, Cooper, & Dupagne, 1993). Furthermore, the social science paradigm showed no signs of shrinking in its prevalence over those 25 years of research published in mainstream journals. Maybe the proliferation of qualitative research took place in books and monographs, but we will not know that until scholars document this trend with evidence.

Still, this claim for growing interest is also seen in sociology and education. For example, in sociology Wuthnow and Witten (1988) observed a dramatic growth in interest in cultural studies, saying "Only a few years ago it would have seemed extremely unlikely that the study of culture might emerge as a major growth industry" . . . "but it has now happened" (p. 49). They said the cause for the change "appears to be a growing dissatisfaction with the state of 'normal science' in the discipline. Ever more obscure statistical innovations have contributed to the discipline's attractiveness to technically minded government bureaucrats, but these have failed miserably to address issues of serious social and cultural significance" (p. 49).

In education, Wolcott (1992) observed that "we seem on the verge of canonizing" qualitative research but that it:

> is not a field of study, and there is no clearly specified set of activities or identifiable group of specialists who practice them. To claim competence in qualitative research is, at most, to claim general familiarity with what is currently being done, coupled perhaps with experience in one or two particular facets (e.g., to "be good at" collecting and interpreting life histories or to "be" a symbolic interactionist). Claims to familiarity often amount to little more than a sympathetic attitude toward descriptive or interpretive work, accompanied by a far more deeply expressed antagonism for that "other kind" of research to which we have begun attaching the negative label "positivist." (p. 4)

And an even grander claim was made by Denzin and Lincoln (1994c), who said, "over the past two decades, a quiet methodological revolution has been taking place in the social sciences. . . . The social sciences and humanities have drawn closer together in a mutual focus on an interpretive, qualitative approach to research and theory" (p. ix) and that "the extent to which the 'qualitative revolution' has overtaken the social sciences and related professional fields has been nothing short of amazing" (p. ix).

How do they know that it has grown? Where is the evidence? This claim must be viewed with skepticism, especially because there is so much trouble defining it. Even Denzin and Lincoln (1994c) had trouble defining it when they observed that "the 'field' of qualitative research is far from a unified set of principles promulgated by networked groups of scholars" (p. ix) but that it is instead "defined primarily by a series of essential tensions, contradictions, and hesitations" (p. ix). This definition does not help us understand what this thing is that has supposedly "overtaken the social science."

Denzin and Lincoln (1994a) also provided another definition:

> Qualitative research is an interdisciplinary, and sometimes counterdisciplinary field. It cross-cuts the humanities, the social sciences and the physical sciences. Qualitative research is many things at the same time. It is multiparadigmatic in focus. Its practitioners are sensitive to the value of the multimethod approach. They are committed to the naturalistic perspective and to the interpretive understanding of human experience. At the same time, the field is inherently political and shaped by multiple ethical and political positions. Qualitative research embraces two tensions at the same time. On the one hand, it is drawn to a broad interpretive, postmodern, feminist, and critical sensibility. On the other hand, it can also be drawn to more narrowly defined positivist, postpositivist, humanistic, and naturalistic conceptions of human experience and its analysis. (p. 576)

With such a broad definition, it is not surprising that this "approach" is viewed as fast growing. However, the growth may be more a function of the change in definitions than in its growing appeal. An analogy would be that of a small city that decides to annex all the surrounding suburban counties, then claims that it is the fastest growing city in the country. In a technical sense this is accurate, because the population has grown; however, the claim makes it sound like huge numbers of people have recently found the city attractive enough to move there from other less attractive cities. And this may not be the case. It also might be the case, but we need evidence to assess that their claims are not just wishful thinking.

Transmission Model

Carey (1977) drew the distinction between social science and critical approaches in terms of how communication through the media is regarded. He said the media can be regarded as either transmitting information (transportation) or maintaining the culture (ritual). The social scientist's view is one of transportation where communication is seen as "a process of transmitting messages at a distance for the purpose of control. The archetypal case of communication then is persuasion, attitude change, behavior modification, socialization through the transmission of information, influence, or conditioning" (p. 412). He explained that his use of the term "transportation" comes from his perception that during the 19th century there was a desire to use communication and transportation to extend influence, control and power over wider distances and over greater populations. On the other hand, the critic (literary, artistic, or aesthetic person) leans toward a ritual perspective where communication is "not directed toward the extension of messages in space but the maintenance of society in time; not the act of imparting information but the representation of shared beliefs" (p. 412).

Carey (1977) further asserted that social science, which is primarily American with a focus on behaviorist, positivist, empiricist, and pragmatist ideas, has been dominated by attempts to create a behavioral science that elucidates the laws of behavior. But, he said, this effort has yielded no formal theories like other social sciences such as modern linguistics (Chomsky), structuralism (Levi-Strauss), systems theory, and cybernetics. This is an incredible position! There are scores of social science theories in psychology, sociology, political science, and economics that are used in communication studies. Also there are many indigenous social science theories of media, including agenda setting, dependency theory, cultivation, cue theory, catharsis theory, excitation transfer, and uses and gratification theory. Some of these are much less developed than others, and scholars argue whether some should be called theories. However, they all (and many others) serve the function of theory by setting out general explanatory propositions that direct researchers to provide empirical tests.

Carey (1977) argued that cultural studies is superior because it does not seek to explain human behavior but to understand it. It does not seek to reduce human action to underlying causes or structures but to interpret its significance. It does not attempt to predict human behavior but to diagnose human meanings. According to him, "A cultural science of communication, then, views human behavior, or more accurately human action, as a text. Our task is to construct a 'reading' of the text" (p. 421).

This is a difficult position to understand because of his notions of understanding and explanation. From a layperson's point of view, it would seem that in order to explain something, you would first have to understand it. If you did not understand something, how could you explain it? From a scientific point of view, explanation means going beyond description by leveraging results conceptually as well as generalizing results to a broader span of people and time. Therefore explanation would seem to be a task of a higher order beyond understanding. With either of these perspectives, explanation both encompasses and goes beyond understanding. So Carey's (1977) position is confusing. How can cultural studies be superior to social science if that superiority is based on a claim that cultural studies seeks understanding whereas social science seeks explanation? Carey must have been using a third point of view in order to see "understanding" as having superior qualities to "explanation." This, of course, is possible because he may have any meaning he likes for these two terms; however, he did not help us understand that meaning, so his argument leaves the reader requiring more explanation from him.

ASSUMPTIONS OF REALITY AND KNOWING

Does a Reality Exist Apart From One's Perception?

This is the ontological question. Some scholars say that communication is a human construction, so therefore it does not exist like other phenomena, such as rocks, trees, planets, and so forth. For example, Pauly (1991) revealed an idealist perspective when he said, "Humans fabricate rather than discover reality. They use symbols to construct the worlds in which they live. In this view, reality is an accomplishment rather than an entity out there, waiting to be uncovered" (p. 2).

Let's accept this idealist position and agree that people do not discover reality but construct it. Let's make this distinction concrete through an example. TV viewers do not discover their interpretations of a program, they construct it. So from an ontological point of view, there is no preconstruction status of the interpretation; that is, the interpretation does not exist until the person has constructed it. However, once the person has constructed the interpretation in his or her own mind, that interpretation exists. Now when the researcher enters the picture there is an interpretation to be found; in fact, that is the purpose of methodologies such as ethnography, ethnomethodology, symbolic interactionism, and ecological psychology—the research focuses his or her efforts on finding out the interpretations of the people they are studying.

This illuminates the ontological split. It is different being a human who is studied (the subject) and a human doing the studying (the researcher). That which is studied exists to be discovered. If it did not exist, then all we would have would be the researcher's interpretation of that which does not exist—a pure fantasy. This is why the ontological position of all scholars must be a material one.

Different Views of Meaning Making

The next problem is with the nature of knowing that existence, and this is an epistemological, not an ontological, concern—that is, can we come to know that existence? It is not useful to look for a categorical answer here—no one would seriously say that we can completely understand a conversation or that there is no way to understand anything about a particular conversation. The answer to the epistemological question is always a matter of degree. Those who would place themselves on the realist side of the belief continuum believe that scholarship can produce explanations that reveal patterns in the phenomenon. With realists, the goal is to provide explanations that fit the patterns in the observations as closely as possible. But even realists understand that the perceptions are limited and that those explanations will always be limited because they will never be able to perceive all the complexity in the human condition. However, the goal is still a worthy target.

In contrast, scholars who would place themselves on the constructivist side of the continuum believe that the research act itself is a construction. However, they would not seriously argue that it is impossible to know anything about the conversation—to do so would render the entire enterprise of interpreting the conversation useless.

The key difference among qualitative theoreticians and researchers is not with the subject being studied, but with the researcher. All qualitative scholars would agree that humans as subjects must interpret their world; they never discover it. And they would agree that researchers, who are also humans, must exercise interpretation in the research process. However, the question is with the degree of interpretation that is necessary in the research process. Constructivists say that research is purely an act of interpretation. Realists say that subjects have their interpretations and that research is primarily a discovery of those interpretations; also researchers are superior in the meaning making to ordinary individuals for two reasons. First, they are more conscious of the process of meaning making, and second, they have more training and experience in discovering meaning making.

The Ontological-Epistemological Separation Problem

Several theoreticians argue that the issues of ontology and epistemology, which are two quite different issues for realists, are the same for idealists. For example, Lincoln and Guba (1985) asserted that in naturalism, the investigator and what is investigated are seen as interdependent; what we treat as real is in large measure mind-dependent. The inquirer and the subject of inquiry interact to influence one another; knower and known are inseparable. In positivism, the inquirer and the object of inquiry are independent; the knower and the known constitute a discrete dualism.

J. K. Smith (1983) argued that for realists, the "ontological questions concerning 'what is' can be kept separate from the epistemological questions about how we come to know 'what is'" (p. 8). But with idealists, the subject and object become one and theory therefore "perceive no reality independent of the shaping of creating efforts of the mind" (p. 8). He said there is a range of positions within idealism from ontological idealism to conceptual idealism. Ontological idealism is that belief that reality does not exist at all independent of people; it is a pure creation of individuals. Conceptual idealism is the belief that reality is shaped by our minds. This contrast can be made at the epistemological level also. Realists believe that explanations should correspond to the external reality that exists. But correspondence has no meaning for idealists who do not believe in a knowable external reality. Instead, idealists have a different version of epistemology. The conceptual idealist uses a standard of coherence in an explanation. Because the explanation is a construction, it cannot represent anything outside itself, but it should be coherent. The ontological idealist looks for agreement with other researchers. If several researchers present the same interpretation, then there is agreement and that interpretation is accepted. But accepted as what? Truth? Reality? He does not say.

Making all these distinction clear is difficult in such an abstract area of thinking. Let's consider an example to make more concrete the issue of: Where is the interpretation? Let's take an ethnography as that example. Are the utterances of the people being observed regarded as facts (those words were actually spoken) or are they regarded as interpretations (the words represent the people's subjective views of something else)? This I call first-order interpretation to refer to the subjective nature in primary human speech and action. When we talk *about* human speech, which is what communication researchers do, I call this second-order interpretation. This raises the question: Does the researcher acknowledge his or her own interpretation of the observations or does the researcher regard himself or herself as superior in training or method and therefore able to ascend above interpretation and provide simple description of the first-order data or provide insightful explanations of what "is really" going on? Theoreticians rarely address this issue, but when they do they regard researchers as humans who have the same limitations as the people they are studying.

The qualitative approach allows for a range of positions, but so does the quantitative approach. The qualitative approach is not as idealist as some of the rhetoric would have us believe. Many qualitative researchers would seem to be materialists ontologically; this can be inferred from their writings and the way the seek and present evidence. Also, many quantitative researchers pursue projects about how humans construct meaning, especially in the information-processing and cognitive sciences areas. Though their selection of methods may differ, their base beliefs are surprisingly similar.

LACK OF GUIDANCE ON METHODS

Until recently, there has been very little guidance even of a general nature about how to conduct qualitative research. Sieber (1976) analyzed the qualitative methods books used in education and found that only about 5% to 10% were devoted to presenting specific guidance in qualitative methods. Miles and Huberman (1984) observed that "most attention went to issues such as gaining access and avoiding bias during data collection" (p. 16). They said this lack of guidance about the details of the method, especially about how to conduct the analyses, did not begin to change until the late 1970s and early 1980s when several texts addressed this issue in more depth (e.g., Bogdan & Biklen, 1982; Guba & Lincoln, 1981; Spradley, 1979). The same lack of methodological guidance was in evidence in the field of communication until the late 1980s when some extended methodological treatments about methods were published (J. A. Anderson, 1987; Berger, 1982; Lindlof, 1995; Pauly, 1991).

Miles and Huberman (1984) said that "many qualitative researchers still consider analysis as 'art' and stress intuitive approaches to it" (p. 16). Of course, the downside is that qualitative researchers have a greater burden in demonstrating the nature and quality of their decisions, because their methods are not routinized. This led Miles (1979) to observe that a researcher who faces a bank of qualitative observations has very few guidelines for protection against self-delusion, let alone the presentation of unreliable or invalid conclusions. But if we regard qualitative research as an art, then we must also realize that there is a lot of technique involved with art. Good artists have a strong foundation of working with materials before they can use them as a springboard for their creative expression.

THE LOCUS OF VALUING

The question about standards on the surface is: Is it possible to provide evaluative criteria for qualitative methodologies when taking a position that all human behavior is personal and idiosyncratic? But the deeper question is: How does qualitative research establish its value? Is value to be based on truth? On accuracy? On usefulness? On resonance?

J. K. Smith (1984) asserted that qualitative research is built on an idealist foundation, which is defined as the position that the human mind subjectively constructs reality. Because there is no objective place to stand, it is not possible to expect qualitative research to be reliable or valid. Why should we expect all people to "see" the same thing (reliability)? And if no one's perception of truth is any better than anyone else's, then what is the truth standard for judging validity? In short, the idealist assumptions of qualitative research do not provide a foundation for setting standards. Smith extended this point by arguing that establishing criteria for qualitative research is impossible, because there cannot be consistency between the assumptions of qualitative research and the nature of criteria. Qualitative research is based on the assumption that there are multiple meanings. Criteria seek to establish a standard that is neutral and nonarbitrary for determining how trustworthy the research is. He said there are only two ways to go in solving this problem of inconsistency. One way is to admit to a singular reality (ignoring the assumption of qualitative research) and develop a single list of criteria. The other way is to "put aside the desire to be foundational" (p. 390) and not quest for criteria. Mere understanding through interpretation is enough. He did not admit that there is a commonality at any level. Also, he did not allow for multiple criteria or types. So we are left in a position where we must regard all interpretations as being equally good.

But other scholars believe that it is possible and important to establish standards for qualitative research (Altheide & Johnson, 1994; J. A. Anderson, 1987; Fortner & Christians, 1981; Howe & Eisenhart, 1990; Lancy, 1993; Lincoln & Guba, 1986, 1990; Marshall & Rossman, 1989; Penman, 1988). For example, Howe and Eisenhart carefully laid the foundation for a nonpositivist set of criteria then presented five: (a) fit between research questions and data collection/analysis techniques, (b) effective application of specific data collection and analysis techniques, (c) coherence of background assumptions, (d) overall warrant—being able to employ knowledge from outside the particular perspective and tradition within which one is working, and being able to apply general principles for evaluating arguments, and (e) value constraints of ethics and answering the "So what?" question. Also, several of these theoreticians have criteria of generalizability of results (J. A. Anderson, 1987; Marshall & Rossman, 1989; Strauss & Corbin, 1990) and replicability (Lincoln & Guba, 1990; Marshall & Rossman, 1989).

Lindlof and Meyer (1987) said there is a need for interobserver reliability, which is "consensus among multiple observers of the same phenomenon" (p. 16). This is desirable because of the assumption "that there are common interpretations of phenomena if observers are carefully trained in what to look for and how to recognize various displays of behavior" (p. 16). But then they contradicted themselves in the next paragraph by saying "for the most part, naturalistic observation rejects the idea of multiple observers producing a single interpretation" (p. 16). Quantitative has method that indicates tests for validity and reliability. Qualitative has only reinterviewing Ss (which is same as quantitative) and triangulation of data (which is same as quantitative). But qualitative gets into trouble with these methods, because they do not rest on their assumptions of context sensitivity. Asking the same person twice should result in two different answers, because the context has changed. Also asking several different data sources (triangulation) should result in different data (again because of the different contexts of the sources). If you do get confirmation across all sources (and qualitative never tells you how much confirmation is needed or how to do the confirmation), then you have reliability; but this also indicates a generalized phenomenon, that is, one whose perception is shared across different people or media, and the stronger this is the greater the case for reliability and quality of qual measures. But the greater the confirmation, the more we must call into question the qual assumption that all situations have a unique context that influences attitudes and behaviors.

Or is qualitative research purely idiosyncratic? In that case, the term *valid* is a label applied to an interpretation or description with which one agrees (J. K.

Smith & Heshusius, 1986). It is simply a matter of what the reader believes. But what does this mean? Does it mean what the reader believes before reading the research report? If this is the case, then only research that confirms a person's already existing beliefs is of any use. Or does it mean how persuasive the research is in changing a person's opinion or somehow adding to his or her knowledge.

The key idea behind the criteria argument is the concept of progression. If a qualitative theoretician genuinely believes that there is no basis for distinguishing among everyone's interpretations, then there can be no sense of progression. However, if a theoretician believes that it is important for a scholarly endeavor to exhibit a progression toward better description, better explanation, or better criticism, then he or she needs to define what better means and how scholars are to make decisions on this criterion.

SUMMARY

The analysis in this section presents a harsh picture of some of the writings about qualitative research. Claims have been made that there is a lack of clarity in defining and using important terms, a lack of precision in illuminating axioms, a lack of guidance on important methodological features, and arguments based on false dichotomies. However, these are problems that can be ameliorated, because these are problems with the execution, not with the basic usefulness of the approach. This criticism is made in an effort to influence the practices, not to argue against the overall approach to research.

The most damaging problem with qualitative theorizing is the negative critical nature of some of the analysis that appears to be more oppositional than constructive. Constructive criticism is oriented in making the object better; in so doing it points out the weak areas and suggests a plan for improvement. It also points out the strong areas, and this serves to reinforce them. Oppositional criticism focuses on differences between the self and the other. It focuses on the areas where the other is weak and concludes that the self is then superior.

The critics who have taken an oppositional tone have constructed some myths to demonize social science. As long as these criticisms use misinformation and straw man arguments, they will mislead scholars with a genuine interest in trying to understand the usefulness of both approaches.

16

CRITIQUE OF
QUALITATIVE RESEARCH

This chapter, like the previous one, takes a critical perspective. In the previous chapter I provided extrinsic criticism; that is, I stood outside the qualitative paradigm and examined the topics about the qualitative way of thinking and the assumptions made. My criticism focused on how well articulated and how useful are the axioms and prescriptions for practice. In this chapter, I provide intrinsic criticism; that is, I accept the qualitative way of thinking. I take the axioms and prescriptions for practice as givens, then seek to determine the extent to which the empirical research exemplifies those tenets.

This chapter deals with five topics. First, I examine the way scholars have positioned their research through the way they lay out the axioms, assumptions, and methodologies. Second, I lay out the problems in that research in terms of how authors inform readers about the selection of their evidence. Third, the focus shifts to the problems with authors informing readers about how that evidence was analyzed and organized. Fourth, I compare the results of the interpretive analyses to the scientific analysis. And finally, I attempt a parsimonious explanation of the major patterns by speculating that there are two tensions that influence qualitative researchers in making their decisions.

PROBLEMS IN POSITIONING THE RESEARCH

Mischaracterizing Methodologies

In the published research literature there are examples of authors not making clear what methodology they are using or of mischaracterizing the methodology they do use. The most problematic of these is ethnography, which is treated by some scholars almost as a synonym for interviewing. In "The Critical Response: The Audience as Nuisance," Lull (1989) complained that ethnography is becoming a buzzword in our field and that many supposed ethnographies are not. For example, Hobson (1989), Radway (1984), and Seiter et al. (1989b) each characterized their studies as ethnographies. But is this an accurate characterization?

What is an ethnography? Definitions of ethnography seem to share two key elements. First, the researcher needs to enter into the world of the other, and this requires significant contact with the other in his or her natural surroundings over a long period of time so that the researcher can become sensitized to the important elements in the environment. Without this sensitization over a long time, the researcher cannot provide much of an interpretive context. Second, it is important that the researcher foreground the culture of the focal subject in the analysis.

Now let's take a look at the three studies whose authors regard their work as ethnographies. Hobson (1989) interviewed six working women informally during lunch in a nightclub in Birmingham, England. The interviews were recorded, and a secretary took notes. Radway (1984) interviewed 17 women for a total of 60 hours about their reading of romance novels. Seiter et al. (1989a) interviewed a total of 64 people in 26 groups in their homes in western Oregon; each interview was conducted by two scholars. Did these researchers establish significant contact with their subjects (first element in the definition)? A researcher who conducts an hour-long interview with a group of people might be able to hear some interesting expressions of media use, but it is doubtful that this degree of contact has been significant given the standards of ethnography. Without observing the people in their natural environment (outside of the artificially constructed focus groupings), the researchers could not observe their actual media usage and use this as important context to compare their statements about media use. Also, with such limited contact, the researchers have no way of knowing what the people actually do during exposure, how they engage in the construction of meaning while the media are present, and how significant others in their environment shape the meaning-making process. Braber (1989, cited in Jankowski & Wester, 1991) also criticized these same three examples as not being ethnographies because of the lack of centrality of the concept of culture, employment of participant observation, and smallness of the research setting. Without significant contact, how can they provide a detailed contextualization of the culture within which the subjects use the media to construct their worlds (second element)?

These three examples just discussed were chosen for criticism here, because they are well-known studies. They are not the only examples that could have been used. Also, this criticism is not directed at their contributions. Each of these makes a major contribution to qualitative thinking about media audiences. The criticism is limited to the argument that their authors have mischaracterized the methodology used in the research. Rather than ethnographies, these are reception studies. A series of interviews or focus groups—if done well as these are—can result in a good reception study. Both the reception study and the ethnographic methodology require researchers to interview people about their media perceptions and habits, then relate patterns found there to the interpretive communities to which those people belong. The ethnography, with its requirement of the researcher observing the people in their communities over a long period of time, gives the researcher the added authority to develop the patterns into trends over time, to check what people say against what they do, and to become more aware of more subtle patterns of meaning. In short, the ethnography methodology requires much more from the researcher, but it also makes possible a much broader and more in-depth analysis.

There are very few true ethnographies in media studies. Four were used as examples in chapters 6 through 12, and in each of these, the researchers were shown to have had significant contact with the focal subjects over long periods of time. For example, Turkle (1984) lived in a computer culture for 6 years, observing and interviewing 400 people. Altheide (1976) spent 3 years in newsrooms examining how the workers there create a community. Fishman (1988) worked on a newspaper for 7 months, then observed the work at another newspaper for 5 months. And Elliott (1979) was a passive observer of a series of seven documentaries produced over several months in Britain.

Other contiguous fields have more, and these can serve as good examples for media scholars planning to conduct an ethnography. The best ethnographies in education are cited as being: Jackson's *Life in Classrooms* (1968), Wolcott's *The Man in the Principal's Office* (1973), and Mehan's *Learning Lessons* (1979). For example, Wolcott "shadowed" one man around for several years. He went to meetings, listened to all his conversations, and interviewed his staff. He then organized his notes into a 300+-page book of 11 chapters plus a preface and an epilogue. In the preface and the first chapter he talked about the ethnographic methodology as well as how he set up and conducted his study. In a later writing, Wolcott (1982) complained that there is a mischaracterization of ethnography in education. He said, "most of what goes on today under the banner of educational ethnography is neither designed nor intended to produce genuine ethnography, although ethnographic techniques may be employed in the data gathering phases" (p. 160). The essence of ethnography is "with cultural interpretations of human social life" (p. 160). Without this goal, the use of ethnographic forms of data gathering or analysis do not make a study ethnography in his view.

Nonillumination of Axioms

Qualitative researchers, like any other kind of researchers, build their work on certain assumptions. However, with qualitative research, the assumptions are less clear and less well understood than the assumptions of, say, quantitative research. If qualitative researchers want readers to understand their work (such as why they framed their questions as they did, how they made decisions about evidence, analysis, and writing), then they need to illuminate their readers about their key assumptions. This task, of course, is important when scholars delineate any form of research, but it is especially important under the rubric of qualitative methods, because there are so may different assumptions. Without a clear articulation of key assumptions, qualitative researchers have a difficult time properly positioning their research in the minds of their readers who are qualitative scholars. And without clear framing, qualitative researchers cannot communicate much insight to those who are not qualitative scholars.

In illuminating the axioms underlying one's work, the qualitative researcher need not construct an argument to try convincing the reader of the *importance* of the assumptions, only that they *exist*. In a research article it is too great a task to ask the author to convince the reader about the value of his or her research approach; that task should be left to the theoreticians. However, excusing the researcher from the task of persuasion is not the same as telling the researcher he or she does not have to describe the foundation of that research project. This description is still very important. It retains importance, because there are so many varieties of qualitative research, and the reader, who is most likely already convinced of the value of the approach, still needs to know which variety within the qualitative approach he or she is reading so as to be better able to judge the claims of the authors and fit their claims into his or her existing structure of knowledge.

In the description of axioms, authors need to be more careful to make the proper distinction between hypotheses and assumptions. Hypotheses are guesses about what might or might not exist; they can be tested. Assumptions are axioms or beliefs; they can never be tested for truth value. To illustrate this distinction, let's take a look at what Pauly (1991) listed as his three philosophical assumptions. First, people communicate like other animals, but unlike other animals they use symbols and language. Second, people do not discover reality, they fabricate it. And third, symbolic acts are public and social, not merely private and individual. The first and third of these are not assumptions. They can be tested and have been. We do not need to assume these. We have evidence that they exist, and no serious scholar would disagree with these points. However, the second is truly an assumption—a very important assumption in qualitative research. For centuries there has been a philosophical debate about whether humans discover or create reality. Because humans can never establish an objective standard of reality and compare their perceptions to it, we will never know whether we are discovering or creating. We must accept one of the two positions (or select from a variety of middle positions) then build our methods on that axiomatic foundation. Christians and Carey (1989) also advanced this axiom by saying that "qualitative studies start from the assumption that in studying humans we are examining a creative process whereby people produce and maintain forms of life and society and systems of meaning and value. This creative activity is grounded in the ability to build cultural forms from symbols that express this will to believe and assert meaning. To study this creative process is our first obligation" (pp. 358–359).

Theoreticians are generally good about illuminating their axioms of qualitative research, but researchers who publish their individual studies will often neglect to illuminate the axioms on which their work is based. This is understandable in short-form writings (such as articles and even book chapters) where space is at a premium, and authors need to use their space as parsimoniously as possible. However, the axioms are so important that their explication should be given the same prominence as the reporting of conclusions. Otherwise, the reader is not given an adequate basis for evaluating the study or even knowing where to stand (conceptually) to judge the study.

The terms of phenomenology, interpretive, hermeneutics, naturalism, or humanism are rarely mentioned. Again, we should not be surprised at this finding. Because axioms are deep foundational concerns, we must allow authors to treat them as assumptions; that is, authors must be able to make the assumption that readers will bring an understanding of certain foundational principles to the reading. Even in longer form writings, such as books and monographs, authors do not have space to address everything that a reader needs know in order to understand the author's perspective. There are always limits. And because the axioms are the most foundational of all the ideas in the qualitative approach, it is safest to leave them as assumptions.

Rarely do authors use the terms *ontology* or *epistemology* in their empirical work, even in their longer writings. These positions must be inferred from the way they write about the phenomenon, their approach to studying it, and their means of establishing conclusions. Although the issue of ontology was not addressed directly in any of these writings, however, it is safe to infer that most of these studies were written from an ontological position of idealism. An example of how to make such an inference in the chapter, "Myth, Chronicle, and Story: Exploring the Narrative Qualities of News," by Bird and Dardenne (1988), who questioned the concept of "truth" when they said "myth, like news, rests on its authority as 'truth.' Television news . . . has coopted the storyteller/myth-maker role so effectively that it is now regarded as the most authoritative and hence 'truthful' source of news" (p. 80). They argued that truth is created, not discovered, so it can be reasonably inferred that they have a constructivist position on epistemology. Also, an epistemological position can be inferred in the work of Silverstone (1988), who wrestled with the problem of how cultural studies scholars make meaning in their work. He said, "we live in an empiricist culture; visibility and value are synonymous; our knowledge must be testable" (p. 27), and this limits cultural scholars from sharing the full range of the meaning they want to communicate. He argued for a hermeneutic perspective that allows for empirical examination but also meets the cultural scholar's belief in subjective interpretation, saying that "however rigorous and however disciplined, the work is a work of interpretation; structure rather than content, the unconscious rather than the conscious, the speculative rather than the immediately testable, the radical rather than the superficial, the ambiguous rather than the certain" (p. 27).

Another example is in the work of Thornburn (1988), who warned researchers to be careful when they examine television texts, because the examination transforms the text and attaches a new meaning to it. "Appropriating television texts for historical or anthropological or aesthetic use, we transform the medium, conferring upon it something of the dignity accorded to the texts and artifacts already elevated into the 'high culture' that is preserved in museums and art galleries and scholarly books and university curricula" (p. 49). Thornburn's argument shows that there are multiple meanings and that the act of researching something inherently changes its meaning.

There are some examples where an author's epistemological beliefs, although still needing to be inferred, are more clear. For example, Ang (1989) revealed her constructivist position when she argued that the purpose of qualitative or cultural research is fundamentally different than science and that one of these fundamental differences is the epistemology; that is, the notion that knowledge is objective. She said that, with qualitative research, all data-gathering activities require the constructions of interpretations that are "always historically located, subjective, and relative" (p. 105). Tulloch (1989) argued, "there is no objectively neutral way for an observer or interviewer to gain understanding from an audience; he or she is part of the process of 'making meaning,' of making practical consciousness discursive" (p. 197).

In contrast, Morley (1989) seemed to take a realist position when he cautioned against the "dangers of the 'speculative' approach" (p. 25) where the qualitative scholar "simply attempts to imagine the possible implications of spectator positioning by the text" (p. 25). He said this speculative approach "can, at times, lead to inappropriate 'universalizations' of analysis which turn out to be premised on particular assumptions regarding the social positioning of the viewer" (p. 25). Therefore, it is important to conduct empirical work to discover the readings by various individuals. Several qualitative scholars exhibit a clear realistic belief in the way they present treat their observations without question and fit their data into preexisting perspectives (Liebes & Katz, 1988, 1989; Wolf, 1987).

There is a problem with the way some qualitative researchers appear to take a constructivist position, but act more from a realist position. For example, Hall (1980) made a distinction between negotiated, dominant, and oppositional readings. He presupposed a fixed dominant reading, and does not tell us how to determine what dominant readings are except to assume that we will look at the text itself and somehow know. A truly constructivist position would be to say that all readings are negotiated, because we each must determine for ourselves the meaning of each element and then the meaning of the set of elements in a text. But Hall said there is something that is dominant as determined by the intention of the author. This presupposes that the author had a preferred reading—if he were unaware of his ideology, then how could he have preferred it? This problem can only be solved by placing the burden of interpretation back on the reader. But then the dominant reading could be different for each reader and there can be no "real" reading in the sense that there is a criterion outside the person (either the author's intention or the prevalent reading). If there is no "real" reading, then there is no defense for a particular reading being dominant or negotiated or oppositional. But Hall believes there is a way of telling whether it is dominant, oppositional, or negotiated, and therefore he must believe in a realist position of readings.

In summarizing this philosophical section, I point out a pair of related ironies. First, there is the ontology irony. If nothing has an independent existence apart from perceiving it, then how can there be scholarship? No matter how eloquently a theoretician argues for a pure idealist position on ontology, his or her words that communicate those thoughts have existence to readers and that existence illustrates a materialist position and thereby refutes the counterposition of idealist, which is what the theoretician is arguing.

Second, there is the epistemological irony. If everyone interprets everything subjectively, then there can be no determination of quality and no standards. How can we ascribe more or better meaning to one interpretation over others? But qualitative scholars do this all the time, especially in their critique of social science. If social science is one of many equally good interpretations of how scholarship should be conducted, then what is their basis for criticizing it as inferior to the qualitative approach?

Finally there is the fundamental problem of multiple *types* of realities. First, there are physical objects (such as chairs, books, and people) in the world. There is no reason to believe that qualitative researchers do not believe in the material existence of such objects. Second, there are social things (such as culture and communication) that are creations of human interpretation. There is no reason to believe that even quantitative researchers would not believe these are human constructions; that is, they are not naturally occurring objects that are waiting to be discovered. Within this second group, there are varying views, but these variations are traceable to misunderstandings that grow from unannounced shifts in writers' arguments. For example, the creation of a conversation means that it does not exist at one instance, then shortly after it does exist—in material form and even preserved if it is taped. The tape then exists waiting for patterns to be discovered on it. Researchers who think they perceive a pattern on such a tape, construct an argument for a pattern and publish their argument in a book. Their argument is a second-order construction, because it is an interpretation of the meaning that was constructed by other people. The argument in the book can then be critiqued by another scholar. The critiquing scholar constructs his or her meaning of the researcher's meaning, which, of course, is an interpretation of the meaning in the original conversation. Thus the critique is a third-order interpretation. The critique then exists in material form and is open to reinterpretation in the fourth order and beyond. With each of these orders, there is a construction process that focuses on meaning and creates a new text at a higher order of interpretation. Therefore, the overall process requires both a belief in constructivism as well as a belief in materialism. The two are not antithetical; rather they are necessary alternating steps in a continuous process. If we take the process apart and focus on any one component, then it makes sense to argue for a single epistemological position. But if we take a wholistic approach, we see that a belief in both positions is required.

Misleading Assumptions

A clear ideology within the qualitative approach is the belief that there is no objective reality that can be known to humans, hence there is no single truth. However, within this qualitative tradition there are instances where scholars will refer to a single truth, and this can be very confusing to readers. For example, some scholars talk about truth and how this truth gets distorted. Gitlin (1987) believes in a reality as evidenced by the statement "Outside the news, the networks have no particular interest in truth" (p. 526). If there is such a thing as truth, then there must be a reality outside of people. This belief is prevalent in the qualitative literature, especially in the ideological writings where the authors talk about a false consciousness among the population. In order for a false consciousness to be possible, there must be a true one that exists external to the population that cannot quite see it yet. Fishman (1988) in his ethnography of the news operation demonstrated a belief in an external reality; that is, the happenings of the day. However, he argued that news workers do not simply show those happenings; instead they construct news stories. This construction is determined by their intersubjectively supported sense of what is news as well as formulas for presenting the news. Therefore, news is manufactured. In essence there is a material reality, but news viewers do not see that reality; news viewers see a manufactured story about the reality. Also, Altheide's (1976) epistemology approaches an argument for objectivity in the sense that news routines are learned so well and are so constraining that there is little room for personal creativity; that is, subjective interpretation. This is not to say that the news itself is an objective presentation of facts—on this point he clearly said that news is not. But once we understand his news perspective as the standard for newswork (not objective reality), then the news does conform objectively to this news perspective standard, hence objectivity. He said that:

> objectivity means reducing or eliminating biases to let the essential phenomenon appear. This is a special problem in field research, because the investigator assumes the important data of the social world to consist of the nature and organization of subjective meanings. Even though one's understandings and definitions may be shared by members in the settings, the investigator is usually an outsider who seeks to learn how the members see their activities. This orientation precludes

a researcher from assuming at the outset that he knows what is relevant or significant; he must withhold judgment until his research uncovers these important meanings. (pp. 198–199)

So Altheide believes that objectivity is possible for researchers even though human beings are subjective; that is, those subjective interpretations of journalists exist to be observed objectively.

PROBLEMS WITH INFORMING THE READER ABOUT EVIDENCE SELECTION

There appear to be five issues that warrant concern. First, a shortcoming here is the lack of clarity in sampling—specifying how the evidence was selected. Second, a distinction is made between balanced and focused evidence. Third, there is the issue of whether the researcher uses primary or secondary sources. Fourth, we should be concerned about the clarity in presenting the methods. And fifth, there is the issue of the nature of collaboration.

Sampling

Most qualitative researchers are generally good about laying out their expectations for the reader, but they are less forthcoming in illuminating their decisions about selection of evidence. When qualitative researchers begin with an expectation, a premise, a thesis, or an argument, it is not surprising that their data selection is oriented toward finding examples to support their case. In this situation, data are regarded as examples used to illustrate that a particular interpretation is possible and plausible.

In contrast, some qualitative researchers want to *document* an occurrence or trend, instead of using evidence to support key points in their argument. When they seek to document some trend, the evidence needs to be a more complete reflection of the trend, so they seek to gather all the evidence available to build as complete a description or interpretation as possible. Thus sampling is avoided in favor of what social scientists refer to as a population study; that is, the researcher seeks to obtain and use all the information from the totality of the phenomenon. For example, Rowland (1983) presumably avoided sampling by trying to get all the information he could about the way research was used by policymakers concerned with violence on television. The data are primarily the "hearings, records, and reports of the various congressional committees and national commissions involved in federal attempts to grapple with television and the question of its content. These records are examined for the patterns of argument advanced by the leading research spokesmen, industry representatives, public interest group leaders, and political figures" (p. 17).

But most often, researchers will not be able to access all the evidence of a particular phenomenon, especially in audience studies where everyone in an audience cannot be observed or interviewed. In these situations, some selection must be made. Within the quantitative approach, the case for representativeness rests with the probability of people being selected. If everyone in the population has an equal probability of being selected, quantitative researchers make the assumption that the resulting sample will be representative of that population. In order to ensure that everyone in the population does indeed have an equal chance, random methods of selection are used. In the context of sampling, *random* means giving every unit an equal chance of being selected.

But there is some confusion over this term among qualitative researchers. For example, Kinder (1987) looked at MTV rock videos saying that she chose her video clips "almost at random to illustrate what is typical rather than what is most powerful aesthetically" (p. 230). What does she mean by *almost* at random? The idea of randomness is categorical—it cannot be almost. Either every unit was given an equal chance or it was not.

Within in qualitative research, it is very rare to see someone follow the quantitative method of sampling. Instead, qualitative researchers will select a sample based on convenience (what is available) and purpose, then make an argument that their sample reflects the total phenomenon. For example, Liebes and Katz (1988, 1989) used a purposive sample that they said was not randomly generated but that "one can make a good case that these are bona fide members of their respective subcultures" (p. 220).

Balanced or Focused Evidence?

An important sampling concern related to representativeness is the issue about whether evidence should be balanced or focused. Balanced evidence shows both sides of an issue then seeks to arrive at a higher level insight, a dialectic moving toward a synthesis. Focused evidence is the selection of cases that support a position or thesis, and there is no counterevidence presented. Focused evidence appears to be selected to support the author's view of the world, and usually the set of evidence is much more limited than it should be to provide a strong interpretation; that is, there are sources left untapped.

With almost all of the qualitative research (with the exception of grounded theory work), there is the failure to present counterargument data. With many articles, it appears that all the evidence points to only one conclusion and that there is no evidence to suggest any other conclusion. This is a relatively weak argumentation method. The argument would be much stronger if scholars would acknowledge evidence counter to their arguments, then through careful analysis, either seek to discredit it or to put it into a context where their argument is supported at a higher level of synthesis.

Primary or Secondary Sources

Another important issue concerning evidence is whether the information is primary or secondary. Primary evidence is from the source closest to the focal subject. Secondary evidence is from sources one or more steps removed from the focal subject. We must be careful not to equate these terms with a type of source—that is, equating primary with people and secondary with written records. This equation does hold when it comes to doing something like a cultural history of a media organization, for example, where interviewing the people who founded the organization and who work in it would constitute the primary sources of information. The memos and reports written by those people would be the secondary source of information. However, if we were conducting a textual analysis of a television program, the video images would be the primary text, and the people talking *about* the program (even if they are the writers and producers) would be the secondary sources.

Primary evidence is almost always superior to secondary evidence. There are cases where secondary evidence might be better than primary. For example, if we were researching an event that happened several decades ago, the use of memos and records recorded at the time would likely be better evidence than the recollections now of someone who wrote those memos and records.

The best set of evidence contains both primary and secondary so that researchers can triangulate the evidence to build a stronger case. For example, if we are investigating a media organization, we could rely on the secondary information about that organization; that is, the memos and reports written by members in that organization. It would be better to interview the people and observe their behavior. And it would be best to examine both. In text-based research, the primary evidence is the text itself. In audience-based and industry-based research, the primary evidence usually comes from people. With audience-based studies, almost all researchers rely exclusively on primary data.

However, with industry-based research, there is a reliance on secondary evidence. For example, Pauly (1988) conducted a study to determine how the actions of Rupert Murdoch's media acquisitions affect the public. But Pauly did not interview Murdoch or any one who works with or for Murdoch; nor did he present primary data on the effects of Murdoch's acquisition patterns on the industry or on society. Instead, he assembled information from secondary sources and filtered this information through his own interpretations. Much of Pauly's evidence is interesting, but it is curious that he did not explain his reasoning for ignoring primary sources of evidence.

Another example is Zynda (1988) who spent the first 11 pages of his 19-page chapter tracing the history of sitcoms and the rise of alternatives such as "All in the Family," "M*A*S*H," and the "Mary Tyler Moore Show." However, in this historical analysis, he relied exclusively on secondary data saying that he did not have access to "diaries, notebooks, memos, and early drafts of writers, editors, producers, directors, and programming executives. We have only their recollections, as voiced to interviewers, about their creative roles and those of their collaborators" (p. 131). This is a curious statement because most of the people involved in the production of those shows were still alive and active. Instead of conducting his own interviews where he could ask important follow-up questions, he relied instead from quotes and insights published in articles written by scholars who did interview the principles.

Clarity in Presenting Methods

Often researchers will not be clear about the methods they used to gather data. This is especially important with the method of participant observation where the researchers need to define what they meant by participation. For example, Altheide (1976) said he used participant observation and spent a lot of time observing in the newsrooms and even went on shoots. From this it is clear that he had opportunities to observe a wide range of newsmaking activity. But what is meant by "participation"? Is it going along with the reporters? Or is it making the news decisions of camera framing, editing, and so on? It would seem that there is an important difference between real participation and active observation. With participation (in undertaking the same activities as those being observed) the researcher would develop a greater sensitivity to the phenomenon; but there would also be a greater risk of "going native."

ILLUMINATING ANALYTICAL PROCEDURES

The heart of any qualitative report is its analysis, because this is where the author constructs the meaning. Because this is such a crucial task, it is important that the author illuminate the meaning-making process so that the reader can appreciate the decisions made and thereby have the context to evaluate the meaning made by the author. In this section, I examine this concern through the illumination of six issues: conceptual leverage, generalizing, contextualization, self-reflexivity, writing, and making a case for quality.

Conceptual Leverage

A high level of conceptual leverage is exhibited by scholars who take the general principles of other scholars and seek to test them on their own areas or attempt to extend those principles. In either case, the focus of the article is much more on the conceptual issues than on the data. There are many examples of a high degree of conceptual leverage in the research examining texts, people, and institutions. And there are also a fair number of examples of research that exhibit a low level of conceptual leverage; that is, where the authors do not attempt to leverage their interpretations of small amounts of evidence into broad general explanations about larger phenomena (see chapter 8).

Although it would seem that studies with a high degree of conceptual leverage have more to contribute than studies with a low level, a low level should not be regarded as a problem. Some studies are primarily descriptive and make good contributions by providing a documentation of some literal occurrences. A mistake is made, however, when a study attempts to display a high degree of leverage, but does not have either the evidence or a powerful enough argument to achieve it. For example, Horowitz (1987) made wild speculations about the health of sitcoms in her idiosyncratic analysis of a few programs. The set of evidence is interesting, but it is far too limited to support the claims made by the author. Also, Chesebro (1978) presented a high degree of inference that is faulty in two ways. First, although his theory of logical types does indeed reveal a "host of subtle communication patterns, images, and models" (p. 48) as he claimed, and this is demonstrated well on five types of television shows, we are never shown how it is demonstrated in real life. Without such a demonstration and an estimation of the proportion of the population who are in each of these five categories, it is not possible to tell the degree to which the TV world reflects real life. Yet he made the claim that "popular television series do not reflect the American culture; they disproportionately dramatize particular lifestyles at the expense of others" (p. 48). This is indeed a large inference. Perhaps his inference is based on his comparison of demographic characteristics of the American population with characters on TV, but this would also be a problem, because demographic characteristics are not the same as "lifestyle." He is on more solid ground methodologically with specific figures that can be compared, but conceptually his conclusions are very shaky.

Generalizing

What does it mean to generalize the findings from a research study? The central idea is that of connection; that is, connecting the findings of a particular study to the patterns in a larger frame. Generalizing is the leveraging of conclusions to groups of people, texts, or institutions beyond what was examined in a particular study.

Scholars have a weak basis for generalizing when the cases they examine are not representative of anything beyond themselves. So many qualitative researchers avoid this problem, and make a point of cautioning the reader that they will not generalize. However, other qualitative researchers do generalize from their evidence. For example, Horowitz (1987) examined a few situation comedies (one episode of "I Love Lucy" in particular), then generalized to all of 1950s sitcoms. Although the Lucy show may have been the best or the most innovative in the 1950s, it hardly represents all situation comedies during the decade. She examined some episodes of "Kate and Allie" and used this to represent the sitcoms of the 1980s. Based on this analysis, she generalized that television has changed. Also, using several small focus groups, Liebes and Katz (1988, 1989) generalized about how people from different cultures and countries interpret "Dallas."

Pauly (1988) illuminated the problem of generalization in his analysis of Rupert Murdoch when he said, "Murdoch's critics condemn him by synecdoche.

At one level, using this rhetorical strategy—letting the part represent the whole—allows journalists to defend their own preferred conception of their occupation. In this mode, critics can portray those tabloids as 'typical' Murdoch publications, and depict his journalists as mere servants of the trivial and demented . . . using synecdoche allows critics to represent Murdoch's papers using those parts they dislike" (p. 254) and then ignore all other characteristics of his papers. This indeed is an unfair practice. In a larger sense, it is also misleading for any researcher to generalize from samples that do not represent the larger set to which they are speaking.

There is a paradox with the issue of generalization in qualitative research. Some theoreticians say that in order to increase the external validity of results (their generalizability), researchers need to provide detailed descriptions of the phenomenon. For example, Fortner and Christians (1981) said that "The more densely textured our specifics, the more we can maintain external validity" (p. 365) and "The objective is representative rather than anecdotal (i.e., spectacular but idiosyncratic) cases" (p. 366). This is a paradox to say that the more specific the descriptions, the more general the results. In common sense, the adding of detail makes things more specific, thus reducing the generalizability. If qualitative research needs more detail and contextualization to achieve quality, the quest for these characteristics would seem to limit its generalizability.

Contextualization

Contextualization usually means providing a great deal of description. But there is something more. The description should be rich, not just long. It should also serve to illuminate the facets of the focal subject by comparing that subject to elements outside itself. If the author focuses solely on a particular subject, like an episode of a TV series, and does not extend the description beyond the focal element, then there is no contextualization. For example, Lull (1987) provided a high degree of description about the punk subculture in San Francisco. He gave a great deal of rich description of his focal subject, but he did not develop a broad contextualization, such as comparing the San Francisco punk culture to punk cultures in other cities or comparing the punk culture to the other cultures in San Francisco. Nor did he develop a deep contextualization, such as putting the elements in his examined culture in the economic, political, or historical frames of the city.

The prescription for qualitative research is for strong contextualization, but this prescription is not always followed. For example, Ang (1989) argued forcefully for the importance of strong contextualization as what distinguishes qualitative from quantitative research and makes qualitative more useful. She argued against "dissecting 'audience activity' into variables and categories in order to be able to study them one by one" and argued instead for "a more historicized insight into the ways in which 'audience activity' is related to social and political structures and processes" (p. 101). However, in her study of viewers of "Dallas" (Ang, 1985), she relied on letters and was therefore partitioned from her sources and unable to assemble the evidence needed to provide strong contextualization.

There are also some examples that illustrate the problems with contextualization. Lindlof (1987) attempted to contextualize the quotes he offered as evidence, but he had very little contextual information to use, because his contact with the prisoners he was studying was so limited. Another type of problem is exhibited by Wolf (1987), who showed that children use a lot of context from the shows they view in order to make sense of television, but she did not really use much context of the children's lives to explain those understandings. And finally, Hobson (1982) provided a lot of description about what people say, and there is some context expressed by some of the interviewees. But the researcher did not build contextualization of her own by laying in background of the interviewees or some other form of interpretive context. Instead she simply let the interviewees speak for themselves.

There are also some instances of interpretation with very little context. For example, Horowitz (1987) ignored the context of programming (what is up against sitcoms) and the cyclical nature of their popularity (by tracing trends over years). Instead she made the linear argument that sitcoms are dying as a genre. She speculated near the end of the article that there may be an upswing, but she did not really develop that point, which would have been an important contextual element. Also, she did not discuss where the audiences are going when they leave sitcoms; this would be important context to understand the popularity of the genre.

Most of the examples of qualitative research illustrated in chapter 11 do provide a strong contextualization. When looking at all these examples of contextualization there seem to be two types. First, there is *broad* contextualization where the author takes a horizontal approach to comparing an element to other elements of the same kind on the same level of generality. For example, an author who is conducting a textual analysis of a particular episode of a TV show can put that episode in the horizontal context of the other episodes in the TV series, thereby showing how it fits into the flow of long-term character and plot development. Or if an author is analyzing a TV series, he or she can put that series in the horizontal context of other series in the genre.

A good example of this *broad* contextualization is Morley (1980), who focused on TV viewers and compared certain kinds of viewers with other kinds of viewers in terms of their demographics (age, gender, race, and class) and cultural identifications (trade unions, political parties, sections of the educational system, etc.).

The other form is *deep* contextualization where the author takes a vertical approach by comparing the focal subject to different kinds of elements at different levels of generality. With this approach, the author who is focusing on a particular TV series would not compare it to other like series but instead would move down into the infrastructure (economic, political, or creative culture) that influenced its production decisions. Or the author could take a historical perspective and show how the series held a place in the overall trend evolving in TV production. A good example of deep contextualizing is Barrios (1988), who presented a good deal of contextualization of TV viewing in Venezuela by providing lots of description about the country's family structures, economy, television systems, TV programs, and history of television audience research. Deep contextualization is a strong element in the work of Lipsitz (1992), who interpreted 1950s working-class sitcoms. Basing his analysis on literary criticism, cultural studies, and a sociological perspective (especially ideas about how capitalist cultures legitimate themselves), he drew interpretations from economic, political, and cultural contexts. Like Lipsitz, Deming (1992) presented a strong contextualization, but Deming was focusing on what happens in the developing of one particular program, "Kate and Allie." But unlike Lipsitz, he looked at the economic and political forces; however, these are played out on a microlevel (within a network) rather than on the macrolevel (the culture throughout the country).

Self-Reflexivity

There are three ways researchers display self-reflexivity: (a) describing decisions that went into selecting methods, (b) laying out limits of knowledge (or threats to validity) in a particular study, and (c) laying out the researcher's personal biases that might influence the conclusions.

There are examples of all three kinds of self-reflexivity. Some scholars will describe the decisions they made in selecting their methods. Some scholars will describe many of the decisions they made in conducting the research, such as gaining access, establishing credibility, and so forth. Others will exhibit a higher degree of self-reflexivity by consciously reflecting on the nature of the methods they used and worrying about the value of the data and their interpretations. And some scholars will be highly self-reflexive by laying out their biases so that the reader can be forewarned about the author's perspective.

An essential key to understanding self-reflexivity is to understand the distinction between the self and the other. This is especially important in audience research where the focal subject is the "other person" who is being studied. There is a lot written about how the other creates meaning. Qualitative researchers are always skeptical about the other's interpretation so they revise the other's interpretation (criticize institutions or social science, etc.). Also, they reinterpret what others say by showing that what they say is really different from what they do.

But the self is largely ignored; that is, researchers do not raise the question about their own interpretations. Instead they present their work as interpretive realism. The appearance is that they are somehow better perceivers of others' follies. Does this come from training or natural insight? Where is the locus of this expertise? Newcomb (1988) and Zynda (1988) showed that real phenomena (TV shows) are open to different subjective interpretations from viewers. But they seem to place themselves above this situation. Newcomb did illustrate some self-reflexivity when he says "my own reading, of course, is also personalized, but the persona is that of the critic attempting to 'see more' than other individualized viewers" (p. 91).

If qualitative research is primarily an interpretive act where researchers acknowledge their own subjectivity through sharing their biases and limitations with readers so readers can make their own interpretations of the work, then researchers should exhibit a high degree of self-reflexivity. But seldom does this happen. Altschull (1984) exhibited this when he said, "the interpretations of historical developments are sometimes at variance with traditional points of view. These shifts in interpretation support my view that traditional journalism history is faulty in its adherence to the folklore of progressive, Great Man views that cannot provide adequate explanations of the direction of the history of journalism" (p. xii). This is an example of no reflexivity, because he did not examine the possibility that his position might also be faulty or limited.

Writing

It is not an evasion to characterize a good deal of the qualitative task as an art. The qualitative research must have the latitude to create a personal interpretation. There must be the freedom to try different forms of expression, even within the same piece of writing. But writers must always keep two things in mind: the goal of the research and the needs of the readers. The goal will determine for the writer what is relevant to communicate about the study's findings. However, there are certain issues that all writers of qualitative research reports should address, and these are: the decisions they make in terms of selecting their evidence; analysis; defending their leveraging of concepts and making generalizations; and being self-reflexive. The needs of the readers are more difficult to discern. How much detail is needed on each point? How should the points be sequenced in the most meaningful way for the reader? These are questions that writers must continually ask, but which answers they can only guess. However, an attempt to address the essential decision-making issues in some depth is necessary.

Although a good part of the writing task is an art, good artists have a strong foundation of working with materials before they can use them as a springboard for their creative expression. Without technique, there can be no rigor. And without rigor, an area is flat of contribution—that is, there appear to be no hills of useful insight nor peaks of accomplishment.

Making a Case for Quality

Qualitative researchers very rarely make a conscious argument for the quality of their work, either the internal quality (evidence) or the external quality (conclusions). This is not surprising given the position of many theoreticians that no quality criteria can be established for qualitative research (e.g., see J. K. Smith, 1984).

Internal Quality. Chapter 12 displayed four types of cases that qualitative researchers have made in arguing for the internal quality of their studies. First, there is the internal cross-checking of observations. Second, researchers can check decisions made by others such as coders. Third, there is a test for plausibility. Fourth, there is prudent judgment. The first three of these are seldom exhibited in the qualitative research literature. The fourth method suggests a very wide latitude. What is prudent judgment? This is a question that readers must answer, but if they do not have information about what options confronted the researcher at each stage and how the researcher ruled out options, they have very little context from which to make a good judgment.

External Quality. There are two types of cases made for external validity. First, the primary technique of making a case for external validity in audience research is to argue for the generalizability of results. But qualitative scholars who argue for the generalization of their conclusions must be careful how the frame their argument or else they will fall prey to a fallacy. To illustrate, Fishman (1988) admitted "the generality of my findings can be questioned" (p. 19). He did generalize and defended this by saying:

> the news organization chosen for study is fairly typical of American newspapers in terms of its internal structure, monopoly over the local news market, and position in the community. Most importantly, the routine news practices I found on this newspaper closely correspond with journalists' practices mentioned by a variety of independent sources: biographies, autobiographies, and other reports by journalists, as well as empirical studies of news practices on other newspapers. (p. 19)

The trap here is: If one's results conform closely to what is already known on the topic, the value of one's study is almost nonexistent, because it contains nothing new and provides no fresh insights. But if one's results are very different from previous studies, then one's study might be faulty. Therefore, researchers who use the argument of conforming patterns for external validity might find themselves arguing for the noncontribution of their studies.

A second argument for external validity is based on the social significance of the study's results. In text-focused research, Silverstone (1988) said "that although meaning is theoretically unlimited, it is empirically limited. It is perfectly possible to imagine as many readings as there are readers ... but in practice only some will be socially significant" (p. 30). So how do we know which will be more significant? He said that we must examine each reading in context of "the intersecting and competing discourses which both the text and reader are placed" (pp. 30–31). He attempted to create a model of textual analysis and said that as he developed it, it grew "more complex, it is hoped also more sophisticated, more adequate, and more useful" (p. 31). It appears, therefore, that the goals of his effort are sophistication, adequacy, and utility, and those then are the standards upon which he feels the model should be judged.

The qualitative approach is still exhibiting a major debate about whether standards should be applied to judge studies, and if so, what those standards should be. In the meantime, studies continue to be written while many researchers attempt to finesse this issue.

CORRESPONDENCE BETWEEN THEORY AND PRACTICE

When we compare the prescriptions of qualitative theoreticians to the practices of the researchers, we find many points where there is little correspondence. This conclusion was presaged by J. A. Anderson (1987), who said, "Little of what is currently available in the communication journals approaches this ideal form" (p. 253). He blamed this lack of correspondence on the influence of quantitative thinking, saying, "there is little doubt that the form of qualitative research is currently distorted by the overwhelming presence of the rationalistic perspective. Most of what we see is not the interpretation of social action, but the content analysis of mundane data" (p. 253).

J. A. Anderson's (1987) argument at first seems to be a useful explanation about why the qualitative prescriptions are not closely followed in the qualitative research published in mainstream journals, which usually have a high percentage of quantitative work. Perhaps he is substantially correct in his perception that the quantitative perspective puts a certain kind of pressure on qualitative researchers who want to see their work published in the mainstream mass media journals. But when we look more closely at Anderson's argument, there are some problems that arise. If there is quantitative pressure, then we should expect to see certain characteristics in the published qualitative research—characteristics like careful descriptions of the analytical procedures used, statements of length of data gathering, and arguments for the internal and external validity. But the patterns illuminated in this study do not provide much support for this guess. For example, fewer than 14% of the published qualitative studies provided any information on the steps taken in their analyses; fewer than 17% provided any information on the length of data gathering; about 15% addressed the issue of internal validity and 21% addressed external validity. From these figures, it does not appear that the editors of the mainstream journals were publishing only those pieces that followed the major rules of quantitative research. If editors of these mainstream journals were pressuring qualitative researchers to adopt the characteristics of quantitative research reports, these figures should be much higher.

Correspondence of Prescriptions and Practices

On some points, there was a relatively high degree of correspondence between prescriptions and practices. For example, qualitative researchers were generally good in describing the expectations for the data, how they approached the subjects (researcher identification), their data-gathering activities, and the contextualization of the findings. These are all key points in theoreticians' prescriptions for qualitative research.

However, there are other prescriptions that researchers seemed to have ignored, such as their failure to describe the length of data gathering (both in terms of the span of time as well as the degree of contact with the phenomenon) and the steps in the process of analysis. As for lack of description of the span of time for the data gathering, fewer than 17% of studies gave the reader a clear sense of how long the span was. For example, researchers who interviewed or observed people should describe whether this was done in one afternoon or over 25 years. But in only 30% of the people-based studies was such information provided. Researchers studying archival material could describe whether they are looking at a current event over 5 days of news coverage or if they are examining a long-term historical trend over 50 years, but only 12% of the archival-based studies provided such information. There was even less information provided about the degree of contact between the researcher and the phenomenon. Also, about 86% of the articles failed to describe how their information was analyzed in order to construct their conclusions. Because qualitative researchers are providing their subjective interpretations of their observations, there needs to be a careful illumination of the process about how they navigated those waters. If readers are to follow the reasoning and therefore derive value from the conclusions, they must see how those interpretations were made. With people-based research, readers are perhaps able to fill in the gaps by imagining themselves in those situations. But with archival- and text-based research, readers need even more guidance to be able to identify with the steps in the reasoning process and arrive at the same conclusions (or at least understand how the authors arrived at their conclusions).

Also, few researchers explicitly addressed foundational issues (axioms, ontology, and epistemology). However, positions could be inferred, and these inferences indicated a middle position on issues of ontology and epistemology. It was very rare to see an author exhibit a strong idealist position on ontology or a purely constructivist position on epistemology.

On several issues, the practices of qualitative researchers closely resemble the practices of quantitative researchers. This is especially clear on expectations, quest for conceptual leverage, and generalizing. The nature of the evidence is not always subjective impressions; there are also examples of ordered elements needing description.

Correspondence Between Qualitative
and Quantitative Practices

There are four key issues where the qualitative research in general does not correspond to the quantitative research. First, qualitative researchers do use numbers, but very rarely is there anything resembling enumeration. Instead, numbers are used to express mathematical properties, not qualities. Second, sampling is almost always purposive. Frequently, researchers will argue for the representativeness of their sample in order to lay a foundation for generalizing the results. Third, qualitative researchers are careful to contextualize their focal subject rather than translate it into numbers thus abstracting it from its context as quantitative researchers do. And fourth, a frequently used locus of argumentation is ethos, or the personal interpretation of the researcher. With the quantitative approach, researchers almost always will use logos or the data themselves as the locus. Qualitative researchers also frequently use logos and data as the locus, but the most prevalent locus is ethos.

There are also some issues where the practices of the two approaches are surprisingly very similar. For example, it was surprising that there was so much empiricism; that is, reliance on evidence external to the researcher. Researchers, of course, transformed the evidence into arguments within their own reasoning processes, but the reasoning was not the only factor in the process—the evidence was also essential, and frequently the evidence appeared more important than the argument. The arguments were presented in an interpretive realist manner, which is fundamentally the same as the mainstream realist manner of quantitative researchers. Few qualitative researchers tried a style of writing more in line with the humanistic approach, such as a literary tale or a confessional tale.

Also very surprising was the very low degree of self-reflexivity. Given the perspective among qualitative researchers that they themselves are their primary research instrument, it is surprising that they would not illuminate themselves more in their writings. There was no example of a scholar placing himself or herself on center stage and fully interacting with the subject. There were only a few examples where the essay was personal to the point of the reader getting a good sense of the values that went into the decisions made by the researcher in approaching his or her subject, gathering evidence, structuring the argument, and writing the report. Very few scholars reflected on any of the decisions they made, instead presenting the decision points as "done deals" and moving on from there. This fits with the interpretive realism tone of the reports.

THE TWO TENSIONS

Early in my analysis, I began observing a very puzzling element that started as a curious trickle then grew to a dominant finding, that is, that the qualitative research does not appear to be more distinct from the quantitative research.

There are some important differences, but there are also some major similarities. Furthermore, it is not likely that these similarities can be traced to pressure applied by journal editors. Even if we could attribute the similarities to the editors of the mainstream journals, this would not account for the similarities that are also found in books and monographs.

What can account for the similarities between the practices of both qualitative and quantitative approaches on these issues? I advance one possible explanation. Perhaps it is attributable to the combination of two simultaneously operating tensions *within* qualitative thinking that strongly influences qualitative research. These tensions, which run through all of the theorizing, form the environment in which researchers must make their decisions about the purpose, evidence, analysis, and arguments.

Each of these two tensions is created by a conflict between a pair of diametrically opposed themes. One tension is the pull between the themes of fluidity and order. The second tension is the pull between the themes of reflection and transformation.

Fluid-Order. Promoting the fluid theme are the theoreticians who believe that the qualitative approach cannot and should not be defined. These scholars believe the qualitative approach is an organic, mutating area of thinking that cannot be dissected. Its vaporous components are in constant ferment, and they defy the structure imposed by any form of categorization or definition. Analyzing the approach by breaking it into component parts destroys its essence. To use an analogy, you cannot understand the nature of a house by taking it apart into its component boards, nails, bricks, and so on. There is much more to the house; in fact, "house" is more the design and the use people have for it than it is any of its materials. Although this analogy might be useful in illustrating a point, theoreticians who espouse this fluid view would most likely even take issue with the likening of the qualitative approach to a house, because this analogy serves to make the idea too concrete by associating it with a particular image.

In direct contrast to the fluid view is the ordered view. Promoting the theme of order are the theoreticians who believe that the qualitative approach does have specific purposes, methods, and procedures. These can be conveyed as guidance to practicing researchers. Theoreticians using this view do not feel the fluid view would guide researchers into meaningful scholarship, so they try to lay out particular rules and standards. These scholars feel that their enterprise is progressive in the sense that new research is better if it builds on the procedures that were found successful in the past and also adds to the base of knowledge built by previous studies. This view leads one to see that some questions are better than others, certain methodologies are more appropriate for certain tasks, and that there are standards upon which a work can be judged.

Reflection-Transformation. Promoting the reflection theme are the theoreticians who believe that the qualitative approach is meant to reflect something that exists outside the researcher; that is, it is not purely a construction. Researchers must spend a great deal of time observing others to determine how they construct the world, and once the researcher understands those constructions, he or she reflects those constructions to the reader. Although the phenomenon is a construction, the research itself (such as language or culture) is a reflection.

In direct contrast to the reflection view is the transformation view. Scholars espousing this transformation view believe that the research itself is a construction and that "the construction is the thing." The building of an argument or a point of view is the purpose of the scholar's thinking and writing. Evidence is secondary to the point of view; evidence illustrates rather than defines the point of view.

When we look at these two tensions together, we can get a clearer sense of the environment of ideas within which a qualitative researcher makes his or her decisions. This environment is graphically depicted in Fig. 16.1. Theoreticians will establish their positions around the perimeter of this environment. A theoretician at the fluid position will talk about the importance of *not* providing a definition for the qualitative approach, the importance of taking a wholistic, nonreductionistic approach, and the subjective, changeable nature of knowledge. A theoretician at the ordered position will argue for the need to clarify the boundaries of the approach, to specify the methodologies and methods, and the importance of having quality standards to guide researchers toward making contributions that will matter. A theoretician at the reflection position will posit the need for close and prolonged contact with that which is being studied and the importance of ferreting out useful insights that are rechecked through further observation. And the theoretician at the transformation position will advocate the dominance of

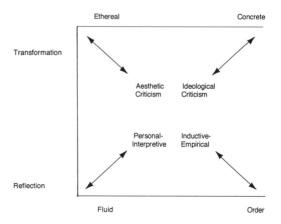

FIG. 16.1. The two tensions in qualitative thinking.

creative constructions in all of human activity and the importance of persuading others of your point of view to energize them into social action.

Qualitative theoreticians carve out their positions in the corners of the figure or articulate visions along the margins. A researcher who reads a variety of theoreticians will then have to reconcile all these points of view when deciding how to approach his or her own research project. Often these points of view are in conflict with one another, so the prospective researcher is pulled in different directions; that is, he or she is simultaneously influenced by the gravity of the polar positions—hence creating a tension. This tension—a pull between the extremes—serves to position the research in a middle ground. Hence, there are very few research studies that serve as good examples of the extreme positions of thinking.

Should qualitative theoreticians maintain their polar positions? I would say yes for several reasons. First, the extreme positions are usually more sharply drawn, and this serves to clarify the deeply held axioms underlying the qualitative approach. It also sets up some very interesting debates and increases the heuristic nature of the approach. Second, given the existing web of tensions, it would be dangerous for the scholars at one extreme to abandon or even moderate their position, unless the scholars at the other extreme did likewise. If only one side moved, the tensions would get out of their current balance and the resulting research patterns might radically change. The maintaining of the current configuration of theoreticians' positions serves to ensure that the research will continue along its traditions.

17

IS CONVERGENCE A POSSIBILITY?

There has been a great deal of thinking and writing about the qualitative approach over the past several decades. Has this scholarly activity been moving in the direction of a creating a greater differentiation between the quantitative and qualitative approaches? Or has it instead moved in the direction of convergence? Recently, Denzin and Lincoln (1994b) organized this activity into what they called "five historical moments" (p. 1), which show a pattern indicating that "a quiet methodological revolution has been taking place in the social sciences.... The social sciences and humanities have drawn closer together in a mutual focus on an interpretive, qualitative approach to research and theory" (Denzin & Lincoln, 1994c, p. ix). They perceived the first moment, the traditional period, as beginning in the early part of this century and ending about World War II. This period is characterized by objective type research in a positivist tradition where researchers are the experts studying cultures that are "alien, foreign, and strange" (Denzin & Lincoln, 1994b, p. 7). The second moment, called the modernist phase, began in the postwar years and extended until the 1970s. "The modernist ethnographer and sociological participant observer attempted rigorous, qualitative studies of important social processes" (p. 8). Although the "social realism, naturalism, and slice-of-life ethnographies" (p. 8) were still valued, this was a period of "creative ferment" where scholars drew from interpretive theories from contiguous fields. Their third moment, which lasted until 1986, is called "blurred genres." During this time, qualitative researchers had a "full complement of paradigms, methods, and strategies to employ in their research" (p. 9). During this time the old approaches of positivism and behavioralism were waning and were replaced by newer approaches such as poststructuralism, neopositivism, micro–macro descriptivism, neo-Marxism, ritual theories of drama and culture, deconstructivism, and ethnomethodology. By the mid-1980s a fourth moment emerged called the "crises of representation," which eroded classical norms and called into question the influence of gender, class, and race on interpretations. Qualitative researchers became more self-reflexive and framed their writings more as personal interpretations than as grounded theories or explanations. The fifth moment is focused on the problem about how qualitative studies are to be evaluated when scholars cannot agree on the meaning of terms such as validity, generalizability, and reliability. This problem is being addressed by the more action- (or activist-) oriented researchers who have replaced the aloof researcher. And social criticism and small-scale theories are replacing grand narratives.

Within the area of media studies, there are no clearly defined moments such as what Denzin and Lincoln (1994b) observed for the qualitative approach in its broadest perspective. Instead, there appears to be a generating dissatisfaction with quantitative methods expressed in the 1970s followed by a lot of rhetoric that the qualitative approach has replaced the quantitative one. For example, Gitlin (1978) was one of the early scholars to express dissatisfaction with what he called the dominant paradigm of media sociology or quantitative work with its focus on effects of:

> broadcast programming in a specifically behaviorist fashion, defining "effects" so narrowly, microscopically, and directly as to make it very likely that survey studies could show only slight effects at most. It has enshrined short-run "effects" as "measures" of "importance" largely because these "effects" are measurable in a strict, replicable behavioral sense, thereby deflecting attention from larger social meanings of mass media production. (p. 206)

He predicted the decomposition of the "administrative" approach, which poses "questions from the vantage of the command-posts of institutions that seek to improve or rationalize their control over social sectors in social functions" (p. 225). Several years later, Corcoran (1987) observed that since the mid-1970s, there "has been a major shift of interest away from the positivist emphasis of the dominant Anglo-American paradigm" to a "textual, anti-empiricist paradigm" (p. 533).

In sociology, Wuthnow and Witten (1988) observed a dramatic growth in interest in cultural studies, saying "Only a few years ago it would have seemed extremely unlikely that the study of culture might emerge as a major growth industry . . . but it has now happened" (p. 49). They said the cause for the change "appears to be a growing dissatisfaction with the state of 'normal science' in the discipline. Ever more obscure statistical innovations have contributed to the discipline's attractiveness to technically minded government bureaucrats, but these have failed miserably to address issues of serious social and cultural significance" (p. 49).

Wolcott (1992) said that in education "we seem on the verge of canonizing" qualitative research even though, he argued, it:

> is not a field of study, and there is no clearly specified set of activities or identifiable group of specialists who practice them. To claim competence in qualitative research is, at most, to claim general familiarity with what is currently being done, coupled perhaps with experience in one or two particular facets (e.g., to "be good at" collecting and interpreting life histories or to "be" a symbolic interactionist). Claims to familiarity often amount to little more than a sympathetic attitude toward descriptive or interpretive work, accompanied by a far more deeply expressed antagonism for that "other kind" of research to which we have begun attaching the negative label "positivist." (p. 4)

Some scholars hold the perception that qualitative research is now the dominant form of research. Denzin and Lincoln (1994c) asserted that "the extent to which the 'qualitative revolution' has overtaken the social sciences and related professional fields has been nothing short of amazing" (p. ix). In media studies, there are examples of qualitative scholars declaring that their approach has replaced the quantitative approach (Allen, 1985; Lewis, 1991). Although these perceptions are certainly exaggerations, there is reason to believe that the qualitative approach is much more popular than it was several decades ago and that it is now regarded by many as a very useful way to examine the media.

The Problem

There is a raging debate over the comparative usefulness of the qualitative and quantitative approaches. By this point in the book, it should be clear to the reader how I have defined the qualitative approach. The "other" in this contrast has not been as well defined. By quantitative, I do not mean positivism, as it has often been defined. Nor is empiricism an adequate synonym. Of course, the quantitative approach is empirical, but that is only part of it; the approach also requires theorizing, that is, speculation, interpretation, and construction. My conception of the quantitative approach is postpositivistic (as characterized by Denzin & Lincoln, 1994c) and strongly influenced by what quantitative researchers actually do (in contrast to what nonquantitative types think they do).

When used in studying the media, the quantitative approach is a perspective on research that has the goal of documenting patterns of textual elements, institutional practices, and human behavior in the aggregate. By aggregate, I mean it is much more concerned with broad patterns that show the regularities than it is with individual anomalies. It is concerned both with constructing general explanations (induction), then operationalizing tests of those general explanations (deduction). The goal of this induction and deduction is to construct better (more useful and more parsimonious) explanations. In the deductive phase, concepts are frequently enumerated, that is, translated into numbers so the resulting data are amenable to mathematical and statistical analysis. The mathematical analyses (such as computing percentages, averages, ranges, indexes, etc.) serve to reduce large quantities of data into relatively simplified indicators of patterns. The statistical analyses indicate the degree of confidence researchers can have in inferring that the patterns in their samples reflect the population parameters. In order to make such inferences, researchers assume that certain types of distributions (patterns of data) exist in the unmeasured population.

Can the debate between the qualitative and quantitative approaches be resolved? Some scholars have tried to show there are several ways to accommodate this debate; that is, warfare is not the only option. Lancy (1993) briefly talked about how the debate is played out and observed six positions in the literature. First, qualitative and quantitative approaches are antagonists where scholars who favor one approach "reject the truth or evidential worthiness of research conducted" by the other (p. 11). Second, there is a complementary view where scholars feel both approaches can contribute. Third, some scholars see qualitative approach as having an antecedent value, that is, helping in an exploratory stage at the beginning of a research project. Fourth, there is an encapsulated view where the qualitative approach (especially in the form of case studies) can contribute insights within an overall quantitative approach to research. Fifth, there is the primary/secondary view where the overall approach is qualitative, and quantitative data are used as background. And sixth, there is the independent view where the "qualitative researcher studies issues that may not attract the interest and attention of a quantitative researcher and vice-versa" (p. 11).

Schwandt (1989) explained that each of the two approaches "holds a radically different view of the nature of reality, values a different kind of knowledge, and promotes a different set of standards for evaluating knowledge claims" (p. 379). According to him, there are six ways scholars have tried to deal with the conflict, but each of these six has been unsuccessful. First, there is denial that there is a problem. Second, there is cooptation where scholars acknowledge that there is a difference but attempt to argue that the two are complementary when the qualitative approach is assimilated into the quantitative approach. Third is the position of supremacy where scholars argue that the quantitative approach is more powerful and is therefore superior. Fourth is the replacement of both approaches with a third one that is a synthesis of the two. Fifth is the primacy of method, which ignores the foundational issues of ontology, epistemology, nature of evidence, and so on, and tells researchers to use a method that is best to solve each individual research problem. And sixth is anarchism, which is an "anything goes" position that allows for relativism. In rejecting all of these as solutions to the problem of conflict between the two approaches, Schwandt argued that each scholar must decide the debate for him or herself by selecting methods that fit his or her values and research needs.

Moving Toward a Solution

In this chapter, I reopen the issue about convergence between the two approaches. This issue raises a series of questions, the most important of which is: What does it mean to achieve a convergence of the qualitative and the scientific approaches? To make this question more concrete: Does it mean that the two approaches must accept the methodologies and use the methods of the other? Does it mean they must share assumptions?

Schwandt's (1989) perspective is to treat the qualitative approach holistically. This is seen in his rejection of partial solutions such as the sharing of methods while ignoring foundational assumptions. Schwandt is correct, of course, in cautioning against ignoring assumptions—they are essential to the approach. However, there are some weaknesses in his perspective. First, there is a weakness with the categorical approach in the implied definition of convergence; that is, either there is a "convergence" or there is not. If we take an either–or categorical approach, then the test for convergence is so conservative that it will be nearly impossible to demonstrate it. With a categorical comparison any difference, no matter how small, would always preempt any argument for convergence; that is, a small difference is all that is needed to show that the two approaches are not identical and therefore there is no convergence. Instead, a comparison made in a continuous manner would focus on the points of similarity and reveal the many characteristics that the two approaches share.

Second, I see a weakness in relying on a holistic comparison. We can, of course, attempt to make a holistic assessment, but beginning with such a task is difficult and can result in misleading conclusions, because both approaches are very complex and consist of many characteristics. It would seem to be more meaningful to begin with an analysis of the issue by breaking it down into component parts first. To illustrate, it is rather like trying to address the question of whether or not television viewing is harmful. We can make an overall, holistic interpretation, but it would be more meaningful to look at types of programming (news, MTV, game shows, situation comedies, religious broadcasts, sporting events, etc.) and first interpret the types of harm from each type of program. With the issue of convergence of the two research approaches, I believe it is more enlightening to conduct an element-by-element examination to determine the *degree* to which the two approaches converge.

Third, I see a weakness in making a judgment on convergence based exclusively on what qualitative theoreticians say. It would be stronger to begin with the theoretical prescriptions but to look at the actual practices as well.

In the analysis that follows, I use a noncategorical, nonholistic comparison by breaking the approaches down into their components as identified by the issues in the analytical templates of chapters 6 through 12. On each of these template issues, both the design (what the theoreticians prescribe) and the practices (as observed in the empirical literature) are considered, and I make a judgment as to the *degree* of convergence, using four levels of degree: none, coexistence, complementary, and integration. When the two approaches are diametrically opposed to each other, then convergence is not possible (none). But on other points, a convergence might be possible but not in the same manner for all of these points. For some, the convergence might be accomplished at a low level by demonstrating that the two approaches can coexist. For some, the convergence might be accomplished at a little higher level by showing that the two approaches are complementary; that is, they not only coexist, but the existence of one might serve to enhance the function of the other. And for some, the convergence might be accomplished at a very high level by arguing that the elements of the two can be integrated, that is fused into a higher order approach.

These decisions are plotted in Table 17.1. The pattern of those plottings reflects the holistic assessment of the *degree* to which convergence is possible.

ANALYSES

What follows in this section is an analysis of 19 issues. These are foundational issues (the phenomenon, purpose, ontology/epistemology, and axioms), issues of evidence (nature, level, and enumeration), issues of data gathering (expectations, researcher activity, sampling), issues of analysis (process, conceptual leverage, generalizability, contextualization, locus of argument, form of expression, and self-reflexivity), and standards for judging quality (internal and external). This section is relatively long and detailed. In this microfocused analysis, the reader might lose sight of the larger picture of convergence. However, this is the risk of any analysis that takes a large phenomenon apart to assess the individual elements. The bigger picture should come back into focus in the next section where the decisions made in this analysis are synthesized.

Foundational Issues

The Phenomenon. Media studies focuses on the phenomenon of how humans create meaning through and from the media. If this definition were common to both approaches, then there would a convergence on this point. But qualitative scholars would disagree that both approaches are looking at the same phenomenon. How do they arrive at their perception? They infer a difference in the phenomenon by looking at the use of methodologies. For example, they look at the use of the methodology of scientific experiment and conclude that the phenomenon must be viewed by scientists to be very atomistic, static, and simple. Seiter et al. (1989b) as well as Morley (1989) perceived science as focused on a quest for simple, direct media effects as characterized by a hypodermic needle. Also, J. A. Anderson (1987) asserted that science seeks to reduce a person

TABLE 17.1
Synthesis Level by Element

Issues	Type of Synthesis		
	Coexistence	Complementary	Integration
Foundational Issues			
1. The Phenomenon		X	
2. Purpose		X	
3. Ontology-Epistemology		X	
4. Axioms		X	
Issues of Evidence			
5. Nature of the Evidence		X	
6. Level of Evidence			X
7. Enumeration	X		
Issues of Gathering Evidence			
8. Expectations		X	
9. Researcher Activity			X
10. Sampling		X	
Issues of Analysis			
11. Process of Analysis		X	
12. Conceptual Leverage		X	
13. Generalizability		X	
14. Contextualization		X	
15. Locus of Argument		X	
16. Form of Expression		X	
17. Self-Reflexivity		X	
Standards for Judging Quality			
18. Internal Quality		X	
19. External Quality		X	

to a set of attributes that can be expressed in a quantitative formula and this presupposes a view that the phenomenon is objective, material, finite, and purified. Qualitative researchers, in contrast, view the phenomenon as subjective, constructed, ever expanding, and made up of individual expressions. But Anderson's contrasting points are themselves simplified characterizations of the situation that is much more complex and much less easily differentiated. Scientists are much more likely to believe in change and flux rather than in a static, finite phenomenon. Also, most scientists (even physical scientists) would identify less with the characteristics of objectivism than with subjective constructivism. For example, physical scientists who study the elementary nature of matter or the origin and nature of the universe know that their phenomena are not finite, nor are they material. For example, the search for basic building blocks of matter has long since gone beyond a point where the "things" being envisioned by the creative minds of scientists will ever be seen by their sense organs. Physical entities are not monolithic but composed of compounds, which are composed of molecules, which are composed of atoms, which are composed of a nucleus among other things. And the nucleus is composed of neurons and protons, which are composed of quarks of which there are six kinds one of which is called a "top." Top only exists for a hundred billionth of a trillionth of a second, then it falls apart into other particles. Can such a short appearance be regarded as an "existence"? Can it be regarded as having materiality when no one has ever seen it or ever will? If no one will ever be able to see it, then how can we know it exists? Scientists say they "know" because of the pattern of traces it leaves behind. So here within the most complex of all physical sciences, at the sub-sub-atomic level, we have a point of convergence with social science. That is, social scientists construct visions about things such as attitudes, motivations, values, and beliefs. But no one has ever seen any of these and no one ever will. Social scientists construct these then look for outward manifestations as support for these constructions. But social scientists in using these constructions are not arguing for their materiality or for their stable, fixed existence. The constructions are regarded as tentative explanations to advance our understanding. Like physical phenomena, social phenomena are very complex—maybe more so, but we will never know because we will never have the ultimate look at each so that a comparison can be made.

Therefore, the way differences have been characterized between the two approaches in terms of the way they view the phenomenon has been misleading. Perhaps a better way to characterize this difference is to think in terms of human thinking and behavior as being a very complex phenomenon with different facets. Some of those facets are parametric whereas others are nonparametric. A facet that is parametric is one that has a parameter that has a physical existence and the purpose of scholar is to document those. For example, parametric facets are things such as the number of households that have at least one television set, the amount of money spent on newspaper advertising, the percentage of support for a political candidate, and the like. These facets exist and can be assessed. This is not to say that they are fixed and stable, but that there is a figure that exists at any given time and that figure can be assessed in a snapshot manner. Also, the movement of those figures over time can be assessed in a time series and the resulting plot shows *how* they have changed. The scientific approach is particularly good at assessing these parameters.

There are also nonparametric facets to the phenomenon. These are the things that do not have a preexistence but must be constructed by the researcher to explain certain things about the phenomenon. Examples are audience, viewing motivation, and violent programming. These things do not exist waiting to be assessed; rather they are constructions of the researcher's mind. A research can point to physical manifestations of these things but those manifestations are not the thing itself. Qualitative theoreticians argue that their approach is very good at dealing with these facets of the phenomenon and that science is not. The theoreticians are half right. The qualitative approach is good with this type of facet, but the scientific approach is also good. When you read the scientific literature it becomes clear that most of the scientific research is concerned with nonparametric facets.

In summary, we can conclude that the two approaches are complementary on the element of phenomenon. Both approaches are concerned with human thinking and behavior as concerns media. And both are interested in nonparametric facets. However, because the quantitative approach is also concerned with parametric facets, its view of the phenomenon has a greater scope. This is not to say that the scientific approach is superior—only that it is interested in a wider part of the phenomenon. In this conclusion, I am not arguing for what Schwandt (1989) called "supremacy" where science is viewed as a more powerful approach. Nor am I arguing for what Lancy (1993) called "encapsulated," because I do not see the qualitative approach as a secondary element under the scientific umbrella. My conclusion of complementary should be interpreted to mean that the scientific approach is focused on the same phenomenon as is the qualitative approach. However, they are not identical because the scientific approach is also concerned with additional facets.

Purpose. Qualitative research has been conceptualized as having a wide range of purpose. It can simply describe something, such as the composition of some audience, conversations about the media by friends over lunch, or the production process of a television series. It can allow for the scholar to foreground his personal interpretations of the quality of television show or of the way meaning is constructed in family television-viewing patterns. It can seek explanation by developing grounded theory or by making a case that the meaning in a culture is determined by an ideology. And it can have an action orientation where the scholar focuses on a problem and argues for a particular solution. All of these are purposes in qualitative thinking, and they are not arrayed in an hierarchy. Although certain scholars favor certain purposes over others, there is no argument here that one of these purposes is more important or more qualitativelike than the others.

With science the avowed purposes are description and explanation. In science, description is useful to convey the composition of an audience, the prevalence of certain characteristics in media texts, and the strength of an attitude in the public. Explanation requires formal theorizing to lay out a construction of the *why* and *how* of the phenomenon then a test of the construction. For example, media scientists seek to explain why there is so much violence on television and how exposure to that violence can alter viewers' perceptions of the real world.

As for action orientation, science does not allow for this purpose. Also, science does not acknowledge interpretation as a purpose in the same way that the qualitative approach does. This does not mean that scientists do not use interpretation; of course they do all the time. They use interpretation in the selection of a research topic, in the construction of a theory, in the way they deduce hypotheses and construct their measures. There is also interpretation in the selection of statistical analyses; in a given situation, some analyses are more appropriate than others but there are always choices among alternatives, and this often requires interpretation. And most prevalently, there is interpretation required in the presentation of the statistical findings. For example, scientists must decide if they should regard 1% error as acceptable or if 5% would do. This decision is an arbitrary one, but it could determine whether their results are statistically significant or not. Also, should a correlation coefficient of .20 be considered meaningful evidence of a relationship? In terms of intercoder agreement, this would be a dismally low relationship; however, with cultivation research, this is a reasonable strong relationship. How do we know this? We must look at the context of the research tradition; that is, we must engage in a hermeneutic process of looking at individual statistics then comparing them to a context that itself is built up of individual statistics over time and continues to be influenced by the addition of new findings. As this context of findings change, the standards for making a contribution change. With theory-driven research, the context of interpreting the contribution of each additional piece of research changes as old propositions are refined, new propositions are added, old measures are discredited, new measures are validated, and old analytical schemes are replaced with more sophisticated and powerful ones. So, a research study that might have made a good contribution a decade ago may not be very useful now. This comparison requires interpretation of both the context, which is itself a construction, and the elements in the study. Therefore, science is structured by interpretations.

The difference between the qualitative approach and the scientific one is not in terms of whether they allow interpretation; both not only allow it but require it. The difference is in the grounding of the interpretation. With science, there is a drive toward showing that each interpretation has an intersubjective basis. This means that a scholar's interpretation either is grounded in the tradition of like interpretations already in the literature, or is the one most likely to be accepted by other scholars seeing the same evidence. In contrast, the qualitative approach allows, at least in the theorizing, for interpretations that are unique to an individual scholar and do not conform to the vision or beliefs of other scholars. The qualitative approach allows for intersubjectively conforming interpretations, but it does not require it, whereas science requires it.

Also, with the element of purpose there is another important distinction between knowing *that* and knowing *why* or *how*. Knowing *that* a person acts a certain way or has a certain reading of a text is relatively easy. The behavior or the reading (as told to the researcher in a conversation) has a material form and can be examined and documented. The ontology of this is material. But the process of construction is the problematic area. We cannot see this directly. People might be able to tell us what they went through, but this is indirect evidence. (This is different from someone telling us what their reading of a text is; in this case the telling is the reading and the reading exists now as the current reading in the viewer's mind.) But the reconstruction of the process behind the reading is a difficult one; that process itself will never have a material reality directly; at best it can only have an indirect recounting—and the recounting can have a material reality, but the recounting is removed from the process a step. With some situations (where the person cannot reconstruct the decision making well or where the researcher is not very skilled) the step removed is a *big* step.

In summary, there is reason to believe that the existing degree of convergence is complementary. With this purpose element, the qualitative approach has a wider scope than does the scientific approach. Both have the purpose of description. Both have the purpose of interpretation and explanation, but the meaning of these purposes is different in the two approaches. And only the qualitative approach allows for an action orientation. Qualitative's action orientation can be viewed as a complement to science. Scientists frequently expect the findings of their work to be used by policymakers or industry managers, although it is not the purpose of a scholar acting like a scientist to do so. And the differences in the meaning of the interpretative and explanatory purposes are also complementary.

The Ontological-Epistemological Nexus. Frequently qualitative theoreticians will prescribe a basis for ontology of idealism. For example, Pauly (1991) revealed an idealist perspective when he said, "Humans fabricate rather than discover reality. They use symbols to construct the worlds in which they live. In this view, reality is an accomplishment rather than an entity out there, waiting to be uncovered" (p. 2). However, this argument sets up an ontological irony. If nothing has an independent existence apart from perceiving it, then how can there be a scholarship? No matter how eloquently a theoretician argues for a pure idealist position on ontology, his or her words that communicate those thoughts have existence to readers and that existence supports a materialist position and thereby refutes the position the theoretician is arguing.

This leads to an epistemological irony. If everyone interprets everything subjectively, then there can be no determination of quality and no standards. How can we ascribe more or better meaning to one interpretation over others? But qualitative scholars do this all the time, especially in their critique of social science. If social science is one of many equally good interpretations of how scholarship should be conducted, then what is their basis for criticizing it as inferior to the qualitative approach?

Finally, there is the fundamental problem of multiple *types* of realities. First, there are physical objects in the world. There is no reason to believe that even qualitative researchers do not believe in the existence of chairs, books, people, and other such objects. Second, there are things called communication and culture that are creations of human interpretation. There is no reason to believe that even quantitative researchers would not believe these are human constructions; that is, they are not naturally occurring objects that are waiting to be discovered. Within this second group, there are varying views, but these variations are traceable to misunderstandings that grow from unannounced shifts in writers' arguments. For example, the creation of a conversation means that it does not exist at one moment, but then it comes into existence. And if it is taped, it stays in a material form. Researchers who think they perceive a pattern on such a tape then construct an argument that such a pattern exists. Their argument is a second-order construction, because it is an interpretation of the meaning that was constructed by other people. A critic of the researcher can then read that researcher's position, which exists in material form as an article. The critic then applies his or her meaning to the meaning of the researcher, which, of course, is an interpretation of the meaning in the original conversation. Thus the critique is a third-order interpretation, and it exists in material form and is open to reinterpretation in the fourth order and beyond. With each of these orders, there is a construction process that focuses on meaning and creates a new text at a higher order of interpretation. Therefore, the overall process requires both a belief in constructivism as well as a belief in materialism. The two are not antithetical; instead they are complementary. They are necessary alternating steps in a continuous process. In order to argue for a single epistemological position (such as realism or idealism), we must take the process apart and focus on only one component in this overall process. But if we take a holistic approach, we see that a belief in both positions is required.

In summary, this issue, which first appears to be characterized as a major difference between the two approaches, is really not much of a difference in practice. My argument just stated leads me to conclude that the two approaches are complementary, because they can be synthesized into a higher order concept of scholarship. Under the umbrella of scholarship the qualitative approach demonstrates an acceptance in the material existence of artifacts of communication and science demonstrates an intersubjective epistemological foundation. Both approaches engage in constructing interpretations or explanations for even the more ephemeral facets of the phenomenon, but these interpretations are never purely idiosyncratic; that is, the subjective interpretations seek to gain credence through their linkage with a tradition of thinking outside the scholar.

Axioms. There are five primary axioms in qualitative research. These axioms are: phenomenology, interpretive, hermeneutics, naturalism, and humanistic studies. Each is presented in the following discussion that illuminates the degree to which each is shared by science:

1. *Phenomenology* is the belief that the phenomenon should be examined without any preconceived notions or a priori expectations. Researchers attempt

to get inside the mind of the actor to attempt an understanding of what the actor sees and believes. This understanding leads the researcher to explain how the actor constructs reality and why the actor behaves as he or she does. This is not an axiom of science, although the position it supports is allowed; that is, science allows for research without an a priori expectation.

2. *Interpretive* is the belief that the researcher should try to see the situation from the point of view of those who are being studied rather than imposing the observer's view upon the situation. To do this, researchers must use subjective methods and their own interpretations to try to understand what is happening in the social settings they observe (Denzin & Lincoln, 1994a; Morris, 1977). As argued previously, there is not a substantial difference here between the two approaches.

3. *Hermeneutics* is the perspective that humans view the world as an interaction of parts and wholes. The part is only understood in the context of the whole, and the whole is constructed of the parts. There is no beginning or end in this circular process of interpretation. As J. K. Smith (1983) explained, "In this circular process, the meaning of any particular part of a text, such as a word or a sentence, requires an understanding of the meaning of the whole and vice versa. Achieving a meaningful interpretation is a process of constant movement between parts and whole in which there is no absolute starting point and no absolute ending point" (p. 12).

This is a shared assumption. The qualitative approach highlights this axiom. Although science does not highlight it in the writings of its theoreticians, the practice of science relies on it very much.

4. *Naturalism* is the belief that the world should be studied in its natural state, undisturbed by the researcher (Denzin & Lincoln, 1994a). Christians and Carey (1989) asserted that researchers must "pitch their tents among the natives, must enter the situation so deeply that they can recreate in imagination and experience the thoughts and sentiments of the observed" (p. 360). Marshall and Rossman (1989) argued that all qualitative approaches assume "that systematic inquiry must occur in a natural setting rather than an artificially constrained one such as an experiment" (pp. 10–11).

There is a difference here, but not so wide as it might first seem. Science does not require naturalism, but neither does science disallow it. Scientific methodologies such as surveys and field experiments can be naturalistic. However, science also allows for laboratory experiments where the researcher controls conditions in a very unnaturalistic setting.

5. *Humanism* highlights language as a demonstration of meaning, and this language must be interpreted in cultural and historical contexts. It focuses on human values as an answer to the question: What does it mean to be human? The goal is to illuminate individual experience, not to generalize.

Science is often contrasted with the humanities in the curricular organization of higher education. At first this appears to be a neat categorization of scholarly activity, but the difference is not as large as it first might appear. The interest in language and meaning is very important to both approaches. The difference is that science has a goal of explaining large classes of behaviors, whereas the humanities does not.

In summary, there is no reason to see no convergence here. However, because of the importance of the axioms of naturalism and humanism, there will never be an integration. The axioms of hermeneutics and interpretive are largely shared, and phenomenology is permitted in science, although science also allows for a nonphenomenological perspective. On balance, the degree of convergence appears to be complementary.

Issues of Evidence

Nature of the Evidence. The key concern with the nature of evidence is with whether it can be objective or if it is subjective. Some social scientists say that there is total subjectivity, whereas others argue that objectivity can be attained under certain conditions. The debate can be traced to the question: What does it mean to be objective? If objectivity means that humans all follow the same process of meaning making that has either been stamped into our brains at birth or that we are all identically conditioned to process information the same way, thereby always arriving at the same conclusions, perceptions, and feelings, then there is no objectivity given this standard. But the other extreme is also equally untenable; each human is not so unique in the processing of information that no one shares any conclusions, perceptions, or feelings. The problem of objectivity is not categorical; it is a problem that is best viewed in terms of degree. The phenomenon of human meaning making is neither totally uniform nor is it totally idiosyncratic; there are elements of both. Qualitative scholars are more concerned with the uniquenesses among individuals, and quantitative scholars are more interested in the regularities across aggregates. The question of Who is right? is the wrong question. It is also wrong to consider the question: Who is more right? This is not a contest, and to cast it as such is to deflect the energy away from the purpose of the scholarship, which should be less about claiming territory from each other and more about cooperatively pushing the boundaries out against the line of ignorance.

Looking at the continuum of belief on evidence, we can illuminate three places where beliefs are fairly prevalent. First, there is the view that evidence can be a creative construction. The phenomenon of interest is unknowable through empirical means, therefore all research must be a subjective interpretation of the researcher. Second, the evidence can be subjective valuing. There are tangible, material artifacts that reflect the phenomenon of interest, but each researcher has his or her own subjective manner for valuing each bit of evidence. And third, the evidence can be viewed with contingent accuracy. Empirical evidence is important and valued. It is checked for accuracy.

The writings of the theoreticians would have us believe that science requires contingent accuracy whereas the qualitative approach requires creative construction. But this was not found to be the case with the qualitative research, which exhibited no examples of creative construction. Instead, all were empirical; that is, all referred to a significant amount of evidence external to the researcher. This places the *research* squarely in the realm of subjective valuing. Even those qualitative authors who wrote a rather personal essay about a particular television show referred to numerous examples of characterization and plot in the shows as well as social, historical, and cultural events outside the show. And there are examples where researchers treat data more objectively and present the data as relatively external to their judgment process. Here, little interpretation is consciously used, and instead, some sort of a case is made for the accuracy of the data. The two approaches therefore appear to be complementary.

Level of Evidence. Qualitative theoreticians talk about the importance of research focusing on the individual level, that is, where the researcher interprets how individuals subjectively construct meaning. There are examples where researchers studied people as individuals, but more typical is research where people are interviewed in groups and the patterns found there are generalized to make statements about how different kinds of people (by gender or ethnic background) construct meaning. Even more prevalent is the large-scale analysis of communities such as the San Francisco punk culture (Lull, 1987) or the computer culture (Turkle, 1984). Industry-focused research exhibited broad-scale perspectives.

Science also allows for the collection of data at all these levels. Therefore, on this point the level of convergence is integration.

Enumeration. A key difference between the qualitative and scientific approaches is with the idea of ennumeration, which science allows (and encourages) and qualitative abhors. There is a difference between the use of numbers and enumeration. Qualitative researchers use numbers. They frequently cite figures that have actual mathematical properties (such as audience sizes, audience compositions, budgets, company profitability, etc.). However, they do not translate a quality of a person (such as an attitude or motivation) or a text (such as entertainment value) into a number. This taboo of enumeration is closely observed by qualitative researchers. On this element, the two approaches coexist.

Issues of Gathering Evidence

Expectations. There is very little difference here between the options of the two approaches. Both allow for an inductive and a deductive approach. With qualitative theory, there is a premium placed on no a priori expectations, but rather letting the observations build up in an inductive way. However, a great deal of the qualitative research is argument-driven where the researcher will have a particular point of view guiding the selection and organization of evidence. In the examination of the qualitative literature in chapters 7 through 10, it appears that almost all of the authors (except for those building grounded theory) had a clear expectation before they began their research. However, from the writing alone, it is almost always impossible to tell for sure if the researcher really did begin with clear expectations or if those expectations developed during the research. Researchers do not usually explain this point clearly unless they write a book that follows the conventions of a diary.

With science there is a premium placed on testing formal theories by deducing hypotheses. However, a great deal of science is exploratory; that is, much of it is inductive. With the qualitative approach (except for ideological research) there is a premium placed on more phenomenological research where there are no prior expectations. Therefore, the two approaches are complementary on this point.

Researcher Activity. With text-based research, the scholar must act like a passive observer. But with audience- or industry-focused research, the scholar has the additional options of being an active observer and an active participant. Qualitative researchers who are guided strongly by the axioms of phenomenology and naturalism will seek to remain passive. However, those who are interested in action-oriented purposes will see a more active participation in the research process.

Science also allows for a range of activity. With the methodologies of content analysis and survey, the research is relatively passive. But with laboratory experiments, the researcher is more active.

On the issue of activity, there is no difference between the two approaches. However, on the more active end of the spectrum, there is a difference in the motivation for their activity. With qualitative researchers, the motivation is to change behavior or attitudes in the direction the researcher thinks is somehow better for the people being examined. The motivation is a therapeutic one. In contrast, with scientific researchers, the motivation is to temporarily alter certain conditions to see if the subjects' behaviors and attitudes are subsequently influenced. The motive is curiosity.

In summary, both approaches allow for a wide range of behaviors on the part of the researcher. Therefore, the two approaches are integrated on this point.

Sampling. Science prescribes probability sampling techniques so that the results will be generalizable. Qualitative theoreticians make no such prescriptions. If we stop the analysis at this point, it appears that there is a big difference between the two approaches. However, if we take the analysis one step further and examine the published literature, we see that there really is very little difference on the issue of sampling. In the qualitative literature, there is no probability sampling. Still, there is a good deal of generalizing, and some qualitative researchers even try to make a case that their sample is representative, although the arguments are largely unconvincing. In scientific research, there is also a great deal of generalizing. But fewer than 27% of the articles using the scientific approach published in the most rigorous journals had a probability sample (Potter, Cooper, & Dupagne, 1993).

In the design of the two approaches there is no chance for integration. However, when we look at the practices of the two approaches, we see very little difference on this element. Therefore, the two appear to be complementary. Both approaches rely largely on nonprobability samples. But science does also have a fair-size minority of studies that do use probability samples, whereas the qualitative approach does not.

Issues of Analysis

Process of Analysis. Both approaches emphasize the importance for researchers to describe the key elements in their designs and to explain how they made their decisions in the selection and analysis of data. However, in practice, scientific research displays the process of analysis much more clearly and to a much greater depth than does the qualitative research. This is attributable to the more formulaic nature of the scientific approach, which allows the authors to convey information about their design decisions in a much more parsimonious fashion. Although qualitative researchers may have as strong an obligation to convey their design decisions, they often are very superficial in addressing this task. Because this element is treated with equally high importance by both approaches, it could be regarded as integrated. But because of the difference in practice, this status will be reduced to complementary.

Conceptual Leverage. To what extent do researchers extend their arguments/findings beyond reporting on the elements of evidence into a more general conceptual level? There are three levels as follows. First, a researcher could present no conceptual leverage where no attempt is made to move beyond describing the literal events in the data. The reporting is limited to description of the actual data themselves. Second, there could be a low level where the researcher constructs patterns (through his or her own processes of inference) to make sense of the literal data. And third, there could be a high level where the researcher infers a connection to an a priori construction such as a theory or ideology.

With science, there is a goal for a high degree of conceptual leverage; that is, the results of a study must fit into a larger body of knowledge and advance the progression of understanding. The results should be used to build theory by using an inductive method or to test theory with a deductive method.

With the qualitative approach, theoreticians espouse a goal of idiosyncratic understanding; that is, they place the focus on the particular. This eliminates conceptual leverage as a goal. However, there is still a prevalence of conceptual leverage in the literature. For example, there are many examples of a high degree of conceptual leverage in the research examining texts, people, and institutions. A high-level inference was exhibited by scholars who take the general principles of other scholars and seek to test them on their own areas or attempt to extend those principles. In either case, the focus of the article is much more on the conceptual issues than on the data.

In summary, researchers seem to place a premium on conceptual leverage in both approaches, even though some qualitative theoreticians would not support such a goal. The two approaches are then considered complementary.

Generalizability. With the qualitative approach, the prescription is for the researcher to gather data at a certain level (the person, the group, etc.) and to pitch his or her conclusions at that level. In contrast, with the scientific approach, there is a drive toward generalizations—this means that the researcher gathers data at a relatively low level (e.g., the individual) and seeks to present conclusions at a higher level (such as the cultural level).

It might help to think of this graphically like a pyramid. Think of the bottom of the pyramid as being composed of each individual person who is regarded as being unique—there is no grouping. At the top of the pyramid is the concept of "human" where all people are regarded as being the same. As we move up the pyramid from the base we must construct concepts that segment individuals; that is, we find ways to arrange people into fewer and fewer segments such that the people in a segment are all the same in some way (by age cohort, by attitude, by gender, etc.) and where there are distinguishable differences among the other segments at that particular level. With science there is a pressure to move up from the base of this pyramid toward the peak by attempting to find explanations about how people are the same. With the qualitative approach there is a pressure to stay near the base and to interpret the uniquenesses among individuals.

In design, the two approaches are very different with their prescriptions for generalization. However, in practice, there is little difference. Sometimes scientific research is low-level exploration or description. In contrast, qualitative researchers frequently generalize, that is, move their conclusions up to a higher level on the pyramid. Therefore, the two approaches have moved to a complementary position on this element.

Contextualization. The prescription for qualitative research is for strong contextualization both broad and deep. Broad contextualization is where the author takes a horizontal approach by comparing an element to the other elements of the same kind on the same level of generality. Deep contextualization is where the author takes a vertical approach by comparing the focal subject to different kinds of elements at different levels of generality. To illustrate, let's say we are interested in interpreting a TV cartoon show. We could provide broad context for our analysis by comparing our cartoon show with other cartoons and showing how it is situated within the cartoon genre. We could also provide deep context by describing the infrastructure (economic, political, or creative culture) that influenced the production decisions. Or we could take an historical perspective and show how this cartoon series held a place in the evolution of different genres on television.

Although the prescription for qualitative research is for strong contextualization, this prescription is not always followed. Sometimes qualitative researchers will not use primary data or use a narrower or shallower scope of data than he or she could have to provide an adequate contextualization. However, most of the qualitative research does provide a good degree of context.

Science does not have a prescription for contextualization in the same sense that the qualitative approach does. However, if we take a broad view of context, we can see that scientific analysis has been moving toward greater contextualization. In science, context is increased by adding variables and subjects to the design, and there has been a trend toward more multivariate designs with greater numbers of research subjects over the years. However, these additions do not lead to rich description. But the addition of variables does deepen the resulting explanations, and the addition of subjects does broaden them.

In summary, contextualization is important to both approaches. But the meaning of the term is different and the goals is achieved in different ways. Therefore, we can consider the position to be complementary.

Locus of Argument. There are four possibilities for where the researcher could place the locus of the argument. Ethos focuses on the authority or expertise of the author/researcher. Pathos is where the presentation is designed to appeal primarily to the emotions, especially anger. Logos focuses on structuring the facts in an orderly manner to convince the reader that this interpretation is the best explanation. And when the focus is on the data, the researcher is demonstrating a perspective that the instances speak for themselves.

With qualitative research we should expect to see ethos, pathos, and logos. Because of the belief in the subjective nature of observations, the data should not be a locus; instead, there is a requirement for the researcher to interpret the data and build an argument (logos), rest the argument on his or her expertise (ethos), or to call for some change using an appeal to the emotions (pathos). But the qualitative research reveals an exception to this expectation; that is, there were no examples of pathos and quite a few examples of data focus.

With science, the prescription is for a focus on data for inductive research and logos for deductive research. The combination of overlap and differences indicate the two approaches are complementary on this element.

Form of Expression. With the science approach, the dominant form of expression is the mainstream realist tale, which is a single-voiced "objective" account of events, persons, and experiences where the researcher maintains a distance from the subject and reifies hypothetical constructs.

The qualitative approach rebels against this type of presentation, favoring more personal styles of expression to illuminate the researcher in the process. In the interpretive realist tale, the author exhibits interpretive omnipotence, which is a no-nonsense manner of presenting representations and accounts as the final word about how the culture is to be interpreted. And in the confessional tale, the focus is far more on the researcher than on the culture studied. This tale uses the first person where events are presented intimately from the fieldworker's point of view, and mistakes are related as well as successes.

Also, qualitative encourages other forms of expression such as the descriptive realist tale and the literary tale to show the phenomenon being studied in a more direct or entertaining manner. The descriptive realist tale uses a journalistic style where the author tries to stay out of the way and let the multiple voices of the subjects speak for themselves. And the literary tale reflects a novelist's sense of narration in bringing alive the culture with concrete characterizations and dramatic tension. The author is trying to show what happened rather than tell about it. Finally, in action-oriented qualitative research, we would expect to see the critical tale where the author shows a problem and argues for a particular solution.

With qualitative research, almost all is written from the interpretive realist form of expression. This is the case whether the focus of the research is audiences, texts, or the industry. However, there were some examples of the critical tale and the confessional tale. Also, if we stretch the definition of the literary tale, we could find some examples of that form of expression as well.

In summary, if qualitative research had lots of examples in each form of expression, then it would be shown to exhibit a great variety compared to the scientific approach. But the practice is for qualitative researchers to favor a narrow band of expression. Thus the two approaches are fairly similar on this element and should be considered as being complementary.

Self-Reflexivity. Theoreticians characterize qualitative research as primarily an interpretive act where researchers acknowledge their own subjectivity through sharing their biases and limitations with readers so readers can make their own interpretations of the work. Researchers should then exhibit a high degree of self-reflexivity. But seldom does this happen.

There are three primary ways that qualitative researchers have displayed self-reflexivity. First, some scholars will describe many of the decisions they made in conducting the research, such as gaining access, establishing credibility, and so on. A second kind of self-reflexivity is where the researcher consciously reflects on the nature of the methods he or she used and worries about the value of the data and his or her interpretations. The third kind of self-reflexivity is demonstrated when a scholar lays out his or her biases, as biases, so that the reader can be forewarned about the author's perspective.

One of the keys to understanding self-reflexivity is to make a distinction between the self and the other in audience research. In this type of research, the focal subject is the "other person" who is being studied. There is a lot written about how the other creates meaning. Qualitative researchers are always skeptical about the other's interpretation so they revise the other's interpretation (criticize institutions or social science, etc.). Also, they reinterpret what others say by showing that what they say is really different from what they do.

But the self is largely ignored; that is, researchers do not raise the question about their own interpretations. Instead, they present their work as interpretive realism. The appearance is that they are somehow better perceivers of others' follies. Does this come from training or natural insight? Where is the locus of this expertise?

If qualitative research is primarily an interpretive act where researchers acknowledge their own subjectivity through sharing their biases and limitations with readers so readers can make their own interpretations of the work, then researchers should exhibit a high degree of self-reflexivity. But seldom does this happen. With science, there is also little self-reflexivity. Scientists feel they are conforming to a well-articulated set of methodologies that are accepted by researchers and readers alike. Therefore, there is no need to reflect on one's use of them in the research report. But the other forms of self-reflexivity are displayed by scientific scholars. For example, they will frequently discuss biasing factors and threats to validity that lead to the limitations of their studies. Because of the importance for researchers using either approach to disclose threats to the quality of their study, the two approaches appear to be complementary.

Standards for Judging Quality

Standards for qualitative research present a very problematic area. Some scholars forcefully argue that discussing of any type of standards is foolhardy (J. K. Smith, 1984). Other qualitative theoreticians disagree and think that standards are very important (Altheide & Johnson, 1994; J. A. Anderson, 1987; Fortner & Christians, 1981; Howe & Eisenhart, 1990; Lancy, 1993; Lincoln & Guba, 1986, 1990; Marshall & Rossman, 1989; Penman, 1988). But there is very little agreement among these supporters of standards about what those criteria should be.

Qualitative researchers very rarely make a conscious argument for the quality of their work, either the internal quality (evidence) or the external quality (conclusions). This is not surprising given the unsettled debate about what should be the criteria.

Internal Quality. The internal quality issue focuses on the evidence or the data themselves. In quantitative research, scholars seek to establish a case for the reliability, validity, and usefulness of their data. Reliability means the consistency and stability of the measures. Validity means the accuracy (or the truthfulness) of the data. And usefulness refers to the appropriateness of the data for the purpose they were gathered.

Some qualitative theoreticians try to emulate these criteria used in social science. For example, Fortner and Christians (1981) stated, "Observations must reflect the genuine features of the situation under study" (p. 366), which requires a faithful account of people's own words. In order to do this, researchers need to immerse themselves deeply enough to be able to establish the principal aspects of the event being studied and to distinguish the main features from the digressions. As Fortner and Christians put it, "If true interiority has occurred, that is, if data accurately reflect the natural circumstances, those data are valid and reliable even though not based upon randomization, repeated and controlled observation, measurement, and statistical inference" (p. 366).

There were some examples of qualitative researchers attempting to establish a case for the internal validity of their research. However, in almost all cases the argument closely followed scientific criteria. Altheide (1976) used an internal process of verification; that is, he checked his observations from one station with what was happening at another station to see if his perceptions of a pattern held up. Also, he checked what he heard with what he saw. But it does not appear that he would check his "findings" with those he observed, only individual data. Turow (1981) trained coders to analyze the characteristics of children's television. To demonstrate that the resulting coded data were good he reported the results of a test of intercoder reliability. Lull (1980) had participant observers write a report about their observations of each family. "Following the writing of the reports, family members were asked to read and confirm the validity of the observations" (p. 200). Jhally and Lewis (1992) raised the issue of internal validity when they said they regarded themselves as a "prudent jury, [who] must use our knowledge and skill to interpret what people tell us rather than accept all testimony at face value" (p. 9).

But there were a few examples where a qualitative researcher would present a nonscientific basis for the internal quality. For example, Silverstone (1988) said "that although meaning is theoretically unlimited, it is empirically limited. It is perfectly possible to imagine as many readings as there are readers ... but in practice only some will be socially significant" (p. 30). So how do we know which will be more significant? According to Silverstone, we must examine each reading in context of "the intersecting and competing discourses which both the text and reader are placed" (pp. 30–31). He attempted to create a model of textual analysis and said that as he develops it, it grows "more complex, it is hoped also more sophisticated, more adequate, and more useful" (p. 31). It appears, therefore, that the goals of his effort are sophistication, adequacy, and utility, and those then are the standards upon which he felt the model should be judged. Also, Elliott (1979) addressed the point of internal validity when he stated, "The important test to apply to the analysis of participant observation data seems to me not to be simply how many other cases is this likely to be true for ... but how plausible is the posited relationship between belief, behaviour and situation in the light of possible alternative explanations?" (p. 174). So he tested his individual observations for plausibility.

It appears that the qualitative approach is struggling here to find a way to be an alternative to the scientific approach. But in the meantime, qualitative researchers borrow the scientific models in order to provide a case for internal quality. Therefore, the condition can best be described as complementary.

External Quality. Some qualitative authors avoid the issue of external validity by saying that they will not generalize their findings to other groups of people. Although most do not address this issue consciously, many still present results in a way that makes it clear that the researchers are generalizing. Very little of the qualitative research makes any case for external validity, but neither does much of the scientific research. With science, there is a requirement of probability sampling as a foundation for generalizing. Therefore, it appears that the situation is one that is complementary.

TOWARD CONVERGENCE?

The Synthesis

The preceding analysis illuminates an interpretation that the two approaches are not as antithetical as much of the debate would have us believe. On only one element (enumeration) was it concluded that the two approaches are very different and that there was no evidence of integration; however, the two approaches could coexist on this element. On several elements (level of evidence and researcher activity), it appeared that there was already an integration between the two approaches. On the remaining 16 elements, the conclusion was that the two approaches were complementary.

What does it mean to be complementary? There were a variety of reasons why the two approaches were considered complementary on an element. One reason was that the differing prescriptions could be synthesized, because there was substantial (but not complete) overlap. Examples of this are phenomenon, purpose, and axioms. Another type of synthesis was possible where the prescriptions differed only in emphasis. An example of this is with the element of expectations. The qualitative approach emphasizes no a priori expectations, whereas the scientific approach emphasizes theory-driven research with clear hypotheses. However, qualitative research frequently presents research with strong expectations (ideological essays) and science displays a good deal of exploratory research. Another type of synthesis was possible where an element was very important to both approaches, but it was defined in a different, but compatible, way in the two approaches. An example of this is the element of self-reflexivity. A final reason was that the synthesis was seen in the practices of researchers. On these examples, which include the elements of nature of evidence, sampling, conceptual leverage, and generalizability, the prescriptions were substantially different across the two approaches, but the practices of the researchers were fairly similar.

When we move from the focus on the elements to a holistic level, we can see that the pattern is a complementary one across the two approaches. How is such a conclusion possible? If we look at only the prescriptions of many of the theoreticians (both qualitative and quantitative) and the guidelines in method-ology texts, we would not arrive at this conclusion. But when we look at the possibilities for synthesis by assessing the degree of overlap and the sharing of a perspective on a higher level of scholarship, we see that some of the prescrip-tions allow for synthesis. Also, when we look at the research itself, we can see patterns that indicate that the practices are much closer than the prescriptions would lead us to believe.

Why the Convergence?

The interpretation just advanced may be surprising to many readers. If this interpretation is taken out of context, it will appear shocking and will be very controversial. So let's explore the reasons for this interpretation, that is, that there might be a relatively high degree of convergence between the two ap-proaches. The reason for the convergence lies primarily in the research, and the reason for the surprise is the difference between the prescriptions and the research. Let's examine each more closely.

The writings of the theoreticians serve to disperse thinking about the quali-tative approach; that is, those writings contain a wide variety of points of view that serve to move thinking outward from a common core of belief. There are two primary reasons for this. First, theoreticians have a very high degree of freedom to be creative and the means to exercise a different vision of things. They do not have an empirical anchor to ground their thoughts, so they can take flights of creativity in any direction. This is a healthy activity, because it expands one's vision and excites the mind. Second, theoreticians, in their argu-ments for the value of the qualitative approach, take an oppositional stance. This stance leads them to hyperbolize. They ignore the fuzzy contours where the similarities lie and instead focus on the more angular areas where the differences jut out. In focusing on these differences, they sharpen them to prickly points and place them in powerful spotlights. That which is left outside the spotlight in darkness seems not to exist. There is nothing wrong with this activity per se; advocates who argue a case must select the strongest evidence to achieve their goal of persuasion. However, readers of these exercises in advo-cacy must realize that they present a very limited view of the phenomenon of qualitative thinking and research. Those who approach their reading with less of an expectation to be persuaded than an expectation to try to experience as much of that phenomenon as possible require exposure to a wider variety of visions of the phenomenon. This is what this book has attempted to do. When the reader considers all this information in total, he or she will realize that there is a considerable variety of positions among the theoreticians and that only a segment is captured in the advocacy writing. However, the advocacy writing is very visible and therefore has a strong effect in constructing a reader's impression of what the qualitative approach is. Readers who accept the interpretation laid out in the advocacy writing will then be most surprised by the conclusions presented in this chapter.

Now, let's turn our attention to the research. There seem to be three reasons why researchers do not follow more closely the prescriptions of the theoreticians. First, researchers must realize that some of the prescriptions cannot be followed. For example, the ontological position of idealism along with the epistemological position of constructivism is a popular prescription. Some theoreticians (e.g., Pauly, 1991) try to convince researchers that the world does not exist but is a pure creation; this prescription gives the researcher complete freedom. However, I found no examples of a researcher using anywhere near this complete freedom. Instead, researchers constructed their interpretations of the "other," which was always regarded as having a material existence outside the researcher. There was not a single research project that failed to refer to the text of a program, the recorded thoughts of other people, or the artifacts of some culture or institution. These references were most often couched in the interpretive realist form of expression, which recognizes the interpretive task of the research where the task is not accomplished through pure creativity but instead grows out of empirical evidence that is treated from a realistic frame.

A second reason why researchers do not follow the prescriptions more closely is because the prescriptions sometimes present conflicting advice on a particular element. This point was raised in the previous chapter when I argued that theoreticians establish their positions around the perimeter of the research environment, so as to define and expand the boundaries of that environment. Some theoreticians plot a fluid position by talking about the importance of *not* providing a definition for the qualitative approach, the importance of taking a holistic, nonreductionistic approach, and the subjective, changeable nature of knowledge. Other theoreticians will plot an ordered position by arguing for the need to clarify the boundaries of the approach, to specify the methodologies and methods, and the importance of having quality standards to guide researchers toward making contributions that will matter. Some theoreticians will argue for a position of reflection, that is, the need for close and prolonged contact with that which is being studied and the importance of ferreting out useful insights that are rechecked through further observation. And others will argue for transformation, that is, the dominance of creative constructions in all of human activity and the importance of persuading others of your point of view to energize them into social action. A researcher cannot satisfy the prescription of all of these positions simultaneously, so he or she must compromise. And in that compromise, he or she tries to accommodate the major ideas at the extremes by moderating them into a middle of the road approach.

And a third reason why the research does not follow more closely the prescriptions of the theoreticians is because some researchers become question-driven rather than approach-driven as they get into their study. They may begin with an approach orientation in the framing of their question and in their initial planning. However, once they become involved in the collection of evidence, the organization of that evidence, and the drawing of conclusions, the question becomes the real guide to the decision making. In short, some researchers may shift their locus away from the approach (and its prescriptions) to the question (and its requirements for building a good answer). Therefore, some researchers may begin with a relatively pure form of a methodology then gradually find themselves bending it to fit their needs and respond to the demands of data collection and analysis. These researchers are not interested in preserving the methodology in pure form; instead, they are guided by the demands of their question so they reshape their "home" methodology, sometimes to the point of creating hybrids or even moving into a wholly different methodology—one that may be part of another approach. A strength of the qualitative approach is that it allows this to happen and even supports this creativity through its variety of perspectives. In the scientific approach, the methodologies are more rigid and require that certain decisions be made; even so, we see that scientific researchers bend the decisions in their drive to make their answers appear as more interesting or compelling responses to their questions. An example of this is the requirement of probability sampling in order to generalize. But scientific researchers who do not have a probability sample will work hard to present a case for generalization because their findings framed as such would appear as a better answer to their questions.

Finally, there is another characteristic that seems to be supporting a synthesis of the two approaches. Like scientific researchers, qualitative researchers exhibit a concern that their individual studies contribute to a progression of their field, even though there are some qualitative theoreticians who reject the notion of progression. In science, the progression is toward more parsimonious explanations, that is, more pithy explanations of a wider scope of human activity over a broader range of people. In qualitative research, the progression is to broaden the perspectives and also to give greater weight to certain perspectives (such as ideological arguments). In this way, an individual research study makes a difference by changing the level of understanding. In order to accomplish this, qualitative researchers know they must be concerned with the context of their field and must make a case for situating their contribution within that context. This form of contextualization along with a drive toward progressively higher levels of understanding of the media are conditions shared by researchers in both approaches. Because these are fundamental perspectives in research communities, the sharing of these perspectives indicates fertile soil to support the growth of a greater degree of convergence.

Forces Supporting Convergence

It is believed for the reasons just stated, that there are many points where the two approaches are complementary. Also, holistically, there appears to be a fair degree of overlap and synthesis. Furthermore, there are foundational reasons that would support a continued movement toward an even greater degree of convergence.

I am not alone in my perception of some convergence. For example, Lindlof (1991) also perceived a complementary relationship between the two approaches. According to him, when "we have a better grasp of their different assumptions . . . and their specific strengths" (p. 33), the qualitative and quantitative designs might be complementary.

Taking an even wider perspective on this issue is Toulmin (1983), who argued that the division between the natural sciences and the humanities is not as strong or rigid as people think. Both employ a hermeneutic process of discovery and interpretation. He said, "the supposed contrast between the scientists' claim to rational objectivity (which requires no interpretation) and the humanists' rival claim to subjective sensibility (in which interpretation is all) shows *on its face* its essential irrelevance to the actual work of art and science. At most, there is a difference of balance or emphasis" (p. 111). Further, Toulmin argued, "We should ask scholars to pay more attention to the elements of interpretation—even of hermeneutics—that have nowadays become essential to both the natural and human sciences and to base their comparisons between the sciences and humanities not on the assumed *absence* of hermeneutic interpretation from natural science but rather on the different *modes* of interpretation characteristic of the two general fields" (p. 101).

Forces Against Convergence

But there are also scholars who argue that it is not possible to have a convergence of the two approaches. For example, Ang (1989) argued against the possibility of convergence by saying there are "fundamental differences not only in epistemological, but also in theoretical and political attitudes toward the aim and status of doing empirical research as such" (p. 100). Although the two approaches agree on the importance of regarding the audience as active, she asserted that the definition of active is different across the two perspectives. She also perceived a lack of convergence methodologically because some phenomena are "too complex to be molded into empirically testable hypotheses"

(p. 103). Ironically, she credited the work of Morley (1980) in his *The "Nationwide" Audience* as producing "an innovative departure within cultural studies, both theoretically and methodologically" (p. 99), because it was an ethnography and exhibited some trappings of science. She also said that some mainstream researchers have picked up on semiological terms of reader and text. She contrasted "mainstream" research with "critical" research showing how they are different, *and* how they are the same. "The basic assumption that the television audience is 'active' (rather than passive) and that watching television is a social (rather than an individual) practice is currently accepted in both perspectives" (p. 101). But despite these points of similarity, she did not perceive a possibility of convergence.

Ang (1989) also argued that contextualization is an important unresolvable difference, saying:

> rather than dissecting "audience activity" into variables and categories in order to be able to study them one by one, so that we could ultimately have a complete and generalizable "map" of all dimensions of "audience activity," which seems to be the drive behind the uses and gratifications project, the aim of cultural studies, as I see it, is to arrive at a more historicized insight into the ways in which "audience activity" is related to social and political structures and processes. In other words, what is at stake is not the understanding of "audience activity" as such as an isolated and isolable phenomenon and object of research, but the embeddedness of "audience activity" in a network of ongoing cultural practices and relationships. (p. 101)

There is another factor that acts against a further convergence—the oppositional nature preferred by many qualitative scholars, especially critical ones. To remove science as a target of criticism would make many of these critics feel less of a sense of community and would take away some of the tools they have grown familiar with using in the establishment of their legitimacy. When we take a historical view on the use of the qualitative approach in media studies, it is understandable that researchers who prefer the qualitative approach have felt that their work has been excluded from traditional scholarly forums by those scholars adhering to the dominant approach of science. So in order to gain entry and legitimize their approach, they have displayed a clear adversarial stance and attacked the scientific approach. For example, they characterized it as being "in grave danger of becoming an almost moribund area of media studies" (Lewis, 1991, p. 23) and even a "thoroughly discredited research philosophy" (Allen, 1985, p. 5). Seiter et al. (1989b) said social science research has "proven quite inadequate to the task of understanding television viewing" (p. 2). Gitlin (1978) argued that it is an approach that defines " 'effects' so narrowly, microscopically, and directly as to make it very likely that survey studies could show only slight effects at most. It has enshrined short-run 'effects' as 'measures' of 'importance' largely because these 'effects' are measurable in a strict, replicable behavioral sense, thereby deflecting attention from larger social meanings of mass media production" (p. 206). But these are many of the same scholars who now say that the qualitative approach is the dominant one in media studies. So they must feel that a sense of legitimacy has been achieved. If this is so, then the need for attacks on science is greatly reduced, and the adversarial mechanism may be dismantling.

The most important force behind convergence is the desire of scholars to want it to happen. If many do not want a movement toward convergence, then it is fruitless to speculate about strategies. If scholars have closed their minds to the possibility, then none of the analyses in this book will have much value. If scholars want to preserve the present condition of separatism, then not much can be said to convince them to change their minds. There are powerful and legitimate forces that keep perceptions of separateness in place. A separateness builds a stronger sense of identity among those creating the separate community. Also, a separateness makes it possible for critical scholars to have an "other" to criticize. Without this other, their essays are not as interesting, and they do not generate as much light as well as heat. Some readers may be perceiving some facetiousness here, but it is not intentional. I have seen students whose personalities and world views make it impossible for them to understand or conform to the tenets of the scientific approach (or to the tenets of the qualitative approach). Without an alternative approach, these students, many of whom are very bright and motivated, would have no alternative and could not be scholars. The qualitative approach gives them that lifeline alternative. It is small wonder then that they feel a fierce sense of identity with the approach and seek to build a solid community with which they can identify.

Types of Synthesis

In the writings of Lancy (1993) and Schwandt (1989), there are essentially four views of convergence laid out. First, there is the antecedent view where qualitative is viewed as a pilot test for the "real" work of science. Second, there is the view where the qualitative approach can be subsumed under the scientific umbrella. Third, there is the view where the scientific approach can be subsumed under the qualitative umbrella. And fourth, there is the approach were both are viewed as complementary to each other. The arguments supporting each of these take place at the methodology or methods levels. That is, scholars will show how the product of one method will fit nicely into the beginning stage of another method. Or scholars will show that differing methods can be fit together in some way so as to accommodate the needs of one or both approaches. Many of these arguments are convincing, because most of the methods of data gathering and analysis are rather generic at base, and they can therefore be used as tools in many different situations.

Do comparisons at the methods level offer satisfying insights into the issue of convergence? Schwandt (1989) in particular cautioned against the arguments that ignore the foundational issues underlying the approaches. A certain method can be used in both approaches, but the way it was used or the product of its use may be very different given the approach's purpose, view of the phenomenon, and axiomatic base. Schwandt, of course, was right to ask for the inclusion of more factors in the analysis, thus making it a higher order analysis by moving it up from the methods or methodologies to the level of the approach.

My perspective is to take the analysis one more step up from the level of approach to a still higher conceptual level that I refer to as scholarship. The approaches are approaches *to* scholarship. When we conduct the analysis at the approach level, the methods and methodologies are treated as tools to the approach, and they are evaluated in terms of how they contribute to the nature of the approach. At the scholarship level, it is the approaches that are the tools, and the approaches themselves must be evaluated in terms of how they contribute to the nature of scholarship.

What is the nature of scholarship? With media studies, scholarship has as its goal the generation of insights in answer to the question: How do humans create meaning in interaction with the media? This is the fundamental question that generates all the research, regardless of approach. Answers to this question can be descriptive, interpretive, explanatory, and action oriented. They can focus on the parametric as well as nonparametric facets of the phenomenon, on audiences, texts, or institutions. In illuminating insights, the answers can rely on all forms of primary and secondary evidence, past and current. They allow for many different voices and perspectives.

Scholars who focus primarily on the question are less bound by the approaches themselves. In contrast, scholars who focus primarily on an approach must continually translate their question into the limitations of the approach, and the resulting answers are correspondingly less insightful. Scholars who focus primarily on the approach limit their understanding of all the possibilities of the question. And finally, scholars who focus primarily on the approach often do not see their limitations, and as they stand inside their approach and look out onto another approach that they do not understand or trust, they see the issue of convergence as hopeless.

Scholars who focus primarily on the question can make a greater contribution. However, they have a greater responsibility, because they will need to learn how to use more tools and even how to create their own hybrid tools to get the answers they need. These are the scholars who are achieving an integration of the approaches. The more scholars in a field who are question focused, the less important the methods debates will become and the more interesting the insights about the phenomenon will be.

APPENDIX

ABSTRACTS OF WRITINGS USED IN INTERPRETIVE ANALYSIS

TEXT-FOCUSED RESEARCH

Examples of Textual Analysis Methodology

Barker, D. (1987). Television production techniques as communication. In H. Newcomb (Ed.), *Television: The critical view* (4th ed., pp. 179–196). New York: Oxford University Press.

This essay focuses on the texts of television and the author's inferences about the production decisions made to encode images. Barker's thesis was that "the communicative ability of any television narrative is, in large part, a function of the production techniques utilized in its creation" (p. 179).

He examined two programs, "All in the Family" and "M*A*S*H." He said he chose 20 episodes of each program randomly and gave them a close reading in order to compare their production techniques. However, his analysis focuses mainly on one episode of each series.

The analysis looks at camera space and performer space in a comparative analysis of the two shows.

Esslin, M. (1987). Aristotle and the advertisers: The television commercial considered as a form of drama. In H. Newcomb (Ed.), *Television: The critical view* (4th ed., pp. 304–317). New York: Oxford University Press.

Esslin argued that the TV ad can be considered drama and analyzed as such. He demonstrated by using various dramaturgical devices, drawing from Aristotle and his Greek terms for the structure, three-beat structures, myth, characterization, and image. He said that the TV commercial universe reflects the fantasies and implied beliefs

333

in the mass of viewers; it is not a creation of producers who are intent on controlling people. "The TV commercial ... is the ritual manifestation of the basic myth of our society and as such not only its most ubiquitous but also its most significant form of folk drama" (p. 316).

Flitterman-Lewis, S. (1992). All's well that doesn't end—Soap opera and the marriage motif. In L. Spigel & D. Mann (Eds.), *Private screenings: Television and the female consumer* (pp. 217–225). Minneapolis: University of Minnesota Press.

Flitterman-Lewis contrasted television, especially soap operas, with film where film moves toward closure in a unifying narrative, whereas television presents a "profusion and dispersal of narrative elements" that fit well with "the varied and casual attention which distinguishes television from film" (p. 217).

She looked at two weddings that took place on "General Hospital." She used a psychoanalytic perspective (dreams, sex, fantasy) model to analyze these texts.

Her conclusions equivocate by saying that the wedding schemes are characteristic and not characteristic of soap opera structure.

Schwichtenberg, C. (1987). *The Love Boat*: The packaging and selling of love, heterosexual romance, and family. In H. Newcomb (Ed.), *Television: The critical view* (4th ed., pp. 126–140). New York: Oxford University Press.

Schwichtenberg criticized "The Love Boat" for presenting an ideology (*a la* Althusser) in which love is made a commodity that is bought with a ticket to the cruise.

Using semiology, she examined the show's opening sequence to determine how the promise of love is put forth. Then she used a narrative analysis of one of the playlets.

She called for sinking the ship, because it makes a false promise to its viewers.

Symbolic Interactionism Methodology

Bird, S. E., & Dardenne, R. W. (1988). Myth, chronicle, and story: Exploring the narrative qualities of news. In J. W. Carey (Ed.), *Media, myths, and narratives: Television and the press* (pp. 67–86). Beverly Hills, CA: Sage.

The purpose of this textual analysis is to look at the narrative qualities of news and to infer what it means to construct such stories. Bird and Dardenne looked at the news genre as a particular kind of symbolic system. They wanted to explore the difference between the reality of events and the symbols that are used to construct stories about that reality.

They examined "news stories as a whole—both as a body of work that is a continuing story of human activity, and as individual stories that contribute to that continuing one" (p. 69).

They argued that news follows a mythological narrative that is ritualistic, communal, and orienting. Myth does not reflect objective reality, but instead builds a world of its own in order to explain baffling or frightening phenomena. "News is a particular kind of mythological narrative with its own symbolic codes that are recognized by its audience" (pp. 71–72). Journalists are governed by the grammar of their culture. If we study the models of news narratives, we can learn about the values and symbols of a given culture.

Cultural Analysis Methodology

Anderson, C. (1987). Reflections on *Magnum, P.I.* In H. Newcomb (Ed.), *Television: The critical view* (4th ed., pp. 112–125). New York: Oxford University Press.

This is an essay of personal reflections on a detective show that is a favorite of the author.

Anderson focused on the series "Magnum, P.I.," and referred to different episodes, but we are not told why he cited the particular episodes he did other than in his opinion some are very good (higher quality "than any movie nominated for an Academy Award this year," p. 112) and some are very bad. He used a narrative analysis.

He asserted that television "has developed a narrative structure based heavily upon formulaic repetition, common cultural codes ... and an emphasis upon narrative fragmentation rather than narrative unity" (p. 121). He attempted to show how "Magnum, P.I." both fits the conventions of television and breaks with those traditions—especially the detective format.

Chesebro, J. W. (1987). Communication, values, and popular television series—A four-year assessment. In H. Newcomb (Ed.), *Television: The critical view* (4th ed., pp. 17–51). New York: Oxford University Press.

Chesebro framed the study by asking four questions: (a) What patterns, types, or kinds of human relationships are portrayed in popular television series? (b) How are human problems and difficulties resolved in popular television series? (c) What images or character references are portrayed in popular television series? and (d) How have popular television series changed, particularly in the last 4 years?

Drawing primarily from the ideas of Herbert Simon and Kenneth Burke, he developed a "theory of logical types" (ironic, mimetic, leader, romantic, mythical) to use in categorizing television shows. He presented an example of each type: ironic - Archie Bunker; mimetic - Fish; leader-centered - Maude; romantic - Charlie's Angels; mythical - Steve Austin, the $6-million man.

He categorized prime-time series to determine changes from 1973 to 1978.

He found that the mimetic type of show grew whereas the leader type of show shrunk. He also looked at the demographic of the characters and concluded that the profile has not changed with the White, single, urban, professional man as the most prevalent character.

D'Acci, J. (1992). Defining women: The case of *Cagney and Lacey*. In L. Spigel & D. Mann (Eds.), *Private screenings: Television and the female consumer* (pp. 169–201). Minneapolis: University of Minnesota Press.

The purpose of this study is to reveal the "cultural struggle over the meanings of femininity as this was played out on prime-time television during the period from 1981 to 1988" (p. 170).

D'Acci focused on the development of "Cagney and Lacey" throughout its run from 1982 to 1988. Examples from individual episodes are cited to support her feminist analysis.

She provided a good deal of context about the show's development and reactions to it from both audience members and network executives. Audience interpretations are not necessarily those intended by the producers. The essay is descriptive and interpretive until the end when it is critical. "I hope we continue to agitate for a greater representation of *difference* in all the mass media ... it is important not to concede television and its representations to the discourses and energies of the New Right" (p. 194).

Deming, R. H. (1992). *Kate and Allie*: "New women" and the audience's television archives. In L. Spigel & D. Mann (Eds.), *Private screenings: Television and the female consumer* (pp. 203–215). Minneapolis: University of Minnesota Press.

This is a cultural analysis of a prime-time television program. Its purpose is to "argue for the ways in which *Kate and Allie* constructs a form of female subjectivity which is constrained by the new-woman sitcom formal, but at the same time, allows for the playing out of cultural and social contradictions" (p. 204). Deming wanted to show that the program "offers various types of involvement for its viewers because it is composed of numerous discourses, ideological propositions and modes of address, which together form a popular, at times progressive, but not necessarily feminist text" (p. 204).

He focused on one television show, "Kate and Allie" during the 1984–1985 season and analyzed several episodes key to making his main point. He also looked at industry trends and expectations for the program.

He provided a good deal of context about the show's development and reactions to it from both audience members and network executives. He demonstrated that the interpretation is an intertextual process; that is, the TV audience draws on a repertoire of images from previous texts to make sense of any one program.

Douglas, S. J. (1993). Will you love me tomorrow? Changing discourses about female sexuality in the mass media, 1960–1968. In W. S. Solomon & R. W. McChesney (Eds.), *Ruthless criticism: New perspectives in U.S. communication history* (pp. 349–373). Minneapolis: University of Minnesota Press.

This is an analysis of texts to demonstrate the changes in the way female sexuality was portrayed during the 1960s. The focus is on popular music, movies, and television shows. Douglas took a feministic point of view.

Haralovich, M. B. (1992). Sit-coms and suburbs: Positioning the 1950s homemaker. In L. Spigel & D. Mann (Eds.), *Private screenings: Television and the female consumer* (pp. 111–141). Minneapolis: University of Minnesota Press.

This cultural analysis of homemakers in situation comedies presents a social history along with a textual analysis of several programs.

Haralovich examined the texts of some 1950s sitcoms, especially "Father Knows Best" and "Leave it to Beaver." She interpreted these texts from a feminist ideology.

She argued that these sitcoms were successful because they presented role models that were popular at the time, although "the working class is marginalized and minorities are absent" (p. 112). The suburban family sitcom was used to position women as homemakers and to naturalize a homogeneous and socially stable community. She concluded that the "durability of the suburban family sit-com indicates the degree of institutional as well as popular support for ideologies that naturalize class and gender identities" (p. 138).

Himmelstein, H. (1984). *Television myth and the American mind.* New York: Praeger.

Himmelstein used myth analysis as a critical strategy in locating the meanings in television programs and ads. His goal was to demythologize the ideology in TV messages so as to reveal the constructed nature of the reality presented by television. He then suggested alternative realities that are "representations rejected outright or coopted by the dominant television apparatus" (p. 7). He defined ideology as "a constructed belief system that explains economic, political, and social reality to people and establishes collective goals of a class, group, or, in the case of a dominant ideology, the entire society" (p. 3). It is the image society gives to itself in order to perpetuate itself. Ideologies make up our commonsenscial views. Myths are regarded as transforming that commonsense into a sacred realm of eternal truth by making them appear to have existed before culture began. But there is another kind of myth besides this "sacred" myth; there are also secular myths, which are described by Marxist critics such as Barthes as "insidious vehicles employed to consolidate the power of the dominant capitalist class" (p. 7). Himmelstein focused on these secular myths and showed that they are not myths in any enduring sacred way, but instead are constructed ideologies.

He focused on eight types of programs: situation comedies, social comedies, melodrama, news and documentaries, sports and live events, religious shows, game shows, and talk shows.

He argued that regardless of the type of program, there are six traditional mainstream values: (a) the sanctity of the "ordinary" American family, (b) triumph of personal initiative over the bureaucratic control and inefficiency of the state, (c) one's gain at another's expense, (d) elevated status of quiet authority in the status hierarchy of power and social control, (e) celebration of celebrity, and (f) conversion of history and the deflection of questions of social structure into the "personal." In his last chapter, he presented some strategies for change.

Horowitz, S. (1987). Sitcom domesticus—A species endangered by social change. In H. Newcomb (Ed.), *Television: The critical view* (4th ed., pp. 106–111). New York: Oxford University Press.

Horowitz analyzed the portrayals on "Kate and Allie" and made generalizations about how situation comedies have changed. Her thesis is that viewer interest in sitcoms waned, because sitcoms have failed to keep pace with the changes in society.

This is a very short and superficial treatment of the subject. Also, there are no scholarly research traditions acknowledged and no literature is cited. It is purely personal speculation.

Joyrich, L. (1992). All that television allows: TV melodrama, postmodernism, and consumer culture. In L. Spigel & D. Mann (Eds.), *Private screenings: Television and the female consumer* (pp. 227–251). Minneapolis: University of Minnesota Press.

Joyrich attempted to "map out the discursive connections forced between melodrama and postmodern consumer culture, focusing on the problems of gender constituted within this field" (p. 229). She defined melodrama as focusing on bourgeois domesticity and passivity; it uses music to convey emotional effects. Melodramas offer no final closure so its narratives "are circular, repetitive and unresolvable" (p. 238).

She referred to a wide variety of television programs ranging from "General Hospital" to "Max Headroom," "Hill Street Blues" to "Dynasty." She used postmodernism, the consumer culture, and feminism as perspectives for interpreting television melodramas.

She examined television as a text and argued that melodrama has become the dominant generic form for television programming. She said, "As a feminist ... I hope it [melodrama] may work to steel women for resistance.... By reading TV melodramas against the grain and providing our own ironic commentaries, feminist criticisms may continue to bring out the contradictions of the TV age" (p. 247).

Kinder, M. (1987). Music video and the spectator: Television, ideology, and dream. In H. Newcomb (Ed.), *Television: The critical view* (4th ed., pp. 229–254). New York: Oxford University Press.

Kinder looked at MTV rock videos as a model of commercial television. She looked at the types of visual images (performance, narrative, and dreamlike). She also examined issues of whether a spectator is present in the video, presence of TV receivers, structural discontinuity, and decentering.

Her sample is limited to rock videos on MTV. There is no information provided concerning how those videos were chosen or how many were in her sample.

She categorized videos by those dominated by performance, those dominated by narrative, and those dominated by dreamlike visuals. She also found that an important characteristic of videos is the omnipresence of the spectator; that is, we are shown people watching the performance. She said that the structural discontinuity of the programming decenters viewers and forces them to fill in the blanks.

Lipsitz, G. (1992). The meaning of memory: Family class, and ethnicity in early network television programs. In L. Spigel & D. Mann (Eds.), *Private screenings: Television and the female consumer* (pp. 71–109). Minneapolis: University of Minnesota Press.

Lipsitz examined 1950s dramas as products of their social and economic history of the times. His thesis is that the working-class sitcoms "evoked the experiences of the past to lend legitimacy to the dominant ideology of the present ... and served important social and cultural functions" (pp. 72–73).

He argued that television was used to legitimate consumption. The 1930s and 1940s included an economic depression, a political shift to a welfare state, and big government involvement in a world war. After the war, the economy shifted to large-scale production of consumer products, and television was the central force to increase consumer spending, not just with ads, but with the values presented in the fictional programming.

Mann, D. (1992). The spectacularization of everyday life: Recycling Hollywood stars and fans in early television variety shows. In L. Spigel & D. Mann (Eds.), *Private screenings: Television and the female consumer* (pp. 41–69). Minneapolis: University of Minnesota Press.

This is a cultural analysis of how film stars were regarded by Americans in the 1940s to the 1950s and how they were introduced into the television world.

The study focuses on two types of TV shows, comedy variety and musical variety, from 1946 to 1956.

Mann said that TV variety shows served to take Hollywood stars and reduce their aura so that they could be seen as common people and thereby enter viewers' homes. She asserted that this was an important part of the negotiation process between the film and TV industries.

Newcomb, H. M. (1988). One night of prime time: An analysis of television's multiple voices. In J. W. Carey (Ed.), *Media, myths, and narratives: Television and the press* (pp. 88–112). Beverly Hills, CA: Sage.

Using a combination of formal and social analysis, Newcomb looked at four particular shows to find the type of voices expressed there. He used this analysis to "illustrate" (generalize?) the storytelling nature of television and the differing interpretations viewers can have.

He took as his text an entire night of prime-time television aired on three commercial networks on October 3, 1985.

He said that audiences "read in such personalized, idiosyncratic, locally determined ways that it becomes impossible to 'read off' the text any totalizing, determining response" (p 90). "Television must be seen as dynamic rather than static, as processural rather than merely as a product, as fissured and contradictory rather than monolithic, polysemic rather than univocal" (p. 90). This leaves the reader with the questions, What is the point of textual analysis? and Should research shift to reception analysis?

Rowland, W. D., Jr. (1983). *The politics of TV violence: Policy uses of communication research.* Beverly Hills, CA: Sage.

The strange relationship between policy and research is examined historically and critically, particularly on the topic of the effects of violence on television. The focus is on "the interaction among the federal, political process of communication policy-making, the broadcasting industry, the public or citizen's interest groups, and the communication research community" (p. 16). The major players are the academy, industry, government, and reformers.

The data are primarily the "hearings, records, and reports of the various congressional committees and national commissions involved in federal attempts to grapple with television and the question of its content. These records are examined for the patterns of argument advanced by the leading research spokesmen, industry representatives, public interest group leaders, and political figures" (p. 17).

Rowland presented a history of mass communication research and how it has changed in terms of its rhetoric and its influence on policymaking.

Schulze, L. (1990). The made-for-TV movie: Industrial practice, cultural form, popular reception. In T. Balio (Ed.), *Hollywood in the age of television* (pp. 351–376). Boston: Unwin Hyman.

This is an analysis of made-for-TV movies set in a cultural history of film and television.

Schulze referred to many made-for-TV movies and used them as examples of certain themes or portrayals. Only one example, "Getting Physical," is analyzed in any detail.

She concluded that made-for-TV movies have emerged "as a privileged site for acknowledging and negotiating some of the most contested issues in American society" (p. 371), especially the social issue movie, which "has taken on a pedagogical function" (p. 371) and which "frequently brings the socially marginalized . . . onto popular terrain" (p. 371). She argued that "the typical TV movie is more than escapist trash or depoliticized fluff" (p. 372).

Zynda, T. H. (1988). The *Mary Tyler Moore Show* and the transformation of situation comedy. In J. W. Carey (Ed.), *Media, myths, and narratives: Television and the press* (pp. 126–145). Beverly Hills, CA: Sage.

Zynda focused on both the text and the institutional history of the "Mary Tyler Moore Show."

He argued that, despite what its producers said, the show does present a political point of view; the politics are not direct like with Norman Lear's shows or with "M*A*S*H," but the show does follow the pattern of socialist realism painting developed in the Soviet Union in the 1930s, which is considered more propaganda than art. He said that the "Mary Tyler Moore Show" is static; that is, characters do not evolve or develop and the settings as well as plots are the same episode after episode. Therefore, he could not use a narrative analysis and instead had to use an aesthetic analysis. In the aesthetic sense, the "Mary Tyler Moore Show" resembles a socialist realist painting that glorifies work, even though the workers are in stifling, static jobs.

AUDIENCE-FOCUSED RESEARCH

Ethnography Methodology

Turkle, S. (1984). *The second self: Computers and the human spirit.* New York: Simon & Schuster.

This is an ethnography of computer cultures. Turkle's purpose was to look at the subjective impact of the computer on individuals. Instead of regarding the computer as an analytical machine (rational, uniform, logical), she treated it as an evocative object—something that disturbs equanimity, fascinates, and precipitates thought. The computer has holding power and this power creates the condition for other things to happen. She dealt with questions of whether the computer is alive in some sense, whether it has intelligence, or whether it can ever "think" like humans.

She lived in computer cultures for 6 years, participating when possible in their lives and rituals. She interviewed people who could help her understand things from the inside. She talked to over 200 children and more than 200 adults (p. 321), broadly so as to get a range of perspectives.

She looked at the differences in how people regard the computer by age, gender, and personality. She looked at what places some people at "risk," that is, getting stuck with the computer. From a sociology of knowledge perspective, she examined how scientific information and concepts move out into the general population.

Her analysis is patterned after ideal types. She chose to describe people who exemplify certain relationships with the computer. She attempted a synthesis but not to construct average or typical types of computer users. Instead, she wanted to identify the significant dimensions along which people differed, then to present some cases that marked those dimensions. Her dimensions of computer usage are metaphysics (life and existence), mastery, and identity. There is a range of behavior within each of these dimensions.

She arrayed her descriptions between two extremes. On the one extreme is technological determinism where technology itself (the computer) determines behavior regardless of the person. At the other extreme is the idea that the influence of a technology can be understood only in terms of the meanings people give to it. She rejected both extremes.

Her templates of analyses are anthropological (computer cultures), Piagetian development, self-reflexivity (Godel, Escher, Bach), and psychoanalysis.

Wolf, M. (1987). How children negotiate television. In T. R. Lindlof (Ed.), *Natural audiences: Qualitative research of media uses and effects* (pp. 58–94). Norwood, NJ: Ablex.

This is an ethnography examining how children understand the characters and stories of television entertainment. Also, Wolf looked at how children negotiated their own television production ideas.

The author and seven research assistants informally observed and interviewed 107 children (ages 4–12 years) in a day-care/summer camp facility over a 10-month period.

There is a detailed description of data collection and analysis. Her main finding is that children are fairly sophisticated in their understanding of the conventions of television and that the level of understanding is not related to age or Piagetian developmental stages.

She showed that there is a variety of ways children negotiate television and these are not related to age. The ways were laid out in a priori schemes, especially by Applebee who provided the team with a structure for the conventions children use in making sense of fictional narratives (story frameworks, theme, fantasy/reality, and ways of constructing reactions to stories).

Ethnomethodology

Rakow, L. F. (1992). *Gender on the line: Women, the telephone, and community life.* Urbana: University of Illinois Press.

This is an ethnomethodology focusing on how various women in a small town make meaning of the telephone in their everyday lives.

Rakow lived in the community of Prospect (fictional name) for 6 weeks in the fall of 1985. She identified herself as a researcher, but kept the fact that she was a feminist hidden. She interviewed 43 women of all kinds in the small town of 1,000. She talked about gaining acceptance: "As a woman, I was a participant; as a feminist I was the observer" (p. 8). She presented a good deal of description of the town, and most of the book (chapters 4 through 8; pp. 83–147) is a description of the stories of six women in their own words.

The major conclusion is that it is extremely important to contextualize gender and technology in order to understand the meanings women hold. It is also important to look at historical changes in the social practices and experiences of the women. The use of the phone is an extension of their place in the community:

> Though the telephone has the technical capacity to level social hierarchies, to end feelings of isolation and loneliness, to provide the liberating function for doing whatever we want with it, technical possibility has not translated into social practice. In part this is because the telephone was introduced into a gendered world, within which it became embedded, and hence it has become a site at which gender relations are organized, experienced, and accomplished in both the family and the larger community and political world. (p. 154)

Traudt, P. J., & Lont, C. M. (1987). Media-logic-in-use: The family as locus of study. In T. R. Lindlof (Ed.), *Natural audiences: Qualitative research of media uses and effects* (pp. 139–160). Norwood, NJ: Ablex.

This is an ethnomethodology focusing on "how social reality is constructed by members of the family household, and how television contributes to the common stock-of-knowledge shared by family members within this process of social construction" (p. 140).

It is a case study of one family and how its five members used television. Researchers visited the home 14 times within 3 months and observed behavior. They also audio-taped interviews and had the family fill out quarter-hour viewing diaries for 2 weeks.

The researchers concluded that "television provides a significant resource for the construction of experiences and knowledge regarding one's self, one's role as a family member, and one's role in life outside the home" (p. 159). Also, "television's presentational logic comes to represent a media consciousness on the part of family members" (p. 159).

Reception Studies

Individual Reception. The authors of these studies presented their findings with the explanation that they are idiosyncratic to the individual; that is, each individual reads the program differently and each has his or her own unique interpretation. There are overlaps in interpretation because there are not an infinite number of unique interpretations; but those interpretations are not identical, nor are they attributed to a group.

Ang, I. (1985). *Watching "Dallas": Soap operas and the melodramatic imagination.* New York: Methuen.

Ang looked at viewers' experience of "Dallas" and the relationship between pleasure and ideology.

She placed an ad in a Dutch newspaper asking for replies from viewers of "Dallas" and got 42 written replies, from a few lines to 10 pages. She said she read the letters symptomatically—"must search for what is behind the explicitly written, for the presuppositions and accepted attitudes concealed within them" (p. 11).

She found a range of reactions to "Dallas." These differences were analyzed from several different perspectives: reality/fiction, melodramatic imagination, ideology of mass culture, and feminism.

Bodroghkozy, A. (1992). "Is this what you mean by color TV?": Race, gender, and contested meanings in NBC's *Julia.* In L. Spigel & D. Mann (Eds.), *Private screenings: Television and the female consumer* (pp. 143–167). Minneapolis: University of Minnesota Press.

This is primarily a reception study even though this presents an analysis of some the scripts of "Julia." Bodroghkozy wanted to explore how racial tension and conflicts by different groups in American society were reflected in the reactions to this program.

The author did not interview viewers; she examined their letters (151 sent to the producers during the 3-year run of the show). She also examined the criticism of the show published in the press.

She concluded that there was "no one preferred, dominant, or definitive set of meanings attached to *Julia*" (p. 164). The interpretations of "Julia" were based on social, cultural, and racial backgrounds of the particular viewers.

Hobson, D. (1982). *"Crossroads": The drama of a soap opera.* London: Methuen.

This book deals with the production of a British serial. Several chapters describe a reception study about how English housewives view soap operas and why.

Hobson did not describe her methods, saying that "this book is not a suitable site for long explanations of the academic research techniques and the theoretical principles on which it is based" (p. 107). However, she appeared to have talked informally (unstructured interviews) with many viewers of the show. In the case of some viewers, she watched the program with them in their homes then interviewed them.

She found that viewers related soap opera happenings to the things in their own lives. The viewers recognized the strategies and identified with the characters. Viewers are in a superior position to producers because the viewers know better if the characters are behaving realistically.

Lewis, J. (1991). *The ideological octopus*. New York: Routledge.

The first half presents a textbooklike treatment of audience research and qualitative (especially semiology and cultural studies) methods. Then Lewis presented two chapters, each of which is an empirical study using reception analysis. In the first of these studies, his purpose was "to explore the precise nature of the ideological power of TV news" (p. 108). He selected a purposive sample of British news viewers representing a range of backgrounds and ages.

His empirical work is based on two samples. In the first were 50 sessions where an individual was shown the news program then interviewed. In the other study, he focused on how groups of people interpreted an episode of "The Cosby Show." The sample included 23 African-American groups and 27 White groups of Americans who were shown an episode of "The Cosby Show" in a person's home, then interviewed.

With his first study, he found that news programs do not communicate the messages they intend to convey (i.e., information about current events) but they do convey an ideological position. With the second study, the ideology is more ambiguous and its effect rests with individual audiences finding something in the show to resonate with their own ideologies; the polysemic nature of the show leads to a variety of readings.

Tulloch, J. (1989). Approaching the audience: The elderly. In E. Seiter, H. Borchers, G. Kreutzner, & E.-M. Warth (Eds.), *Remote control: Television, audiences, and cultural power* (pp. 180–203). New York: Routledge.

This is a reception study examining the meanings soap operas hold for elderly people in England.

The sample consisted of 20 elderly people interviewed in their homes twice. Each interview, which was about 1–2 hours, were about a year apart. Tulloch presented the information as case studies. He asked them about their "television likes and dislikes, their viewing habits, daily routine, and little of their past background" (p. 184).

His main finding is that the elderly exhibit a wide range of motives and habits of viewing soap operas. They are rather isolated from one another so they do not form interpretive communities like other age viewers often do. He displayed a good amount of self-reflexivity in talking about his project; that is, he talked about why he made the decisions he did and presented his biases.

Group-Level Analysis of Reception. The authors of these studies place a primary emphasis on explaining their findings as being attributable to social groups with which people associate.

Hobson, D. (1989). Soap operas at work. In E. Seiter, H. Borchers, G. Kreutzner, & E.-M. Warth (Eds.), *Remote control: Television, audiences, and cultural power* (pp. 150–167). New York: Routledge.

This reception study looks at the way soap operas "are incorporated into the lives of viewers outside their home, at their workplace. It also explores the way that fiction is interwoven with events in the 'real' world" (p. 150).

Six working women were interviewed informally during lunch in a nightclub in Birmingham, England. The interviews were recorded, and a secretary took notes.

Soap opera viewers are active viewers, discussing the events and characters in the shows with their coworkers. They continually compare the portrayals to their own lives. These conclusions are very weak; in fact the article is not very scholarly with no literature cited, no intellectual history developed, and a conversational (but highly readable) tone.

Jhally, S., & Lewis, J. (1992). *The Cosby Show, audiences, and the myth of the American dream*. Boulder, CO: Westview Press.

The purpose of this study was to interpret viewers' reactions to "The Cosby Show" in terms of race, gender, and class.

Jhally and Lewis interviewed viewers in 52 small (did not say how many people) focus groups, each composed by race (23 African-American, 3 Hispanic-American, and 26 White). People were shown a videotape of an episode then asked questions about their attitudes toward race, gender, and class. The transcribed audiotapes were analyzed by the authors.

They said they began the study with a positive reaction to the show and thought that audiences would like the portrayals. However, they found that African-Americans did not see the show as a celebration of African-American upward mobility. In contrast, Whites liked the idea of seeing African Americans succeed without affirmative action help.

Liebes, T., & Katz, E. (1988). *Dallas* and genesis: Primordiality and seriality in popular culture. In J. W. Carey (Ed.), *Media, myths, and narratives: Television and the press* (pp. 113–125). Beverly Hills, CA: Sage.

This is part of a larger research program that examines how people around the world decode "Dallas." In this essay, Liebes and Katz looked at the text itself for why people are attracted to the show and they focused on the semantic element of primordiality and the syntactic element of its seriality.

Interviews were conducted with people from four Israeli ethnic communities (Moroccan Jews, Arabs, Russian Jews, and people living in Israeli kibbutzum) and nonethnic Americans in Los Angeles. People were interviewed in groups of six friends in private homes. People were shown an episode of "Dallas" then asked to discuss it.

The conclusions were developed inductively through interviews. They found that American programs like "Dallas" "invite multiple levels of understanding and involvement, offering a wide variety of different projects and games to different types of viewers" (p. 114). They found three major patterns in the decodings. First were the traditional viewers who remain in the "real" world and "mobilize values to defend themselves against the program" (p. 116). Second, the more Western groups deal with its reality in a playful fashion. And third, the Russians are the most serious as they focus on the underlying message rather than the structure of the program. Finally, the authors explained the show's appeal in terms of its primordiality (echoing fundamental myths) and its seriality (familiarity builds from repeated contact with characters and situations).

Liebes, T., & Katz, E. (1989). On the critical abilities of television viewers. In E. Seiter, H. Borchers, G. Kreutzner, & E.-M. Warth (Eds.), *Remote control: Television, audiences, and cultural power* (pp. 204–222). New York: Routledge.

Liebes and Katz wanted to determine the critical abilities that viewers use when making sense of an American television show such as "Dallas." Viewers have diverse strategies for defense against the perceived message of the show.

Method: Same as Liebes and Katz (1988).

They found that Western viewers were more critical—as defined by being aware "of the semantic elements of the text and/or of the roles of the reader as processor of the text" (p. 208). They focused on the forms of criticism: semantic criticism (theme, messages, and archetypes), syntactic criticism (genre, dramatic function, and business), and pragmatic criticism (awareness of the nature and causes of involvement in the semantics and syntactics).

Lindlof, T. R. (1987). Ideology and pragmatics of media access in prison. In T. R. Lindlof (Ed.), *Natural audiences: Qualitative research of media uses and effects* (pp. 175–197). Norwood, NJ: Ablex.

The purpose of this study was to look at how the institution and its ideology shape the inmates' media habits.

Lindlof conducted intensive interviews with 16 inmates as well as some administrative and line officers. He also examined documents but was not allowed to observe in the prison.

The primary findings are: (a) Media provide them with a way to measure the distance between their previous world and the institutionalized world, and (b) the use of personal media give inmates the power to control their information flow.

Lull, J. (1980). The social uses of television. *Human Communication Research, 6,* 197–209.

The purpose of this reception study was to determine how family members use television for social purposes in their homes.

A team of participant observers (students) visited more than 200 families in their homes in Wisconsin and California. The families, who were contacted through social agencies such as scouts and religious groups, were each visited from 2 to 7 days. Each visit began at midafternoon and extended until bedtime. After the last session, each family member was intensively interviewed independently. A report was written for each family and these were shown to the family as a validity check.

The results of the observations were inductively analyzed and arranged into a social uses of television typology that was composed of two major components: structural and relational. The structural component included environmental use (background noise, companionship, and entertainment) and regulative use (punctuation of time and activity and talk patterns). The relational component had four subcomponents of communication facilitation (agenda for talk, experience illustration), affiliation/avoidance (relationship maintenance, family solidarity), social learning (behavior modeling, legitimazation, substitute schooling), and competence/dominance (role reinforcement, argument facilitation).

Morley, D. (1980). *The "Nationwide" audience: Structure and decoding.* London: British Film Institute. (167 pages)

The purpose of his book is to construct a typology of the range of coding viewers have for a particular British TV show, to analyze how and why they vary, to demonstrate how different interpretations vary, and to relate those variations to cultural forces (p. 23). Morley began by criticizing media studies thinking in America (normative paradigm) and argued for the interpretive paradigm. He said that the discourses on TV follow ideologies, but that not all viewers accept the dominant ideological position. He said that producers can encode a message in a variety of ways. He asked: How and why do certain production practices and structures tend to produce certain messages? On the decoding side, he looked at why certain messages prefer certain readings (although all messages are polysemic—allow for a range of readings). He wanted to see who had dominant, oppositional, and negotiated frameworks for decoding.

He began with hypotheses about different readings made by different types of people according to demographics (age, gender, race, and class) and cultural identifications (trade unions, political parties, sections of the educational system, etc.).

He used a purposive sample of 29 groups of from 2 to 13 people each. He showed each group an episode of "Nationwide," a British news program. He then ran a focus group and recorded the 30-minute discussions. He analyzed the audiotapes, and this analysis results in a primarily descriptive presentation that is the longest part of the book (pp. 40–133), organized to show the salient quotes for each of the 29 groups.

His results focus on a comparative analysis of decodings across groups and an argument for his theory that the interpretive discourses are related to, but not determined by social-structural position.

Radway, J. A. (1984). *Reading the romance: Women, patriarchy, and popular literature.* Chapel Hill: University of North Carolina Press.

This is a reception study that examines why certain women read romance novels and what they get out of it.

Radway identified a woman in a local bookstore who had developed a network of customers who relied on her recommendations about romance novels. Radway interviewed this woman (Dot) and 16 of her regular customers for a total of 60 hours of interviews. She also got 42 responses to her 53-item questionnaire, which was fairly quantitative in nature. Her qualitative analysis was primarily semiotic with a feminist ideology.

She concluded that women read romances to create their own space in their confining daily routines as wives and mothers. The reading is a gesture of protest against the strictures of a patriarchal society.

Rogge, J.-U., & Jensen, K. (1988). Everyday life and television in West Germany: An empathic-interpretive perspective on the family as a system. In J. Lull (Ed.), *World families watch television* (pp. 80–115). Beverly Hills, CA: Sage.

The purpose of this reception study is to look at the media rituals of German families and to determine how family members consume TV and interpret the meaning of the messages.

Rogge and Jensen did not talk much about data gathering, but it appears from the analysis that they interviewed 10 families. They focused much more on data analysis methods. They said they took an empathic-interpretive method, which is "an approach that enters into the everyday worlds of families and seeks to understand families within the context of their individual and social frameworks and then to describe those particular actions" (p. 85).

Their results show that psychological stress in families is caused by and negotiated through media use. Control of the set and interpretations of its messages are reflections of power in the family.

Rogge, J.-U. (1989). The media in everyday family life: Some biographical and typological aspects. In E. Seiter, H. Borchers, G. Kreutzner, & E.-M. Warth (Eds.), *Remote control: Television, audiences, and cultural power* (pp. 168–179). New York: Routledge.

This is a reception analysis focusing on how families use media in their everyday lives. Rogge tried to explain media use in the context of work, family communication patterns, psycho-social, economic, and ecological background of the family.

The sample was 420 West German families. Data were gathered using a standardized questionnaire, participant observation, a media journal, and the qualitative interview, which "addressed the multiple aspects of concrete living situations of everyday life" (p. 174).

Changes in family condition and structure alter members' feelings about TV. She presented generalizations at the end that are very much like uses and gratifications propositions, but they were unattributed to that theory. Instead, she made an interesting distinction between objective and subjective media reality. Objective media reality has a formative influence on lifestyles and patterns of communication. Subjective media reality deals with "people's everyday knowledge about he media, the patterns of behavior adopted" (p. 178).

It is an essay with no footnotes or attributions to scholarly literature. It is a reception study, but it borders on ethnomethodology with its strong focus on the meaning people make of media in their everyday lives. However, it is not strong ethnomethodology, because it does not focus on the question of *how* that meaning is made. Also, it does not focus on the "reading" of any particular program or genre.

Seiter, E., Borchers, H., Kreutzner, G., & Warth, E.-M. (1989a). "Don't treat us like we're so stupid and naive": Toward an ethnography of soap opera viewers. In E. Seiter, H. Borchers, G. Kreutzner, & E.-M. Warth (Eds.), *Remote control: Television, audiences, and cultural power* (pp. 223–247). New York: Routledge.

This is a reception study examination of how women who work in their homes view soap operas. In their overall project, Seiter et al. were interested in the relationship between social conditions of housewives and the soap opera discourse. They focused on how "media schedules influence and interest with the temporal organization of their work" (p. 228). They contrasted text with genre then provided a feminist analysis to examining the place of the mother in the soap operas.

A total of 64 White people (49 women) were interviewed in 26 groups in their homes in western Oregon. Each interview was conducted by two scholars.

Viewing is organized around the women's work in their homes. They seek to construct a uniquely female space for viewing. They see the women as the primary characters, whereas the men are there in support roles.

Ecological Psychology

Barrios, L. (1988). Television, telenovelas, and family life in Venezuela. In J. Lull (Ed.), *World families watch television* (pp. 49–79). Beverly Hills, CA: Sage.

This study focuses on the nature of the family and how those environments influence television use.

Thirteen families were interviewed and observed in their natural settings through participant observation and open-ended interviews. Each family was observed from 16 to 46 hours.

Factors influencing television use were availability of space, number of sets, and location of set(s) in the home. Children were found to be passive when viewing alone, but active when viewing with others; viewing for children is a time for playing, joking, dancing, and so forth. People schedule their lives around television programs.

Pardun, C. J., & Krugman, D. M. (1994). How the architectural style of the home relates to family television viewing. *Journal of Broadcasting & Electronic Media, 38,* 145–162.

The purpose of this study is to "explore the relationship between the physical environment of the home and families' television viewing behavior."

The 20 families (61 people) were chosen in a purposive manner so as to get 10 families living in traditional-style homes and 10 families in transitional-style homes. Data gathering took 2 hours per home during which the interviewer took pictures, talked to the family members, and administered a questionnaire about demographics. The interviews were audiotaped then transcribed into a 528-page document that was then analyzed in a three-step procedure. First was the step of open coding, which was a line-by-line examination to identify potential categories to guide subsequent steps. Second was axial coding, a procedure of fitting data to the eight main themes identified in the first step. Third was selective coding that focused on identifying an overarching core concept for the study.

The analysis is a good illustration of building grounded theory. Pardun and Krugman's overarching core concept was that families regard the TV as either a magnet or a retreat. Families who live in transitional-style homes treat the TV as a common hearth for family gatherings. In contrast, families who live in traditional-style homes treat the TV as a retreat; that is, individuals use the TV to get away from the family.

Symbolic Interactionism

Lull, J. (1987). Trashing in the pit: An ethnography of San Francisco punk subculture. In T. R. Lindlof (Ed.), *Natural audiences: Qualitative research of media uses and effects* (pp. 225–252). Norwood, NJ: Ablex.

This study focuses on communication within the San Francisco punk subculture "including both the domains of symbolic interaction, where so many of their images are nurtured, and the social processes that constitute their modes for living" (p. 226).

Lull spent 2 months (hundreds of hours) of participant observation and interviewing in locations where punks congregate, such as where they live, eat, hang out, and attend music shows.

His results are a descriptive and interpretive account of what punk is, its lifestyle, its music, and one special subgroup called the skinheads. This is presented in "the natural contexts of its occurrence" (p. 226). He defined the punk lifestyle in terms of their appearance, clothing, living quarters, food, school, religion, money, drugs, gender relations, enemies, music, and media habits. He showed that their symbols have a special meaning to the members of that community and this shared meaning is opposite to how outsiders would interpret the meaning. For example, their talk appears very aggressive and violent, but to insiders, the meaning is the opposite.

Cultural Studies

Hoover, S. M. (1988). Television myth and ritual: The role of substantive meaning and spatiality. In J. W. Carey (Ed.), *Media, myths, and narratives: Television and the press* (pp. 161–178). Beverly Hills, CA: Sage.

This is a cultural analysis of the way the mass media have changed audiences for religious institutions. Hoover used a kind of mythic analysis mainly based on Turner's concept of *liminality* as a means of explaining how television viewers engage in religious rituals. They use television to make "religious pilgrimages" into a feel of community with others.

His method is to assemble a conglomeration of information (survey results, audience ratings, insights from interviews, findings of previous research studies of all kinds) and perspectives (cultural, historical, religious, positivist). There is no thesis or consistent argument. He raised questions he did not answer. The most consistent thread in this book chapter is the repeated mention of Turner's ideas of liminality and communitas.

He argued that there is a parachurch religiosity that is supported by the mass media. This parachurch is a means whereby individuals can become part of a network that gives them religious experiences beyond what they would be able to get in their conventional churches. He drew from Victor Turner's concept of liminality to look at threshold experiences between the secular world and the sacred world.

INSTITUTION-FOCUSED RESEARCH

Ethnography

Altheide, D. L. (1976). *Creating reality: How TV news distorts events*. Beverly Hills, CA: Sage.

This is ethnography about how people in the newsroom create a community to get their news work done. Altheide's central thesis is "events become news when transformed by the news perspective, and not because of their objective characteristics" (p. 173).

He provided a 20-page methodological appendix where he described his three settings, gaining entree, gaining trust, nature of data, and verification. He spent a year in a network affiliate newsroom (and 2 more years in other newsrooms) while he was a participant observer. He presented his "news perspective" early as an explanation then used it structure his book; but it is obvious that he did not begin his *investigation* that way; that is, the construct was developed over the course of the data gathering.

He developed a construct called "news perspective" to explain how the staff select and treat the news. News perspective is a sort of bias that helps journalists simplify and organize the overwhelming amount of material they must sift through. This news bias is influenced by the constraints of commercialism, scheduling, technology, and competition. He argued that "the organizational, practical, and other mundane features of newswork promote a way of looking at events which fundamentally distorts them" (p. 24). "In order to make events news, news reporting decontextualizes and thereby changes them" (p. 25). The biggest influences on the news scene are commercialism (ratings and the drive for profit), competition (from other media), and the community context (especially political ties).

Elliott, P. (1979). *The making of a television series*. London: Sage.

This is regarded as the classic, beginning point for ethnographies on television production. This case study looks at the making of a series of seven programs for an adult education project entitled, "The Nature of Prejudice." Elliott said, "the central aim of this book is to throw light on the relationship between culture and social structure as it is mediated through television" (p. 6).

He used a participant observation method to gather data and an extended case study structure that "incorporates the dynamics of behaviour and process while allowing beliefs and organization to be explored in more static, structural terms" (p. 8).

He attempted to generalize his findings to dramatic television. He also worked at carefully inducing general statements to theories. Highly self-conscious in reporting methods.

Fishman, M. (1980). *Manufacturing the news*. Austin: University of Texas Press.

This ethnography focuses on how journalists construct social reality for audiences.

There is a very good explication of methods (pp. 18–26) in the first chapter. Fishman worked as a journalist on one newspaper for about 7 months, then went to a competing newspaper where he observed for about 5 months. He argued that his experience was typical of all newspapers so he could generalize the results. Also, he talked about how he gained access to the newspapers and the reporters and how he collected data.

Fishman argued that journalists develop routines so they do not have to invent new methods of reporting the world on every occasion they confront it. He made a distinction between routine journalism and manipulated journalism. Routine journalism is the "good, plain, solid, honest, professional news reporting" that is produced through the "daily methods and standard practices of journalists" (p. 15). In contrast, manipulated journalism is the product of a political game where the news is produced to service certain interests. Even routine journalism displays an ideological hegemony, which can be traced to "the routines of news detection, interpretation, investigation, and assembly" (p. 18).

Ethnomethodology

Tuchman, G. (1978). *Making news: A study in the construction of reality*. New York: The Free Press.

This is an ethnomethodology that is an "applied study in the sociology of knowledge" (p. 2). Tuchman looked at how news work draws on aspects of everyday life to make sense of the world and tell stories. She placed this work within the ethnomethodological tradition of Schutz, Husserl, Goffman, and Berger and Luckmann.

She gathered her data over a 10-year period (not continuously) at four sites in New York City (pp. 9–12).

The primary theme of the book is "the act of making news is the act of constructing reality itself rather than a picture of reality" (p. 12). A secondary theme is that "professionalism serves organizational interests by reaffirming the institutional processes in which newswork is embedded" (p. 12). The central concept is "news frame," which is what news workers use to put up to events to determine whether those events "fit" as news.

The selection of news is a negotiated activity throughout the bureaucracy. Time, place, and classifications are essential ingredients in this construction process. As for time, organizations create deadlines and rhythms of work. As for place, certain institutions and sources are appropriate locations for news whereas others are not. Classifications are developed for stories to help simplify the process of selection and development of news stories.

The news is a construction that represents an ideology shaped by trends in the 19th century: rise of journalistic professionalism and news organizations based on corporate capitalism. This ideology serves to legitimate the "intertwining of political and corporate activity" (p. 14).

Symbolic Interaction

Altheide, D. L. (1985). *Media power*. Beverly Hills, CA: Sage.

The purpose is to explore "how mass media, and especially TV, provide formats, or templates for perception, expectation, and action" (p. 7). By diffusing formats and perspectives, the media hold power. Formats are defined as the "rules and procedures for defining, selecting, organizing, and presenting information and other experiences" (p. 9).

Altheide said he drew from symbolic interaction, phenomenology, and ethnomethodology to look at how the world is constructed through communication. He characterized his work as ethnography, but there is no direct contact with people for this particular study; instead he drew from his observations of newsroom workers from a previous study; no apparent fresh data.

He provided a methods section (pp. 234–237). His analysis really focuses on decoding the symbols from the media. He did mention the process of analysis as a process of guessing and confirmation and reformulating general explanations from the patterns in the specifics.

The primary effect of these formats is to influence the "basic temporal and spatial relationships we tend to take for granted" (p. 10). He dealt "with mass communication, and especially television, as a piece of culture" (p. 12). He tried to get beyond the political ideological arguments to look at whether there is "a cultural consideration lurking within the symbolic, semantic, and syntactic structure of these media" (p. 12).

Altheide, D. L., & Snow, R. P. (1979). *Media logic*. Beverly Hills, CA: Sage.

The central premise is that media is culture. "Media are such pervasive phenomena that they are the dominant institutions in contemporary society" (p. 9). The way to understand media as a social force is to treat them as if they have a logic of their own. However, this logic is not imposed on audiences; instead, there is an interactive process where people interpret the media messages and provide feedback to the media. Media logic can be inferred from the formats of communication used by the media. "Format consists, in part, of how material is organized, the style in which it is presented, the focus or emphasis on particular characteristics of behavior, and the grammar of media communication. Format becomes a framework or a perspective that is used to present as well as interpret phenomena" (p. 10).

There are no explicit details about method.

Altheide and Snow examined the consequences that arise from the media logic and this requires an examination of the media culture, which is defined as the character of institutions. They said that "when media logic is employed to present and interpret institutional phenomena, the form and content of those institutions are altered" (p. 11). They looked at the cultures of entertainment, news, politics, religion, and sports from a mediacentric perspective.

Snow, R. P. (1983). *Creating media culture*. Beverly Hills, CA: Sage.

Snow's central construct is "media culture," which is a "culture being constructed and altered continuously through the linguistic and interpretive strategies of media" (p. 7).

There is no explicit treatment of methods.

The main part of the book shows the grammar of various media: newspapers, novels, magazines, radio, television, and film. He argued that each medium has its own "grammatical structure," which is composed of syntax, inflection, and vocabulary. Because humans are symbol users, they must know how to "read" the grammar of the media in order to interpret their experience and construct meaning.

Cultural History

Altschull, J. H. (1984). *Agents of power: The role of the news media in human affairs*. New York: Longman.

This is an historical reinterpretation of the categories of press throughout the world.

There is no explicit treatment of methods.

Altschull argued that there are three press systems: market, Marxist, and advancing. The market press is the Western model and runs on a profit motive with professional journalists striving for openness and objectivity. The Marxist press is designed to mold views and change behavior. The advancing press (in the third world) attempts to unify people into a common community and bring about social change.

Auletta, K. (1991). *Three blind mice: How the TV networks lost their way*. New York: Random House.

This is a journalistic history of the TV networks, focusing primarily on the period from 1984 to 1990, during which cable and VCRs ate away at their dominance for the mass audience. Auletta tried to show a balanced view of how the networks operated during that period.

His primary data were from personal interviews and observations at meetings. In all, he conducted 1,500 interviews with 350 people (pp. 6–7).

He described the decisions that were made by the networks in order to maintain their prominence in the media industries.

Barnouw, E. (1975). *Tube of plenty: The evolution of American television.* New York: Oxford University Press.

This is a condensation and updating of Barnouw's *A History of Broadcasting in the United States,* which is composed of three books, each with its own title: *A Tower of Babel* (broadcasting up until 1933), *The Golden Web* (1933 to 1953), and *The Image Empire* (1953 to 1970).

There is no explicit description of methods, but it is clear that he relied on existing documents to piece together this historical narrative.

This history focuses on the development (from technological, regulatory, and market-ing points of view). His organization follows a growth metaphor progression of fore-bears, toddler, plastic years, prime, and elder. There is a great deal of detail here—but the sources are rarely identified and never challenged. Therefore the tone is descrip-tive, not critical and not interpretive.

Baughman, J. L. (1990). The weakest chain and the strongest link: The American Broad-casting Company and the motion picture industry, 1952–60. In T. Balio (Ed.), *Hollywood in the age of television* (pp. 91–114). Boston: Unwin Hyman.

This is a cultural history of the television industry's shifting production to California in the early 1950s.

There is no explicit description of methods, but it is clear that Baughman relied on existing documents to piece together this historical narrative.

It traces ABC's rise to power by its use of Hollywood film studios production, which reduced costs and garnered high ratings.

Brown, L. (1971). *Televi\$ion: The business behind the box.* New York: Harcourt Brace Jovanovich.

This is a journalistic account of what happened with the three commercial TV net-works during 1970.

As a reporter for *Variety,* Brown interviewed people in the business.

The journalistic description focuses on a variety of topics in its 15 chapters. Topics include the three commercial networks, advertisers, sales forces, the audience, profits, and public service.

Innis, H. A. (1950). *Empire and communications.* Oxford University Press.

This is a cultural history of the empires of Egypt, Babylonia, Greece, and Rome. Innis examined the significance of communication on these large-scale political institutions. His thesis is that each empire has its own form of communication that makes it cohesive and distinguishes it from other empires. However, this creates a bias that makes it difficult for empires (or countries) to communicate with one another.

He did not consciously address the topic of methods. He was clearly using a historical method, but did not discuss how he selected or authenticated his data.

He argued that the "effective government of large areas depends to a very important extent on the efficiency of communication" (p. 7). He credited writing as being a significant factor in the development of civilizations. "Individuals applied their minds to symbols rather than things and went beyond the world of concrete experience into the wold of conceptual relations created within an enlarged time and space universe. The time world was extended beyond the range of remembered things and the space world beyond the range of known places. Writing enormously enhanced a capacity for abstract thinking which had been evident in the growth of language in the oral tradition" (p. 11).

Litman, B. (1990). Network oligopoly power: An economic analysis. In T. Balio (Ed.), *Hollywood in the age of television* (pp. 115–144). Boston: Unwin Hyman.

Litman's essay is an economic analysis of the structure of the television industry and how it paralleled the TV and film industries in terms of cost efficiencies, product differentiation, and vertical integration. These led to network oligopoly control. The treatment is descriptive without quantitative analysis.

There is no explicit treatment of method. He presumably relied on existing documents; there is no evidence of interviewing or direct observation.

He looked at the degree of concentration among the networks and how this leads to efficiencies and influences product differentiation. The idea of vertical integration is examined from an economic and policy perspective. He characterized the structure as a monopsony that requires competition among a few players while at the same time requiring them to cooperate. He said that the broadcast networks resemble the film industry in their structural development. But the future will be disruptive to this structure as new technologies become major factors.

Metz, R. (1975). *CBS: Reflections in a bloodshot eye*. Chicago: Playboy Press.

This is a history of the CBS television network. It is very descriptive in a breezy journalistic manner.

Metz said he conducted 120 major interviews and recorded his notes on a typewriter. He warned the reader not to look for footnotes. But he did include a bibliography.

He traced the origins and development of CBS mainly in terms of Bill Paley's vision and influence.

Pauly, J. J. (1988). Rupert Murdoch and the demonology of professional journalism. In J. W. Carey (Ed.), *Media, myths, and narratives: Television and the press* (pp. 246–261). Beverly Hills, CA: Sage.

This is a cultural history of Rupert Murdoch's media acquisitions and the public's reaction.

There is no explicit treatment of method. Pauly presumably relied on existing documents; there is no evidence of interviewing or direct observation.

After giving a brief history of the man, the focus shifts to his newspapers and how critics have characterized them over time.

Spigel, L. (1993). Seducing the innocent: Childhood and television in postwar America. In W. S. Solomon & R. W. McChesney (Eds.), *Ruthless criticism: New perspectives in U.S. communication history* (pp. 259–290). Minneapolis: University of Minnesota Press.

This is a cultural history of how children were regarded during the early days of television.

There is no explicit treatment of methods. It appears that Spigel relied exclusively on existing documents, especially publications.

She began with the perspective that children were presumed innocent and television was seen as innocent also. But then television was viewed as showing children undesirable messages that served to make them grow up prematurely.

Turow, J. (1981). *Entertainment, education, and the hard sell: Three decades of network children's television.* New York: Praeger.

This book provides an analysis of the diversity of programming for children from 1948 to 1978. It is very empirical and almost purely descriptive. There is no a priori expectations (purely exploratory) and no grounded theory.

The book presents a content analysis of 30 years of children's programming. The analysis is quantitative, but the numbers represent numerical properties (such as numbers of programs per genre and network) and not enumerative translations.

A series of tabulations show the frequency of children's shows across networks and over time. There are also breakdowns by subjects, type of characters, nature of continuing characters, and presentation methods. The concluding chapter contains a summary of each preceding chapter then presents questions about the future of children's television and networks' responsibilities.

Cultural Interpretation

Allen, R. C. (1985). *Speaking of soap operas.* Chapel Hill: University of North Carolina Press.

Allen examined the American soap opera as a narrative form, cultural product, and advertising vehicle. He presented a strong ideological position in the introduction and first two chapters; he is antiscience, but he called it antiempiricism. This is the overriding point of the book. He tried to demonstrate that the use of critical methods conveys better understanding about the phenomenon of soap operas.

To gather the evidence for his arguments, he combed through the trade and general press for material on the history of soap operas. He also interviewed the cast and staff of a major soap opera and analyzed scripts.

He described how soap operas are produced as commodities, the texts as open and displaying codes (stylistic, generic, textual, intertextual, and ideological). He presented an institutional history, then a history of how they have been received.

Berman, R. (1981). *Advertising and social change.* Beverly Hills, CA: Sage.

This interpretive article focuses on the issue of social change and the influence of television advertising. Berman illuminated much of the general criticism directed at advertising.

There is no explicit treatment of methods. He said that the book began as an article written for the 50th-anniversary issue of *Ad Age.*

He said that traditional institutions of family, religion, and education have grown weaker whereas the world has grown more complex. Advertising fills the void by providing guidance about style, morality, values, and behaviors. He asserted that advertising serves to "give us a great deal of advice about work, maturation, marriage, and other aspects of social life" especially "information about living that life in conditions of incessant change" (pp. 12–13). He said that advertising has created a psychology of consumption in order to drive the economy, but it goes beyond creating desires for goods to creating impossible desires for ourselves. He explored the critical positions directed at advertising and concluded that the government is not in a position to do anything useful about it.

Bernhard, N. E. (1993). Ready, willing, and able: Network television news and the federal government, 1948–1953. In W. S. Solomon & R. W. McChesney (Eds.), *Ruthless criticism: New perspectives in U.S. communication history* (pp. 291–312). Minneapolis: University of Minnesota Press.

This is a cultural history exploring the main institutional parameters of network television news production during its first 5 years. Specifically, Bernhard looked at how the news divisions' relationships with advertisers and government agencies shaped news form and content.

The methods issues are not explicitly described. However, it appears that she relied exclusively on written documents.

She argued that "as television marginalized other forms of discourse, the narrow range of political contention it portrayed became the entire range most viewers encountered, and the availability of alternative worldviews diminished" (p. 292). There is an underlying criticism here based on a Marxist perspective against capitalism.

Cantor, M. (1980). *Prime-time television: Content and control.* Newbury Park, CA: Sage.

Cantor is a sociologist who says she is doing work in the sociology of mass communications and the popular arts. Her study is a look at the production of television drama, how it is produced, by whom, under what conditions, and for whom. She developed a model that is "historical as well as systemic and interactive" (p. 14), which is an advancement over the Lasswellian model that is one-directional, not interactive and not historical.

This study is based on interviews with actors, directions, writers, and producers over a 10-year period up until 1976. Her work is sometimes regarded as ethnography, but it is not. She interviewed many people, but she did not "live" with them.

Her model focuses first on content. The content sits inside concentric circles of influence: (a) the legal system, (b) organizational and economic controls from the networks, advertisers, and local stations, (c) occupational and creative controls, and (d) audience. Each set of influences is examined in a historical and contextual analysis. The model does not emphasize stability over change; and it is not deterministic. She said the networks are the most powerful influence in the model.

Cantor, M. (1988). *The Hollywood television producer: His work and his audience.* New Brunswick, NJ: Transaction Books.

This cultural interpretation is grounded in traditional occupational sociology. It is strongly contextualized in terms of the wider television industry.

After a pilot testing procedure of interviewing six television producers, Cantor got a list of all life-action filmed drama television shows currently being produced in southern California. She sent a letter to the producer of each show and personally interviewed 59 producers, recording most interviews. Several years later, she also interviewed 20 producers and 4 writers of children's shows. She also examined private and public documents and observed in the field (studios).

She described how decisions are made in the preproduction process and showed how that process is influenced by networks, advertisers, ratings, and pretesting of ideas. She profiled producers and developed a typology: film makers, writer-producers, and online producers. She then examined the relationships producers have with their coworkers (writers, directors, and actors) and with the business types (network people). The producers' reactions to changes in content and perceptions of the television audience are illuminated. Her main conclusion is that the producers operate under many constraints that limit their creativity.

Clark, E. (1988). *The want makers: Inside the world of advertising.* New York: Penguin Books.

This is a journalist's cultural interpretation of the advertising industry. At times it is very critical, but Clark said he remains proadvertising, so on balance, this is more interpretation than criticism.

He said that "hundreds of individuals and organisations in a number of countries helped me in the preparation of this book" (p. 11), but there is nothing more specific about methods than this statement.

This is a very readable journalistic account of the advertising industry primarily in America and Britain. He also focused on advertising targets and the media.

Douglas, S. J. (1993). Will you love me tomorrow? Changing discourses about female sexuality in the mass media, 1960–1968. In W. S. Solomon & R. W. McChesney (Eds.), *Ruthless criticism: New perspectives in U.S. communication history* (pp. 349–373). Minneapolis: University of Minnesota Press.

This is a cultural interpretation (Douglas called it history) of changes in the way female sexuality was portrayed during the 1960s.

There is no explicit dealing with method. Examples are from popular music, movies, and television shows. The primary tool of analysis is feminism.

Douglas argued that popular culture during the 1960s was not as monolithic and oppressive as feminists might think. Instead, there was a "discourse of ambivalence and contradiction" (p. 353) where young girls where given messages and role models about conforming and being different. Advertisers targeted messages to the 11.7 million girls between the ages of 12 and 18 years and this "helped cultivate a highly self-conscious sense of importance and difference among these girls" (p. 350). Finally, she said that by the 1970s women who had been exposed to this culture wanted real power for themselves; that is, the success of the feminist movement grew out of this culture.

Ewen, S., & Ewen, E. (1992). *Channels of desire*. Minneapolis: University of Minnesota Press.

This is a cultural history of selected aspects of the mass media broadly defined to include dress and fashion. Its five chapters are standalone essays, most of which were originally published in 1982. The longest (115 pages) is about how people dress.

There is no explicit treatment of method. Ewen and Ewen seem to have relied primarily on existing documents.

They said that "historians and cultural analysts have, in the last twenty-five years, zeroed in on 'the problem of representation' as the cardinal issue of our time" (p. 190) and that is the focus of their book. They said the media have created a culture of choice, violence, and ignorance. Their essays provide examples of the creation of these images in society by movies, fashion, and tabloid journalism.

Jowett, G., & Linton, J. M. (1980). *Movies as mass communication*. Beverly Hills, CA: Sage.

This is primarily a description of some elements of the movie industry.

There is no explicit treatment of method. Jowett and Linton seem to have relied primarily on existing documents.

They purported to present a new perspective of movies as mass communication. In the first chapter, there is a graphic model with lots of boxes (movie, production, distribution, marketing/promotion, exhibition, attendance, viewing process, and evaluation) and lots of arrows, but the text does not develop the information in all these boxes and it is very weak on demonstrating the relationships. So this model is neither grounded theory nor even an organizing device for the presentation of information, which is essentially citations of the ideas of others. There is nothing new here except to see all this particular information all in one book. The most interesting idea is the "audience image," which comes from McQuail and Gans. It is the mental image the industry has of audiences as it develops and markets its products. This image is different for different movies. This image serves to reduce the complexities in the decision-making processes and ritualize the action.

Meehan, E. R. (1993). Heads of household and ladies of the house: Gender, genre, and broadcast ratings, 1929–1990. In W. S. Solomon & R. W. McChesney (Eds.), *Ruthless criticism: New perspectives in U.S. communication history* (pp. 204–221). Minneapolis: University of Minnesota Press.

This is a cultural interpretation of the broadcast ratings industry. Meehan provided a history of the industry then contextualized it within the larger broadcasting industry that regards audiences as commodities. Underlying the interpretation is a feminist ideology that criticizes broadcast ratings for treating women as a commodity.

There is no explicit treatment of methods. She relied primarily on existing documents.

She said that broadcast and cable are only interested in manipulating the "consumerist caste" and not the entire population, so they cannot be regarded as mass media. "The artifacts manufactured within that structure are designed to assemble the consumerist cast for measurement and sale" (p. 217).

Reeves, J. L. (1988). Television stardom: A ritual of social typification and individualization. In J. W. Carey (Ed.), *Media, myths, and narratives: Television and the press* (pp. 146–160). Beverly Hills, CA: Sage.

This is a cultural interpretation of the television star system. Reeves addressed "issues related to how media stardom assists in the production, repair, and transformation of social reality" (p. 147). He said "a star is the *discourse* of an *individualized social type*—and as such, the star represents a *strategic socioideological worldview*" (p. 154).

There is no explicit treatment of methods. It appears that he relied primarily on existing records.

He showed how the stardom ritual contributes to the maintenance of society through the interactions of three types of people: the layman, the expert, and the well informed.

Spigel, L. (1992). Installing the television set: Popular discourses on television and domestic space, 1948–1955. In L. Spigel & D. Mann (Eds.), *Private screenings: Television and the female consumer* (pp. 3–38). Minneapolis: University of Minnesota Press.

This is a cultural history of how the television set moved into American living rooms and the discourses this inspired. Specifically, Spigel focused on what the media suggested about how people should use television.

She said she searched popular books and magazines, especially middle-class women's home magazines, magazine advertisements for television ... and early television narratives, especially family situation comedies" (p. 4) for her evidence.

She argued that the media show an ambivalent posture toward television. On the one hand, popular media presented utopian discourses idealizing television "as an ultimate expression of technological and social progress" (p. 3). On the other hand, the media represented TV as an isolating agent that would "have devastating effects on family relationships and the efficient function of the household" (p. 3).

Turow, J. (1984). *Media industries: The production of news and entertainment*. New York: Longman.

This is an analysis of the culture of the media industries from a resource dependency perspective. Turow used Kluckhohn's very general definition of culture "the distinctive way of life of a group of people, their designs for living" (p. 2). The resource dependency approach comes from Howard Aldrich, who said that resources are not randomly distributed throughout organizations, but are concentrated in certain areas. This use of resources is not simply based on exchange. People develop relationships where others are dependent on them for resources. This gives them leverage in gaining compliance from others (pp. 8–10).

He relied on existing documents (no interviews, observations, or primary documents) to build and support a framework for making sense about how the players in the industry use power. He used a comparative case study method. Instead of focusing on general industry-wide patterns, he selected several subindustries; then through a process of *retroduction*, he attempted to determine the differences in patterns in their cultures. "Retroduction is the activity of deductively applying ideas from certain bodies of knowledge and emerging frameworks to case studies and then inducing from findings of the case studies the extent to which (and the manner in which) the bodies of knowledge and emerging frameworks should be altered" (p. 71). This works well in his analysis of children's book publishing, where there were found to be very different production practices for the library market compared to the mass market.

Turow's framework includes 13 power roles: producer, authority, investor, patron, auxiliary, creator, union, distributor, exhibitor, linking pin, facilitator, public advocacy, and the public. He used a resource dependency approach to illuminate patterns of interaction among these groups of players. These patterns create the culture. He said "the creation of mass media culture cannot be truly understood without reference to the broad industrial and social environment in which the production of symbols takes place" (p. 38).

At the heart of the culture are the producers whose major goals are to avoid dependence on others and to make others dependent on them. They recognize that in order to gain the resources they need, they must give resources in return. In deciding how much to give they consider the importance of the resources, the power of the entities that control the resources, competition, and alternative ways of gaining the resources (p. 81). "They continually produce mass media material that actually reflect and validate the right of those organizations and groups to remain powerful, to control resources and hold leverage" (pp. 116–117). This is the process of legitimation.

In his scheme, the key interaction is between producers and patrons. The patrons (exhibitors, distributors, and advertisers who finance the productions) set general boundary conditions for day-to-day production activity. This sets up routines that allow production people to work more efficiently than they would if they had to consider every task anew. In contrast, the public is relatively powerless to influence producers, but there are examples of mass media production firms bending to the interests and perspectives of socially powerful organizations and movements.

His 1981 book is a nice, little beginning; descriptive. His 1984 book is the best as far as presenting a fresh new conceptual framework that can guide future analyses. His doctor (1989) book uses his 1984 conceptual scheme as the foundation of analysis of doctor shows; his analysis provides further support for his scheme.

Turow, J. (1989). *Playing doctor: Television, storytelling, and medical power.* New York: Oxford University Press.

This cultural interpretation focuses on the circuits of power that unite television, the institution of medicine, and the viewing public. Turow said his "aim is to explore the way powerful forces within an American institution try to guide TV's fictional images of their institution" (p. xiii). Again, he took a resource dependency approach, saying that organizations that make up institutions (such as medicine, law, education) must compete with one another and with organizations outside the institution for resources, such as money, people, supplies, permission, prestige, and information. Control of these resources means power, and power is the ability of an actor (organizations or people) to use its resources to affect activities in its environment. The mainstream organizations hold the most power within an institution because of their ability to draw resources from the wealthiest elements in society (government, elites, huge segments of the population). The strongest pressure comes from the networks who want to have a product delivered on time and on budget and will appeal to the widest audience.

He is also very empirical by interviewing 109 actors, producers, and members of the medical profession. He read scripts or viewed tapes of the 55 medical programs aired on network prime time. And he looked at the writings about these shows in the popular press over 40 years.

He said that "prime-time fiction is especially compelling as a vehicle for portraying the rules of the game. With the intensity that newscasts cannot match, TV fiction brings millions of viewers behind the scenes to outline vividly acceptable forms of behavior by the organizations that make up an institution" (p. xiv). Therefore TV fiction "can have a major effect on the perception of, and the clout of, an institution in society." A key task of research on television fiction should be to investigate how portrayals of institutions get established, reinforced, and changed.

Although the effect is often direct, it is most likely highly complex, especially when influences are conflicting. So the resulting shows are not "platforms for the democratic presentation of a wide gamut of ideologies. But neither are TV's programs mere channels that transmit the established powers' versions of their world" (pp. xvii–xviii). Instead, he said, the relationship between the institutions and the storytellers is symbiotic and "threaded with strong tensions that will force ongoing conflict" (p. xviii).

He demonstrated a belief in the concept of truth. This is illustrated in the following way. He began his book with an example of how a doctor influenced the plot of a show for his own personal business gain (Jarvik heart). He later said, "It is true that the Jarvik story . . . shows how a powerful organization can use its resources to guide content" (p. xv).

Critical Analysis

Ang, I. (1991). *Desperately seeking the audience.* New York: Routledge.

The purpose of this critical analysis is to deconstruct the audience-seeking process by examining the discourses of the institutions in context. Ang's ideology is that the audience does not exist, "at least not in the unified and controllable mode in which it is generally envisioned" (pp. ix–x). She argued against the institutional point of view, which is a belief in the existence of audiences.

There is no explicit treatment of methods. She criticized the industry's emphasis on decontextualized quantitative data and recommended ethnographic work instead. But her study is not an ethnography.

She undertook a short historical analysis of the economic and cultural development of television. She then argued against the current conception of audience, which she said is only "a shared orientation toward some focal point—a centre of transmission, a centre of attraction—that turns them into 'audience members'. In this context, the idiosyncracies of the individual people making up an audience, as well as the specific interrelations between these people, do not matter: audience as taxonomic collective is in principle a term of amassment" (p. 35).

What she presented as the institutionalized definition of audience is a distortion and serves as a straw man argument. In some places she wrote clearly, but in others (where she attempted to make the real points of her argument) her prose becomes opaque with jargon, very long complex sentences, double negatives, and convoluted logic.

Bagdikian, B. H. (1972). *The effete conspiracy and other crimes by the press.* New York: Harper & Row.

This book is 15 essays criticizing the press for examples of unfairness or incompetence.

Bagdikian's method is that of a newspaper columnist. He interviewed people and read documents then worked the evidence to fit his opinions, which are critical.

Bagdikian, B. H. (1987). *The media monopoly* (2nd ed.). Boston: Beacon Press.

This is a criticism of the degree of concentration (and trend toward even more concentration) in the ownership and control of the media.

There is no explicit treatment of methods. It is clear that Bagdikian relied primarily on existing documents.

His analysis reveals that there are 25,000 media outlets, but that 29 corporations control most of the business in all the major media, down from 50 in 1983. He argued that this monopolistic control limits the news and commentary in the major newspapers, magazines, and broadcasting operations. The public is presented only what serves the economic and political interests of the corporations that own the media. He rejected a conspiracy theory as unnecessary. The drive toward concentration is done for "pragmatic business reasons" (p. 12). News workers have developed conventions that favor large corporations. These conventions include a reliance on official sources of news, a lack of context for the news, which serves to reduce its meaning, and the selective pursuit of stories (p. 212).

He called for "the restoration of genuine competition and diversity" (p. 224) and argued for "severe limits on cross-ownership of the media" (p. 228). He also called for a "progressive tax on advertising" (p. 230).

Barnouw, E. (1978). *The sponsor: Notes on a modern potentate*. New York: Oxford University Press.

In contrast to Barnouw's *Tube of Plenty*, which is a descriptive history, this book is a *critical* history of the sponsorship of broadcasting. He reused a fair amount of information from his previous book.

There is no explicit treatment of methods, but it is clear that he relied on existing documents.

Part I (about half the book) is a fairly descriptive treatment of the way broadcasting first allowed advertising, then courted it, then became totally dependent on it. Part II is fairly critical. He said that the word *commercial* is a euphemism, because sponsors go way beyond trying to sell products to promote a way of life, a view of the world, a philosophy. The major value propagated by advertising is conspicuous consumption. He said advertising over time changes our values from thrift to a duty to buy; from a work ethic to a consumption ethic; sexuality over modesty. Nature (especially the human body) is faulty and can be improved with the use of advertised products. Whereas the government is a very weak and slow regulator, sponsors are very powerful shapers of entertainment. Sponsors will not allow content that is controversial or will upset the viewers and thereby make their products look bad. Part III is very critical as he blamed advertising for creating a culture that squanders the world's resources and pollutes the planet with industrial waste and obsolete products in a mad rush to produce and consume more. He also lamented the weak public television system.

Browne, N. (1987). The political economy of the television (super) text. In H. Newcomb (Ed.), *Television: The critical view* (4th ed., pp. 585–599). New York: Oxford University Press.

This is an implied criticism of textual research of television. Browne's thesis is that television is different than film, so its analysis must be different. Because of the ads in programs, the nature of viewing is different and it should be examined from a political economic perspective.

There is no explicit treatment of methods, but it appears that he used existing documents although there are very few citations.

He argued that it is not programs that inform us best about the medium's significance; it is the large patterns of programming, the schedule itself, as a text for analysis. But the text should not be analyzed from an aesthetic point of view; instead an economic perspective is most appropriate for the TV text, because it is primarily a business in America.

Collins, J. (1989). *Uncommon cultures: Popular culture and post-modernism.* New York: Routledge.

This is a critical interpretation that focuses on popular culture and postmodernism "as a continuum because both reflect and produce the same cultural perspective—that 'culture' no longer can be conceived as a Grand Hotel, as a totalizable system that somehow orchestrates all cultural production and reception according to one master system" (p. xiii). Collins said the goal of the book is to examine how the "decentering and recentering processes occur and to explore their ramifications for notions of textuality, intertextuality, audience, ideology, and the history of narrative" (p. xiii).

There is no explicit treatment of method.

He argued that the concepts of "mass culture" and "the dominant" should be questioned and said that there is a complex of conflictive power relations that constitute culture.

Corcoran, F. (1987). Television as ideological apparatus: The power and pleasure. In H. Newcomb (Ed.), *Television: The critical view* (4th ed., pp. 533–552). New York: Oxford University Press.

This is an implied criticism of television research. First he argued against the positivist approach, then said it is a mistake to treat the analysis of television the same as the analysis of film.

There is no explicit treatment of methods, but it appears that he used existing documents although there are very few citations.

He argued that the television audience is indifferent to TV content and is therefore not active. Also, the dominant mode of narration is different in film and television. He argued that "the ideological critique of television should proceed along lines quite different from those evolving within film studies" (p. 537). However, he did not say what those lines of criticism should be. Instead, he was satisfied that his essay culminates "in questions rather than conclusions about the subtle connections between the ideological 'power' of television and the 'pleasure' which, in the culture of consumerism, acts as incentive to motivate the massive, voluntary use of a medium supposedly functioning as an agent of social control" (p. 537).

Dates, J. L., & Barlow, W. (Eds.). (1990). *Split image: African Americans in the mass media.* Washington, DC: Howard University Press.

This is a critical treatment of the media using a racial ideology. The introduction, conclusion, and most of the nine essays in between were written by the editors.

There is no explicit treatment of methods, but there is a reliance on other published scholarship.

Dates and Barlow's central point is that the definition of control of African-American images in the mass media is determined by a hegemonic influence. "In American society, by reproducing the ideological hegemony of the dominant white culture, the mass media help to legitimate the inequalities in class and race relations" (p. 4). One way of doing this is through presenting stereotypes. "Stereotypes are especially effective in conveying ideological messages because they are so laden with ritual and myth, particularly in the case of African Americans" (p. 5).

Gandy, O. H., Jr. (1982). *Beyond agenda-setting.* Norwood, NJ: Ablex.

This is a critical analysis about how dominant corporate, political, and bureaucratic powers have benefited from information subsidies in broadcasting, advertising, health, education, and science.

There is no explicit treatment of method. Gandy relied primarily on published books and articles as well as government documents.

First he showed how decisions are made about public policy then showed how these decisions have resulted in subsidies to health, education, and science/technology. He argued that the powers-that-be have sought to further influence public policy, thus forcing the citizen consumer to the sidelines. Wealthy parties (such as governments and corporate agencies) often offer TV storyteller subsidies (such as free advice, equipment, etc.) and this gives them the ability to shape media portrayals to their liking. This tends to move stories away from antiestablishment themes. This argument is for a rather direct effect that results in an information inequality.

Gitlin, T. (1980). *The whole world is watching: Mass media in the making and unmaking of the New Left.* Berkeley: University of California Press.

This is a cultural history of the New Left and how this social movement was helped and influenced by the mass media.

Gitlin drew on his experiences as an active member of the Students for Democratic Action from about 1963 to 1969. He studied CBS news coverage during that period and conducted close readings of *The New York Times.* He dissected news reports, photographs, and editing techniques using ideological critical theory based on Gramsci's idea of hegemony.

He argued that the mass media are the "core systems for the distribution of ideology" (p. 2). He talked about media frames, which are "persistent patterns of cognition, interpretation, and presentation, of selection, emphasis, and exclusion, by which symbol-handlers routinely organize discourse, whether verbal or visual" (p. 7). He said that the central command structures in our culture are the "privately controlled corporate economy and its intimate ally, the bureaucratic national security state, together embedded within a capitalist world complex of nation-states" (p. 9).

Gitlin, T. (1983). *Inside prime time.* New York: Pantheon.

This is a critical analysis of how television constructs social reality. The purpose is to determine how television executives and creatives select their images by addressing the question of: Who puts the images on the screen and for what reasons? "I wanted to see whether the industry 'knew' what 'it' was doing when it came up with these images" (p. 13).

Gitlin used a snowball technique of contacting people in the television industry and ended up with over 200 interviews with producers, actors, writers, and executives along with observations are the database. "I began interviewing network executives, writers, agents, actors, and anyone else who would talk to me about what shaped TV's images of the wider world" (p. 13). He hung around sets for weeks, read successive versions of scripts. He taped or took notes for interviews then analyzed them later.

He presented a dynamic picture of conflict and contradiction. He said there is a direct influence on television by the giant advertisers and ad agencies who are the heart of the modern capitalist system. Therefore, TV executives are unlikely to offend any of the mainstream institutions for risk of losing revenue. This leads to a stifling of debate about institutions and instead continually reflects the perspective of society's existing power structure. He used thick description. He said that "Anecdote is the style of industry speech, dialogue its body, and narrative its structure" (p. 14).

Gitlin, T. (1987). Prime time ideology: The hegemonic process in television entertainment. In H. Newcomb (Ed.), *Television: The critical view* (4th ed., pp. 507–532). New York: Oxford University Press.

Gitlin posed the question: What do television programs mean? He said this must be determined before scholars can address the question of effects. To answer his question of meaning, he used Gramsci's idea of hegemony and sought to translate that idea into the realm of television.

There is no explicit treatment of methods, but he appears to have relied on existing documents.

He concluded that the structure of the medium limits television's capacity for critical disclosure and thereby supports the status quo. The structure is determined by the formats, formulas, rules of genre, settings, character types, slants on problems, and solutions to conflicts shown on television.

Kellner, D. (1987). TV, ideology, and emancipatory popular culture. In H. Newcomb (Ed.), *Television: The critical view* (4th ed., pp. 471–503). New York: Oxford University Press.

Kellner examined "*how* television constructs and conveys hegemonic ideology and induces consent to advanced capitalism" (p. 473).

There is no explicit treatment of methods. But it is clear that he relied on existing documents for his evidence in his arguments.

He showed that television images, narrative codes, and methodologies convey this hegemonic ideology and thereby legitimate American society. However, he also showed that some images and narratives contain contradictory messages. He perceived the political structures as determinants of the content offered which he saw as very limited. This is a Marxist analysis, but it seeks to correct some mistakes and limitations of other Marxist research, by extending the argument from print to television and by showing that the messages are not a uniform support for the hegemonic ideology but also contain conflicting messages.

Mander, J. (1978). *Four arguments for the elimination of television.* New York: Morrow.

This is a criticism of television by a former ad man who begins the book with a history of himself—ethos as a foundation. Mander's central thesis is that the belief that television is essentially a window (a conduit of information) is totally wrong.

He showed his argument as developing over 15 years' experience working in advertising. His data are personal observations and from informal conversations. Also, he hired some researchers to look at the scholarly literature.

His four arguments show that TV has characteristics that are not reformable; that is, "there is an ideology in the technology itself" (p. 47). The first argument is that TV accelerates an already existing condition of humans being disconnected from their environments in our complex world. Thus we all experience artificial realities. Second, TV is dominated by a small number of corporate powers. Third, TV produces neurophysiological responses that could cause addiction and illness. And fourth, information on TV is very limited due to the technology and the control by the corporate owners. He called for the complete elimination of television.

McChesney, R. W. (1993). Conflict, not consensus: The debate over broadcast communication policy, 1930–1935. In W. S. Solomon & R. W. McChesney (Eds.), *Ruthless criticism: New perspectives in U.S. communication history* (pp. 222–258). Minneapolis: University of Minnesota Press.

This is a critical reassessment of the scholarship about the public's reaction to the setup of commercial broadcasting in this country. McChesney said that much good criticism was written about the decision-making period prior to 1930, but that after that time, scholars assumed that the public was happy with the system. He argued that the opposite is the case; that is, there was a lot of dissatisfaction with the system, but that policymakers had taken the issue off the agenda.

There is no explicit methods treatment, but it is clear that as a historian he relied on existing documents.

He concluded that there was a broadcast reform movement in the period 1930–1935 but that it was not able to accomplish anything. He said, "it is an error to argue that the system was thoroughly consolidated by the middle 1920s or to assume that the American people were ignorant, apathetic, or even enthusiastic about commercial broadcasting. The commercial broadcasters and their allies did everything within their (substantial) powers to keep people and even Congress ignorant of their right and ability to determine broadcast policy throughout the period in question" (p. 248). He said further that it is a myth that our system is the perfect one or the only logical one given our political and cultural situation. Instead, there were many conflicts and the business interests won.

Parenti, M. (1986). *Inventing reality: The politics of the mass media.* New York: St. Martin's Press.

This is criticism of the way the media create messages. Parenti said, "this book is an attempt at understanding how and why the media are the way they are so that we might better defend ourselves not only by talking back in the privacy of our living rooms but by organizing and struggling to become active agents of our own lives and the creators of our own reality" (p. xii).

He relied primarily on evidence "gathered from extensive and detailed studies produced by academic scholars, journalists, and other independent investigators" (p. xii).

He began with an explanation about capitalism and how that has influenced the development of the media. He argued that media do not meet their own standards of objectivity, informativeness, truthfulness, or independence. Using Gramsci's notion of hegemony, he pointed out that the media are creating a false consciousness that is accepted by society.

Schiller, H. I. (1989). *Culture, Inc.: The corporate takeover of public expression.* New York: Oxford University Press.

Schiller asserted that this is not a historical study. "Its aim is to mark out, at least minimally, where the social order is at this time and how it has arrived there" (p. 10).

There is no explicit treatment of methods, but it is clear that he relied on existing documents.

He began his "nonhistory" with the post-WWII culture and showed how it has changed (for the worse in his argument). He was primarily concerned about how big business has grown in size and power over the culture. He argued that the profit motive and government have changed the culture industries. Information has been privatized, moving from government and higher education to businesses who control and sell it. He called for an "expansion of publicly supported facilities for information and creative expression . . . which will confer a new and richer meaning on the idea of the free flow of information" (p. 173). His ideological position is that diversity should replace homogeneity.

Wajcman, J. (1991). *Feminism confronts technology.* University Park: Pennsylvania State University Press.

The central thesis is that technology is influenced by gender and serves to influence gender. Gender relationships in the workplace affect the direction and pace of technological (especially in the area of human biological reproduction) change. Wajcman argued that gender divisions are built into houses, urban systems, and transportation systems.

There is no information about methods used.

REFERENCES

Allen, R. C. (1985). *Speaking of soap operas*. Chapel Hill: University of North Carolina Press.

Allen, R. C. (1987). Reader oriented criticism and television. In R. C. Allen (Ed.), *Channels of discourse: Television and contemporary criticism* (pp. 74–112). Chapel Hill: University of North Carolina Press.

Altheide, D. L. (1976). *Creating reality: How TV news distorts events*. Beverly Hills, CA: Sage.

Altheide, D. L. (1985). *Media power*. Beverly Hills, CA: Sage.

Altheide, D. L., & Johnson, J. M. (1994). Criteria for assessing interpretive validity in qualitative research. In N. K. Denzin & Y. S. Lincoln (Eds.), *Handbook of qualitative research* (pp. 485–499). Thousand Oaks, CA: Sage.

Altheide, D. L., & Snow, R. P. (1979). *Media logic*. Beverly Hills, CA: Sage.

Altschull, J. H. (1984). *Agents of power: The role of the news media in human affairs*. New York: Longman.

Anderson, C. (1987). Reflections on *Magnum, P.I.* In H. Newcomb (Ed.), *Television: The critical view* (4th ed., pp. 112–125). New York: Oxford University Press.

Anderson, J. A. (1987). *Communication research: Issues and methods*. New York: McGraw-Hill.

Anderson, J. A., & Meyer, T. P. (1988). *Mediated communication: A social action perspective*. Newbury Park, CA: Sage.

Ang, I. (1985). *Watching Dallas: Soap operas and the melodramatic imagination*. New York: Methuen.

Ang, I. (1989). Wanted audiences: On the politics of empirical audience studies. In E. Seiter, H. Borchers, G. Kreutzner, & E. Warth (Eds.), *Remote control: Television, audiences, and cultural power* (pp. 96–115). New York: Routledge.

Ang, I. (1991). *Desperately seeking the audience*. New York: Routledge.

Atkinson, P., & Hammersley, M. (1994). Ethnography and participant observation. In N. K. Denzin & Y. S. Lincoln (Eds.), *Handbook of qualitative research* (pp. 248–261). Thousand Oaks, CA: Sage.

Auletta, K. (1991). *Three blind mice: How the TV networks lost their way*. New York: Random House.

Bagdikian, B. H. (1972). *The effete conspiracy and other crimes by the press*. New York: Harper & Row.

Bagdikian, B. H. (1987). *The media monopoly* (2nd ed.). Boston: Beacon Press.

371

Barker, D. (1987). Television production techniques as communication. In H. Newcomb (Ed.), *Television: The critical view* (4th ed., pp. 179–196). New York: Oxford University Press.

Barnouw, E. (1975). *Tube of plenty: The evolution of American television.* New York: Oxford University Press.

Barnouw, E. (1978). *The sponsor: Notes on a modern potentate.* New York: Oxford University Press.

Barrios, L. (1988). Television, telenovelas, and family life in Venezuela. In J. Lull (Ed.), *World families watch television* (pp. 49–79). Beverly Hills, CA: Sage.

Barthes, R. (1972). *Mythologies* (Annette Lavers, Trans.). New York: Hill & Wang.

Baughman, J. L. (1990). The weakest chain and the strongest link: The American Broadcasting Company and the motion picture industry, 1952–60. In T. Balio (Ed.), *Hollywood in the age of television* (pp. 91–114). Boston: Unwin Hyman.

Becker, H. S. (1985). *Writing for social scientists: How to finish your thesis, book, or article.* Chicago: University of Chicago Press.

Bennett, T. (1982). Theories of the media, theories of society. In M. Gurevitch, T. Bennett, J. Curran, & J. Woollacott (Eds.), *Culture, society and the media* (pp. 30–55). London: Methuen.

Berger, A. A. (1982). *Media analysis techniques.* Beverly Hills, CA: Sage.

Berman, R. (1981). *Advertising and social change.* Beverly Hills, CA: Sage.

Bernhard, N. E. (1993). Ready, willing, and able: Network television news and the federal government, 1948–1953. In W. S. Solomon & R. W. McChesney (Eds.), *Ruthless criticism: New perspectives in U.S. communication history* (pp. 291–312). Minneapolis: University of Minnesota Press.

Bird, S. E., & Dardenne, R. W. (1988). Myth, chronicle, and story: Exploring the narrative qualities of news. In J. W. Carey (Ed.), *Media, myths, and narratives: Television and the press* (pp. 67–86). Beverly Hills, CA: Sage.

Blumer, H. (1969). *Symbolic interactionism: Perspective and method.* Englewood Cliffs, NJ: Prentice-Hall.

Bodroghkozy, A. (1992). "Is this what you mean by color TV?": Race, gender, and contested meanings in NBC's *Julia.* In L. Spigel & D. Mann (Eds.), *Private screenings: Television and the female consumer* (pp. 143–167). Minneapolis: University of Minnesota Press.

Bogdan, R., & Taylor, S. J. (1975). *Introduction to qualitative research methods: A phenomenological approach to the social sciences.* New York: Wiley.

Bowen, S. P., & Wyatt, N. (1993). Visions of synthesis, visions of critique. In S. P. Bowen & N. Wyatt (Eds.), *Transforming visions: Feminist critiques in communication studies* (pp. 1–18). Cresskill, NJ: Hampton Press.

Breen, M., & Corcoran, F. (1986). Myth, drama, fantasy theme, and ideology in mass media studies. In B. Dervin & M. J. Voigt (Eds.), *Progress in communication sciences* (Vol. 7, pp. 195–223). Norwood, NJ: Ablex.

Brown, H. I. (1977). *Perception, theory and commitment: The new philosophy of science.* Chicago: Precedent.

Brown, L. (1971). *Television: The business behind the box.* New York: Harcourt Brace Jovanovich.

Browne, N. (1987). The political economy of the television (super) text. In H. Newcomb (Ed.), *Television: The critical view* (4th ed., pp. 585–599). New York: Oxford University Press.

Burgess, R. (1984). *In the field: An introduction to field research.* Boston: Unwin Hyman.

Burke, D. (1966). Language as symbolic action.

Campbell, D. T. (1963). *Experimental and quasi-experimental designs for research.* Chicago: Rand McNally.

Cantor, M. (1980). *Prime-time television: Content and control.* Newbury Park, CA: Sage.

Cantor, M. (1988). *The Hollywood television producer: His work and his audience.* New Brunswick, NJ: Transaction Books.

Carey, J. W. (1977). Mass communication research and cultural studies: An American view. In J. Curran, M. Gurevitch, & J. Woollacott (Eds.), *Mass communication and society* (pp. 409–425). Beverly Hills, CA: Sage.

Chatman, S. (1978). *Story and discourse: Narrative structure in fiction and film*. Ithaca, NY: Cornell University Press.

Chesebro, J. W. (1987). Communication, values, and popular television series—A four-year assessment. In H. Newcomb (Ed.), *Television: The critical view* (4th ed., pp. 17–51). New York: Oxford University Press.

Christians, D. G., & Carey, J. W. (1981). The logic and aims of qualitative research. In G. H. Stempel III & B. H. Westley (Eds.), *Research methods in mass communication* (pp. 342–362). Englewood Cliffs, NJ: Prentice-Hall.

Christians, D. G., & Carey, J. W. (1989). The logic and aims of qualitative research. In G. H. Stempel III & B. H. Westley (Eds.), *Research methods in mass communication* (2nd ed., pp. 354–374). Englewood Cliffs, NJ: Prentice-Hall.

Clark, E. (1988). *The want makers: Inside the world of advertising*. New York: Penguin Books.

Collins, J. (1989). *Uncommon cultures: Popular culture and post-modernism*. New York: Routledge.

Condit, C. M. (1991). The rhetorical limits of polysemy. In R. K. Avery & D. Eason (Eds.), *Critical perspectives on media and society* (pp. 365–386). New York: Guilford.

Cooper, R., Potter, W. J., & Dupagne, M. (1994). A status report on methods used in mass communication research. *Journalism Educator, 48*(4), 54–61.

Corcoran, F. (1987). Television as ideological apparatus: The power and pleasure. In H. Newcomb (Ed.), *Television: The critical view* (4th ed., pp. 533–552). New York: Oxford University Press.

Craig, R. T. (1989). Communication as a practical discipline. In B. Dervin, L. Grossberg, B. J. O'Keefe, & E. Wartella (Eds.), *Rethinking communication* (pp. 97–122). Newbury Park, CA: Sage.

Curran, J., Gurevitch, M., & Woollacott, J. (1982). The study of the media: Theoretical approaches. In M. Gurevitch, T. Bennett, J. Curran, & J. Woollacott (Eds.), *Culture, society and the media* (pp. 11–29). London: Methuen.

D'Acci, J. (1992). Defining women: The case of *Cagney and Lacey*. In L. Spigel & D. Mann (Eds.), *Private screenings: Television and the female consumer* (pp. 169–201). Minneapolis: University of Minnesota Press.

Dates, J. L., & Barlow, W. (Eds.). (1990). *Split image: African Americans in the mass media*. Washington, DC: Howard University Press.

Deming, R. H. (1992). *Kate and Allie*: "New women" and the audience's television archives. In L. Spigel & D. Mann (Eds.), *Private screenings: Television and the female consumer* (pp. 203–215). Minneapolis: University of Minnesota Press.

Denzin, N. K. (1970). *The research act: A theoretical introduction to sociological methods*. Chicago: Aldine.

Denzin, N. K. (1978). *The research act* (2nd ed.). New York: McGraw-Hill.

Denzin, N. K. (1994). The art and politics of interpretation. In N. K. Denzin & Y. S. Lincoln (Eds.), *Handbook of qualitative research* (pp. 500–515). Thousand Oaks, CA: Sage.

Denzin, N. K., & Lincoln, Y. S. (1994a). The fifth moment. In N. K. Denzin & Y. S. Lincoln (Eds.), *Handbook of qualitative research* (pp. 575–586). Thousand Oaks, CA: Sage.

Denzin, N. K., & Lincoln, Y. S. (1994b). Introduction: Entering the field of qualitative research. In N. K. Denzin & Y. S. Lincoln (Eds.), *Handbook of qualitative research* (pp. 1–17). Thousand Oaks, CA: Sage.

Denzin, N. K. & Lincoln, Y. S. (1994c). Preface. In N. K. Denzin & Y. S. Lincoln (Eds.), *Handbook of qualitative research* (pp. ix–xii). Thousand Oaks, CA: Sage.

Douglas, S. J. (1993). Will you love me tomorrow? Changing discourses about female sexuality in the mass media, 1960–1968. In W. S. Solomon & R. W. McChesney (Eds.), *Ruthless criticism: New perspectives in U. S. communication history* (pp. 349–373). Minneapolis: University of Minnesota Press.

Elliott, P. (1979). *The making of a television series*. London: Sage.

Esslin, M. (1987). Aristotle and the advertisers: The television commercial considered as a form of drama. In H. Newcomb (Ed.), *Television: The critical view* (4th ed., pp. 304–317). New York: Oxford University Press.

Evans, W. A. (1990). The interpretive turn in media research: Innovation, iteration, or illusion? *Critical Studies in Mass Communication, 7,* 147–168.

Ewen, S., & Ewen, E. (1992). *Channels of desire.* Minneapolis: University of Minnesota Press.

Feurer, J. (1987). Genre study and television. In R. C. Allen (Ed.), *Channels of discourse: Television and contemporary criticism* (pp. 113–133). Chapel Hill: University of North Carolina Press.

Fisher, W. R. (1987). *Human communication as narration: Toward a philosophy of reason, value, and action.* Columbia: University of South Carolina Press.

Fishman, M. (1980). *Manufacturing the news.* Austin: University of Texas Press.

Fiske, J. (1987). British cultural studies and television. In R. C. Allen (Ed.), *Channels of discourse: Television and contemporary criticism* (pp. 254–289). Chapel Hill: University of North Carolina Press.

Fiske, J. (1994). Audiencing: Cultural practice and cultural studies. In N. K. Denzin & Y. S. Lincoln (Eds.), *Handbook of qualitative research* (pp. 189–198). Thousand Oaks, CA: Sage.

Fiske, J., & Hartley, J. (1978). *Reading television.* New York: Methuen.

Flitterman-Lewis, S. (1992). All's well that doesn't end—Soap opera and the marriage motif. In L. Spigel & D. Mann (Eds.), *Private screenings: Television and the female consumer* (pp. 217–225). Minneapolis: University of Minnesota Press.

Fortner, R. S., & Christians, D. G. (1981). Separating wheat from chaff in qualitative studies. In G. H. Stempel III & B. H. Westley (Eds.), *Research methods in mass communication* (pp. 363–374). Englewood Cliffs, NJ: Prentice-Hall.

Fry, D. L., & Fry, V. H. (1986). A semiotic model for the study of mass communication. In M. L. McLaughlin (Ed.), *Communication yearbook 9* (pp. 443–462). Beverly Hills, CA: Sage.

Gandy, O. H., Jr. (1982). *Beyond agenda-setting.* Norwood, NJ: Ablex.

Garfinkel, A. (1967). *Studies in ethnomethodology.* Englewood Cliffs, NJ: Prentice-Hall.

Gee, J. P., Michaels, S., & O'Conner, M. C. (1992). Discourse analysis. In M. D. LeCompte, W. L. Millroy, & J. Preissle (Eds.), *The handbook of qualitative research in education* (pp. 227–291). New York: Academic Press.

Gerbner, G. (1983). The importance of being critical—In one's own fashion. *Journal of Communication, 33*(3), 355–362.

Giddens, A. (1989). The orthodox consensus and the emerging synthesis. In B. Dervin, L. Grossberg, B. J. O'Keefe, & E. Wartella (Eds.), *Rethinking communication* (Vol. 1, pp. 53–65). Newbury Park, CA: Sage.

Gitlin, T. (1978). Media sociology: The dominant paradigm. *Theory and Society, 6,* 205–253.

Gitlin, T. (1980). *The whole world is watching: Mass media in the making and unmaking of the New Left.* Berkeley: University of California Press.

Gitlin, T. (1983). *Inside prime time.* New York: Pantheon.

Gitlin, T. (1987). Prime time ideology: The hegemonic process in television entertainment. In H. Newcomb (Ed.), *Television: The critical view* (4th ed., pp. 507–532). New York: Oxford University Press.

Glaser, B. G., & Strauss, A. L. (1967). *The discovery of grounded theory: Strategies for qualitative research.* Chicago: Aldine.

Gove, P. B. (Ed.). (1986). *Webster's Third International Unabridged Dictionary.* Springfield, MA: Merriam Webster.

Guba, E., & Lincoln, Y. (1981). *Effective evaluation: Improving the usefulness of evaluation results through responsive and naturalistic approaches.* San Francisco: Jossey-Bass.

Hall, S. (1980). Encoding/decoding. In S. Hall et al. (Eds.), *Culture, media, language* (pp. 128–139). London: Hutchinson.

Hamilton, D. (1994). Traditions, preferences, and postures in applied qualitative research. In N. K. Denzin & Y. S. Lincoln (Eds.), *Handbook of qualitative research* (pp. 60–69). Thousand Oaks, CA: Sage.

Hammersley, M., & Atkinson, P. (1983). *Ethnography: Principles and practice.* London: Tavistock.

Haralovich, M. B. (1992). Sit-coms and suburbs: Positioning the 1950s homemaker. In L. Spigel & D. Mann (Eds.), *Private screenings: Television and the female consumer* (pp. 111–141). Minneapolis: University of Minnesota Press.

Harvey, D. (1989). *The condition of postmodernity: An enquiry into the origins of cultural change.* Cambridge, MA: Basil Blackwell.

Head, S. W., & Sterling, C. H. (1990). *Broadcasting in America.* 6th ed. Boston: Houghton Mifflin.

Himmelstein, H. (1984). *Television myth and the American mind.* New York: Praeger.

Hobson, D. (1982). *"Crossroads": The drama of a soap opera.* London: Methuen.

Hobson, D. (1989). Soap operas at work. In E. Seiter, H. Borchers, G. Kreutzner, & E.-M. Warth (Eds.), *Remote control: Television, audiences, and cultural power* (pp. 150–167). New York: Routledge.

Holstein, J. A., & Gubrium, J. F. (1994). Phenomenology, ethnomethodology, and interpretive practice. In N. K. Denzin & Y. S. Lincoln (Eds.), *Handbook of qualitative research* (pp. 262–272). Thousand Oaks, CA: Sage.

Hoover, S. M. (1988). Television myth and ritual: The role of substantive meaning and spatiality. In J. W. Carey (Ed.), *Media, myths, and narratives: Television and the press* (pp. 161–178). Beverly Hills, CA: Sage.

Horowitz, S. (1987). Sitcom domesticus—A species endangered by social change. In H. Newcomb (Ed.), *Television: The critical view* (4th ed., pp. 106–111). New York: Oxford University Press.

Howe, K., & Eisenhart, M. (1990). Standards for qualitative (and quantitative) research: A prolegomenon. *Educational Researcher, 19*(4), 2–9.

Innis, H. A. (1950). *Empire and communications.* London: Oxford University Press.

Jackson, P. (1968). *Life in classrooms.* New York: Holt, Rinehart & Winston.

Jacob, E. (1987). Qualitative research traditions: A review. *Review of Educational Research, 57,* 1–50.

Jacob, E. (1988). Clarifying qualitative research: A focus on traditions. *Educational Researcher, 17,* 16–24.

Jankowski, N. W., & Wester, F. (1991). The qualitative tradition in social science inquiry: Contributions to mass communication research. In K. B. Jensen & N. W. Jankowski (Eds.), *A handbook of qualitative methodologies for mass communication research* (pp. 44–74). New York: Routledge.

Jensen, J. K. (1993). The consequences of vocabularies. *Journal of Communication, 43*(3), 67–74.

Jensen, K. B. (1991a). Humanistic scholarship as qualitative science: Contributions to mass communication research. In K. B. Jensen & N. W. Jankowski (Eds.), *A handbook of qualitative methodologies for mass communication research* (pp. 17–43). New York: Routledge.

Jensen, K. B. (1991b). Introduction: The qualitative turn. In K. B. Jensen & N. W. Jankowski (Eds.), *A handbook of qualitative methodologies for mass communication research* (pp. 1–11). New York: Routledge.

Jensen, K. B., & Jankowski, N. W. (Eds.) (1991). *A handbook of qualitative methodologies for mass communication research.* New York: Routledge.

Jhally, S., & Lewis, J. (1992). *The Cosby Show, audiences, and the myth of the American dream.* Boulder, CO: Westview Press.

Jick, T. D. (1979). Mixing qualitative and quantitative methods: Triangulation in action. *Administrative Science Quarterly, 24,* 602–611.

Jowett, G. (1976). *Film, the democratic art.* Boston: Little, Brown.

Jowett, G., & Linton, J. M. (1980). *Movies as mass communication.* Beverly Hills, CA: Sage.

Joyrich, L. (1992). All that television allows: TV melodrama, postmodernism, and consumer culture. In L. Spigel & D. Mann (Eds.), *Private screenings: Television and the female consumer* (pp. 227–251). Minneapolis: University of Minnesota Press.

Kaplan, E. A. (1987). Feminist criticism and television. In R. C. Allen (Ed.), *Channels of discourse: Television and contemporary criticism* (pp. 211–253). Chapel Hill: University of North Carolina Press.

Kellner, D. (1987). TV, ideology, and emancipatory popular culture. In H. Newcomb (Ed.), *Television: The critical view* (4th ed., pp. 471–503). New York: Oxford University Press.

Kinder, M. (1987). Music video and the spectator: Television, ideology, and dream. In H. Newcomb (Ed.), *Television: The critical view* (4th ed., pp. 229–254). New York: Oxford University Press.

Kozloff, S. R. (1987). Narrative theory and television. In R. C. Allen (Ed.), *Channels of discourse: Television and contemporary criticism* (pp. 42–73). Chapel Hill: University of North Carolina Press.

Krippendorf, K. (1989). On the ethics of constructing communication. In B. Dervin, L. Grossberg, B. J. O'Keefe, & E. Wartella (Eds.), *Rethinking communication* (Vol. 1, pp. 66–96). Newbury Park, CA: Sage.

Lancy, D. F. (1993). *Qualitative research in education: An introduction to the major traditions.* New York: Longman.

Leiter, K. (1980). *A primer on ethnomethodology*, New York: Oxford University Press.

Lewis, J. (1991). *The ideological octopus.* New York: Routledge.

Liebes, T., & Katz, E. (1988). *Dallas* and genesis: Primordiality and seriality in popular culture. In J. W. Carey (Ed.), *Media, myths, and narratives: Television and the press* (pp. 113–125). Beverly Hills, CA: Sage.

Liebes, T., & Katz, E. (1989). On the critical abilities of television viewers. In E. Seiter, H. Borchers, G. Kreutzner, & E.-M. Warth (Eds.), *Remote control: Television, audiences, and cultural power* (pp. 204–222). New York: Routledge.

Lincoln, Y. S., & Guba, E. G. (1985). *Naturalistic inquiry.* Newbury Park, CA: Sage.

Lincoln, Y. S., & Guba, E. G. (1986). But is it rigorous? Trustworthiness and authenticity in naturalistic evaluation. In D. D. Williams (Ed.), *Naturalistic evaluation* (pp. 73–84). San Francisco: Jossey-Bass.

Lincoln, Y. S., & Guba, E. G. (1990). Judging the quality of case study reports. *Qualitative Studies in Education, 3*(1), 53–59.

Lindlof, T. R. (1987). Ideology and pragmatics of media access in prison. In T. R. Lindlof (Ed.), *Natural audiences: Qualitative research of media uses and effects* (pp. 175–197). Norwood, NJ: Ablex.

Lindlof, T. R. (1991). The qualitative study of media audiences. *Journal of Broadcasting & Electronic Media, 35,* 23–42.

Lindlof, T. R. (1995). *Qualitative communication research methods.* Thousand Oaks, CA: Sage.

Lindlof, T. R., & Meyer, T. P. (1987). Media use as ways of seeing, acting, and constructing culture: The tools and foundations of qualitative research. In T. R. Lindlof (Ed.), *Natural audiences: Qualitative research of media uses and effects* (pp. 1–30). Norwood, NJ: Ablex.

Lipsitz, G. (1992). The meaning of memory: Family class, and ethnicity in early network television programs. In L. Spigel & D. Mann (Eds.), *Private screenings: Television and the female consumer* (pp. 71–109). Minneapolis: University of Minnesota Press.

Litman, B. (1990). Network oligopoly power: An economic analysis. In T. Balio (Ed.), *Hollywood in the age of television* (pp. 115–144). Boston: Unwin Hyman.

Lofland, J. (1971). *Analyzing social settings: A guide to qualitative observation and analysis.* Belmont, CA: Wadsworth.

Lofland, J., & Lofland, L. H. (1984). *Analyzing social settings: A guide to qualitative observation and analysis* (2nd ed.). Belmont, CA: Wadsworth.

Lont, C. M. (1993). Feminist critique of mass communication research. In S. P. Bowen & N. Wyatt (Eds.), *Transforming visions: Feminist critiques in communication studies* (pp. 231–248). Cresskill, NJ: Hampton Press.

Lull, J. (1980). The social uses of television. *Human Communication Research, 6,* 197–209.

Lull, J. (1985). Ethnographic studies of broadcast media audiences. In J. R. Dominick & J. E. Fletcher (Eds.), *Broadcasting research methods* (pp. 80–88). Newton, MA: Allyn & Bacon.

Lull, J. (1987). Trashing in the pit: An ethnography of San Francisco punk subculture. In T. R. Lindlof (Ed.), *Natural audiences: Qualitative research of media uses and effects* (pp. 225–252). Norwood, NJ: Ablex.

Lutz, R. J. (1989). positivism, nauturalism and pluralism in consumer research: Paradigms in paradise. *Advances in consumer research, 16*, 1–8.

Mander, J. (1978). *Four arguments for the elimination of television.* New York: Morrow.

Mann, D. (1992). The spectacularization of everyday life: Recycling Hollywood stars and fans in early television variety shows. In L. Spigel & D. Mann (Eds.), *Private screenings: Television and the female consumer* (pp. 41–69). Minneapolis: University of Minnesota Press.

Manning, P. K. (1982). Analytic induction. In R. B. Smith & P. K. Manning (Eds.), *Qualitative methods: Volume II of Handbook of social science methods* (pp. 273–302). Cambridge, MA: Ballinger.

Manning, P. K., & Cullum-Swan, B. (1994). Narrative, content, and semiotic analysis. In N. K. Denzin & Y. S. Lincoln (Eds.), *Handbook of qualitative research* (pp. 463–483). Thousand Oaks, CA: Sage.

Marshall, C., & Rossman, G. B. (1989). *Designing qualitative research.* Newbury Park, CA: Sage.

McChesney, R. W. (1993). Conflict, not consensus: The debate over broadcast communication policy, 1930–1935. In W. S. Solomon & R. W. McChesney (Eds.), *Ruthless criticism: New perspectives in U.S. communication history* (pp. 222–258). Minneapolis: University of Minnesota Press.

Meehan, E. R. (1993). Heads of household and ladies of the house: Gender, genre, and broadcast ratings, 1929–1990. In W. S. Solomon & R. W. McChesney (Eds.), *Ruthless criticism: New perspectives in U.S. communication history* (pp. 204–221). Minneapolis: University of Minnesota Press.

Mehan, H. (1979). *Learning lessons: Social organization in the classroom.* Cambridge, MA: Harvard University Press.

Metz, C. (1974). *Film language: A semiotics of the cinema* (M. Taylor, Trans.). New York: Oxford University Press.

Metz, C. (1982). *The imaginary signifier: Psychoanalysis and the cinema.* Bloomington: Indiana University Press.

Metz, R. (1975). *CBS: Reflections in a bloodshot eye.* Chicago: Playboy Press.

Miles, M. B. (1979). Qualitative data as an attractive nuisance: The problem of analysis. *Administrative Science Quarterly, 24*, 590–601.

Miles, M. B., & Huberman, A. M. (1984). *Qualitative data analysis: A sourcebook of new methods.* Beverly Hills, CA: Sage.

Morley, D. (1980). *The "Nationwide" audience: Structure and decoding.* London: British Film Institute.

Morley, D. (1981). Industrial conflict and the mass media. In S. Cohen & J. Young (Eds.), *The manufacture of news: Social problems deviance and the mass media* (pp. 368–392). London: Constable.

Morley, D. (1989). Changing paradigms in audience studies. In E. Seiter, H. Borchers, G. Kreutzner, & E.-M. Warth (Eds.), *Remote control: Television, audiences, and cultural power* (pp. 16–43). New York: Routledge.

Morris, M. B. (1977). *An excursion into creative sociology.* New York: Columbia University Press.

Newcomb, H. M. (1988). One night of prime time: An analysis of television's multiple voices. In J. W. Carey (Ed.), *Media, myths, and narratives: Television and the press* (pp. 88–112). Beverly Hills, CA: Sage.

Nord, D. P. (1989). The nature of historical research. In G. H. Stempel III & B. H. Westley (Eds.), *Research methods in mass communication* (pp. 290–315). Englewood Cliffs, NJ: Prentice-Hall.

Olesen, V. (1994). Feminisms and models of qualitative research. In N. K. Denzin & Y. S. Lincoln (Eds.), *Handbook of qualitative research* (pp. 158–174). Thousand Oaks, CA: Sage.

Orr, L. (1991). *A dictionary of critical theory.* New York: Greenwood Press.

Pardun, C. J., & Krugman, D. M. (1994). How the architectural style of the home relates to family television viewing. *Journal of Broadcasting & Electronic Media, 38*, 145–162.

Parenti, M. (1986). *Inventing reality: The politics of the mass media.* New York: St. Martin's Press.

Pauly, J. J. (1988). Rupert Murdoch and the demonology of professional journalism. In J. W. Carey (Ed.), *Media, myths, and narratives: Television and the press* (pp. 246–261). Beverly Hills, CA: Sage.

Pauly, J. J. (1991). A beginner's guide to doing qualitative research in mass communication. *Journalism Monographs, 125.*

Penman, R. (1992). Good theory and good practice: An argument in progress. *Communication Theory, 2*, 234–250.

Potter, W. J., Cooper, R., & Dupagne, M. (1993). The three paradigms of mass media research in mainstream communication journals. *Communication Theory, 3*, 317–335.

Potter, W. J., Troiano, C., Riggs, K., & Robinson, M. (1993, August). *A content analysis of published qualitative research.* Paper presented at the meeting of the Communication Theory and Methodology Division of the Association for Education in Journalism and Mass Communication, Kansas City, MO.

Potter, W. J., & Ware, W. (1987a). An analysis of the contexts of antisocial acts on prime-time television. *Communication Research, 14*(6), 664–686.

Potter, W. J., & Ware, W. (1987b). Traits of perpetrators and receivers of antisocial and prosocial acts on television. *Journalism Quarterly, 64*, 382–391.

Potter, W. J., & Ware, W. (1989). The frequency and context of prosocial acts on primetime television. *Journalism Quarterly, 66*, 359–366, 529.

Powers, J. (1982). *Philosophy and the new physics.* New York: Methuen.

Radway, J. A. (1984). *Reading the romance: Women, patriarchy, and popular literature.* Chapel Hill: University of North Carolina Press.

Rakow, L. F. (1992). *Gender on the line: Women, the telephone, and community life.* Urbana: University of Illinois Press.

Real, M. R. (1986). Demythologizing media: Recent writings in critical and institutional theory. *Critical Studies in Mass Communication, 3*, 459–486.

Reason, P. (1994). Three approaches to participative inquiry. In N. K. Denzin & Y. S. Lincoln (Eds.), *Handbook of qualitative research* (pp. 324–339). Thousand Oaks, CA: Sage.

Reeves, J. L. (1988). Television stardom: A ritual of social typification and individualization. In J. W. Carey (Ed.), *Media, myths, and narratives: Television and the press* (pp. 146–160). Beverly Hills, CA: Sage.

Reinharz, S. (1992). *Feminist methods in social research.* New York: Oxford University Press.

Richardson, L. (1990). Narrative and sociology. *Journal of Contemporary Ethnography, 19*(1), 116–135.

Richardson, L. (1994). Writing: A method of inquiry. In N. K. Denzin & Y. S. Lincoln (Eds.), *Handbook of qualitative research* (pp. 516–529). Thousand Oaks, CA: Sage.

Rogers, E. M. (1982). The empirical and critical schools of communication research. In M. Burgoon (Ed.), *Communication yearbook 5* (pp. 125–144). New Brunswick, NJ: Transaction Books.

Rogge, J.-U. (1989). The media in everyday family life: Some biographical and typological aspects. In E. Seiter, H. Borchers, G. Kreutzner, & E.-M. Warth (Eds.), *Remote control: Television, audiences, and cultural power* (pp. 168–179). New York: Routledge.

Rogge, J.-U., & Jensen, K. (1988). Everyday life and television in West Germany: An empathic-interpretive perspective on the family as a system. In J. Lull (Ed.), *World families watch television* (pp. 80–115). Beverly Hills, CA: Sage.

Rosengren, K. E. (1989). Paradigms lost and regained. In B. Dervin, L. Grossberg, B. J. O'Keefe, & E. Wartella (Eds.), *Rethinking communication* (Vol. 1, pp. 21–39). Newbury Park, CA: Sage.

Rowland, W. D., Jr. (1983). *The politics of TV violence: Policy uses of communication research.* Beverly Hills, CA: Sage.

Schensul, J. J., & Schensul, S. L. (1992). Collaborative research: Methods of inquiry for social change. In M. D. LeCompte, W. L. Millroy, & J. Preissle (Eds.), *The handbook of qualitative research in education* (pp. 161–200). New York: Academic Press.

Schiller, H. I. (1989). *Culture, Inc.: The corporate takeover of public expression.* New York: Oxford University Press.

Schulze, L. (1990). The made-for-TV movie: Industrial practice, cultural form, popular reception. In T. Balio (Ed.), *Hollywood in the age of television* (pp. 351–376). Boston: Unwin Hyman.

Schwandt, T. A. (1989). Solutions to the paradigm conflict: Coping with uncertainty. *Journal of Contemporary Ethnography, 17,* 379–407.

Schwandt, T. A. (1994). Constructivist, interpretivist approaches to human inquiry. In N. K. Denzin & Y. S. Lincoln (Eds.), *Handbook of qualitative research* (pp. 118–137). Thousand Oaks, CA: Sage.

Schwartz, H., & Jacobs, J. (1979). *Qualitative sociology: A method to the madness.* New York: The Free Press.

Schwichtenberg, C. (1987). *The Love Boat:* The packaging and selling of love, heterosexual romance, and family. In H. Newcomb (Ed.), *Television: The critical view* (4th ed., pp. 126–140). New York: Oxford University Press.

Seiter, E. (1987). Semiotics and television. In R. C. Allen (Ed.), *Channels of discourse: Television and contemporary criticism* (pp. 17–41). Chapel Hill: University of North Carolina Press.

Seiter, E., Borchers, H., Kreutzner, G., & Warth, E.-M. (1989a). "Don't treat us like we're so stupid and naive": Toward an ethnography of soap opera viewers. In E. Seiter, H. Borchers, G. Kreutzner, & E.-M. Warth (Eds.), *Remote control: Television, audiences, and cultural power* (pp. 223–247). New York: Routledge.

Seiter, E., Borchers, H., Kreutzner, G., & Warth, E.-M. (1989b). Introduction. In E. Seiter, H. Borchers, G. Kreutzner, & E.-M. Warth (Eds.), *Remote control: Television, audiences, and cultural power* (pp. 1–15). New York: Routledge.

Sieber, S. D. (1976). *A synopsis and critique of guidelines for qualitative analysis contained in selected textbooks.* New York: Project on Social Architecture in Education, Center for Policy Research.

Silverstone, R. (1988). Television myth and culture. In J. W. Carey (Ed.), *Media, myths, and narratives: Television and the press* (pp. 20–47). Beverly Hills, CA: Sage.

Slack, J. D., & Allor, M. (1983). The political and epistemological constituents of critical communication research. *Journal of Communication, 33*(3), 208–218.

Smith, J. K. (1983, March). Quantitative versus qualitative research: An attempt to clarify the issue. *Educational Researcher,* pp. 6–13.

Smith, J. K. (1984). The problem of criteria for judging interpretive inquiry. *Educational Evaluation and Policy Analysis, 6,* 379–391.

Smith, J. K., & Heshusius, L. (1986, January). Closing down the conversation: The end of the quantitative-qualitative debate among educational inquirers. *Educational Researcher,* pp. 4–12.

Smith, M. J. (1988). *Contemporary communication research methods.* Belmont, CA: Wadsworth.

Smith, M. L. (1987). Publishing qualitative research. *American Educational Research Journal, 24*(2), 173–183.

Snow, R. P. (1983). *Creating media culture.* Beverly Hills, CA: Sage.

Spigel, L. (1992). Installing the television set: Popular discourses on television and domestic space, 1948–1955. In L. Spigel & D. Mann (Eds.), *Private screenings: Television and the female consumer* (pp. 3–38). Minneapolis: University of Minnesota Press.

Spigel, L. (1993). Seducing the innocent: Childhood and television in postwar America. In W. S. Solomon & R. W. McChesney (Eds.), *Ruthless criticism: New perspectives in U.S. communication history* (pp. 259–290). Minneapolis: University of Minnesota Press.

Spradley, J. (1981). *The ethnographic interview.* New York: Holt, Rinehart & Winston.

Stevens, J. D., & Garcia, H. D. (1980). *Communication history.* Beverly Hills, CA: Sage.

Strauss, A., & Corbin, J. (1990). *Basics of qualitative research: Grounded theory procedures and techniques.* Newbury Park, CA: Sage.

Thornburn, D. (1988). Television as an aesthetic medium. In J. W. Carey (Ed.), *Media, myths, and narratives: Television and the press* (pp. 48–66). Beverly Hills, CA: Sage.

Toulmin, S. (1983). The construal of reality: Criticism in modern and postmodern science. In W. J. T. Mitchell (Ed.), *The politics of interpretation* (pp. 99–117). Chicago: University of Chicago Press.

Traudt, P. J., & Lont, C. M. (1987). Media-logic-in-use: The family as locus of study. In T. R. Lindlof (Ed.), *Natural audiences: Qualitative research of media uses and effects* (pp. 139–160). Norwood, NJ: Ablex.

Tuchman, G. (1978). *Making news: A study in the construction of reality.* New York: The Free Press.

Tuchman, G. (1994). Historical social science. In N. K. Denzin & Y. S. Lincoln (Eds.), *Handbook of qualitative research* (pp. 306–323). Thousand Oaks, CA: Sage.

Tulloch, J. (1989). Approaching the audience: The elderly. In E. Seiter, H. Borchers, G. Kreutzner, & E.-M. Warth (Eds.), *Remote control: Television, audiences, and cultural power* (pp. 180–203). New York: Routledge.

Turkle, S. (1984). *The second self: Computers and the human spirit.* New York: Simon & Schuster.

Turner, M. B. (1965). *Philosophy and the science of behavior.* New York: Appleton-Century-Crofts.

Turow, J. (1981). *Entertainment, education, and the hard sell: Three decades of network children's television.* New York: Praeger.

Turow, J. (1984). *Media industries: The production of news and entertainment.* New York: Longman.

Turow, J. (1989). *Playing doctor: Television, storytelling, and medical power.* New York: Oxford University Press.

Vande Berg, L. R., & Wenner, L. A. (1991). Approaches to television criticism. In L. R. Vande Berg & L. A. Wenner (Eds.), *Television criticism: Approaches and applications* (pp. 18–43). New York: Longman.

Van Maanen, J. (1988). *Tales of the field: On writing ethnography.* Chicago: University of Chicago Press.

Vidich, A. J., & Lyman, S. M. (1994). Qualitative methods: Their history in sociology and anthropology. In N. K. Denzin & Y. S. Lincoln (Eds.), *Handbook of qualitative research* (pp. 23–59). Thousand Oaks, CA: Sage.

Wajcman, J. (1991). *Feminism confronts technology.* University Park: Pennsylvania State University Press.

White, M. (1987). Ideological analysis and television. In R. C. Allen (Ed.), *Channels of discourse: Television and contemporary criticism* (pp. 134–171). Chapel Hill: University of North Carolina Press.

Wimmer, R. D., & Dominick, J. R. (1991). *Mass media research* (3rd ed.). Belmont, CA: Wadsworth.

Wolcott, H. F. (1973). *The man in the principal's office: An ethnography.* New York: Holt, Rinehart & Winston.

Wolcott, H. F. (1982). Differing styles of on-site research, or, "If it isn't ethnography, what is it?" *Review Journal of Philosophy and Social Science, 7*(1/2), 154–169.

Wolcott, H. F. (1990). *Writing up qualitative research.* Newbury Park, CA: Sage.

Wolcott, H. F. (1992). Posturing in qualitative inquiry. In M. D. LeCompte, W. L. Millroy, & J. Preissle (Eds.), *The handbook of qualitative research in education* (pp. 2–52). New York: Academic Press.

Wolf, M. (1987). How children negotiate television. In T. R. Lindlof (Ed.), *Natural audiences: Qualitative research of media uses and effects* (pp. 58–94). Norwood, NJ: Ablex.

Woods, P. (1992). Symbolic interactionism: Theory and method. In M. D. LeCompte, W. L. Millroy, & J. Preissle (Eds.), *The handbook of qualitative research in education* (pp. 337–404). New York: Academic Press.

Wuthnow, R., & Witten, M. (1988). New directions in the study of culture. *Annual Review of Sociology, 14,* 49–67.

Zynda, T. H. (1988). The *Mary Tyler Moore Show* and the transformation of situation comedy. In J. W. Carey (Ed.), *Media, myths, and narratives: Television and the press* (pp. 126–145). Beverly Hills, CA: Sage.

AUTHOR INDEX

A

Allen, R. C., 9, 10, 20, 54, 55, 90, 100, 129, 178, 180, 261, 268, 269, 305, 330, 357, 371

Allor, M., 10, 379

Altheide, D. L., 76, 77, 89, 98, 99, 101, 103, 111, 114, 119, 120, 128, 129, 132, 143, 164, 166, 179, 182, 184, 188, 189, 192, 193, 196, 200, 203, 262, 268, 277, 281, 286, 290, 323, 324, 351, 353, 371

Altschull, J. H., 77, 90, 114, 129, 179, 182, 187, 295, 354, 371

Anderson, C., 75, 89, 140, 178, 180, 181, 182, 184, 187, 335, 371

Anderson, J. A., 16, 19, 20, 40, 43, 67, 101, 103, 115, 117, 122, 123, 155, 162, 163, 165, 184, 193, 194, 228, 276, 277, 297, 308, 323, 371

Ang, I., 20, 78, 96, 102, 119, 128, 129, 132, 167, 170, 178, 179, 180, 181, 186, 189, 202, 253, 263, 284, 292, 329, 330, 343, 364, 371

Atkinson, P., 51, 52, 99, 102, 105, 118, 122, 127, 160, 176, 188, 198, 371, 374

Auletta, K., 77, 90, 92, 98, 101, 103, 114, 162, 180, 182, 184, 354, 371

B

Bagdikian, B. H., 78, 90, 92, 129, 170, 172, 178, 179, 180, 364, 371

Barker, D., 75, 87, 118, 128, 140, 166, 179, 181, 184, 187, 333, 372

Barlow, W., 78, 111, 119, 129, 172, 179, 181, 366, 373

Barnouw, E., 77, 90, 92, 96, 143, 162, 170, 179, 180, 182, 183, 259, 355, 365, 372

Barrios, L., 73, 89, 92, 100, 101, 104, 107, 112, 113, 128, 153, 166, 182, 185, 187, 202, 294, 349, 372

Barthes, R., 135, 372

Baughman, J. L., 77, 90, 92, 164, 178, 181, 355, 372

Becker, H. S., 167, 372

Bennett, T., 136, 372

Berger, A. A., 5, 6, 147, 276, 372

Berman, R., 90, 129, 178, 181, 358, 372

Bernhard, N. E., 90, 129, 178, 181, 358, 372

Bird, S. E., 75, 89, 118, 128, 131, 150, 170, 181, 184, 188, 283, 334, 372

Blumer, H., 58, 372

Bodroghkozy, A., 88, 89, 96, 102, 127, 132, 164, 178, 182, 185, 189, 202, 343, 372

Bogdan, R., 4, 14, 15, 18, 20, 21, 22, 40, 43, 53, 54, 57, 58, 105, 117, 122, 127, 131, 160, 164, 171, 198, 276, 372

Borchers, 9, 98, 101, 107, 111, 113, 139, 139, 149, 168, 170, 178, 182, 185, 190, 252, 257, 261, 267, 280, 308, 330, 349, 379

Bowen, S. P., 5, 6, 146, 372

Breen, M., 5, 150, 372

Brown, H. I., 29, 180, 264, 372

Brown, L., 77, 90, 92, 101, 114, 162, 182, 183, 184, 355, 372

Browne, N., 78, 90, 92, 172, 179, 365, 372

Burgess, R., 159, 372

C

Campbell, D. T., 196, 372

Cantor, M., 78, 100, 106, 112, 114, 119, 125, 129, 133, 143, 179, 193, 184, 358, 359, 372

Carey, J. W., 8, 14, 16, 18, 20, 22, 44, 61, 62, 102, 131, 154, 161, 162, 163, 164, 169, 177, 271, 272, 282, 315, 372, 373

Chatman, S., 140, 373

Chesebro, J. W., 88, 89, 92, 108, 111, 113, 119, 124, 128, 131, 165, 179, 181, 187, 335, 373

SUBJECT INDEX